# ROBERT LOUIS STEVENSON AND THE APPEARANCE OF MODERNISM

# Robert Louis Stevenson and the Appearance of Modernism

## A Future Feeling

Alan Sandison

First published in Great Britain 1996 by
**MACMILLAN PRESS LTD**
Houndmills, Basingstoke, Hampshire RG21 6XS
and London
Companies and representatives
throughout the world

A catalogue record for this book is available
from the British Library.

ISBN 0–333–62067–4

First published in the United States of America 1996 by
**ST. MARTIN'S PRESS, INC.,**
Scholarly and Reference Division,
175 Fifth Avenue,
New York, N.Y. 10010

ISBN 0–312–15968–4

Library of Congress Cataloging-in-Publication Data
Sandison, Alan.
Robert Louis Stevenson and the appearance of modernism / Alan
Sandison.
p. cm.
Includes bibliographical references and index.
ISBN 0–312–15968–4 (cloth)
1. Stevenson, Robert Louis, 1850–1894—Criticism and
interpretation.   2. Modernism (Literature)—Scotland.   I. Title.
PR5496.S185    1996
828'.809—dc20                                                  95–50589
                                                                    CIP

10   9   8   7   6   5   4   3   2   1
05   04   03   02   01   00   99   98   97   96

Printed and bound in Great Britain by
Antony Rowe Ltd, Chippenham, Wiltshire

To Helen M. Henderson, the best of teachers, and
*in memoriam* J. A. H., the best of students

# Contents

*Acknowledgements*                                                    viii

*Introduction: 'A Future Feeling'*                                       1

1    A Crisis of Paternity                                              18

2    *Treasure Island:* The Parrot's Tale                               48

3    Arabesque                                                          82

4    *Prince Otto:* To Write and Obliterate                            145

5    *Kidnapped* and *Catriona:* The Missing Storey                    179

6    *Jekyll and Hyde*: The Story of the Door                          215

7    'No Other Father': Title Deeds in *The Master of Ballantrae*      270

8    *The Ebb-Tide*: A Modernist in the South Seas                     317

9    *Weir of Hermiston*: The Horizon of Silence                       369

*Select Bibliography*                                                  415

*Index*                                                                421

# Acknowledgements

For their valuable assistance in reading drafts and their constructive criticism, I am indebted to Alison Hoddinott, Elaine and Kenneth Moon, David Evans and Robert Dingley. The latter, in particular, has sacrificed a great deal of time and given freely of his own large store of knowledge of Victorian life and letters in the furtherance of this study. I should also like to record the help I received by being given access to the Beinecke Library and from discussions with John Scally of the National Library of Scotland.

To go back to where Henry James, and Browning, and Swinburne and Meredith had come. ...

The others all stayed where they were, it was where they had come but Henry James knew he was on his way.... And so although they did in a way the same thing, his had a future feeling and theirs an ending.

Gertrude Stein

...in the early seventies there came a kind of awakening. ...

Gertrude Jekyll

# Introduction:
## 'A Future Feeling'

Since we have explored the maze so long without result, it follows, for poor human reason, that we cannot have to explore much longer; close by must be the centre, with a champagne luncheon and a piece of ornamental water. How if there were no centre at all, but just one alley after another, and the whole world a labyrinth without end or issue?

'Crabbed Age and Youth'

A critic is a reader who ruminates. Thus, he should have more than one stomach.

Friedrich Schlegel

...to break a butterfly on the wheel, or make it walk the plank.

Alastair Fowler

It is very tempting to begin by paraphrasing D. C. Muecke on irony and say that so many critics have already not defined Modernism that there seems to be little point in not defining it all over again. Equal circumspection about its beginnings would then be enjoined upon one as a matter of course. The trouble is that the argument against such an elegant evasion of the issue has been compellingly set out by Stevenson himself. In a devastating review of J. Clarke Murray's *The Ballads and Songs of Scotland* he writes: 'Now, modesty is a good thing in itself; but the same modesty which withholds a man from resolving a question, should certainly keep him back from publishing the fact of his indecision to the world in more than two hundred pages of type.'

Clarke Murray was certainly culpable to the degree that he had a well-defined corpus to work on unlike anyone seeking to ascribe a character to Modernism. To survey what has been done already is to recognise the magnitude of the task. Thus Harry Levin's stimulating essay 'What was Modernism?' was answered by Maurice Beebe in 'What Modernism Was', and both contributions were helpfully 'perspectivised' by Michael Levenson's *A Genealogy of Modernism*, subsequently rivalled by Ricardo Quinones' *Mapping Literary Modernism*. In the middle of these 'definitive' accounts had come, *inter alia*, Richard Ellmann's and Charles Fiedelson's anthology *The Modern Tradition*, Malcolm Bradbury's and James MacFarlane's perennially valuable collection of essays, *Modernism 1890–1930* and David Lodge's *The Modes of Modern Writing*. Clearly maps and genealogies are going to provide an indispensable *vade mecum* for a traveller venturing into this terrain.

So far as I know there isn't an essay called '*When* was Modernism?' but it is, of course, a question subsumed in most of the writings alluded to though the answers are remarkably various; and naturally so since *when* Modernism appeared depends on *what* it appears to the writer to be. Thus Ricardo Quinones announces – in a generous spirit of give or take a few years – that he has no objections to the beginnings of Modernism being pushed back to the 1890s. But even with the built-in proviso of 'as a movement' this is still rather niggardly. After all Stephen Spender (who almost seems to have been *there*), discussing what he capitalises as the Modern Movement in *The Struggle of the Modern*, sees it as *having reached its climax* 'just before the First World War'. David Lodge inexplicably uses the wrong metaphor when he writes in *The Modes of Modern Writing* that after the Great War 'the Edwardian certainties and complacencies were unable to reassert themselves and *the stage was set* for that astonishing burgeoning of Modernism in English Literature'. If the stage is only being set then, there's going to be very little time for performance before Bradbury and for MacFarlane to ring down the curtain in 1930.

The early 1880s would seem to be a popular starting-date though some commentators opt for the 1870s. Roland Barthes is much more expansive and delivers his verdict with something of the panache of Virginia Woolf when she, in pursuit of the watershed, advanced the proposition that 'on or about December 1910 human nature changed...'. 'Around 1850', writes Barthes, 'classical writing therefore disintegrated, and the whole of literature, from Flaubert to the present day, became the problematics of language.'[1] Perhaps more reassuringly, Louis Kampf in *On Modernism* declares, after the obligatory genuflection in the direction of *Tristram Shandy*, and in a slightly odd sentence, that 'modernism is, and has been for some years, a permanent state of mind';[2] while Michael Levenson lets us all off the hook by informing us that '[p]art of all the difficulty with modernism is that it has suppressed its origins. As it became an established cultural preserve, it revised its history in line with its present inclinations.'3

It is Louis Kampf, however, who offers the latecomer a way out, and one which is so dignified as to come within a whisker of the mandarin. His opening sentence is enviable in its masterful resolution: 'I do not wish to discuss the *nature* of modernism.' So there. The reasons he then gives can readily be sympathised with: 'Whatever the nature of the parent, we are all too sure of the diversity of the offspring.' Confronted by the 'dizzying variety of philosophies, social and political systems, and styles of art which constantly assault our intellects and feelings', he decides to 'leave the task of defining our age to some of our deeper philosophers, theologians and social thinkers'.

In truth, Kampf has, in his preface, already supplied successors with all the essentials of a *modus operandi* by quoting William Empson's simple definition of the critic's duty which is 'to follow his nose'. 'Surely,' writes Kampf, 'one's own direction depends on one's sense of smell.' Precisely; and because my own sense of smell assures me that Robert Louis Stevenson's work has, in Gertrude Stein's phrase, 'a future feeling' highly compatible with what I construe to be Modernist sentiments, I have presumed to look at his achievement through the spectacles Modernism provides me with. (Of course it helps to know that writers like Nabokov and Borges have also recognised in Stevenson that same future feeling.)

The moment any such argument gets down to detail, however, one has to recognise that, no matter how many disclaimers and qualifications one enters, there will always be those to cry out, 'Shakespeare said (did) that three-and-a-half centuries ago.' And if it is not Shakespeare it is Cervantes or Rabelais. In some ways one is lucky to come within reach of their gravitational pull since one is liable to be swallowed up in the insatiable black hole which is *Tristram Shandy*. Or, even more humiliatingly, one is stuck in a distinctly sub-lunar sphere by others claiming that what has been painstakingly assembled as evidence of Modernist sentiment is really just Romance (or Romantic) sediment. There is no way of decisively winning such an argument and so one settles for an attempt to provide evidence of a proto-Modernist 'future feeling' in Stevenson's work which, to some, may happily suggest affinities with those innovative developments which have come to characterise a substantial and important part of later nineteenth and early twentieth-century writing whereby greater freedom of expression has been vouchsafed modern consciousness.

When William Archer, the champion and translator of Ibsen (and himself an 'Ibsenite' Modernist), described Stevenson as 'a modern of moderns' he knew what he was saying. In 1885 the word 'modern' was itself modern for, though Baudelaire had an essay entitled 'The Modern Artist' in *The Salon of 1859*, and, in *Painter of Modern Life* (1863) had noted conflicting tendencies which were later to be seen as an expression of Modernism (one half of the moderns were concerned with the 'transitory, the fugitive and the contingent' and the other with the 'eternal and immutable'), his tone was often hostile and disparaging. It is only after 1883 that the term begins to appear with any frequency and with positive associations, this being the year of Georg Brandes' *Men of the Modern Breakthrough*.

Thus Archer is using what would have been recognised at the time as an *avant-garde* term and, as his phrase implies, sees Stevenson both as a bold exponent of the new dialectic and as one liable to carry the nascent doctrine to uncongenial extremes. Archer was already a highly-regarded critic associated with those who were engaged in challenging traditional artistic (and particularly literary), values so his endorsement of Stevenson's lower-case modernism is significant as were the grounds for his classification. In particular Archer (who stood for a morally committed art) identified his 'alert self-consciousness' as putting him 'in the front rank of our new school of stylists', but he regrets that this particular emphasis on the new aesthetic is deliberately calculated so that 'his readers shall look first to his manner, and only in the second place to his matter'.[4]

I shall return to William Archer in the next chapter but would like to focus attention first on this alert self-consciousness which Archer has singled out as Stevenson's most noticeable characteristic. In fact, in this brief introduction I should like to look at Stevenson's putative Modernism under three broad headings chosen because their components will reappear in the subsequent discussion of different texts. These are: self-consciousness, textuality and authority.

Writing of the period between 1880 and the turn of the century, Malcolm Bradbury and James MacFarlane have this to say about it: 'if anything distinguishes these decades and gives them their intellectual and historical character, it is a fascination with evolving consciousness: consciousness aesthetic, psychological and historical'.[5] And, one could say, if any single thing distinguishes Stevenson's writing it is his intense artistic self-consciousness. It manifests itself in a number of ways but principally, perhaps, in an abiding concern with matters of form and metafictional structures. For art's role as a purveyor of moral truth designed to equip readers with rules for life, he has as much distaste as D. H. Lawrence expressed in his celebrated letter to Garnett for that 'certain moral scheme' within which he felt he was expected to conceive his characters.[6] In those works which, in their moral and psychological realism might seem to be responding to such expectations (for example, *The Master of Ballantrae*), there is always, as this study will show, an accompanying subversive, deconstructive undertow.

Artistic self-consciousness is for Stevenson the *sine qua non* of the contemporary writer; and it is the yardstick by which he measures the performance of others. Victor Hugo, for example, is seen to be superior to Walter Scott precisely because of 'the advance of self-consciousness' perceived in his work. 'There never was artist more unconscious than Scott and there have been not many more conscious than Hugo', he writes in his essay, 'Victor Hugo's Romances'; and he goes on to praise Hugo for showing 'how organically he had understood the nature of his own changes' (7). It is, in fact, Scott's failure in self-consciousness which lies behind Stevenson's belittling of his predecessor at the end of 'A Gossip on Romance'.

> As his books are play to the reader, so were they play to him. ... He was a great day-dreamer, a seer of fit and beautiful and harmonious visions, but hardly a great artist; hardly in the manful sense, an artist at all. ... Of the pleasures of his art he tasted fully; but of its toils and vigils and distresses never man knew less. A great romantic – an idle child (131).

That Stevenson should have written with such condescension about Scott when himself only thirty-two and a writer of still limited achievement, shows how much he wanted to distance himself from Scott and the tradition he represented. It also shows, however, how very seriously Stevenson took his work and himself as artificer. The distinction which he draws between the sort of 'play' indulged in by his predecessor and the highly contrived 'play' which he strategically deploys in his own novels is sharp enough to be cutting. That Scott does not deserve to be called an artist 'in the manful sense' is a clear allusion to the absence of that strenuous attention to his craft – with all the 'toils and vigils and distresses' that entailed – which Stevenson, with unremitting effort, lavished on his own.

That his remarks on Hugo could very well be applied to himself is surely obvious, for, among British writers of the period there was

certainly no more conscious artist than Stevenson; and from his
constant interrogation of the nature of his own changes comes his
extensive theorising on the means and integrity of art. From this, too,
comes his endless experimenting which also links him to the modernist
temper. Talking of the 'special nature of the modernist response',
Peter Keating in his important book *The Haunted Study* finds it in part
exemplified in 'that permanent state of formal experimentation which
manifests itself within an author's work not as traditional development or change but as an unstoppable reaction against the self...'.[7]
Stevenson's experiments, his ceaseless questing among forms,
ensured that of all his contemporaries his works show the greatest
and most radical diversity. *New Arabian Nights* could not be more
different in conception from *Weir of Hermiston,* or *The Master of
Ballantrae* from *Prince Otto,* or any of those from *The Ebb-Tide.* What
all of them do have in common, however, is a profound interest in
formal categories and the relationship between them. So intense is
the interest that at times (as in the case of *The Ebb-Tide* and *New Arabian
Nights*) it becomes a large part of the subject.

Writing of the Modernist attempt to break down genres and transcend limitations of form, Maurice Beebe in his essay 'What
Modernism Was' suggests that this implies 'a preoccupation with
form itself' which he sees as 'a major distinguishing feature of
Modernism'.[8] It is a preoccupation which Stevenson fully reflects, as
Henry James notes when reviewing a volume of his letters. Unable
to recall any instance of Stevenson 'expressing' a subject *'as* a subject',
that is, talking of 'the idea out of which it springs', he observes that,
instead, it is '[t]he form, the envelope, [which] is there with him,
headforemost, *as* the idea'.[9]

When I described Stevenson as questing among forms I did not,
of course, mean that his was a quest for a particular form. To the
contrary, Stevenson delights in the polyphonic coexistence – even
within one text – of a number of forms, articulating themselves in a
number of 'voices'. This is demonstrable not just in the novels I have
mentioned but also in *Jekyll and Hyde* and, less obviously, *The Master
of Ballantrae.* At times the effect is more polysemic than polyphonic
but Stevenson himself is too vital a consciousness (and too committed
to telling a story for his own and other people's pleasure) to allow
these different voices to cancel each other out, negating all realities
bar the linguistic (though it is fair to say that the idea hovers, from
time to time, at the edge of his mind). Either way, polyphonic or
polysemic, it shows Stevenson embracing an open-endedness in his

view of the art of fiction which in turn leads to notions of contingency and indeterminacy.

In his introduction to *An Old Song* Roger Swearingen observes that 'even in his twenties Stevenson had the same view of fiction that by the end of the century, in part due to his own arguments for it from *Victor Hugo's Romances* (1874) onward, was all but universally accepted: that the writer's job was to render, not explain, to depict rather than also draw practical and moral conclusions'.[10] To Stevenson, re-directing attention from the novel as 'treatise' (to use Lawrence's derogatory term) to formal priorities, from mimesis to the abstract and non-representational, was to confer on the artist a greater freedom:

> Art is not like theology; nothing is forced. You have not to represent the world. You have to represent only what you can represent with pleasure and effect, and the only way to find out what that is is by technical exercise.[11]

The criterion that is involved in 'with pleasure and effect' is far from clear but the key lies in 'technical exercise' and leaves no doubt that a new constraint has arrived in the premium which technique now bears. (We recall the earlier reference to 'toils and vigils and distresses' which the artist, serious about his craft, is committed to.)

In his essay 'Fontainebleau' Stevenson is again to be found encouraging the aspiring artist (or writer – for Stevenson the terms are explicitly interchangeable) to ignore those who 'prate to him about the lofty aims and moral influence of art' and concentrate on technique: 'To work grossly at the trade, to forget sentiment, to think of his material and nothing else, is, for a while at least, the King's highway to progress' (102). And he stresses again that it is 'the love of form and not a novel reading of historical events [which] mark[s] the vocation of the writer and the painter'. He then adds: 'The arabesque, properly speaking, and even in literature, is the first fancy of the artist...'; and by 'arabesque' he means, I believe, form for its own sake.

The emphasis on technique is a natural concomitant of that high degree of artistic self-consciousness which characterises Stevenson's writing and it again helps to confirm his literary relations: 'One of [the word Modernism's] associations', write Bradbury and MacFarlane, 'is with the coming of an era of high aesthetic self-consciousness and non-representationalism in which art turns from realism and human representation towards style, technique and spatial form...'.[12] Stevenson's predilection is very much for the abstract. Denying Henry James's contention that literature *can* successfully 'compete with life' he goes on to argue in 'A Humble Remonstrance' that '[t]he arts, like arithmetic and geometry, turn away their eyes from the gross, coloured and mobile nature at our feet and regard instead a certain figmentary abstraction'. Rejecting mimesis (James had argued that 'the air of reality (solidity of speci-fication) seems to me to be the supreme virtue of the novel'), Stevenson holds that '[s]o far as [literature] imitates at all it imitates not life but speech: not the facts of human destiny, but the emphasis with which the human actor tells of them'. And he goes on: 'Our art is occupied, and bound to be occupied, not so much in making stories true as in making them typical', concluding with his well-known coda: 'A propo-sition of geometry does not compete with life; and a proposition of geometry is a fair and luminous parallel for a work of art. Both are reasonable, both untrue to the crude fact; both inhere in nature, neither represents it' (135–6).

One of the reasons why Herbert Spencer appealed to him so much, he tells us in 'Books Which Have Influenced Me', is that 'there dwells in his pages a spirit of abstract joy, plucked naked like an algebraic symbol but still joyful' (64). In 'A Note on Realism' he traces the contemporary taste for details and 'facts' back to Scott, before whom, in, for example, the hands of Voltaire, the story was 'as abstract as a parable'. Now '[a] photographic exactitude in dialogue is ... the exclu-sive fashion; but even in the ablest hands it tells us no more – I think it even tells us less – than Molière, wielding his artificial medium, has told to us and to all time of Alceste or Orgon, Dorine or Chrysale' (70). He would thus have been very pleased had he known of the company George Moore placed him with: 'Romantic! He's about as romantic as Voltaire, and would have been a much greater writer if he had lived in the reign of Anne.'[13]

So Stevenson, stressing in his own work the importance of the abstract, of artifice and the repudiation of old conventions, illus-trates well what Bradbury and MacFarlane contend to be part of any working definition of Modernism, namely 'a quality of abstraction and highly conscious artifice, taking us behind familiar reality, breaking away from familiar functions of language and form'.[14] At times Stevenson goes further than one might expect. In 'Some Gentlemen in Fiction' he describes those 'verbal puppets' as he twice calls the novelist's characters, as 'only strings of words and parts of books; they dwell in, they belong to, literature; convention, technical artifice, technical gusto, the mechanical necessities of the art, these are the flesh and blood with which they are invested' (110). That technical gusto is everywhere in Stevenson's own art and it is what makes books like *New Arabian Nights* and *The Dynamiter* a pleasure to read. It is also an important source of the regard felt for him by as innovative a writer as Mallarmé (who dubbed him *un maître*) and of his influence on later writers like Nabokov and Borges. One of the compliments paid to him which he must have found particularly gratifying came from Sir John Millais, who as well as being one of the foremost painters of his day, was also, according to Sidney Colvin, 'a shrewd and independent judge of books'. Buttonholing Colvin, Millais is recorded as saying:

> I wish you would tell [Stevenson] from me, if he cares to know, that to my mind he is the very first of living artists. I don't mean writers merely, but painters and all of us. Nobody living can see with such an eye as that fellow, and nobody is such a master of his tools.[15]

Though Millais' remark recognises Stevenson's technical skill it also helps to remind us that there are limits to his taste for the abstract and it is something to be kept in mind throughout the discussion which follows. As Kenneth Graham judiciously notes in his essay 'Stevenson and Henry James: A Crossing', there is 'a saving contradictoriness' in much of what Stevenson says. Thus his aestheticism 'frequently comes up against his inalienable sense of experience. ... His very description of the "life" with which "emasculate" art must never compete is a paean to experience.' From this Graham goes on to argue that 'so *un*self-contained is his art ... that its most florid and highly-formed rhetoric is directly occasioned by the perception and the pressure of life's shapeless variety'.[16] That said, however, it is still the case that Stevenson's work illustrates well one of the 'Modernist' contentions of 'The Name and Nature of Modernism': that 'the task of art is to redeem, essentially or existentially, the formless universe of contingency. ... The act of fictionality thus becomes the crucial act of imagining.'[17] Immediately this recalls part of Stevenson's disquisition in 'A Gossip on Romance' where he contemplates the unfinished 'reality' of the Hawes Inn:

> There it stands, apart from the town, beside the pier, in a climate of its own, half inland, half marine – in front, the ferry bubbling with the tide and the guardship swinging to her anchor. ... But you need not tell me – that is not all; there is some story, unrecorded or not yet complete, which must express the meaning of that inn more fully (122).

In *Experiment in Autobiography* H. G. Wells wrote:

Throughout the broad smooth flow of nineteenth century life in
Great Britain, the art of fiction floated on [an] assumption of social
fixity. The Novel in English was produced in an atmosphere of
security for the entertainment of secure people who liked to feel
established and safe for good. Its standards were established within
that apparently permanent frame and the criticism of it began to
be irritated and perplexed when, through a new instability, the
splintering frame began to get into the picture.[18]

Curiously enough Gertrude Stein in her 1906 essay on Picasso had
used just this image to signify the necessary break with the past
which would allow cubism to flourish: 'the framing of life, the need
that a picture exist in its frame, remain in its frame, was over'.[19] For
her, too, the frame began to get into the picture, but in a sense rather
more 'advanced' than Wells intended, for in her avowed aim 'to kill
the nineteenth century' she advocated an art that was pluralised or
'de-centralised' and expressed 'in a conceptual iconography which
itself ultimately becomes the object of the composition'.[20] Applied to
literature (as, indeed, Stein meant it to be) what this amounted to
was a recognition of the appropriateness of metafictional writing to
those who considered themselves part of the *avant-garde*.[21]

As one would expect in 'a modern of moderns' whose most conspicuous literary feature was his acute artistic self-consciousness,
Stevenson's interest in metafictional process was very marked. He
took a great deal of pleasure in exposing the fictionality of his fictions
by 'laying bare the device' and, as Chapter 3 makes clear, earned the
disapproval of his own contemporaries and even some of ours for
doing so. And it has to be admitted that he can, at times, be highly
provocative in the extravagance of his performance, sporting his
*mise-en-abyme* device like a piece of costume jewellery.

'As our arts come to reflect on themselves more and more', writes
Louis Kampf in *On Modernism*, 'their real subject seems to be the
theory of their own composition, and the concern for the nature of
their own reality becomes quite obsessive.'[22] Ricardo Quinones makes
the point more moderately and more sympathetically:

Given its overwhelming sense of change Modernism is suspicious
of standpoints. ... Its expansive consciousness must always pass
beyond itself and reflect the fact of its own reflecting. This accounts

for what has been called the 'reflexive' nature of Modernism, its sense of form turning back on itself as the panorama of multiplicity gives way to circularity.[23]

The first part of this is well said and Stevenson's writing, with its constant self-appraisal and restless search for new forms, fits the description more than adequately. Quinones' last sentence, however, seems to me to underestimate the extent to which the form, in turning back upon itself, can be seen to be interrogating (not simply confirming) its own constructive principles. In Stevenson, as in others, this turning back upon itself was often a prelude to de-creation or deconstruction, as is evidenced in, for example, *New Arabian Nights* and the 'Bibliographical Postscript' at the end of *Prince Otto*. Further, when Stevenson's texts manifest their reflexivity in the tale-within-a-tale (as they often do), it cannot be said without qualification that 'the panorama of multiplicity gives way to circularity'. The fact is that the reflexive object continues to multiply itself in an endless succession (or recession), prolonging and expanding the life of the narrative with philoprogenitive ardour. Hence Stevenson's frequent call upon the model offered by *The Thousand and One Nights* and his occasional recourse to biblical parable (by definition a tale-within-a-tale) and exemplary biblical episode traditionally grounded in a welter of begetting.

A further objection to Quinones' comment as it stands is that it appears to ignore that rhetorical device so ubiquitous in Modernist writing where it is often what adds particular significance to form turning back on itself: that is, irony. Quinones talks very rightly about 'Modernism's need at once to create a world and to stand outside of it'[24] but, as Stevenson's work demonstrates, what allows writers to do so is their manipulation of the ironic device and the ironic perspective. Peter Brooks in his valuable critique, *Reading for the Plot*, accepts that 'from Flaubert onward into Modernism the self-reflexive ironies of the novelistic enterprise have been a major preoccupation'.[25] So are they with Stevenson, most of whose major fiction reflects it to a greater or lesser degree. In some works, notably *New Arabian Nights* and *The Dynamiter*, it is crucial to his undertaking and achievement. As Chapter 3 demonstrates, Stevenson manipulates the ironic voice with consummate skill and a great deal of wit and humour, and, more generally, very much in accord with that 'stance of irony and non-commitment' which Maurice Beebe holds to be 'one of the features which most clearly distinguishes Modernist literature from that of other periods'.[26]

The 'four cardinal points of Modernism' which Beebe identifies in his essay help to summarise the relationship of Stevenson to this new movement. They are: its formalism and the aesthetic autonomy of the work of art; its attitude of detachment and non-commitment which he, following the New Critics, calls irony; the use it makes of myth; its reflexivity. Of course Beebe enters all the proper qualifications acknowledging that these four characteristics are in no way 'the unique property of the Age of Modernism'.[27] Nonetheless, in their concurrence and coherence these features do help to differentiate Modernist writing from what had preceded it though one is also inclined to stress Clement Greenberg's sensible view that what makes all this new is 'its explicitness, its self-consciousness, and its intensity'.[28] This is certainly what strikes one about the manifestation of these characteristics in Stevenson's writing.

At times, however, it seems that Stevenson carries his Modernist sympathies further than might be expected, reaching out beyond the Modernism of the *fin-de-siècle* to anticipate some (but only some) of the characteristics of Postmodernism. Earlier I quoted Peter Brooks on the self-reflexive ironies of Modernism but that was only part of his argument. What he was in process of doing was to contend that the difference between Modernism and Postmodernism is largely one of degree. Though there will be plenty of critics who disagree with this, Ricardo Quinones is surely right when he argues that Postmodernists 'do not define themselves by a counter-Modernity in the way Modernists defined themselves by a counter-Romanticism'.[29] The difference Brooks finds between the two is 'a greater explicitness in the abandonment of mimetic claims, a more overt staging of narrative's arbitrariness and lack of authority, a more open playfulness about fictionality'.[30]

What is of particular interest here is that Brooks lists three areas which Stevenson returns to from time to time in his work and develops to a point which renders the Modernist label insufficient and inexact. Something else (not mentioned by Brooks) encourages one occasionally to go beyond Modernism for one's parallels and that is Stevenson's at times ostentatious desertion of mimesis for a self-engrossed textuality where whatever reality exists has its unstable dwelling-place in the dazzling interplay of texts. It is important to stress, however, the fitfulness, even the capriciousness, with which such a mode makes its appearance and to note that it can coexist with others of a quite different character. Thus, while we can have *New Arabian Nights*, which might seem to illustrate Barthes' celebrated onion metaphor for the text, in which the text is to be likened not to a fruit with a kernel, but to an onion, 'a construction of layers (or levels or systems) whose body contains ... nothing except the infinity of its own envelopes – which envelop nothing other than the unity of its own surfaces'[31], we also have *The Master of Ballantrae* where the inter-textual, polyphonic play seems to conform more to a Bakhtinian model since, notwithstanding the importance of formal interests and the plurality of 'voices', it continues to offer the reader ready access to a recognisable world. In fact, Bakhtin's description of the specific qualities which the novel has brought to other genres reveals that they are those which are at the forefront of Stevenson's fictional works, reassuring us that we do not have to follow Lévi-Strauss and conclude that 'to reach reality we must first repudiate experience':[32]

> The other genres become dialogized, permeated with laughter, irony, humour, elements of self-parody and finally – this is the most important thing – the novel inserts into these other genres a certain semantic open-endedness, a living contact with unfinished, still evolving contemporary reality (the open-ended present).[33]

The Modernist emphasis on change, on discontinuity, on the need to 'make it new' involves a more than usually decisive rupture with the past. The first step was to admit the evidence of dislocation; to recognise that, in the words of Edward Said, '[w]here once stood a *pater familias*, or an unfolding plot, or a single image (like a Platonic idea of the father) that bred successive and genealogically related 'children' we have instead a break in the sequence'.[34] Though he does not harp on it Stevenson was well aware of discontinuity, incoherence and instability: 'The obscurest epoch is today;' he wrote in 'The Day After Tomorrow', 'and that for a thousand reasons of inchoate tendency, conflicting report, and sheer mass and multiplicity of experience; but chiefly, perhaps, by reason of an insidious shifting of landmarks' (113). Bradbury and MacFarlane are more specific, and more explicit about the consequences for art:

> The communal universe of reality and culture on which nineteenth-century art depended was over; and the explosively lyrical, or else the ironic and fictive modes, modes which included large elements not only of creation but of de-creation, were inevitable.[35]

But Stevenson was no passive or fearful monitor of change; like other Modernist writers he not only welcomed change but loudly called for it. That this entailed conflict with what had gone before he well knew; indeed, it could be said that he sought out such conflict – at times almost obsessively.

Concern about authority and origins (and originality) lie very near the heart of Modernism (always assuming that the latter has a constitution different from that of Roland Barthes' onion) and Stevenson's work reflects this. Additionally, however, there is, as the next chapter will show, a hostility towards traditional authority (or the authority of the tradition) which goes beyond intellectual and aesthetic considerations. Perhaps for this reason his hostility is not always consistent in its implacability, occasionally being found contending with another more accommodating instinct. There is, for example an interesting moment in 'Lay Morals' when he tries to square the circle by detaching God, the Supreme Authority, from the tradition which is upheld in his name at the expense of what constitutes 'truthfulness' for the individual: 'For the voice of God, whatever it is, is not that stammering inept tradition which the people holds' (32–3).

Maurice Beebe, in discussing some of the more vacuous and clichéd definitions of Modernism ('an age of crisis', 'the end of innocence', 'the inability to communicate') also includes among the recurrent themes the quest for the father. But this theme is neither vacuous nor vitiated by facile usage. To the contrary, it is of central significance: in the Modernist context the generational conflict is vital and vitalising. It is, however, necessary to acknowledge that the theme of the father is important in English literature well before the last quarter of the century. For example, in her essay on Thackeray in *The English Novel*, Dorothy Van Ghent indicates the important difference between the father in eighteenth-century fiction and his appearance in nineteenth-century novels. In the earlier period she notes that he was, in general, 'a reflection of social trust' who embodied 'a general social system of values' and expressed a coherent world-view.[36] In nineteenth-century writing, fathers stand for conflict, for the betrayal of trust, for the absence or abuse of authority. Peter Brooks in *Reading for the Plot* sees paternity as 'a dominant issue within the great tradition of the nineteenth-century novel … a principal embodiment of its concern with authority, legitimacy, the conflict of generations, and the transmission of wisdom'. So central are these issues of authority and paternity to the literary imagination of the century that he sees them providing 'not only the matter of the novel but also its structuring force, the dynamic that shapes its plot'.[37]

More recently Peter Keating in *The Haunted Study* places the changed concept of the father in the context of the Victorian family which was 'not just an important institution: it was the age itself'. Thus '[r]ebellion against Victorianism meant, unavoidably, rebellion against the family; and the enemy, just as unavoidably, was the father of the house'. Keating recognises that the theme of conflict between parents and children 'was present in Stevenson's work from the beginning' culminating in his last novel, *Weir of Hermiston,* where it found 'its most savage expression'. There, if the author's intention to have Weir preside over his son's trial and condemn him to death had been carried out, 'it would have been an appropriate comment on a problem that had come to be seen as soluble only by a violent struggle to the death between the generations'. And Keating adds: 'This assumption was carried effortlessly into the work of those novelists who are usually classified as the founders of fictional modernism in Britain.'[38]

For Modernist writers the antagonism towards the father – or fathers – is very often subsumed in, or expressed as, antagonism towards the literary tradition against which they are in revolt. It may also have wider social and political implications as it does in Stendhal or Balzac. But among all those writers in whose work the theme of the father figures centrally from, say, the two writers just mentioned to Samuel Butler, there is no more fervent an antagonist than Robert Louis Stevenson. True, the antagonism is of a strangely mixed sort, as even a cursory reading of *Treasure Island* would tell us, yet it fuels a subversiveness towards all authority and what he calls its 'dead jargon', a hostility towards the dominant precursors and a sustained assault on the themes, forms and moral bases of 'the literary tradition' – that is, those who would uncritically peddle the received wisdom of the art of fiction.

It is quite remarkable that in all the accounts of the generational warfare of the later nineteenth century, Stevenson's contribution has gone virtually unnoticed. Because of its seminal importance for an understanding of his work, as well as for its more general significance, I have prefaced my study with a discussion of what calls for recognition as a long-running crisis of paternity or authority in a context which will, I trust, amplify Stevenson's Modernist credentials.

In each of the chapters which follow one (or, in the case of Chapters 3 and 5, two) works will be discussed in an approach which is designed

to bring out their Modernist affinities without swamping them in
'dead jargon'. The study is, to borrow one of Malcolm Bowie's happy
phrases, 'a work merely of theory-tinged literary criticism' in which
I hope it will not seem as though I am taking a spade to a soufflé or
making a butterfly walk the plank.

**Notes**

All references to Stevenson's writings (including letters) are to the Tusitala
edition (1924).

1. Roland Barthes, *Writing Degree Zero* (1967), p. 9. Quoted in 'The Name
   and Nature of Modernism' in *Modernism 1890–1930*, ed. Malcolm
   Bradbury and James McFarlane (1976), p. 21.
2. Louis Kampf, *On Modernism: The Prospects for Literature and Freedom*
   (Cambridge, Mass., 1967), p. 9.
3. Michael Levenson, *A Genealogy of Modernism: A Study of English Literary
   Doctrine 1908–1922* (Cambridge, 1986), p. xi.
4. William Archer, 'Robert Louis Stevenson: His Style and his Thought'.
   Quoted in Paul Maixner, *Robert Louis Stevenson: The Critical Heritage* (1981),
   pp. 160, 161.
5. Op. cit., p. 47.
6. Quoted in Peter Faulkner (ed.), *A Modernist Reader: Modernism in England
   1910–1930* (1986), p. 23.
7. Peter Keating, *The Haunted Study: A Social History of the Novel 1875–1914*
   (1989), p. 97.
8. Maurice Beebe, 'What Modernism Was' in *Journal of Modern Literature*,
   Vol. 3, 1974, p. 1072.
9. See Janet Adam Smith (ed.), *Henry James and Robert Louis Stevenson: A
   Record of Friendship and Criticism* (1948), p. 267.
10. Roger Swearingen (ed.), *An Old Song and Edifying Letters of the Rutherford
    Family* (Paisley, 1982), p. 15.
11. *Letters*, vol. 2, p. 252.
12. Op. cit., p. 25.
13. Quoted in Maixner, *op. cit.*, p. 476.
14. Op. cit., p. 24.
15. Sidney Colvin, Introduction to *Letters*, vol. 1, p. XV.
16. Kenneth Graham, 'Stevenson and Henry James: A Crossing', in *Robert
    Louis Stevenson*, ed. Andrew Noble (1983).
17. Op. cit., pp. 30–31.
18. H. G. Wells, *Experiment in Autobiography* (1934), vol. 2, pp. 494–5.
19. Gertrude Stein, *Picasso: The Complete Writings*, ed. Edward Burns (Boston,
    1970), p. 38.
20. Ibid., p. 16.
21. The sense in which I am using this term is explained in Note 18 at the
    end of Chapter 1.
22. Op. cit., p. 10.

23. Ricardo J. Quinones, *Mapping Literary Modernism: Time and Development* (Princeton, 1985), p. 118.
24. Ibid., p. 117.
25. Peter Brooks, *Reading for the Plot: Design and Intention in Narrative* (New York, 1985), p. 317.
26. Op. cit., p. 1070.
27. Ibid., p. 1070.
28. Clement Greenberg, 'The Necessity of "Formalism"' in *New Literary History*, vol. 3, no. 1, Autumn 1971, p. 172.
29. Op. cit., p. 254.
30. Op. cit., p. 317.
31. Roland Barthes, 'Style and its Image'. Quoted in David Lodge, *The Modes of Modern Writing: Metaphor, Metonymy, and the Typology of Modern Literature* (1979), p. 63.
32. Claude Lévi-Strauss, *Tristes Topiques* (New York, 1961). Quoted in David Lodge, op. cit., p. 64.
33. M. M. Bakhtin, *The Dialogic Imagination: Four Essays by M. M. Bakhtin*, ed. Michael Holquist, trans. Caryl Emerson and Michael Holquist (Austin, 1981), p. 7.
34. Edward W. Said, *Beginnings: Intention and Method* (Baltimore, 1975), p. 171.
35. Op. cit., p. 27.
36. Dorothy Van Ghent, *The English Novel: Form and Function* (New York, 1953), p. 147.
37. Op. cit., pp. 63, 65.
38. Op. cit., pp. 228, 235, 236.

# 1

# A Crisis of Paternity

Death of the Father would deprive literature of many of its pleasures. If there is no longer a Father, why tell stories? Doesn't every narrative lead back to Oedipus? Isn't storytelling always a way of searching for one's origin, speaking one's conflicts with the Law, entering into the dialectic of tenderness and hatred?

Roland Barthes, *The Pleasure of the Text*

'Who doesn't desire his father's death?'

Ivan in Dostoevsky's *The Brothers Karamazov*

Leslie Fiedler, commenting on Stevenson's inclination to play the role of child and to fall in love with older women, says of his marriage to the forty-year-old Fanny van de Grift that 'there can be little doubt that one of Stevenson's motives in marrying was to become a child – and finding himself at the age of 30 at long last a child enabled him unexpectedly to become for the first time a real creative writer'.[1] Having delivered himself of this assured analysis of Stevenson's psycho-sexual drives and the nature of the literary imagination, Fiedler doesn't really attempt any very serious justification. Which is probably just as well since his colourful diagnosis, while it may be winsomely paradoxical, seriously misrepresents Stevenson's problems with authorship – literary and biological.

It is, of course, perfectly true that Stevenson was attracted to women older than himself (although this did not exclude flirtations, perhaps even affairs, with women of his own age). His attraction to the American Fanny van de Grift (whom he had met at the artists' colony at Grez) had been preceded by his apparently one-sided love affair with Mrs Sitwell, twelve years his senior, and with Mme Garschine, who was older still. It is also true that when Mrs Sitwell, the estranged wife of a clergyman 'of unfortunate temperament and uncongenial habits',[2] decisively rejected his importunities, Louis' letters to her tended to begin 'Dear Mother' and end 'Your Loving Son'. To

18

Mme Garschine he was explicit: 'What I want is a mother', adding very surprisingly and unjustly that he had never really had one.

This hardly amounts to proof of a Fiedlerian mother-fixation though Michael Levenson might regard it as exemplifying what he sees as a typically Modernist inability to separate from the mother; gaining freedom from the mother being, he tells us in *A Genealogy of Modernism*, the real problem for the Modernist. The mother, after all, stands for continuity which the Modernist seeks to rupture: more than that, she 'has become for Modernism the voice of submission to that which is conventionally social, to the larger general processes of life, foremost among which, for her, is the procreative'.[3]

For Stevenson, however, this is too simplistic a solution, his problem being more an inability to break free from the father rather than the mother. A helpful comparison could be made between Stevenson and Kafka who writes in his celebrated *Letter to the Father*: 'It is true that Mother was inimitably good to me, but for me all that was in relation to you...' and he adds that his mother was 'too devoted and loyal to you to have been able to constitute an independent spiritual force, in the long run, in the child's struggle' – that is, in the struggle to grow up.[4] Kafka compares his parents' interaction with him to a hunt in which the beaters drive the game into the range of the hunters' guns: 'Mother unconsciously played the part of a beater during a hunt' so, in the words of Peter Blos's study, 'driving the little boy into the father's domination'. Only with 'violence and revolution', Kafka argues, would there have been a chance of 'breaking away from home... assuming that Mother wouldn't have worked against it'.[5]

I shall return to this issue later but I should like first to deal with the second point in Fiedler's statement: the child-therefore-a-creative-writer sequence. If this is, as it seems, a version of the artist-as-child figure, it might be said again to help to identify Stevenson as a proto-type Modernist. Levenson instances Ford Madox Ford as a writer who deploys the notion of the artist as child as a 'rhetorical stratagem'. He says of Ford's rather studied accentuation of himself as someone who never grew up ('I have always the feeling that I am a little boy who will be either "spoken to" or spanked by a mysterious *They*') that this pose of the naif is a Modernist expression of the 'shift in attention from large things to small, from public responsibility to private expression, from an "adult" earnestness and self-seriousness to "childlike" intimacy, sincerity and amoralism'. Certainly Ford sounds not untypical of a number of his contemporaries in his insis-

tence that his childhood had been blighted by the great Victorian
father-figures like Carlyle, Arnold and Browning 'and the gentlemen
who built the Crystal Palace':

> These figures were perpetually held up to me as standing upon
> unattainable heights, and at the same time I was perpetually being
> told that if I could not attain these heights I might just as well not
> cumber the earth.

Against these authoritarian figures he warns his children in a sub-
Wildean paradox:

> 'Do not desire to be Ruskins or Carlyles. Do not desire to be great
> figures. It will crush out all ambition; it will render you timid... .'[6]

What is subsumed in this repudiation is a distrust of the magisterial figures who dominated the tradition, and an apparent inclination
towards the alternative morality and aesthetic of the artist as child.
But Levenson is right, I believe, to call this a 'rhetorical stratagem'
and in doing so he opens a sizeable gulf between a response such as
Ford's and that of Stevenson. Ford's alleged 'embracing of childhood insignificance and irresponsibility' is as calculated and paraded
as Harold Skimpole's in *Bleak House*. It is hard to believe that it ever
emanated from a crisis of paternity, whereas for Stevenson it is a
crisis which inscribes itself on all his doings (and *de*-scribes himself).
Again the comparison with Kafka is instructive for he was a life-long
'prisoner of his childhood'. In a letter to a friend, Kafka writes: 'I
shall never grow up to be a man; from being a child, I shall immediately become a white-haired ancient.'[7] Both the sentiment and the
tone are Stevensonian for whom (*pace* Fiedler) the problem was not
how to become a child again but, like many of his literary contemporaries (and countrymen), how to grow up. Moreover, Stevenson's
distressed perception of himself as genuinely and irredeemably
trapped in, if not childhood, at least late adolescence, authenticates
him as a proto-modernist every bit as well as does Ford's attraction
to the aesthetic of the artist-as-child, particularly given the fact that
he himself relates this stasis to unresolved conflicts in his attitude to
procreation and heredity not just in the biological and psychological
arenas but also as they reveal themselves in his writing and literary
theory.

The preoccupation of writers with issues of origin and generation
(frequently conflated in the nexus of 'originality') is nothing new,
one of the clearest examples being also one of the earliest of modern

times – the work of Rabelais. As Carla Freccero has shown in her outstanding book *Father Figures: Genealogy and Narrative Structure in Rabelais*, just such a preoccupation fuels and structures Rabelais's masterpiece. In outlining its ramifications Freccero makes the text sound almost Modernist:

> Thus a predicament of filial succession structures Rabelais's narrative, even as it constitutes the themes: of the writer as author of 'his' book, of the narrator as royal historiographer, of the son Pantagruel and his gigantic father Gargantua. The predicament is theological and linguistic as well: many chapters enact the search for and the impossibility of finding a transcendent guarantee or reference outside language that will authorize meaning, at the same time that the text seems to celebrate the very contingency implied by the failure of such a search.[8]

Much of the felicitous wording of this discriminating judgement can be applied with altogether notable appositeness to Stevenson's 'predicament of filial succession' as that emerges in his writing. But what confirms him as a Modernist is the dominating role these issues play in his consciousness and his explicit incorporation of them into all forms of his discourse (fiction, essays, letters) and his readiness to theorise on the basis of this consciousness.

Robert Louis Stevenson was the only child of devout Calvinist parents who doted on him and on each other: the latter to a degree which appeared to a highly sensitive child to exclude him. Later he found a characteristically succinct, penetrating and memorable phrase to describe his reaction, confiding to Mrs Sitwell that 'the children of lovers are orphans' – and this despite the fact that his mother was both deeply loving and assiduous in her caring for her son; which does not, of course, exclude the possibility that she, like Kafka's mother, was too devoted to her husband to assist in her son's efforts to grow up, though the relationship between the two was, for the most part, warm and close. Though he perceived her to be 'cold and unresponsive' in the family rows over Louis' alleged atheism when she always sided with her husband against their son, he could still write of a lunch he had with his mother in that same year of turmoil (1873) in these terms: 'We had lunch together, and were very merry over what people at the restaurant would think of us – mother and son they could not suppose us to be.'[9]

For whatever reason (and the mother's rather fragile health which led her to spend most mornings of Louis' early life in bed might have been a factor) there was, for the son, some sort of felt deficiency in the relationship. Perhaps in compensation he allows himself to be attracted to, and sets out to attract the love of,. women significantly older than himself. As the recounting of the impact made on other diners by the appearance of himself and his mother would suggest, there is clearly more to it than this, however; and, equally clearly, at the heart of the matter is the oedipal complex. In fact, complicate it as one may, it is very hard not to see Stevenson's case as a classical example. Just as Kirstie Elliott had perceived there to be at the end of every passage which might lead Archie Weir out of his 'maze of difficulties' the 'flinty countenance of Hermiston', so does the figure of the father appear to Stevenson to lie across the path of his own moral and intellectual progress. Kafka saw himself in a similar predicament and visualised it in a striking image:

> Sometimes I imagine the map of the world spread out flat and you stretched out diagonally across it. And what I feel then is that only those territories come into question for my life that either are not covered by you or are not within your reach. And, in keeping with the conception I have of your magnitude, these are not many and not very comforting territories, and above all marriage is not among them.[10]

A few months before his death, in a letter to his cousin Bob in September 1894, Stevenson admits that among the things – he calls them 'the commonest things' – he cannot get used to are procreation and heredity. In his explicitness he goes a long way towards identifying the root of the tension which informs his work so comprehensively that it seems to structure it. So acute is his consciousness of the inhibiting paternal presence (far in excess of anything actually perpetrated by Thomas Stevenson), so aware is he of the need to throw off such constraints if he is to secure his independence and his own dominion, and so doubtful about ever fully doing so, that his work seems to be the product of a sustained and unresolved crisis of authority. It is this crisis that I should like to give some attention to now though its impact on Stevenson's fiction will be examined more fully in the following chapters.

The best way to compress some of the most significant ramifications inherent in the concept of authority in the present context is to quote again from Edward Said's *Beginnings*:

*Authority* suggests to me a constellation of linked meanings: not only, as the OED tells us, 'a power to enforce obedience,' or 'a derived or delegated power,' or 'a power to influence action,' or 'a power to inspire belief,' or 'a person whose opinion is accepted'; not only those, but a connection as well with *author* – that is, a person who originates or gives existence to something, a begetter, beginner, father, or ancestor, a person also who sets forth written statements. There is still another cluster of meanings: *author* is tied to the past participle *auctus* of the verb *augere;* therefore *auctor,* according to Eric Partridge, is literally an increaser and thus a founder. *Auctoritas* is production, invention, cause, in addition to meaning a right of possession. Finally, it means continuance, or a causing to continue. Taken together these meanings are all grounded in the following notions: (1) that of the power of an individual to initiate, institute, establish – in short, to begin; (2) that this power and its product are an increase over what had been there previously; (3) that the individual wielding this power controls its issue and what is derived therefrom; (4) that authority maintains the continuity of its course.[11]

At the beginning of *The Madwoman in the Attic* Sandra Gilbert and Susan Gubar also use what they call Said's 'miniature meditation on the word *authority*' as a summary of the means by which (in Said's words) 'narrative fiction asserts itself psychologically and aesthetically through the technical efforts of the novelist', noting that his four 'abstractions' can also be used 'to describe both the author and the authority of any literary text'. In the way that male writers use the metaphor of literary paternity, Gilbert and Gubar find confirmation of the thesis that in patriarchal western culture 'the text's author is a father, a progenitor, a procreator, an aesthetic patriarch whose pen is an instrument of generative power like his penis'. Observing that implicit in this metaphor of paternity is an idea of 'ownership', they conclude:

if the author/father is owner of his text and of his reader's attention, he is also, of course, owner/possessor of the subjects of his text, that is to say of those figures, scenes, and events – those brain children – he has both incarnated in black and white and 'bound' in cloth or leather. Thus, because he is an *author*, a 'man of letters' is simultaneously, like his divine counterpart, a father, a master or ruler, and an owner: the spiritual type of a patriarch, as we understand that term in Western society.[12]

For Stevenson, however, as we shall see, there were insurmountable problems in his assuming the role of patriarch.

To his claims to having been orphaned by being the child of lovers, and his apparent tendency to turn lovers into mothers, Stevenson adds a great many allusions to his being and remaining a child or youth. If on occasions he does so with an element of self-congratulation, more often the tone is one of self-criticism and frustration. In the letter to his cousin already referred to, he tells him that he has 'become more of a bewildered child', and in his last letter to Edmund Gosse (possibly his last letter of all), and thinking of Gosse the family man, he contrasts himself as 'a childless, rather bitter, very clear-eyed blighted youth': a string of adjectives which bears much scrutiny. A childless youth might not form much of a paradox but add bitter, clear-eyed and blighted, and premature sterility threatens to become a sterile (or aborted) maturity. It also recalls David Balfour who in both *Kidnapped* and its sequel *Catriona* shows himself extraordinarily aware of himself as a youth (in *Catriona* almost an impotent youth), repeatedly stating his unreadiness for fatherhood. Quite early in the story and aware of his attraction to Catriona, he reproves himself in these words: 'I knew that he was quite unfit to be a husband who was not prepared to be a father also; and for a boy like me to play the father was mere derision' (60).

The anxiety and uncertainty about fatherhood expressed here centres on David's perceived unreadiness for it, and many of Stevenson's principal characters suffer a similar paralysis, arrested in a phase of late adolescence, as Blos says of Hamlet, 'lingering and loitering in the borderland that lies between youth and manhood': one needs only to instance Robert Herrick in *The Ebb Tide*, Prince Otto and Archie Weir. Only in *Weir of Hermiston*, however, is there a direct confrontation between son and father although this is the *actual* locus of antagonism in nearly all the novels. As Freudians would expect, the father is himself often absent and it is another adult who fills the paternal role by attracting the usual mixture of hostility and dependence. In *The Ebb Tide* it is the sinister, murderous figure of the monomaniac evangelist Attwater and in *Kidnapped* it is Uncle Ebenezer who tries to bring about David Balfour's death. In *Treasure Island* it is the surrogate father Long John Silver who performs an extreme version of the same role: extreme because he polarises the incest-threat and death.

Despite the fact that Stevenson represents many of his characters as trapped on an island of aborted maturity – something which quite literally happens twice to David Balfour, once in *Kidnapped*, where his mood of desolation on the island of Earraid is never fully accounted for, and again on the Bass Rock in *Catriona* – this depiction goes hand in hand with a fierce repudiation of the literary fathers when he talks *in propria persona* of the role of the writer. What this suggests is that, again like Kafka, it is in the literary act that Stevenson most success-fully bids for his own freedom, his own powers of generation and, more or less successfully, contains his enfeebling father-complex. Kafka is explicit: ' in my writing, and in everything connected with it, I have made some attempts at independence, attempts at escape, with the very smallest success'. Paradoxically, however, as Peter Blos points out, 'writing not only offered him an escape from the emotional bondage to his father but also kept the writer in constant closeness to him, albeit in a transfigured mode. He says "My writing was all about you; all I did there after all was to bemoan what I could not bemoan upon your breast. It was an intentionally long-drawn-out leave-taking from you."'[13] Given all the surrogate father-figures in Stevenson's fiction, much the same could be said of him.

For all that, Stevenson was never in any doubt as to the impera-tive which ruled artistic integrity: it was to be radically innovative, which, of course, entailed a conscious and deliberate break with the past, with the 'fathers'. His refusal to be cabined and confined by the architects of literary Crystal Palaces expresses itself in an antago-nism towards the elders of the literary tradition which he perceives himself to be expected to inherit. In fact, his argument with them is trenchant and sustained and conducted in terms which justify the description of him as a Modernist.

One of the best and most concise of these arguments takes place with William Archer who, being a Modernist of an Ibsenite sort himself, saw himself as something of a champion of what he described as 'the reigning ethical school'. The source of Stevenson's offence in his eyes and in the eyes of those with similar views is pinpointed in two of the former's letters. In the first of these (to Henry James) Stevenson deplores that part of his audience who think that 'striking situations or good dialogue are got by studying life: they will not rise to understand that they are prepared by deliberate artifice and set off by painful suppression'.[14] In the second letter (to another admirer, Trevor Haddon), he elevates technique to a level guaran-teed to affront the traditionalists of the realist school:

In your own art, bow your head over technique. Think of technique when you rise and when you go to bed. Forget purposes in the meanwhile: get to love technical processes: to glory in technical successes; get to see the world entirely though technical spectacles.[15]

Clement Greenberg argues in his essay 'Beginnings of Modernism' that it is precisely in the emphasis that it gives to technique 'in its most concrete sense' that Modernism defines itself, and he quotes Fromentin's attack on the painter Manet on just this score, which strikingly resembles Archer's on Stevenson.[16] Certainly sentiments such as those communicated to Haddon, devoid of all redeeming reference to life and moral purpose, were guaranteed to elicit a broadside from Archer, and they did: 'To be less concerned about what a man says than about how he says it', he wrote accusingly, 'is unutilitarian, unprogressive, not to say reactionary: for the world is not to be regenerated by a nice arrangement of epithets.' From the standpoint of Ibsen's translator, Stevenson could well have appeared reactionary: he certainly was provocative as he demonstrated in his essay 'Fontainebleau', already referred to, where, talking of the 'intelligent bourgeois' who 'prate to the [young artist] about the lofty aims and moral influence of art', he goes on:

> And this is the lad's ruin. For art is, first of all and last of all, a trade. The love of words and not a desire to publish new discoveries, the love of form and not a novel reading of historical events, mark the vocation of the writer and the painter (102).

The truth surely is that he was 'ahead' of Archer and his school. In fact, the latter, as I have indicated in the Introduction, had more than a suspicion that Stevenson was the voice of the future, and we might recall here the words quoted earlier: 'Stevenson is a modern of moderns both in his alert self-consciousness and in the particular artistic ideal which he proposes to himself.'

Being 'a modern of moderns' Stevenson does not believe that art can regenerate the world: at best, in his view, what the modern writer can do is to regenerate the *word*, though not, of course, in a way that will permit it to calcify in a new prescriptive linguistic order, since he believes in language's perpetual renewal. In this context it is worth quoting Greenberg again: 'It is what happened to the medium in every art, that I consider most decisive in fixing the beginnings of Modernism. The renovation of the medium has brought about a revaluation of aesthetic quality. Away from such renovation Modernism evaporates.'[17] Stevenson's confidence in his role of innovator – even originator – in the theoretical context makes an interesting contrast with all those references in the letters to himself as a child or youth and, in his fiction, with his near-obsession with characters who betray a crippling weakness, immaturity or irresponsibility. These characters may set themselves to challenge authority but they mostly fail.

Stevenson's inclination to portray himself and his male characters as perpetual adolescents or youths clearly reflects a crisis which is only partly resolved in the degree of freedom he secures in becoming an author of fictions. It is impossible to ignore the fact that the failure of crippled 'orphans' like David Balfour and Robert Herrick or Prince Otto to supply an authority of their own has a lot in common with Stevenson's personal difficulties with procreation and heredity. On the one hand Stevenson is the young, aspiring writer determined to be radically innovative, which, he readily acknowledges, means repudiating or at least distancing himself from his precursors; on the other, he appears greatly troubled at the prospect of exercising the authority which would make his usurpation effective and secure and confirm his newly-asserted independence. The dilemma thus described is very much a Modernist one. Indeed, it is part of Irving Howe's felicitous definition of Modernism:

> The modern world has lost the belief in a collective destiny. Hence, the hero finds it hard to be certain that he can possess – or that anyone possesses – the kind of powers that might transform human existence. Men no longer feel themselves bound in a sacred or even, often enough, a temporal kinship. Hence, the hero finds it hard to believe in himself as a chosen figure acting on behalf of a divine commandment or national will.[18]

The rupturing of these links of sacred and temporal kinship have a considerable bearing both on Stevenson's problems and his Modernist character. By extending the examination of Stevenson as innovator, this should become clearer.

For Stevenson, art has to be new in every moment and this constant renewing and refreshing is a continuous process infused with an alert radicalism that will subvert any recidivist tendency towards reliance on the given order. 'God', he says in that gloomy and sententious piece 'Lay Morals', (immediately entering the qualification 'if there be a God'), 'speaks daily in a new language by the tongues of men; the thoughts and habits of each fresh generation and each new-coined spirit throw another light upon the universe and contain another commentary on the printed Bibles.' For the son of a funda-mentalist follower of Calvin to whom the Biblical word was fixed and unalterable, such a defiant dedication to revisionism was a remarkable deviation from the paths of righteousness. In a final sentence he presses the point home, enterprisingly if not, indeed, paradoxically, connecting the moral order with this discontinuous and tentative linguistic process which rejects the 'given' and fash-ions a transient shape for itself out of distrust, novelty and conflict, so ensuring that full formal self-realisation and completion will be infinitely deferred: 'every scruple, every true dissent, every glimpse of something new, is a letter of God's alphabet' (32). Such an alphabet is going to guarantee that the new language will perpetually de- and re-construct itself.

For Stevenson words are anything but fixed and unalterable – or even reliable; and the problematics of language can be seen to be a recurring concern throughout his work. 'As a matter of fact', he writes in his essay on Walt Whitman, 'we make a travesty of the simplest process of thought when we put it into words; for the words are all coloured and foresworn, apply inaccurately, and bring with them from former uses, ideas of praise and blame that have nothing to do with the question in hand' (60). That we must not put our trust in words is part of the message of 'Lay Morals'. 'When many people perceive the same or any cognate facts, they agree upon a word as symbol; and hence we have such words as *tree, star, love, honour,* or *death;* hence also we have this word *right*, which, like the others, we all understand, most of us understand differently, and none can express succinctly otherwise' (26). The result is that, as he puts it in one of his notes (collected by Colvin at the end of *Memories and Portraits*), '[w]e can never argue on anything beyond the relations between certain words; and if you and I understand by our words a different substrate of thought – if we have different values for the same symbols and yet have no means of actually explaining this disagreement – we cannot wonder that we reach different solutions …' (176). At times he expresses a real frustration at the inadequacy of language as in these sentences from 'Victor Hugo's Romances': 'The fact is that art is working far ahead of language as well as of science, realising for us, by all manner of suggestions and exaggerations, effects for which we have as yet no direct name… we are not used to consider anything clear until we are able to formulate it in words, and analytical language has not been sufficiently shaped to that end' (8). Freud was, of course, to help to remedy this, but Stevenson accepts that we may never have a direct name for these effects since they 'do not enter very largely into the necessities of life'.

With a revisionist God at the head of affairs, received opinion and the precepts of the elders (in which, by neat and ironic contrast, he tells us, 'the letter is not only dead but killing') are anathema and he firmly commits himself to experiment, innovation and change, central tenets in the Modernist creed, and to theorising on their implications for the craft of writing. But it is, perhaps, in his intense awareness of his own theories, and his constant reappraisal of them, that he is most obviously Modernist. William Archer recognised this – though it did not alter his opinion of Stevenson: 'Mr Stevenson has no lack of theories to express, but his beliefs are not weighty enough, his truths are not true enough to demand emphasis.'

As crushing as one of Dr Leavis's ponderations, this judgement is followed by one equally misconceived: 'By instinct or design', he writes, 'he eschews those subjects which demand constructive patience in their describer.'[19] As one would expect, but still greatly to his credit, Stevenson refuses to be patronised (I choose the word advisedly), replying that it was by instinct and design that he avoided traditional and currently-approved processes of construction, adding in another revealing sentence: 'my theory is that literature must always be most at home in treating movement and change; hence I look for them'.[20] He had to look fairly hard, it seems, for what he found himself surrounded by was, in his own words 'an art that is like mahogany and horsehair furniture, solid, true, serious and dead as Caesar'.[21] Stevenson thus draws a very clear line between himself and his precursors (which can, of course, also be taken to distinguish him from many of his conservative contemporaries, and the whole of what Archer described as the 'reigning ethical school'). The vigorousness of his repudiation, however, and the clear perception of himself as of the *avant-garde* may come as something of a surprise.[22]

So he consciously sets up the artist/author as the foe of what is safely traditional which simply means (to use his own words from a letter to Edmund Gosse in March, 1884) 'sinking into rank conformity and pouring forth cheap replicas'. Art and novelty are synonymous for him: putting one's trust in the habitual and the familiar is a kind of death. As he writes in 'Lay Morals': 'familiarity has a cunning disenchantment; in a day or two she can steal all beauty from the mountain-tops; and the most startling words begin to fall dead upon the ear.... Our attention requires to be surprised... ' (10).

It would take a fairly ingenious argument to make a strong case for any resemblance between Stevenson and D. H. Lawrence, but on this subject their feelings are identical and Stevenson would have been delighted with Lawrence's tirade against the habituated ear:

> If your ear has got stiff or a bit mechanical, don't blame my poetry. That's why you like Golden Journey to Samarkand – it fits your habituated ear, and your feeling crouches subservient and a bit pathetic. 'It satisfied my ear,' you say. Well, I don't write for your ear. This is the constant war, I reckon, between new expression and the habituated mechanical transmitters and receivers of the human constitution.[23]

Stevenson's writing provide us with one of the best early examples of what Irving Howe in *The Decline of the New* describes as Modernism's 'commitment to an aesthetic of endless renewal'.[24] He would certainly have accepted Lawrence's metaphor of a constant war; the 'cunning disenchantment' of familiarity being an insidious enemy and one with whom his audience will often side. For him defamiliarisation is an activity not just proper for, but essential to, the artist; and his fiction displays a remarkable variety of devices which further this objective. Some of these have been touched on already and many of them overlap: his refusal to allow his readers to be passive and wallow in illusion or the familiar; his preference for the galvanic; his nearly-constant challenge to the reader through the intrusiveness of a highly-cultivated artistic 'personality'; his scorn for the realists with (in yet another interesting phrase) their 'insane pursuit of completion'.[25]

The freshness of vision that Stevenson so applauds will be an antidote to the torpor (a favourite word of his) which is such a blight upon the spirit. (Restfulness, he says, in 'Talk and Talkers' is a quality for cattle.) And in fiction a great deal of the artificer's effort will be expended on stimulating – even startling – the reader into a fuller awareness of, not so much the world as the word, for that reinvigorates everything. In Stevenson's eyes, to be conscious of oneself as a radical innovator committed thereby to challenging the wisdom of the fathers is the special perquisite of youth and the *sine qua non* of the artist. In 'Letter to a Young Gentleman Who Proposes to Embrace the Career of Art' while singling out contentment as the near-relative of indifference and a threat to all that is truly living, he hails youth as the repository of hope in that it is the natural enemy of 'rank conformity'. Youth for whom the 'razor-edge of curiosity' is never dulled, is, he insists, 'wholly experimental'.

From this it is a natural progression to link trail-blazing, authority-repudiating youth with the tendency to theorise. The adolescent is, after all, 'the individual who begins to build "systems" or "theories" in the largest sense of the term ... [who] is able to analyse his own thinking and construct theories'.[26] What might be construed as youthful follies, Stevenson argues, may simply be a protest against the defects of the society the young have inherited. Provoked by such an inheritance, the youth's protest may very well turn into a theory and theories are, of course, an attempt to understand the present and map the future. They are the matrix of new authority; agents of discontinuity and a bid for originality. Youth will not go with the flow of the mainstream: 'When the torrent sweeps the man against a boulder, you must expect him to scream, and you need not be surprised if the scream is sometimes a theory.'

Not that there will be any special stability or consistency in one's theories any more than there will be an impregnable system as their end-product; life itself is too random and changeful for that:

> We have no more than glimpses and touches; we are torn away from our theories ... we take a sight at a condition in life, and say we have studied it; our most elaborate view is no more than an impression... It is vain to seek for consistency or expect clear, stable views in a medium so perturbed and fleeting.... This is no cabinet science, in which things are tested to a scruple; we theorise with a pistol at our head....

Nonetheless, when one considers the complacent, unthinking alternative (which produces art like mahogany and horsehair furniture), it is better if one's agony is expressed, and one's involvement in this perturbed medium and one's commitment to change thus authenticated:

> It is better to emit a scream in the shape of a theory than to be entirely insensible to the jars and incongruities of life and take everything as it comes in a forlorn stupidity. Some people swallow the universe like a pill; they travel on through the world like smiling images pushed from behind.[27]

Again, Stevenson is voicing sentiments very characteristic of the Modernist who, in Irving Howe's words in 'The Idea of the Modern', 'regards settled assumptions as the mask of death'. That perceptive and under-rated Modernist, Yevgeny Zamyatin (born in 1884) expressed this in words which would have appealed to Stevenson: 'most people suffer from hereditary sleeping sickness, and those who are sick with this ailment must not be allowed to sleep or it will be their final sleep, death'. Stevenson might even have agreed with him that 'harmful literature is more useful than useful literature', since in using the word 'harmful' Zamyatin is really referring to all heretical literature which challenges dogma. Such literature is 'a means of combating calcification, sclerosis, crust, moss, quiescence. It is utopian, absurd... '.

Stevenson's work, particularly, but by no means exclusively, in its formal aspect, is similarly heretical and with much the same objectives. In 'Books Which Have Influenced Me' Stevenson, in fact, says something very similar to Zamyatin:

> A human truth, which is always very much a lie, hides as much of life as it displays. It is men who hold another truth, or, as it seems to us, perhaps, a dangerous lie, who can extend our restricted field of knowledge, and rouse our drowsy conscience (68).

Zamyatin strengthens the comparison by continuing in the same essay: 'The formal character of a living literature is the same as its inner character: it denies verities.... It departs from the canonical tracks, from the broad highway.' This links with yet another interesting comparison to be made between the two. In 'Crabbed Age and Youth' Stevenson writes that even youth's capacity for error is a healthy sign, for it teaches us that all error and not just verbal error is simply 'a strong way of stating that the current truth is incomplete'. Even if he had delivered himself of no other wise saw, it seems to me that this prescient remark entitles Stevenson to be regarded as having a Modernist sensibility and outlook. Just as he had enshrined discontinuity in the constant dissent which regenerates God's alphabet, so incompleteness is to be found at the heart of truth itself, leaving open an infinity of possibilities. Doors will be there for the opening at the end of passages which we may or may not take into the rose garden. By arguing *against* the resolution of error, he is liberating the dialogic imagination, he is de-centring truth and he is even de-centring self, for this 'error' is not a Cartesian 'J'erre donc je suis' in which the 'cogito' is subsumed and therefore 'merely a deviation from an assured truth', but is something which 'aggressively calls into question the status of truth itself' and by implication undermines Cartesian structures of self. The attempt to *eradicate* error (as Georges Van Den Abbeele argues in his stimulating book *Travel as Metaphor* from which these quotations come) seeks to establish a self-sufficient economy of the self. But to institute this ideal economy, the self 'must mark itself off from all else, trace a clear line of demarcation between itself and what is other'.[28] Stevenson's refusal to condemn or eradicate error shows that for him as for other Modernists, the self is a much more fluid and unstable quantity than is implied in this particular construct.

Zamyatin, proceeding along similar lines, chooses a metaphor more natural to a Russian engineer and redefines truth, in the process – and particularly in his conclusion – dotting a few of Stevenson's i's and crossing his t's: 'errors are more valuable than truths: truth is of the machine, error is alive; truth reassures, error disturbs. And if answers be impossible of attainment, all the better!'[29] In fact, Stevenson had declared himself almost as forcefully, though with a slight adaptation of the metaphor, on the subject of the mechanical for, in 'Lay Morals', he condemns those who allow themselves to be seized by an 'arctic torpor' (the equivalent of Zamyatin's sleeping sickness), the result of which is that 'consciousness becomes engrossed among the reflex and mechanical parts of life'. This, he says, 'is temporal damnation, damnation on the spot' (28).

For Stevenson, it is explicitly through youth that the creative force of error declares itself, which is far from the backhanded compliment it might seem since youth is that moment of revisionary truth which is most likely to challenge the authorised version. At any rate, for the artist there is, in Stevenson's eyes, no alternative to preserving the youthful vision if he is to avoid 'rank conformity' and make his proper mark upon the world. 'Cling to your youth,' he had advised his correspondent Trevor Haddon, 'it is an artistic stock in trade'; and when in a later letter to Haddon he talked about preferring galvanism to acquiescence in the grave, he had added airily, 'All do not: 'tis an affair of tastes and mine are young.'[30]

Upon the youthful artist, then, self-conscious of his role, there falls the mantle of divination, manifesting itself in the urge, even the need, to theorise and in the conviction that this, too, assists in 'making it new.' 'Darwin', wrote Stevenson to Henry James, 'said no-one could observe without a theory: I suppose he was right: ... but I will take my oath, no man can write without one – at least the

way he would like to'. For Stevenson it was a never-ending quest to
find a form or forms that would march with his evolving theories,
and often he despaired of bringing the two together. In this letter to
James he reveals just how integral to his writing his theories were:
'my theories melt, melt, melt, and as they melt, the thaw-waters
wash down my writing and leave unideal tracts – wastes instead of
cultivated farms'.[31] It is worth recalling at this point Malcolm
Bradbury's remarks on the significance of the Modernists' concern
with theory and literary form:

> The search for a style and a typology becomes a self-conscious
> element in the Modernist's literary production; he is perpetually
> engaged in a profound and ceaseless journey through the means
> and integrity of art. In this sense, Modernism is less a style than a
> search for a style in a highly individualistic sense; and indeed the
> style of one work is no guarantee for the next.[32]

Stevenson does not give up the search to 'make it new', which entails
a repudiation of the hegemony of the past and results in the discovery
of a new theoretical base as a *point de départ*. To a practising poet,
Stephen Spender, the confrontation of past and present was 'the
fundamental aim of Modernism'.[33]

It is obvious, of course, that the influence of the past can neither
be comprehensively denied nor ever fully escaped from. In several
of his essays Stevenson readily acknowledges this, emphasising,
indeed, its cultural and personal necessity. (Without it, he writes in
'A Chapter on Dreams', man would be left a 'naked nullity' for it is
only through his connection with the past, real or imaginary, that he
knows himself.) This awareness does, however, produce a certain
tension in the Modernist artist (perhaps for the artist throughout
most of the nineteenth century). This is how Louis Kampf describes
the situation:

> The artist's awareness that the history of his art has a logic has
> brought about an unusual, and problematic, attitude towards that
> history. He is historical, yet he feels no sense of progressive
> development in his particular art; there is no feeling of event
> following event, form fusing into form, with the artist's own work
> emerging at the end. Rather than seeing the past as a number of
> events developing in time, the tendency is to see those events
> concatenated in space.

Or, to put it as Stevenson does in 'A Chapter on Dreams', the past is reduced to a proliferation of 'incontinuous images'. For the Modernists, however (Kampf continues), '[t]o be aware of history is to be aware of its destructiveness' and thus to many it seemed that they had 'to be rid' of the past if the possibilities of the future were to be realised.[34]

Stevenson, as the young iconoclast and innovator, lauding youth with its razor-edge of curiosity and promise for the future, seems to furnish the very figure of what Wallace Stevens called the youth as virile poet. ('I am myself part of what is real and it is my own speech and the strength of it, this only, that I hear or ever shall.'[35]) The difficulty is that along with this thrusting and theorising experimentalist we get the contradictory figure of youth as arrested development, youth refusing to exercise authority despite having repudiated the ancestral tradition. Clear-sighted enough to see the need for, and to commit himself to, a radical departure from the canonical tracks, but, at the same time, a blighted youth.

Why blighted, why this constant evocation of inhibited growth in the child or youth? Is it that the artist has been made too literally and comprehensively synonymous with youth and the transition to adulthood portends defeat? Is it for the reason given by Howe – that the modern world has lost its belief in a collective destiny and so deprives the hero (or the artist) of any confidence that he *can* exercise authority as a chosen figure, no longer driven or supported by certain authority-structures and cultural imperatives? Is it that, having repudiated ancestral authority, there is simply nothing else to believe in but one's self and no reason to believe in that: an artificer but without the least shred of divinity to strengthen a belief in his high calling to be a leader of the minds of men? Is it that the act of parricide paralyses and he can do no more than young Jack in 'The House of Eld' who, after slaughtering his parents, 'sat in the lone house and wept beside the bodies'? Some such reflection prompts Harold Bloom to ask a pertinent question in *The Anxiety of Influence*:

> Do strong poets gain or lose more, as poets, in their wrestling with their ghostly fathers? Do ... all [the] revisionary ratios that misinterpret or metamorphose precursors help poets to individuate themselves, truly to be themselves, or do they distort the poetic sons quite as much as they do the fathers?[36]

With Stevenson the first stage of self-assertion is clear enough: a vigorous denial by him of the authority of his precursors; but the second stage does not fully ignite and so the new challenger can not wholly escape the gravitational pull of the fathers: 'what divides each poet from his Poetic Father (and so saves, by division)', says Bloom, 'is an instance of creative revisionism'.[37] The revisionism, the dividing, would seem, in Stevenson's case, not to have been complete enough so that the ephebe, as Bloom, following Stevens, designates the young artist about to achieve full-blown artistic self-realisation, is going to be prevented from reaching his full development. This makes sense as far as it goes. Stevenson is, without question an excellent example of that crisis of authority and legitimacy referred to by Peter Brooks in *Reading for the Plot*. Brooks uses Stendhal's *Le Rouge et Le Noir* in a brilliant exposé of the crisis of paternity; but if one is looking for an example of a British writer who graphically illustrates the crisis in his own creative processes (and his literary theory), Stevenson should be an obvious choice.

Despite what has been said here about a crisis of authority and paralysis, and despite Stevenson's fictionalising of that crisis, it should be noted that he does *not* give up and settle for rank conformity. He continues to experiment with new forms quite literally to the day of his death. Nonetheless, he shows himself convinced that, however much he may have taken arms against the fathers, and despite his marriage, he himself has still not fully entered manhood, is still not, in his own mind, a paterfamilias. And no amount of dressing his large Samoan household in tartan kilts will hide the fact: rather, as so often with kilts, it exposes the deficiency. He is, in his own mind, still a youth, still unable to accept the commonest things 'like heredity and procreation'.

One of his most interesting statements in the light of these comments is his passionately-expressed desire to detach the physical being from the artist altogether: to strip himself of his physical identity and become one, in utter freedom, with artistic process – an abstract personality wholly defined by the needs and processes of art – indeed created by it, creature of the Muse:

> O the height and depth of novelty and worth in any art! and O that I am privileged to swim and shoulder through such oceans! Could one get out of sight of land – all in the blue. Alas not, being anchored here in the flesh and the bonds of logic being still about us.

Son of the Muse then, perhaps, but a son who seeks to become his own Originator, taking the Muse, whose death would be *his* death, to wife:

I sleep upon my art for a pillow; I waken in my art. I am unready for death, because I hate to leave it. I love my wife, I do not know how much, nor can, nor shall, unless I lost her, but while I can conceive myself being widowed, I refuse the offering of life without my art. I am not but in my art; it is me; I am the body of it merely.[38]

Alas, again; he *is* 'anchored here in the flesh', and artistic self-realisation is inextricably bound up with self-realisation *tout court*. For both, the problem is what is to be done about father and fatherhood (not mother). Stevenson, in seeing it as essential for the emerging artist explicitly to repudiate the precursors, was expressing an attitude characteristic of the Modernists, but in so relentlessly returning to it, it seems safe to conclude that the attack upon the fathers also embodied an attack upon the father.

In a remarkable and tantalising fragment (whose unfinished state is *almost* as much a matter for regret as that of *Weir of Hermiston*) he brings the two, innovative artist and hostile son, together. *Edifying Letters of the Rutherford Family* purports to be letters exchanged between father and son and various acquaintances. They are, of course, explicitly concerned with the father and son relationship and are plainly autobiographical. (Stevenson was twenty-six or twenty-seven at the time of their composition.) Most of William Rutherford's talk is about shaking off the constraints of Edinburgh and the paternal restraints, but the idiom he uses is unmistakably that of the young *artist* seeking his freedom by means of energetically repudiating the past. 'I feel', says the lightly-disguised Stevenson, 'as if the wisdom I have been taught is no more than shadows and jargon.' Having decided, for all his propensity for Great Thoughts, that he is only 'a cipher in the sum, a soldier in the vast array of mankind', he is, at the same time, passionately convinced of his own originality and his dedication – unlike his predecessors presumably – to truth:

I, who am quite a common young man with no transcendencies to plume myself upon, am something almost sublime for the moment because I am at the height of my position, a young man such as young men ought to be, vehemently scornful of what is past, vehemently aspiring after what is still before.

Characteristically of the ephebe, the new-comer making his way, he is aware of his isolation and that he is the standard-bearer of truth: 'I am all alone in the dark; no-one is by to encourage or direct me;

they all snore and grovel around me on their rubbish heaps, gorged with sawdust and dead verbiage.'[39]

Freudians would be inclined to argue that the image Stevenson uses here is one which fits well with what he is himself doing: devouring the father, so destroying the god, and decisively breaking the continuum. Which is as it should be, if there is to be a conflation of the artistic and the biological ephebes. 'The God of poets', says Bloom, 'is not Apollo, who lives in the rhythm of recurrence, but the bald gnome Error, who lives at the back of a cave; and skulks forth only at irregular intervals, to feast upon the mighty dead, in the dark of the moon.' This is the same Error we came across earlier – that wandering from the traditionally straight-and-narrow which, to Stevenson, led literally to a dead end: the departure from the canonical tracks, the transgressing enlargement which proves that current truth is incomplete and so ensures perpetual deconstruction and radical new possibilities. Such a quest will mean 'feasting upon the mighty dead', or, more prosaically, going against the paternal grain to map out one's own country and so become one's own Originator. Bloom concludes: 'The largest Error we can hope to meet and make is every ephebe's fantasia: quest antithetically enough to live to beget yourself.' The need to repudiate the precursors and to prefer error to the straight, well-trodden paths of ancestral wisdom is part and parcel of the customary displacement of the father in what Freud called the family romance; which Harold Bloom, in turn, describes as the only poem that even unpoetical natures continue to compose.

In the passage where Stevenson claimed 'I am not but in my art', I have drawn attention to the fact that while he can envisage separation from his wife (in death) it would appear that he is eternally wedded to his Muse. We could go further. Falling in love with older women and eventually marrying one could be construed, in the simple version of the family romance, as reflecting the son's wish to displace the father and become the mother's lover. If, now, mother, shading into wife, shading into Muse is, in accordance with Freudian theory, to be seen as being *rescued*, what is she being rescued from? Initially, of course, from the father who will be, for the poet, the precursor. Freud, in a passage quoted by Bloom, writes that:

> rescuing the mother acquires the significance of giving her a child or making one for her – one like himself of course… all the instincts, the loving, the grateful, the sensual, the defiant, the self-assertive and independent – all are gratified in the wish to be the *father of himself.*

And to be the father of himself is, in the view of others besides Bloom, the objective of the poet – indeed, the *sine qua non* of the poet of serious aspiration, who will thus at last free himself from the anxiety of influence. (We should perhaps recall Stevenson's assertion that a large part of the artist's design is 'to verify his own existence'.) All that it needs, says Bloom, to make Freud's family romance apply to the sodality of poets is to place less emphasis upon phallic fatherhood and more upon priority, 'for the commodity in which poets deal, their authority, their property, turns upon *priority*. They own, they are, what they become first in naming'. (He concludes by adding 'All quest-romances of the post-Enlightenment, meaning all Romanticisms whatsoever, are quests to re-beget one's own self, to become one's own Great Original.')[40]

We can now return to Fiedler's remark about Stevenson marrying Fanny van de Grift in order to become a child and hence a writer. To his proposition as it stands we must, I think, say 'no' (or even 'No! in Thunder'). If we are to be Freudian in our reading of this scion of Edinburgh's New Town, perhaps we should go the whole hog and advance this proposition. Stevenson, if in little else conformist, was, so the theory would run, conformist in Freudian terms. He seeks to displace the father by becoming the mother's lover and so father himself. A variant of this, espoused by Bloom, translates mother/lover into Muse and the young poet, begetting on her his own self, can become, as a writer, his own Great Original, allowing the ephebe to pass into full artistic selfhood, full fatherhood, even full Godhood.

If, however, Stevenson had completed all these stages, there would be no explanation for his perceived entrapment in the late adolescent phase: indeed it would be surprising if any such perception existed. But that evidence is there not just in his perception of entrapment, but in his problems with fathers and paternity in general, in his concern for his literary inheritance and the pressing need to establish originality. What this suggests is that he also conforms to that syndrome identified by Peter Blos as an inability to deidealise the father and transcend the symbiotic relationship enjoyed in the pre-oedipal stage with the dyadic father which, in Blos's words 'proves such a lasting influence on the life of every man'. Failure to complete the deidealisation of the father – 'the task of adolescence' for Blos – means that the progression from childhood to maturity will be blocked. When one of Blos's patients (an older male adolescent) discovered during analysis this source for his sense of entrapment, he commented: 'It feels like being accepted for the first time in my father's arms or to have a life of my own, not just playing at it.'[41] And he later describes the route out of his impasse in these terms: 'If I'll ever be able to let anything or anybody go for good – and what else is growing up all about – I have first to say goodbye to my father' (which Blos suggests should be amended to 'dyadic father').

I believe that Stevenson was never fully able to say goodbye to his father. And here one has to say that, unlike Kafka's parent, Thomas Stevenson was a loving father though severe in his judgements – particularly theological – and frequently critical of his son's way of life. (At one stage he announced his intention, not unlike Mr Pontifex in *The Way of All Flesh*, of disinheriting Louis since, each holding the views he did, he was sure that both would feel such an inheriting to be immoral. Louis concurred.) Though he once or twice referred to his father as a Jekyll and Hyde figure, Louis' memorial essay on him strives for a balanced view.[42] He describes him as being a blend of 'sternness and softness that was wholly Scottish', capable of being both 'shrewd and childish; passionately attached, passionately prejudiced; a man of many extremes, many faults of temper, and no very stable foothold for himself among life's troubles'. As an obituary written by an only son, the essay is remarkably reserved, even guarded, though we know that, however much he inveighed against literary precursors and however often he arranged wounding encounters between his fictional sons and their fathers, Louis loved his father deeply. All that this means, however, is that, in Andre Bleikasten's words, 'contrary to the simplistic assumptions of vulgar Freudianism, the father–son relationship is reducible in none of its stages to mere antagonism'.[43] Unable to complete the final act of what Blos calls 'symbolic patricide', Stevenson resembles the youth who cannot transcend his isogender complex and pass into adulthood. He is stuck forever at the cross-roads confronting Laius, shouting at him from a safe distance even, but unwilling to sever the link with the necessary stroke. The impasse is well described by Blos:

[T]wo sets of enticements and urges are beckoning him in opposite directions. They are those of emotional retreat to earlier childhood positions, when parental idealisation rendered life dependable and predictable, and those of aggressive self-determination and independence, leading into the unknown and unpredictable future.

Writing of the theme of 'the search for the loving and loved father' – a search which is often so intense that it has been described as a 'father hunger' – Blos notes that 'this facet of the boy's father complex assumes in adolescence a libidinal ascendancy that impinges on every aspect of the son's emotional life'. In seeking to renounce this libidinal bond with the father, the adolescent's progress is marked by ambivalence. On the one hand he seeks vigorously to repudiate his submissiveness; on the other, overtly or clandestinely, directly or symbolically, he may seek out these 'submissive modalities' as Blos describes them. Analysis of the latter discovers that they are expressed towards 'males, father and father substitutes as well as brother and brother–substitutes [revealing] a fixation on the dyadic and triadic father which can become responsible for deviant character formation and emotional immaturity'.[44]

There is much recourse to these 'submissive modalities' in Stevenson and we may select our examples from David Balfour's relation to Alan Breck, Prestongrange, or even Catriona, Henry Durisdeer's to his father, Archie Weir's to his and Jim Hawkins' to a galaxy of father-figures. Interestingly, both in his fictions and his own life, the rebellions or repudiations of submissiveness are more than a little half-hearted and usually end in defeat.

Even Stevenson's marriage is not really the rebellion, or at least the farewell, it might properly be seen to be. Kafka, for example, sees marrying and becoming the founder of a family as rendering him equal with his father. (John T. Irwin in 'The Dead Father in Faulkner' reiterates the view that the only hope of the son revenging himself on the father's priority lies in his becoming a father himself.)[45] But Kafka clearly recognises this intrusion into his father's realm for the prohibited fact it is: 'marrying is barred to me because it is your very own domain', he writes in the *Letter*. Stevenson does marry but his wife is already a mother whose eldest daughter is herself an adolescent and whose age makes it unlikely that she will bear Louis any children. He is therefore entering into his father's dominion in a limited sense only.

Where Stevenson 'rebels' most successfully – that is, establishes his independence – and becomes an originator and creator is, like Kafka, in his writing and his literary theory: through his marriage to the Muse with whom is fused lover and mother. Nonetheless, one has to remember his preoccupation in his fiction with immature sons and potent father-figures. So ubiquitous are these allusions and themes that they amount, almost, to the subversion or denial of that authorial mastery – what Bleikasten calls 'the ultimate stake in the writing game' – which would appear to be the realm in which he has achieved some sort of freedom and maturity. No one as sensitive as Stevenson to the theoretical implications of his art and who dwells so knowingly among fictions – the phrase is from Malcolm Bowie's admirable book *Freud, Proust and Lacan: Theory as fiction* – can write so much about crippled and crippling fathers without being aware of the questions thus posed about the integrity of his own authorship. Andre Bleikasten puts the point very well in his essay on Faulkner's *Absalom! Absalom!*: 'sonship and fatherhood as we come to realise in reading the novel are not merely capital issues in the fictional world it represents; they relate back to the writer as fiction-maker and designate the very stakes of his perilous game with language'.[46]

The evidence for the profound tension which underlay the relationship between this father and son, who loved each other so much, is everywhere, though it is never presented as directly as it is in Kafka's *Letter to the Father*; the nearest Stevenson gets to this being the Rutherford letters. In a letter of 2 February 1873, describing to his friend Charles Baxter the miserable atmosphere at 17 Heriot Row, he writes 'I confess I cannot exactly swallow my father's purpose of praying down continuous affliction on my head', and in a later communication (4 November 1873) he is at his gloomiest: 'My parents utterly puzzle me; I have sometimes a notion that the atheist son is almost in the way'.[47] The subject of what the son owes to the father comes up in a very interesting way again in one of his entries in his note-books:

> Nothing so thoroughly brings back to us the unthinkable moralities of the past, as the story of Abraham and Isaac. It is strange enough that this grown man should have consented to follow his father on such a fool's errand and, when he learned at last the object of the journey, should have meekly suffered himself to be bound for the sacrifice; but it is far stranger to think that, while we have plenty of praise of Abraham's faith, we hear not a syllable of comment on Isaac's obedience, that the whole of his conduct in the matter was too much *matter of course* for commendation. This comparison gives us an *aperçu* at the same time into the contemporaneous theology. A man was evidently expected to do much more for his parents than for his God; and this is natural enough; for there was a large choice of deities out of which a man could make his selection, but he never could have another father. All

through the earlier part of the Old Testament there are incidents and expressions that can only be understood in the light of this *competition of Godheads* (180).

Nowhere is the conflict between Louis and his father more conspicuously on display, however, than in those bruising quarrels between the pair over religious doctrine which left Louis prostrate with exhaustion and often in tears. Ostensibly, the quarrel was over Louis' refusal to accept his parents' greater emphasis on God the Father at the expense of the teachings of Christ the Son. In reality, for Louis, the father he was seeking to unseat, in a symbolic sense if in no other, was his own.

In the Rutherford family letters, 'William Rutherford' laments his position as that of a bird in a cage or a prisoner in his cell. 'Just let me see a crevice, and I will show my heels to this dismal city in a trice', he writes 'and land where the sun shines and neighbours mind their own business.' Perhaps there is no such place he concludes, 'no such place, all the wide world over; and nothing but rain and carping and sour looks, and the damned wearisome ten commandments, and their ten million corollaries, dinned in people's ears to perpetuity'. But, he consoles himself, there's always the grave 'where the elders cease from troubling and the wicked are at rest'. In the end Stevenson, of course, does find such a place far away from the Law-giver, where he presides like a paternalistic clan chieftain over his Samoan retainers and like an indulgent father over, not his own, but *his wife's* children.

The book he was working on in Samoa when he wrote his last letters to Gosse and Bob Stevenson, was, of course, *Weir of Hermiston*. Progress on the novel had been slow and one of his difficulties in composing it had much to do with the father/son relationship. Archie Weir has committed murder and Stevenson's problem was how to square with Scottish legal practice his intention of having Lord Hermiston, a judge of the High Court, try *and condemn* his son for murder. It is not surprising to find him writing to his cousin at the time acknowledging that he always had had difficulty with 'commonest things' – like procreation and heredity.

But the evidence for the extraordinary tension abounds in his fiction, in, for example, the number of absent fathers, surrogate fathers (who are not above attempting to murder their 'sons', like David Balfour's Uncle Ebenezer), or maimed but threatening father-figures like the one-legged Long John Silver or the impotent, equivocating Lord

Durisdeer. It is also there in a story which never got published. In 'A Chapter on Dreams' he describes how the story had come to him much in the way *Jekyll and Hyde* did. The dreamer is a young man who, having lived abroad for some time 'on purpose to avoid his parent', returns home to find that his father (a widower) has re-married. They meet to discuss some matter to do with the young wife (who hates her husband) and, in the course of a quarrel, the son kills the father. Afterwards he continues to live in the same house as his stepmother who, in due course, discovers all. She does not destroy him, however, because she has fallen in love with him (47–50).

The antagonism and the violence towards parents comes out more comprehensively in one of his macabre fables, 'The House of Eld', where young Jack, to free his society literally from its shackles, kills the sorcerer apparently responsible for this state of affairs, even though he takes successively the phantasmagoric shape of Jack's father and mother and his uncle the catechist, and has to be killed in each mani-festation. When Jack returns home it is to find these people are indeed dead, the bodies bearing precisely the same wounds as those he had inflicted on each of the phantoms. Killing the law of the elders is not to kill a chimaera: it means killing the elders themselves in the shape of the mother, father and catechist-uncle. (Incidentally, Jack discovers that the people have indeed lost the gyve from their right foot but now wear it on their left, dismissing the earlier prac-tice as superstition – humanity's willingness to shackle itself in conformity seems irredeemable.) The verse-moral appended to the fable is quite explicit.

> Old is the tree and the fruit good,
> Very old and thick the wood.
> Woodman, is your courage stout?
> Beware! the root is wrapped about
> Your mother's heart, your father's bones;
> And like the mandrake come with groans.

So apposite is the fable and its moral that it serves to illustrate Malcolm Bowie's point that '"Theory" and "fiction" are, after all, alternative names for the verbal productions of those who indulge in "as if" thinking about the world.'[48]

As for Stevenson's capacity to turn lovers into mothers, we might look again at that passage in *Catriona* where he declares his love for

Catriona:

> I kneeled down before her in the sand, and embraced her knees, and burst into that storm of weeping that I thought it must have broken me. All thought was wholly beaten from my mind by the vehemency of my discomposure. I knew not where I was, I had forgot why I was happy; only I knew she stooped, and I felt her cherish me to her face and bosom, and heard her words out of a whirl (279–280).

But the image presented to us here is a highly complex one in which lover, mother *and father* seem all to have a part. Certainly it is difficult to think of *this* Catriona, without some effort, as simply a young woman (younger, in fact, than David); and embracing her knees is not the most obvious gesture for the passionate lover to make, be they never so alluring. As Catriona stoops to 'cherish' him she seems to suggest, rather, the benevolent Father who speaks both reproachfully and reassuringly out of the whirlwind. (Incidentally, what the voice out of the whirlwind said to Job – as Stevenson would certainly have known – was 'Gird up thy loins now like a man'.) Perhaps this is the reason why we are less disconcerted than we might otherwise be when Catriona later reassures David (who has accidentally wounded her slightly with his sword) in these words: '"See!" she said, showing me a bleeding scratch, "See you have made a man of me now."'

For a moment one is surprised that Stevenson with his fondness for theory hasn't advanced one in anticipation of his contemporary Sigmund Freud, some of whose own problems deriving from his relationship with his mother and the Jewish tradition parallel Stevenson's with his father and the Scottish Calvinist tradition. Then one realises that much of the theory is there buried in a shallow grave in his ardently-promulgated theories on the art of fiction – which make him so much of a Modernist. André Bleikasten, writing on Faulkner's novel, arrives at a summarising sentence which, in uniting various strands, serves very well to illustrate the problematics of paternity as these manifest themselves in Stevenson's fiction:

> fatherhood and sonship are not to be seen merely as themes on the level of mimetic representation... they are deeply involved in the *writer's* venture and relate back to his maddest desire: the desire to seize the authority of an original *author* – the authority that is of an origin, a founder, a father.[49]

## Notes

1. Leslie Fiedler, 'R. L. S. Revisited' in *No! in Thunder*, printed in The *Collected Essays of Leslie Fiedler*, vol. 1 (New York, 1971), pp. 299-300.
2. Quoted in Frank McLynn, *Robert Louis Stevenson: A Biography* (1993), p. 70.
3. Michael Levenson, op. cit., p. 50.
4. Franz Kafka, *Letter to the Father* in *Wedding Preparations in the Country and other Prose Writings*, trans. E. Kaiser and E. Wilkins (1954), pp. 176, 173.
5. Peter Blos, *Son and Father: Before and Beyond the Oedipus Complex* (New York, 1985), p. 69. See also Kafka's letter in *Wedding Preparations in the Country...* , pp. 176, 178.
6. Ford Madox Hueffer, *Memories and Impressions* (1911), pp. xiii, xiii–xiv.
7. Blos, op. cit., p. 84.
8. Carla Freccero, *Father Figures: Genealogy and Narrative Structures in Rabelais* (Ithaca, 1991), pp. 6–7.
9. *Letters*, vol. 1, pp. 218, 76.
10. Kafka, op. cit., pp. 211–12.
11. Edward Said, op. cit., p. 83.
12. Sandra M. Gilbert and Susan Gubar, *The Madwoman in the Attic* (New Haven, 1984), pp. 4–7.
13. Blos, op. cit., pp. 109, 89-90. See also Kafka's *Letter* in *Wedding Preparations in the Country* ..., pp. 213, 197.
14. *Letters*, vol. 3, p. 24.
15. *Letters*, vol. 2, p. 251.
16. Clement Greenberg, 'Beginnings of Modernism' in *Modernism: Challenges and Perspectives*, ed. Monique Chefdor, Ricardo Quinones and Albert Wachtel (Illinois, 1986), p. 19.
17. Ibid., p.19.
18. Irving Howe, 'The Idea of the Modern', in *Selected Writings 1950–1990* (New York, 1990), p. 161.
19. Quoted in Maixner, op. cit., p. 161.
20. Ibid., p. 171.
21. *Letters*, vol. 2, p. 305.
22. It needs to be made clear that I am using the term *avant-garde* according to what Renato Poggioli in *The Theory of the Avant-Garde* sees as the more guarded (and variable) Anglo-American formula rather than the Gallic: i.e. as less theoretical and more 'intuitive and empirical'. At the end of his study of the *avant-garde* 'as a centre of tendencies and ideas', and having found, through 'a system of analogies', a way of including in his chain of definition 'concepts both like and unlike', he summarises these as follows: 'These concepts are activism, antagonism and nihilism, agonism and futurism, antitraditionalism and modernism, obscurity and unpopularity, dehumanization and iconoclasm, voluntarism and cerebralism, abstract and pure art'. And he adds: 'Almost all have been summed up in the central formula of alienation, as reflected in one or another of the variants of that alienation: social and economic, cultural and stylistic, historical and ethical' (pp. 3, 8, 226). While it is clear that Stevenson's writing shares the characteristics of a relatively limited

number of these links in the chain, nevertheless some of its constituents
find a perfectly legitimate place among them.

23. Letter to Edward Marsh, 19 November 1913. Quoted in Stephen Spender, *The Struggle of the Modern* (1965), p. 104.
24. Irving Howe, *Decline of the New* (New York, 1970), p. 30.
25. 'A Note on Realism' in *Essays Literary and Critical*, vol. 28, p. 74.
26. B. Inhelder and J. Piaget, *The Growth of Logical Thinking from Childhood to Adolescence* (New York, 1958), p. 337. Quoted in Blos, op. cit., p. 54.
27. 'Crabbed Age and Youth', in *Virginibus Puerisque*, vol. 25, pp. 48, 43, 49.
28. Georges Van Den Abbeele, *Travel as Metaphor: From Montaigne to Rousseau* (Minneapolis, 1992), pp. 46, 47, 58.
29. Yevgeny Zamyatin, 'On Literature, Revolution, Entropy and Other Matters', in *A Soviet Heretic: Essays by Yevgeny Zamyatin*, ed. and transl. Mirra Ginsburg (Chicago, 1975), pp. 112, 109, 110.
30. *Letters*, vol. 2, pp. 252, 305.
31. *Letters*, vol. 4, pp. 44-5.
32. Op. cit., p. 29.
33. Stephen Spender, op. cit., p. 80.
34. Louis Kampf, op. cit., pp. 13, 15.
35. Wallace Stevens, 'The Figure of the Youth as Virile Poet' in *The Necessary Angel: Essays on Reality and the Imagination* (1960), p. 63.
36. Harold Bloom, *The Anxiety of Influence: A Theory of Poetry* (Oxford, 1975), p. 88.
37. Ibid., p. 42.
38. *Letters*, vol. 2, pp. 248-9.
39. *An Old Song and Edifying Letters of the Rutherford Family*, ed. Roger Swearingen (Paisley, 1982), pp. 84-5.
40. Harold Bloom, op. cit., pp. 78, 79, 64.
41. Blos, op. cit., p. 120.
42. *Letters*, vol. 3, pp. 89, 90. In these letters we are left to draw the inference that the Jekyll-and-Hyde behaviour might be linked to his father's ill-health. At the same time from the tone of the second letter (to his mother) it is fairly clear that this is by no means the first time that the comparison of his father to Hyde has been made. The essay, 'Thomas Stevenson: Civil Engineer' is printed in *Memories and Portraits*, vol. 29, pp. 65-70.
43. André Bleikasten, 'Fathers in Faulkner' in *The Fictional Father: Lacanian Readings of the Text*, ed. Robert Con Davis (Amherst, 1981), p. 119.
44. Blos, op. cit., pp. 32, 33, 44.
45. John T. Irwin, 'The Dead Father in Faulkner' in Robert Con Davis (ed.), op. cit., p. 154.
46. André Bleikasten, op. cit., pp. 136-7.
47. Printed in full in *RLS: Stevenson's Letters to Charles Baxter*, ed. DeLancey Ferguson and Marshall Waingrow (1956), pp. 24-30.
48. Malcolm Bowie, *Freud, Proust and Lacan: Theory and Fiction* (Cambridge, 1990), p. 6.
49. André Bleikasten, op. cit., p. 14.

# 2

# *Treasure Island*:
# The Parrot's Tale

'Were you never taught your catechism?' said the Captain. 'Don't
you know there's such a thing as an Author?'
'The Persons of the Tale'

'You could say that the parrot ... was Pure Word. If you were a
French academic, you might say that he was *un symbole du Logos.*'
Julian Barnes, *Flaubert's Parrot*

In *Treasure Island* a parrot gets the last word, and turns out to be a
two-hundred-year-old deconstructionist. Moreover, these last verbal
fragments uttered by an uncomprehending fowl, while they effortlessly rupture conventional relations between signifier and signified,
are, firstly, the fine but troublesome summation of a composition
which signifies Jim Hawkins' accession to authority via authorship,
and, secondly, the surprising means of galvanising Jim out of his sleep
and having him sit up in bed in fear and horror of that 'accursed
island' on which, one might have thought, he had enjoyed his finest
hour.

So we have a problem. Jim tells us at the outset that he has taken
up his pen at the behest of his companions 'to write down the whole
particulars' of the treasure-island adventure. Can we now accept
the narrative-composition as proof of his having achieved the estate
of Author – of independent, mature authority – or do we find our
expectations confounded by a raucous old parrot screeching the
eviscerated words of a defunct pirate?

One way of reading *Treasure Island* is as carnivalesque masquerade
where traditional authority, in a variety of categories, is gleefully
subverted. Such an approach would foreground Long John Silver
as chief 'masker' – appropriately enough for he is a master of (moral)
disguise – but it would also have to include his cherished parrot
which is also a dissembler, for 'Cap'n Flint', that cornucopia of naval

48

history and bad language, is, in fact, a lady. Gender reversal is almost a standard component in Stevenson's fiction: we have only to think of the 'old maid' Mackellar, or of Colonel Geraldine in *New Arabian Nights*, or of David Balfour playing wife to Alan Breck's fiddler in their long and inconclusive march, or Ramsey in 'The Castaways of Soledad' who makes the immodest suggestion that he should become the official hostess to the oddly-named Captain Crystal, the better to entertain the crew.

Whatever caprice drove Stevenson to endow his parrot with the female gender, it is clearly more than a courtesy for her to be given the last word. Roosting securely in Jim Hawkins' dreams, with a life-tenure the equal of his, she declines to be written out of the story; so helping to secure the survival of her master, who has been. (The awful possibility has to be faced that the parrot's gender may have survived from her original and improbable incarnation *as a hen* in an earlier version of the tale; but Stevenson's characteristically assiduous re-writing would, I am sure, have removed all accidental vestiges of such an ignoble descent. The trio of females in *Treasure Island* are alike in embodying certain contradictions: Jim's mother is materialist rather than maternal, Silver's black wife is, despite the colour-coding, an accomplice and Cap'n Flint is a female masquerading as a male parrot.)

So is it Jim's word against the parrot's? In a hell devised by French theorists the parrot can be seen as undeconstructible: an ageless allusion (to a dead pirate), the language of its discourse can never be at variance with itself since it signifies nothing to its subject. Howbeit, she is, at the same time, well-nigh, indestructible: 'Now that bird', says Silver 'is, may be, two hundred years old, Hawkins – they lives forever mostly; ...' (63). Notwithstanding her great age and vast experience, Cap'n Flint appears no more than a 'babby'. Moreover, despite having been present at innumerable naval engagements and learning to speak the language of such events, she is still Long John's 'poor old innocent bird' protected from contamination by incomprehension. Is this meant to comfort us as perusers of Jim's book? Or is it meant to comfort Jim who may be similarly protected from his exposure to Long John Silver? Is he still an innocent after witnessing, and in truth participating in, innumerable gruesome killings and sundry other bad deeds? Or is he parroting the parrot, so to speak, who/which had learned to scream 'Pieces of eight!' on another treasure hunt which had turned up 'three hundred and fifty thousand of 'em'. Jim's scream is modified into a memoir but there may be a covert allusion to that first hoard when he dilates on the contrasting variety of coinage in Flint's treasure – and on the pleasure it gave him: 'It was a strange collection, like Billy Bones' hoard for the diversity of the coinage, but so much larger and so much more varied that I think I never had more pleasure than in sorting them' (215). At any rate, we can quite properly think of Jim as No. 2 parrot on the grounds that he is responsible for sustaining the memory – if not, indeed, the presence – of Silver by *his* words. Silver, we are told, 'can speak like a book when so minded' (62) and maybe that is just what he's doing through Jim, courtesy of 'Cap'n Flint'.

All the foregoing questions, probing various possibilities, could be rolled up into one general question: what kind of text is this? Is it, for example, a 'mere' adventure-story, or is it a *Bildungsroman* with Modernist anxieties about the problematics of language and textual authority? Should the carnivalesque option be pursued? That there are carnivalesque elements is, I believe, undeniable and these, it could be argued, have some responsibility for the ambiguity in the text towards authority. Thus while Jim's gradual acquisition of authority (or Authority, if we are thinking of Lacan's symbolic order) is a serious matter and, insofar as it reflects the dynamic which drives the adolescent adventurer to take the action he does, constitutes the tale's bed-rock, Long John Silver frequently comes near to burlesquing authority – at least in its excessively conventional embodiment on the *Hispaniola* in those three archetypes of social hierarchy, the Squire, the doctor and the ship's captain.

Nonetheless the carnivalesque does not seem to provide an adequate focus within which *all* the story's parts can be seen to come together, nor does it make sufficient allowance for the seriousness of Jim's quest. Before any attempt to establish one which does, an objection has to be anticipated. It has been said (by *Punch*) that to attempt a serious critique of P. G. Wodehouse is to take a spade to a soufflé. Alastair Fowler at the end of a penetrating analysis of *Treasure Island*, and perhaps mindful of *Punch*'s scorn (and of Alexander Pope), similarly cautions readers against breaking a butterfly on the wheel, or making it walk the plank. Yet Stevenson's attitude to his texts is a sophisticated one and part of his perfectly evident relish in writing derives from his gleeful participation in subverting his own text. What he is doing, however, goes well beyond mere mischievousness or self-indulgence. Authority (or authorship) in all its variety is a constant preoccupation with him: he yearns for its legitimation in him – the blessing, in the biblical sense even though he knows that it will only come, if it comes at all, by an act of self-assertion, even usurpation, for which he, unlike Jacob, lacks resolve.

In the excellent essay already referred to, Alastair Fowler is surely right when he notes that what Jim finds particular pleasure in, in sorting the coinage, are the figures of authority which are imaged in these coins, for what he is appreciatively running through his fingers are 'the pictures of all the kings of Europe for the last hundred years'. Fowler also notes the Jungian 'treasure hard to attain' archetype – 'selfhood, independence, identity' – and, in suggesting that this is more truly Jim's objective, describes the book as being for the most part not really about treasure or the search for it; rather, it 'recounts a series of contests for power'.[1]

In another excellent essay Wallace Robson, pondering the reasons for the treasure-hunt being somewhat marginalised, discreetly favours Freud over Jung and advances the argument that '[t]he avoidance of the 'treasure' theme ... may have something to do with Stevenson's personal stabilisation at that time'. He is thinking, of course, of Stevenson's recent marriage and the 'degree of resolution' he had achieved in the difficult relationship with his father.[2] It has, I believe, a great deal to do with this *and* with Jim's role in the 'contests for power' which together account for the serious theme of the book and explain why Jim should be frightened by a parrot.

All Stevenson's major fiction involves some form of tension or conflict between sons and 'figures of authority from the class of fathers'.[3] Many, if not indeed most, of these stories have to do with a young man unable to attain that level of maturity and independence necessary for him to meet the obligations imposed on him by the adult world. In the most serious cases, these young men are trapped in a limbo between adolescence and manhood. *Weir of Hermiston, Kidnapped, Prince Otto, The Ebb-Tide* all have central characters who are, in this sense, 'failures'.

Jim Hawkins, however, is not in this category. Here in *Treasure Island* we have one of the few cases where the adolescent *does* win through to transcend his condition; so much so that he is invested by his much older companions with responsibility for 'authoring' the text of their adventures, a charge of some significance from a writer on the threshold of Modernism. Jim's development is notable for being the first and very nearly the last such achievement by someone in his position in Stevenson's work. If there is the hint of a shadow lying across it in the closing sentences, it is nothing to the great question-mark which hangs over the comparable case of David Balfour in *Catriona* whose epiphany as a piece of hormone-deficient ivy wrapping himself round Catriona's knees is parasitic rather than priapic and carries little conviction that he has at long last proved himself capable of that individuation which will allow him to take his place in the adult world.

That Jim succeeds to man's estate is almost certainly a reflection of Stevenson's 'personal stabilisation' as Robson calls it. After the agonies of the 1870s where his hopeless infatuation with Mrs Sitwell was compounded by an apparently endless sequence of shattering rows with his father, Stevenson had finally married, though the effort to do so nearly cost him his life. *Treasure Island* – or the bulk of it – was composed in the bosom of his new family; Fanny and her son Lloyd Osborne were both there, and the composition enjoyed the benevolent participation of his father since both parents were also part of the holiday ménage sojourning in the Scottish Highlands.

In conventional Freudian psychology, *Treasure Island* is easily seen to be a *locus classicus* in the representation of the adolescent confronted by the castrating father-figure who, however, already bears the marks of the son's desire to turn the tables on him by being himself maimed, that is symbolically emasculated. This extends even to the image of authority in the effigy of Admiral Benbow (a hero of Stevenson's incidentally), hanging as a sign in front of the inn which takes the sabre-cut Bill Bones aims at Black Dog, a cut so deep that '[y]ou may see the notch on the lower side of the frame to this day' (12).

Bones, like so many of Stevenson's father-substitutes, is a man of fine physique: he is 'a tall, strong, heavy, nut-brown man' with, however, the mark of a sabre-cut across one cheek, 'a dirty, livid white' (3). He exudes authority, 'looking as fierce as a commander' and is recognised by young Jim as a man 'accustomed to be obeyed or to strike'. Jim's response to him might be described as pleasurably fearful and a sort of intimacy is quickly established between them. That Bones lives in some dread of visiting seafarers is soon obvious to the inn-keeper and his family, and Jim becomes sufficiently partisan to describe himself as 'a sharer in his alarms' (5). Already, it would seem, there is a hint of fluidity in the boundaries between Jim's and the pirates' moral world.

Bones' domination of the 'Admiral Benbow's' patrons – he 'tyrannised' over them, we're told – is synchronised with the rapid decline in Jim's father's health. In fact, Jim believes his father's death to have been hastened by his fear of Billy who effectively displaces him as *patron*. As the natural father continues to fade, another substitute, Black Dog, appears. He is distinguished by a maimed left hand, having lost two 'talons', and he, too, exerts a menacing degree of authority over Jim. However, he alternates between threats and attempts at ingratiating himself: "'I have a son of my own", said he, "as like you as two blocks, and he's all the pride of my 'art. But the great thing for boys is discipline, sonny – discipline"' (11). Later, Jim is 'this dear child here, as I've took such a liking to' (12).

The next in this almost phantasmagoric sequence of threatening authority-figures or bad fathers is Blind Pew, a 'horrible, soft-spoken, eyeless creature' (20) who terrifies Jim much more than the other two. As a result of his visit, Billy Bones dies, his death occurring on the day after the funeral of Jim's father. Jim himself links the two events in a way which begs an interesting question:

> It is a curious thing to understand, for I had certainly never liked the man … but as soon as I saw that he was dead, I burst into a flood of tears. It was the second death I had known, and the sorrow of the first was still fresh in my heart (21).

This contrasts sharply with the prosaic, almost off-hand account Jim gives of his father's death:

> But as things fell out, my poor father died quite suddenly that evening, which put all other matters on one side. Our natural distress, the visits of the neighbours, the arranging of the funeral, all the work of the inn to be carried on in the meanwhile, kept me so busy that I had scarcely time to think of the captain, far less to be afraid of him (18).

There is not much sign of mourning in this matter-of-fact description of his 'natural distress'; any outburst of grief seemingly, and indeed curiously, having to wait the expiry of Billy Bones. Yet his tears then are perhaps as much a sign of his growing maturity as their (apparent) absence at his father's death, for what Jim is learning is something about the unreliability of appearances and the ambiguities of the moral order – as reflected in himself as well as in others.

Billy Bones has unquestionably perpetrated atrocious acts of wickedness, but through him Jim makes a number of discoveries about himself – one being that 'he was far less afraid of the captain himself than anybody else who knew him' (5), and another that he could still feel some pity for this bloodthirsty old pirate who had so comprehensively offended against a Christian society's most cherished values. Jim is even mature enough already to recognise (unlike his father) that the captain's presence, notwithstanding his wickedness, did the inn no harm, that he might even help to energise the community and at the same time assist it in its self-definition:

> I really believe his presence did us good. People were frightened at the time, but on looking back they rather liked it; it was a fine excitement in a quiet country life; and there was even a party of the younger men who pretended to admire him ...(6).

Jim is sharply distinguishing his own from his father's over-anxious and imperceptive reaction, as he does again when he tells how his father 'never plucked up the heart' to ask the captain for the money due to him, and describes him as living in terror of his obstreperous guest (6).

The most notable and powerful of all the surrogate and maimed fathers does not, of course, make a physical appearance in this sequence. Much more tellingly, Long John Silver haunts Jim's dreams. A little later in the book Smollett sharply criticises Trelawney for telling the secret of their voyage to the parrot, meaning that everyone knows it. (The Squire thinks he's referring to Silver's parrot and Smollett has to explain that 'It's a way of speaking' [55].) Here in the account of his dream Jim broadcasts his own secret almost as promiscuously and with as little comprehension as the parrot – or so we are led to assume.

> How that personage haunted my dreams, I need scarcely tell you. On stormy nights, when the wind shook the four corners of the house and the surf pounded along the cove and up the cliffs, I would see him in a thousand forms, and with a thousand diabolical expressions. Now the leg would be cut off at the knee, now at the hip; now he was a monstrous kind of a creature who had never had but the one leg, and that in the middle of his body. To see him leap and run and pursue me over hedge and ditch was the worst of my nightmares (5).

There is more here than 'simply' the Oedipal castration of the father or the fear of personal castration: there is also the ambiguous fear on the part of the son that the potency of the father will be incestuously visited upon him.[4]

Set over against the collection of threatening 'fathers' found among the pirates, we get a trio of authority-figures in Smollett, Trelawney and Livesey. Initially, we might assume that Trelawney the Squire, as the social superior of the other two, would be the principal of the group and when Jim first visits him at the Hall this seems about to be confirmed:

> The servant led us down a matted passage, and showed us at the end into a great library, all lined with bookcases and busts upon the top of them, where the squire and Dr Livesey sat, pipe in hand, on either side of a bright fire (34).

Nothing, it appears, could be more conspicuously redolent of accepted hierarchical authority, literary, historical and social, than such a scene. Yet as the tale unfolds we come to realise (as does Jim) that things are not quite what they at first seem.

It becomes clear fairly quickly, for example, that Trelawney is sorely lacking in personal authority. He cannot keep his own or other people's counsel – 'you cannot hold your tongue', Livesey tells him roundly – is highly irresponsible and gullible to a degree. He gets at odds with his captain almost immediately and, had it not been for Livesey's intervention, would have dismissed him. The contrast between Trelawney and Smollett could hardly be more marked. Smollett is uncommunicative, authoritarian in all matters under his command, forthright and decisive. In fact, of the three he is the only one who truly conforms to the stern, uncompromising, judgemental father whom we often find the young Stevenson hero pitting himself against – or perhaps, on occasion, even creating. It is of more than passing significance, then, that this father-figure is disabled by a wound in the middle of the adventure and thereafter poses no further threat to Jim's freedom of action. Eventually he is made subject (as all the others are) to Jim's pen – a highly effective form of subjugation whether we think of him as Alexander Smollett, captain of the *Hispaniola*, or Tobias Smollett, precursor-author.

When Smollett is wounded, the man who takes over the leadership of the Squire's party is not Trelawney himself but Dr Livesey. From the start of the book whether asserting himself over Billy Bones in the 'Admiral Benbow' or comfortably sharing in the privileged surroundings of the Squire's library, Livesey is a figure of quiet but confident authority. Drawn in sharp contrast to the unbending, unsympathetic Smollett, he exercises over Jim an influence grounded on benevolence and – significantly – a generous readiness to recognise Jim's deserts.

On several occasions Livesey is brought into conflict with other father-figures and shown to be their superior. When he refuses to be silenced by Billy Bones, obstreperously presiding over the 'Admiral Benbow's' parlour, the beached pirate draws a knife. Livesey orders him to put it away or he will see that he hangs: 'Then followed a battle of looks between them; but the captain soon knuckled under, put up his weapon, and resumed his seat, grumbling like a beaten dog' (8). The doctor's authority is further underlined by his disclosure in this episode that he is also a magistrate; which, incidentally, offers another instance of the imbrication of medicine, the father-figure and the law which is to be found elsewhere in Stevenson's fiction (in particular in *Jekyll and Hyde*).

Livesey is equally undaunted when he confronts the ruthless and treacherous Long John Silver. In everything the doctor is Silver's polar opposite: a man of the utmost integrity, hating deception, steadfast and loyal. He makes no bones about his abhorrence of all Silver stands for and cheerfully admits to his willingness to have seen him cut down by his enraged followers at the empty treasure-site had Jim Hawkins not been in the way. Again, the contrast between these two authority-figures is brought out when Livesey's innate compassion is contrasted with Silver's inhumanity. The doctor, hearing the sounds of (as he thinks) delirium coming from the camp of the few remaining pirates, tells Silver that he is half-inclined to go and treat the sufferers, and this exchange follows:

'... if I were sure they were raving ... I should leave this camp, and, at whatever risk to my own carcase, take them the assistance of my skill'.

'Ask your pardon, sir, you would be very wrong,' quoth Silver. 'You would lose your own precious life, and you may lay to that ... these men down there, they couldn't keep their word ... and what's more, they couldn't believe as you could.'

'No,' said the doctor. 'You're the man to keep your word – we know that.' (216–17)

It is, of course, Livesey who brings about Silver's defeat.

If these confrontations between Livesey and the others might seem to suggest a contest between good and bad fathers and the kind of authority they assert, there may be another example in

Smollett's attitude to Jim when he brusquely orders the latter to the galley with the words 'I'll have no favourites on my ship.' He, the quintessentially harsh and repressive father, addresses these words not to Jim but, almost as a challenge, to the doctor, who is possessed of a rival *moral* authority based not, perhaps, on showing favour, but at least on kindness and consideration. Just as he asserts himself over Bones and Silver, Livesey, in effect, repeats his success with Smollett by assuming the direction of the Squire's party when the captain is disabled. All the decisions are his and everything is managed with understated self-confidence: '... I did what I thought best ...' (212).

It could be argued that it is Smollett's resentment at Jim's success in finding in Livesey another 'father', an alternative moral authority which will nurture his (Jim's) own, which impels him to make his rather gnomic remark to Jim at the end: 'You're a good boy in your line, Jim; but I don't think you and me'll go to sea again. You're too much of the born favourite for me' (214). To look with favour on any 'son' is more than this autocratic 'father' can bring himself to do since it is a step towards his own disempowerment. Significantly, having dismissed Jim, he immediately turns his attention to Silver, to whom he reacts quite neutrally: ' "What brings you here, man?" "Come back to do my dooty, sir," returned Silver. "Ah!" said the captain, and that was all he said.' The difference in his attitude to Silver is drawn to our attention by these last few words. Smollett, having cast off or disinherited the intrepid Jim for being too much of the born favourite, now extends favour to the reprobate pirate and accepts his return to 'dooty' without demur. There is clearly a sense in which these two surrogate fathers are on the same side.

Livesey's behaviour suggests a very different paternal model. Even in the face of Jim's desertion of their party in the stockade, the doctor conspicuously refuses to condemn his action out of hand. His criticism is muted yet very much to the point:

> 'Heaven knows I cannot find it in my heart to blame you; but this much I will say, be it kind or unkind: when Captain Smollett was well, you dared not have gone off; and when he was ill, and couldn't help it, by George, it was downright cowardly!' (193)

Pinpointing Jim's lack of scruple as this does, highlights the authenticity of Stevenson's portrayal of the adolescent negotiating his rite of passage. In seeing his opportunity to circumvent the 'father's' authority and taking it, Jim, *does* display selfishness; yet his act is a necessary one if he is eventually to learn to take responsibility for his own decisions and his own life. Throughout the story Jim's acceptance of Livesey's authority is instinctive if tacit, but at the reproof administered here (not angrily but 'sadly'), Jim becomes a boy again – and a repentant one at that – and bursts into tears.

This telling exchange invites comparison with another between a 'real' father and son: that of Adam Weir and Archie in *Weir of Hermiston*. Livesey's assertion of authority is of a kind diametrically opposed to Weir's but is extremely close kin to Lord Glenalmond's. These two men exercise great influence with tact, restraint and affection over a young man growing up. Each views the young man's aspirations to an independent position for himself sympathetically and in doing so is contrasted with a father-figure who does not.

In Livesey's case the figure in question is primarily Silver (who, in the last section of the book, literally ties Jim to himself with a length of rope), but, as has been implied, shadowed-in behind him is Captain Smollett who also has a good deal in common with Adam Weir. While Livesey admires the Captain (as Glenalmond does Weir) he does not share his idea of authority based on rigorous demarcations uncompromisingly enforced. Smollett, first described as 'a sharp-looking man, who seemed angry with everything on board', delivers an ultimatum to the Squire's party before they leave Bristol requiring that things be done on the *Hispaniola* exactly according to his wishes or he will resign his command. His attitude is not an unreasonable one in his position but it puts him at the extreme of the range and makes him not just an uncompromising enforcer of the law but something of a martinet. It is notable that it is only by Livesey's quietly but effectively interposing his own kind of authority between Smollett and Trelawney that Smollett is reconciled to his post.

Dr Livesey is, in fact, a father-figure of a kind we encounter throughout Stevenson's fiction. As such he can easily be seen as a son's apology for the antagonistic portrayal of the father as harsh, uncaring and judgemental: for characters like Attwater in *The Ebb-Tide*, Ebenezer in *Kidnapped*, Weir in *Weir of Hermiston*. It is something of a commonplace of Freudian analysis to see the representation of the father in these terms as a sort of parricide for which the 'oedipal regressive' must do penance:

> An Oedipus, to atone for his crime, must put out the eyes that have gazed on the mother he has wed and the father he has slain. An author has other means of propitiation and penance. He can

perform the comforting miracle of restoring his father to life in the most exalted form; he can re-create the father in the image that he (the son) loved best; he can call into existence a father-ideal toward whom no 'son' could have the slightest objection.[5]

Dr Livesey is just such an ideal father whom no son could object to, as are in varying degrees, Alan Breck in *Kidnapped*, Davis in *The Ebb-Tide* and Glenalmond in *Weir of Hermiston*. The latter is of particular significance (as we shall see in a later chapter) for in this book Stevenson exposes quite clearly the son's role in *creating* such an accommodating surrogate. Livesey has in full measure what all of these men have to some extent: a protective, affectionate concern for the 'son', a willingness to recognise his merits and no inclination whatsoever to put obstacles in the way of his development. 'Every step, it's you that saves our lives', he says to Jim, acknowledging the effect of the latter's initiatives and so of his progress towards equality of participation in the responsibilities of adulthood. All that said, a caveat still needs to be entered when we are marshalling good and bad father-figures: in *Treasure Island* there is no clear-cut division allocating the 'bad' father-figures to the pirates and the 'good' to the Squire's party. Jim expresses more grief at the death of the murderous Billy Bones than he does at that of his own father, while Smollett's hostility towards him remains to the end implacable. Silver's, as we shall see, is a highly complex case.

Finally, one might note that even Livesey may have a mote in his compassionate eye for he prides himself on having served with the Duke of Cumberland at Fontenoy. The year was 1745: in the next year this able general acquired his notorious sobriquet 'Butcher' Cumberland for what were seen as his brutal tactics in the battle of Culloden which ensured the decimation of the Jacobite forces and the disfavour of romantic nationalists like Stevenson. And one truly last point for Freudians: nearly all the ideal fathers (including Livesey) are bachelors, for which reason alone they are less challenging to 'penitent' sons.

I have said that in *Treasure Island* we have almost the only example of a young Stevensonian hero who safely negotiates the shoals of adolescence to the extent of becoming 'Captain' Hawkins (even if only to Israel Hands), *and* his own author. Nevertheless there are one or two clues scattered around to suggest that the carapace of adult-

hood may not, even by the end of the composition, be quite complete.
One, already referred to, is the allusion to nightmares about the
island in the last sentence of the book, but another, more significant
one resides in the fact that there is one father-figure whom Jim never
quite transcends, and that is, of course, Long John Silver. Hawkins
senior dies, Billy Bones dies and so does Blind Pew, but Silver
escapes. When Jim tells us that 'the formidable sea-faring man with
one leg has gone clean out of my life' (219), it is clear that he has not
gone clean out of his dreams. Unless we are to assume an unreasonable fear of psittacosis on Jim's part, the fact that the parrot is
part of his nightmare testifies to its capacity to revive memories
of Long John and all that he stands for. Telling one's secrets in
recounting one's dreams becomes complicated when part of that
secret is conveyed in a few seemingly unimportant words spoken by
a parrot.

The relationship between Jim and Long John is at the very heart
of the book and in its sophisticated nature shows us just how remiss
it is to think of *Treasure Island* as a 'mere' adventure-story for children. Adventure there is, of course, and brilliantly constructed too,
but we should never forget that in this case it feeds into the genre of
the *Bildungsroman* (with which it is far from being incompatible) where
a youth is subjected to a variety of experiences which will test his
capacity and readiness for the sort of responsibilities that go with
adulthood. It is in the hazard of this enterprise that the more substantial drama is played out and it involves the painful rupturing of
relationships, the confrontation with unsuspected moral ambiguities
which make choosing exceptionally difficult yet crucial to the growth-
process, and the recognition that independence, though a prime
objective, will bring with it loneliness and isolation. This drama begins
in the second paragraph of the book with the arrival of Billy Bones
and is so skilfully blended with the adventure that its existence has
even been denied. The concentration of so many menacing authority-
figures does not succeed in crushing the boy's growing self-confidence,
however, and he emerges with credit from the trial. He is helped in
this by having already begun to distance himself from his father,
clearly seeing himself as more able to cope with their unwelcome
visitors. When his father's death duly occurs, it is something which
he can then take in his stride.

The final step in this phase is taken when he decides to leave England
with the squire and his companions in search of the treasure, but that
decision is rendered irrevocable when, on returning to the inn after

his brief stay in the squire's house, he discovers another boy – the new apprentice – in his place:

> It was on seeing that boy that I understood, for the first time, my situation. I had thought up to that moment of the adventures before me, not at all of the home that I was leaving; and now, at sight of this clumsy stranger, who was to stay here in my place beside my mother, I had my first attack of tears. I am afraid I led that boy a dog's life; for as he was new to the work, I had a hundred opportunities of setting him right and putting him down, and I was not slow to profit by them (46).

He is therefore already launched upon his voyage even before he reaches Bristol or sets his foot upon the deck of the *Hispaniola*.

Once on the ship Jim encounters yet another authority-figure in the person of Captain Smollett. The captain turns out to be as much a disciplinarian as Black Dog and declines to modify his authoritarian temper in any way in his dealings with Jim. Not only does he order him about very roughly – 'Here, you ship's boy … out of that! Off with you to the cook and get some work' – he also takes care to make his adjuration (addressed, as I have said, to Dr Livesey) audible to Jim: 'I'll have no favourites on my ship.' Jim is going to have to earn his passage as well as to accept unequivocally his subordination to an uncompromising ship's master.

It is a paradigm which this boy who has already glimpsed what lies beyond the adolescent's horizon is going to find it difficult to conform to, so it is unsurprising that he should tell us here (though in no very serious tone) that he 'hated the captain deeply' (59). In fact neither Jim nor the Captain gives ground and tension remains between them for the whole of the expedition. Twice Jim absents himself from the Captain's command and the Captain, on his part, makes it clear at the end that he will never permit Jim any privileges which would diminish his authority over him.

Jim does, however, get the last word – literally, for he becomes the author of the Captain in writing the account of their travels. Nor is one being arbitrary in crossing barriers in conflating the world of the book with the act of its inscription, for Stevenson has already set a precedent. Not only has he written one of his fables, 'The Persons of the Tale', in which the characters step outside their fictional world in order to talk about the author, but he has also given his Captain the name of Smollett.

Tobias Smollett was a Scotish writer who could have been predicted to attract Stevenson's interest. Having joined the navy at an early age, he rose to become surgeon's mate, sailed the Spanish Main and, as a young man of twenty, took part in an expedition against the Spaniards in the West Indies in 1741. He was a consumptive and because of his poor health and exiguous means took to spending substantial periods of time travelling in France and Italy, eventually dying at fifty in his home at Leghorn in 1771. Smollett was the author of, *inter alia, The Adventures of Roderick Random, The Expedition of Humphry Clinker* and *The Adventures of Peregrine Pickle,* and could be regarded as a contemporary of Long John Silver since the latter tells the gullible squire that he lost his leg in a naval action under the command of 'the immortal Hawke'. Hawke (1705–81), having first distinguished himself in action at Cape Finisterre in 1747, earned his 'immortality' by a celebrated victory at the battle of Quiberon Bay in 1759.[6] (Note 6 offers some speculations on the life and career of Long John Silver.)

It is impossible, therefore, to regard Smollett's name as accidental any more than is Herrick's in *The Ebb-Tide* or Hoseason's in *Kidnapped.*[7] Nor is it simply an example of Stevenson innocently sporting with the idea of reflexivity so that he can enjoy exposing the fictionality of his fictions (something which he *does* enjoy doing). As will become obvious, Stevenson has all the Modernists' disdain for the fathers of the tradition, which masks no small measure of Harold Bloom's anxiety of influence; so that Jim's refusal to knuckle down to 'Captain' Smollett and the latter's strenuous insistence that he will not abate a jot of Jim's apprentice-position as 'ship's boy', reflects a battle of literary generations. It is a battle Jim decisively wins when he has the privilege of 'inscribing' the Captain in his account of their voyage, but, arguably, the Captain has already lost it when he refuses to admit that Jim *is* privileged, whether he likes it or not – privileged, that is, by being the succeeding generation. Jim, therefore, establishes his maturity by becoming the author of the ship's master, thus indirectly affirming that, Kafka-like, one way *his* author could gain independence from *his* father was by becoming a writer.

If this relationship shows Jim as achieving the independent status aspired to by the adolescent, that with Silver is a very different matter. From the start it is more intimate and more physical. Jim's dream of Silver's sexual potency is a mixture of fear and desire: fear of the castrating domination of this father-figure, desire for his potency (or, possibly, desire to submit to that potent sexuality). There is nothing outlandish in the suggestion that behind this particular fictional relationship can be discerned the complex relationship between Stevenson *père et fils*. In the last year of the author's life, his correspondence shows him as father-haunted as ever: 'He now haunts me, strangely enough, in two guises: as a man of fifty, lying on a hill-side and carving mottoes on a stick, strong and well; and as a younger man, running down the sands into the sea near North Berwick, myself – *aetat 11* – somewhat horrified at finding him so beautiful when stripped!'[8]

No sooner is Silver mentioned on the third page of *Treasure Island* than he realises himself in Jim's subconscious awareness: 'How that personage haunted my dreams, I need scarcely tell you'; and, despite Jim's equivocation, he is there in the dreams of a much older Jim at the end of the tale. In between, Jim is subjected to the full range of attentions Stevenson allows his fictional fathers to visit upon their 'sons' – from assiduous wooing to an overt threat upon their lives. The first stage – the wooing – is highly successful, assisted as it is by Jim's naivety. Having been put on his guard against one-legged men by Billy Bones, his suspicions are roused at 'the very first mention of Long John in Squire Trelawney's letter' (48). When he sees him, however, his fears are at once allayed:

> one look at the man before me was enough. I had seen the captain, and Black Dog, and the blind man Pew, and I thought I knew what a buccaneer was like – a very different creature, according to me, from this clean and pleasant-tempered landlord (49).

Clearly Jim has a long way to go before he learns the Stevensonian lesson implicit in this misreading of signs. Not that he can be blamed unduly, for Silver is one of the astutest in his class. The speed of his recovery and the quickness of his invention when Jim recognises Black Dog at the 'Spy-glass' is highly impressive, as is the way Stevenson judges the scene's potential for comedy to a hairsbreadth. The upshot of the whole incident, however, is that Silver, after flattering Jim ('You're a lad, you are, but you're smart as paint') puts himself on the same level, convincing Jim that 'here was one of the best of possible shipmates' (52). However it is as well to remember that Silver leaves Dr Livesey and the Squire with the same impression: '"The man's a perfect trump", declared the Squire' (53).

To Jim he is 'unweariedly kind', making much of him on his visits to the galley: 'Nobody more welcome than yourself, my son', he tells him and we see why the crew should respect and obey him as Jim has himself just observed them to do. When it suits him he can wear his authority very lightly even while reminding others of it in the most casual expressions – like 'my son' (62). What makes him an attractive figure, at least to Jim, is the way in which he relishes his own performance. Some of that was evident in the Black Dog incident, but even in introducing Jim to his parrot he indulges himself in a way that makes the youth think him 'the best of men' (63).

One of the most appealing things about Stevenson's writing is the manifest pleasure it gave him – and his almost provocative exposure of the fact. It is a point of some significance since it gives a fair indication of his refusal to endorse the established view that the objective of the art of fiction was to create a moral reality, structured on high principle and discriminating sensibilities, which would be capable of teaching life a lesson. In his essay, 'A Humble Remonstrance' Stevenson flatly rejects the Jamesean claim that literature can 'compete with life' and identify its essential truths. For him its product will remain the 'phantom reproductions of experience' which have little to do with factual experience which 'in the cockpit of life, can torture or slay'. When we are expressing our admiration of such reproductions what we are really doing is '[commending] the author's talent': that is, admiring artifice rather than 'real life'.

Though he is highly capable of giving us the illusion that what we are enjoying *is* like 'real life', Stevenson also enjoys deliberately showing his hand; he puts on a performance, and frequently has his characters do the same (James Durie, Alan Breck, as well as Long John Silver, come to mind). It is a sophisticated process of deconstruction: by all sorts of strategies of the narrative voice – inflections, wild extravagances (Dr Livesey's snuff-box full of parmesan), reflexivities – the text becomes a *soi-disant* performance. Stevenson draws our attention to his performance as author and has his characters frequently draw attention to *their* performance as characters. The later fable 'The Persons in the Tale' is, in this respect, entirely of a piece with the book to which it provides a coda.

Silver's performance in his introduction of 'Cap'n Flint' is a bravura piece of play-acting and Jim is captivated by it. At the conclusion of his performance 'John would touch his forelock with a solemn way he had' which delighted Jim and completely won him over (63). Silver's defence of his parrot's innocence and his respect for a theoretically outraged clergy – 'Here's this poor old innocent bird o' mine swearing blue fire, and none the wiser, you may lay to that. She would swear the same, in a manner of speaking, before chaplain' – are alike tongue-in-cheek. Whether Jim relishes – or even recognises – the play-acting for what it is, is by no means clear, but achieving maturity has a great deal to do with *not* suspending one's disbelief too easily, and Jim's inexperience certainly allows him too readily to believe in Silver.

The degree to which he has read Silver as a man of sincerity, genuinely fond of him, and willing to talk to him 'like a man', comes out unequivocally in his reaction to his overhearing Silver's wooing of another young man in precisely the same terms:

> You may imagine how I felt when I heard this abominable old rogue addressing another in the very same words of flattery as he had used to myself. I think, if I had been able, that I would have killed him through the barrel (67).

Jim's trust in words has been naive – despite the demolition-job done in his presence on the sanctity of inherent verbal meaning by a loquacious 200-year old parrot. As he goes through with the adventure he becomes much more aware of ambiguities until he can deal verbally in them himself. 'And now, Mr Silver,' he says when he becomes the pirates' prisoner, 'I believe you're the best man here ...', and Long John agrees: 'I'm cap'n here because I'm the best man by a long sea-mile' (78, 179). But what does Jim mean by 'best' now, and is it what Silver means? This is the dialogue which ends with Silver's famously enigmatic remark 'Ah you that's young – you and me might have done a power of good together!' Jim is the only one, it seems, who has not been surprised or puzzled by the remark for he makes no comment on it. While the 'power of good' will remain a mystery, the reason for Silver's show of favour to Jim is at least partly explained by his seeing in the youth a reflection of his younger self: 'I've always liked you, I have, for a lad of spirit, and the picter of my own self when I was young and handsome' (176). Even allowing for Silver's characteristically mocking flattery, the allusion merits attention for it is picked up again in 'Ah, you that's young ...' Is this an expression of a sentiment much quoted by Stevenson – *si Jeunesse savait, si Vieillesse pouvait* – that is, the desire of the older man to yoke to his adult experience the vigour and drive of his youth? If so is it a way of empowering or emasculating surrogate youth? In exchange for the youth's potency he would give him his knowledge – but the 'power of good' they might do together remains Silver's to define, and *that* is a sinister degree of *dis*empowerment.

What I think this shows is how serious a threat to Jim's freedom and moral growth Silver has actually been. He has offered him power by talking to him 'like a man' and treating him as an equal, but he was always going to ensure that that power and that growth remained firmly circumscribed. The appeal in the offer has been almost dazzling to Jim – on his way to manhood but not observing the castrating knife in Long John's sleeve. What the latter has offered him has been a share in, or access to, his own mature sexual power as well as that residing in his whole mind and personality and Jim hasn't perceived that this is a trap which will, in the event, emasculate rather than empower him, for Silver is giving nothing up.

The high point of Silver's fascination for Jim is to be seen in an incident which seems to exceed the parameters of a boy's adventure story, though it is arguably the best piece of description in the whole book. This is that moment when Silver exerts his powers of seduction on another member of the crew to persuade him to join the pirates. His approach is the familiar one, and Jim, concealed close by, can hear it all:

> 'Mate', he was saying, 'it's because I thinks gold dust of you – gold dust, and you may lay to that. If I hadn't took to you like pitch, do you think I'd have been here a-warning of you?' (88)

As they argue, the sound of a scream from across the marsh signalling the death of another loyal seaman brings Tom to his feet, but Silver 'had not winked an eye. He stood where he was, resting lightly on his crutch, watching his companion like a snake about to spring. "John!" said the sailor, stretching out his hand.'

The appeal to this figure poised to strike (in the suggestive image of the snake) is ineffectual and when Tom defies Silver and turns to walk away, Silver strikes in a manner that is more like a sexual assault:

> With a cry, John seized the branch of a tree, whipped the crutch out of his armpit, and sent that uncouth missile hurtling through the air. It struck poor Tom, point foremost, and with stunning violence, right between the shoulders in the middle of his back. His hands flew up, he gave a sort of gasp, and fell.
>
> Whether he were injured much or little, none could ever tell. Like enough, to judge from the sound, his back was broken on the spot. But he had no time given him to recover. Silver, agile as a monkey, even without leg or crutch, was on top of him next moment, and had twice buried his knife up to the hilt in that defenceless body. From my place of ambush, I could hear him pant aloud as he struck the blows (89).

In many ways the description is a realisation of Jim's nightmare when he first dreamed of Silver: 'a monstrous kind of creature who had never had but the one leg, and that in the middle of his body', and who had pursued him 'over hedge and ditch'.

At the culmination of Silver's attack, Jim faints. Wallace Robson, a very astute (if reticent) commentator, has this to say: 'What makes this scene powerful is our intimate closeness to Silver during the murder: he is referred to twice as 'John' – unusually for *Treasure Island*.' He goes on to note that 'the older reader' will be struck by the moment when Silver 'twice buries his knife in Tom's body, and Jim says, 'I could hear him pant aloud as he struck the blows'. And Robson concludes:

> The *obvious* force of this scene lies in Jim's identification with the victim; its less obvious force is the secret participation of Jim (because of his *closeness* to Silver) and hence the reader .[9]

Nothing could be clearer than that Silver's enticement of Jim to share in his potency exerts an almost irresistible appeal for the adolescent (whose fainting may not be precisely what it seems). Nor could anything be clearer than the fact that it is, for this youth's develop-ment, a dead end in every sense of the term. It is no wonder, then, that Jim is ambiguous in his attachment to, and admiration of, Silver, even after the latter's exhibition of his brutal lust for murder. What he has to do is to escape Silver's powerful temptation and find his own way to the empowerment that goes with manhood.

In alluding to the saying, *si Jeunesse savait, si Vieillesse pouvait*, in his essay 'Crabbed Age and Youth', Stevenson takes issue with it for while he agrees that it is 'a very pretty sentiment', he believes that it is not always right: 'In five cases out of ten, it is not so much that the young people do not know, as that they do not choose.' Jim *does* choose, however, very publicly and at great risk to himself. Silver has presented him with an ultimatum to join the pirates or be killed: 'I always wanted you to jine and take your share, and die a gentleman, and now, my cock, you've got to ... you can't go back to your own lot, for they won't have you; and without you start a third ship's company all by yourself, which might be lonely, you'll have to jine with Cap'n Silver' (176).

Jim has apparently been excluded from 'the treaty' as Silver calls the deal he did with Dr Livesey and the others, so his back is to the wall:

'And now I am to choose?'

'And now you are to choose, and you may lay to that', said Silver.

Jim, of course, chooses to defy Silver which leads, interestingly, not to his death but to his life being saved by Silver. As a result they become, for the time being, genuinely dependent on each other and neither Jim's sympathy for Silver nor his appreciation of the clever game he sees him as playing is diminished. He even admits that his 'heart was sore for him, wicked as he was' when he considered 'the shameful gibbet that awaited him' (188) – which may, or may not, be an excuse for not facing up to the real source of his sympathy. Yet the completely unprincipled Silver remains an acute threat, for Jim knows that he cannot be trusted, particularly after having heard him tell the pirates of his brutal plan should they get the treasure and re-take the *Hispaniola*. Silver reminds Jim of just how much he is at his mercy by tying the youth to him with a length of rope. As they approach the hiding-place of the treasure, Jim, tied to the rope's end, '[f]or all the world … like a dancing bear', finds Silver directing 'murderous glances' towards him and is left in no doubt about his intentions: 'Certainly he took no pains to hide his thoughts; and certainly I read them like print' (207). However, after the discovery that the treasure has gone, Silver instantly changes sides again and this time, having no alternative, stays with the Squire's party until he makes his escape (presumably *confident* of making his escape).

Jim's lesson has been a substantial one. Essentially he has had to come to terms with the fact that growing up involves some painful and daunting discoveries – most notably that the world is charac-terised by the proliferation of misleading signs whereby duplicity and treachery (particularly from figures of authority) are initially concealed from the youth seeking access to the adult male world. He has to learn that moral categories are not clear-cut; that the same face can bespeak both affection and murder and render classification of its owner impossible.

As a psychological archetype the island is a lonely place, and those who venture upon it will either emerge from the trial triumphant against all the forces that would seek to deny selfhood and sustain the authority of the patriarchy; or, like David Balfour, be marooned in their sense of existential worthlessness, abject and malleable before the forces of authority. Jim does triumph – to the point where he can participate in the marooning of others. As the ship, that symbol of the resolved self, sails out through the narrows on its way home, its occupants catch a last sight of the pirates they had made castaways:

> we saw all three of them kneeling together on a spit of sand, with their arms raised in supplication. It went to all our hearts, I think, to leave them in that wretched state; but we could not risk another mutiny (217).

The island has been for Jim a challenge to his own nascent self-sufficiency and he must meet that challenge alone – hence his two desertions from the comforting support of the ship and the stockade, each of which is, of course, commanded by Captain Smollett.

In the iconography of *Treasure Island* knives play a considerable role making clear the nature of the trial facing Jim. On each occasion of desertion Jim is threatened by one: the first is wielded by Silver on the prostrate body of Tom, the second by yet another father-figure, the particularly disreputable Israel Hands (whom Stevenson also found in Defoe's *A General History of the Robberies and Murders of the Most Notorious Pyrates)*. The knife that pins Jim to the mast is literally almost the last throw of the father-figures and it is altogether ineffectual. Predictably so, one might say, for Jim's authority has grown steadily in this his second desertion from Captain Smollett's command. He has himself used a knife to advantage, cutting the *Hispaniola's* cable before taking command of the vessel. And take command he undoubtedly does: 'I've come aboard to take possession of this ship, Mr Hands; and you'll please regard me as your captain until further notice' (165), and Hands dutifully, if not without some irony, calls him 'Cap'n Hawkins' thenceforth.

It is easy to agree with Robson that 'In so far as the book describes the "growing up" of Jim, this is an important episode' (91). Jim himself is 'to the adult eye more experienced and psychologically secure in his handling of this new and grim anti-father'. But, as usual, this figure is not so easily disposed of. Even in Jim's moment of triumph when he makes his 'great conquest' of the ship, the baleful influence of the hostile father is felt: 'I should, I think, have had nothing left me to desire but for the eyes of the coxswain as they followed me derisively about the deck, and the odd smile that appeared continually on his face.' It might have been 'a haggard, old man's smile', but there was still danger in it: 'there was, besides that, a grain of derision, a shadow of treachery, in his expression, as he craftily watched, and watched, and watched me at my work' (158). The derision in

Hands' expression is one of the many strategies of emasculation practised by the old upon the young in Stevenson, while treachery seems to be second nature to unideal fathers.

Jim wins this confrontation, too, however, though the menace in the father-figure seems never to be quite extirpated. The 'quivering' of the water above Hands' body makes him seem to move a little 'as if he were trying to rise' despite the fact that he has been 'both shot and drowned' (167). Jim sends the dead O'Brien over the side to join him and the internecine strife of fathers and sons is again mirrored in O'Brien – 'still quite a young man' – finally resting on the bottom with his prematurely bald head 'across the knees of the [old] man who had killed him'. And the drama seems set to be enacted eternally as Jim looks down upon the bodies 'both wavering with the tremulous movement of the water' (168).

Through his integrity and resolution, Jim has vindicated himself triumphantly, thwarting the pirates by his rock-like steadfastness – 'First and last we've split upon Jim Hawkins' (179) – and saving his friends: 'There is a kind of fate in this', we may recall Dr Livesey saying. 'Every step it's you that saves our lives' (194). From the start, however, Jim's readiness to shoulder responsibility and to act (or, Stevenson might say, to *choose*) has been obvious. Lying hidden in the apple-barrel he had realised after the first words from the pirates 'that the lives of all the honest men on board depended on me alone' (65). That 'alone' has singular force. To Jim, acting responsibly means, in these circumstances, acting alone, as though he is aware that the challenge confronting him is a deeply personal trial. Which is one reason why, despite his achievements, Treasure Island is still to him that 'accursed island' rather than Silver's 'sweet spot'.

Jim's revulsion is, however, evident even before he sets foot on the island. The sight of it, 'with its grey, melancholy woods, and wild stone spires', discomposes him to the extent that, he tells us, 'from that first look onward, I hated the very thought of Treasure Island' (81–2). It is not the reaction we expect from this adventurous youth and we won't find an explanation in the superficies of a boy's adventure-story. Stevenson's islands are, by and large, traps for the self-tormented where the traveller's moral adequacy (usually as that is reflected in his aspirations to manhood) is put under severe stress with results which are often less than flattering. The truth of this is obvious in, for example, *Kidnapped, The Ebb-Tide, Treasure Island* and even exotic tales like *The Isle of Voices*.

The active involvement of the sub-conscious is signalled in a number of such stories by the draining away of colour from the landscape and by the association of the landscape with dreaming. Jim first sees the island 'almost in a dream' (73) and then describes the 'grey, melancholy woods'. The dream-landscape runs strikingly true to psychoanalytical form and is heavily imbued with Freudian symbolism:

> Grey-coloured woods covered a large part of the surface. This even tint was indeed broken up by streaks of yellow sand-break in the lower lands, and by many tall trees of the pine family, out-topping the others – some singly, some in clumps; but the general colouring was uniform and sad. The hills ran up clear above the vegetation in spires of naked rock. All were strangely shaped, and the Spy-glass, which was by three or four hundred feet the tallest on the island, was likewise the strangest in configuration, running up sheer from almost every side, and then suddenly cut off at the top like a pedestal to put a statue on. (81)

In the manuscript draft (clearly a very early one) of the unfinished *The Castaways of Soledad*, another youth, the seventeen-year-old Walter Gillingly, awakes to catch his first glimpse of the Isle of Solitude 'through the break of the mist, up a sort of funnel of moonlit clouds'. But he, too, seems scarcely awake. 'Next moment a little flying shower had blurred it out, and I laid me down again to see the same peaks repeated in my dreams'. When the sun rises and Walter awakens again he finds no great improvement in the prospect before him. The island

> rose out of the sea in formidable cliffs, and it was topped by an incredible assembly of pinnacles, more like the ruin of some vast cathedral than the decay of natural hills; and these rocks were no less singular in colour than in shape; the most part black like coal, some grey as ashes and the rest of a dull and yet deep red. Nowhere was any green spot visible....

It strikes Walter as a 'quite dead and ruined lump of an island' and its 'infinitely dreary, desert and forbidding air' puts the castaways 'notably out of heart' and the reader in mind of Earraid.

If the sight of such islands as Soledad, Earraid and Treasure Island sends the hearts of these youths into their boots (which is how Jim puts it), it is because they instinctively realise that they are a tightly-contained theatre of action which they must enter if they are to prove their fitness for the adult world. Treasure Island, however, departs in one important particular from the accepted archetype. As a number of critics have noticed, there is – in Wallace Robson's words – 'an absence of emotional pressure in the winning of the treasure' [10] and very little appearance of the meaning that is often held to accrue round the search for buried treasure, that is, the desirability of the mother's body. Nonetheless it is far from true to say, as Robson does, that 'its geography is purely functional, mere stage-setting'.[11] The last quoted extract, with its description of the almost painfully-truncated Spy-glass, suggests that Jim's anxiety has everything to do with his psychosexual development and bespeaks a troubled awareness of a highly vulnerable masculine identity. Though we should not dismiss out of hand the archetypal equation of buried treasure with the mother's body (Ben Gunn's cave where the treasure has been re-buried accords well with the conventional delineations of the symbol – with the additional detail of Captain Smollett being already ensconced there), there is another latent meaning in buried treasure which alludes to 'selfhood, independence, identity'.[12] Thus while for the pirate-crew 'the very sight of the island had relaxed the cords of discipline' (82) for Jim it signals the need to establish his *own* discipline in defiance of that imposed by the father-figures. Yet their potency – concentrated in Silver – is formidable and Jim's reaction, as witnessed at the time of Tom's murder, for example, is an authentic mixture of half-pleasurable terror and envy.

The earlier nightmares which had been induced by the description of Long John Silver have a subterranean link to Jim's dream-like vision of the island. In fact, the island is to be the focus of the struggle presaged in the first dream and one which will be decisive for Jim's development and independence. As Fowler notes, 'Jim chose to face the terrible father.... And the reward for his boldness was not only that Silver kept him alive, but that the good father's party cut the tether of dependence and ratified the free self-hood that he had stolen.' Had Jim chosen as Silver wanted, 'he would indeed have become the son of a sea-cook'.[13]

The island thus becomes Jim's Peniel where he struggles, like Jacob, for a new identity. It is a life-and-death struggle for selfhood with the youth having to meet challenge after challenge. Not only does he surmount them, he also becomes hardened by them so that when the time comes for him to have to dispose of the dead O'Brien, he does so with some degree of equanimity:

> as the habit of tragical adventures had worn off almost all my terror for the dead, I took him by the waist as if he had been a sack of bran, and, with one good heave, tumbled him overboard (168).

He may well be surrounded by dogs and murderers as the quotation from Revelations on the back of the 'black spot' handed to Silver suggests; but that he has come safely through their 'dark and bloody sojourn on the island' (218) means that he has served out the adolescent's apprenticeship. As Ben Gunn promised (95), finding the treasure has made a man of him though his new status has been earned in the process, not bought by the proceeds.

But always there is a Long John Silver who will not be transcended. He is, if you like, both the residual self-doubt in Jim's mind and residual desire; sentiments which will persist long after the action even to the time when Jim is himself an author in command of his crew of characters. For though Jim assures us at the end that Silver has gone 'clean out of [his] life', he is indubitably present as a mocking echo in the voice of the parrot which invades Jim's dreams and ends his narrative.

By far the most insidious of the father-figures in *Treasure Island*, Long John Silver is also the most seductive. We recognise him as such, in part at least, because we have come to appreciate that Jim has reached a vulnerable and decisive stage of growth. His susceptibility to Silver's ingratiating tactics is therefore natural as is his response to the latter's self-command and command over others. ('All the crew respected and even obeyed him' [62].) What Silver *seems* to Jim to be offering him through his intimacy and confidences is a share in his power and a certain enfranchisement which comes with it. But the degree of freedom he offers is illusory for he is a far more ruthless defender of his authority than Captain Smollett ever was, with no scruples about invoking the supreme sanction against recalcitrants. Smollett will eventually cut Jim adrift, so to speak, in an act which mirrors Thomas Stevenson's repeated threat to disinherit his son. Silver would go about things with less equivocation: he would simply kill him.

Nonetheless, in Silver, there is unquestionably an appeal. His persuasive wooing is as confident as Lovelace's or Richard III's and for much the same reason: he knows that there is a response in the object of his attention. And Jim's behaviour confirms the accuracy of his perceptions. Even when he is expressing his 'horror' at Silver's planned treachery, the terms in which he does so are significant: he had acquired, he tells us, 'a horror of his cruelty, duplicity and power' (73). The third term is a little surprising and makes us look again at that rather ambiguous word 'horror', which Stevenson uses a lot. It is ambiguous because it often seems *not* to mean unalloyed revulsion but to include fascination or even desire as well. (He was 'somewhat horrified', we may recall, at finding his father 'so beautiful when stripped'.)

At this stage in the adolescent's growth, power is going to attract and Silver's seductive potency will prove particularly irresistible. Initially Jim, with a degree of conceit appropriate to his age, is inclined to interpret his apparent admission into Silver's confidences as a kind of power-sharing. A certain disingenuousness might be thought to be present in this, for no son ever thinks of this sort of access to power as remaining at the level of a mere share – any more than a father thinks to draw attention to the areas which are quarantined from such access and sequestrated in the small print of the patriarchal mind. A very good example of both 'father' and 'son' playing this game occurs in *Kidnapped* when David Balfour prides himself on his ability to 'smell out [Ebenezer's] secrets one after another, and grow to be that man's king and ruler', while his uncle, apparently willing to admit David's claims, is secretly planning his transportation.

It is not long before Jim realises that any such offer to share power is, contrary to what it first looks like, a ruse to *disarm* him. When he re-enters the stockade and is confronted by Silver instead of his friends, he soon realises that a crucial choice has to be made. The offer that Silver makes him is not without its attractions, nor has the affinity he has always felt for Silver lost all its potency. He would, for one thing, enjoy the Conradian solace of being one of a crew, particularly comforting when one is beginning to contemplate the problematics of manhood and the loneliness such an aspiration brings with it. Long John's temptation is real because the position it ascribes to Jim is accurate: he *is* at a cross-roads in his development, and his dilemma is a recognisable one for the growing adolescent, though it is not often realised in such a picturesque way. Silver's words deserve to be weighed well:

'the short and the long of the whole story is about here: you can't
go back to your own lot, for they won't have you; and, without
you start a whole ship's company all by yourself, which might be
lonely, you'll have to jine with Cap'n Silver' (176).

In some ways the short and the long of the whole story *is* about here,
for it is Jim's moment of decision: whether to maroon himself like
David Balfour, in abject submissiveness, or to take arms against a
sea of troubles and, in transcending them, achieve independence
and his own authority – or oblivion. In fact, we have had a very good
indication of what is likely to happen in that Jim has, it could be
argued, already started his own ship's company *and*, as 'Cap'n
Hawkins', put down his first mutiny in so capably despatching O'Brien
and Israel Hands (the latter characterised by his 'old man's smile'
and 'shadow of treachery').

It is, however, also true that loneliness is endemic in this situation
as so many of Conrad's characters found out, and isolation can destroy
moral integrity. So Jim may defy Silver and eventually see him
bested – but he will not be able to lay his ghost. The slightly mocking,
paternalistic figure who flatters him with compliments about his *savoir
faire* as though he were already a man ('I never saw a better boy than
that. He's more a man than any pair of rats of you in this here house
...' [180]) is a reminder that such a 'caring' person (with, of course,
an alternative game-plan) is not just a comfort but a necessity, given
that no one's integrity is quite proof against fears of its own inadequacy.

Another, more substantial, reason for Silver's durability is to be
found, paradoxically, in his repeated acts of treachery and duplicity.
In them lies much of the secret of his power, for they are the product
of a total and shameless absence of any firm commitment or principle. Whatever lip-service he may pay to such notions, it can be no
more than this, for he is prepared to sacrifice any or all of them on
the instant should the *summum bonum*, his own self-preservation, be
threatened. 'Dooty is dooty' is a sentiment he never tires of repeating
but it is the stuff of his brazen effrontery, for he is as far from
believing in that fixed standard of conduct which governs Conrad's
mariners, for example, as it is possible for any man, seafaring or
landlubber, to be.

The net result, however, is that there inheres in him an irreducible
sense of his own being. Others may take seriously notions of duty,
loyalty and honest-dealing and agonise over them, espousing certain

ethical and moral principles in the process – all of which are capable of eroding their self-certainty. For Silver, no compromise is neces-sary: struggle and conflict are simplified and externalised under his Gloucester-like credo: 'I am myself alone.'

The power which derives from the total absence of principle is, as the foregoing allusion reminds us, the power that animates some of Shakespeare's most charismatic villains – Iago, Edmund, Richard III – as well as Milton's Satan, to whom James Durie, for example, is frequently compared in *The Master of Ballantrae*. What gives this power additional glamour is the freedom it appears to bring with it, which is, in truth, its justification in the eyes of its exponents. It may, of course, be freedom to go to the devil as the penultimate paragraph of *Treasure Island* suggests (or freedom to *be* the devil, as Milton's Satan portrays it), but it is immensely attractive nonetheless and perhaps not least to those who believe that there *is* a higher order of society than the piratical and are prepared to accept certain constraints on their freedom in order to sustain it.

An important factor which adds to the charisma of the Shakespearian and Miltonic villains is their almost demonic energy. Their position demands it and so, in a similar way, does Silver's, for his sort of freedom depends on his mobility, on his repudiation of all fixed principle, even on a fluidity of personality which amounts to a constant reconstruction of 'self'. In the tale, perhaps the two most striking things about Silver are his remarkable physical agility, given his missing limb, and a parallel and equally notable mental agility which allows him to change his position in a flash, as he does when he discovers the treasure to be gone, or to exploit the unex-pected to the full, as he does with Jim's return to the stockade. Power and mobility clearly go together, a nexus which receives its most dramatic rendering in the scene where Silver kills the loyal seaman, Tom. It is worth a moment's pause to reflect on Stevenson's imagi-native achievement in the characterisation of Silver: to observe how the amputation of a leg and its substitution by a crutch actually *increases* the character's apparent mobility, power and dangerous unpre-dictability. Worth noting too, perhaps, is the fact that the most impressive of recent productions of *Richard III* had Anthony Sher play Richard on crutches, giving him a devastating speed of attack at any moment from the most unexpected quarter, confounding and cowing his opponents with his protean versatility.

For both these characters, their crippled condition is turned to advantage: their mobility and their freedom are, it seems, enhanced to a pitch which makes of their actions a relished performance. Free – indeed, conditioned by their unrelenting egotism – to manipulate every situation and to play a multiplicity of roles, however incompatible or extravagant they may be, they find themselves given natural access to the matter of comedy. So for Silver in his 'knowing' exchange with Jim on the very subject of mobility when they come in sight of the island. Jim is deeply apprehensive about what their landfall will mean to him whereas Silver, whose interest in it is very different, dilates enthusiastically on the attractions of this 'sweet spot':

> 'You'll bathe and you'll climb trees, and you'll hunt goats, you will; and you'll get aloft on them hills like a goat yourself. Why, it makes me young again. I was going to forget my timber leg, I was. It's a pleasant thing to be young, and have ten toes ...' (73–4).

Mobility is indeed the key, so that there is much irony in Silver solemnly telling the crew-member he is attempting to subvert that, with middle-age looming, he is going to settle down as a pillar of genteel society: 'I'm fifty, mark you; once back from this cruise, I set up gentleman in earnest' (67). For a middle-aged pirate to put out a prospectus offering superannuated security in good society as an inducement to recruits to sail under his skull-and-cross-bones flag adds a Gilbertian touch which everyone (including Silver) enjoys and no one believes. The fact is that his ethic makes movement essential and 'settling down' a fatal contradiction. Shark-like, when he stops swimming, he drowns. So it is appropriate that he quits the story in a shore boat having stolen some of the treasure 'to help him on his further wanderings' (219).


Stevenson's scepticism about the capacity of language to sort out moral categories and define truth ('words are for communication, not for judgement', he says in his essay on Walt Whitman) also gets ventilation in *Treasure Island*. For example, Long John's supposed surname serves too many functions for it to be taken simply as an inherited patronymic – he is quick-silver when we think of his agility, silver-tongued when we think of him as a persuasive talker, unredeemed bar-silver when we think of the treasure.[14] He masks his duplicity by a handling of language so adroit that it makes words his accomplices in the grossest deceptions. Thus when we hear that he could 'speak like a book when so minded' (62) or that Jim could 'read [his thoughts] like print' (207) we recognise Stevenson again indulging a mischievous taste for sly deconstructive jabs at his own text which, cumulatively, amount to something significant.

The realisation that words 'are all coloured and foresworn', as he says in the Whitman essay, that they are among the world's most *misleading* signs, is the beginning of wisdom for many a Stevenson character. When Silver lays outrageous claim to being *un homme de parole* – brazenly telling Dr Livesey not to trust the word of the other pirates – the doctor's sneer is justified: 'No ... you're the man to keep your word – we know that' (217). But Silver is, it appears, not at all discomfited for he is at one with James Durie and Captain Hoseason in deriding the notion of inalienable verbal truth. It is quite fitting, therefore, that many years later when Jim is frightened out of his sleep, it is not by a voice which 'speaks sense' but by the gabbling of a parrot – *un perroquet des paroles*, one might say – whose voice burlesques the fundamentals of language and meaning yet still succeeds in summoning the ghost of Long John Silver.

There is no chance that Silver will disappear from Jim's dreams for he is bred in the bones of his adolescence. When this figure of the 'terrible father' receives the black spot from his crew, he tosses it derisively to Jim who reads the word 'Depposed' written in wood-ash. But we know that Silver will never be deposed, as an older Jim now occupied in constructing him anew in his memoir clearly indicates: 'I have that curiosity beside me at this moment; but not a trace of writing now remains beyond a single scratch, such as a man might make with his thumb-nail' (188). Texts which vanish are surprisingly frequent occurrences in Stevenson's work but on this occasion disappearance leaves the subject not less but more 'real'.

After so much evidence of duplicity and treachery, Jim's total condemnation of Silver would have been a foregone conclusion in a run-of-the-mill boy's adventure story.[15] That this doesn't happen challenges the reader to develop a more sophisticated explanation of the motivating psychology. That it has everything to do with the adolescent's struggle to escape the circumscribing edicts of paternal authority and arrive at a mature independence has been the ground of the foregoing argument. Jim has at first been won over by this, to him, powerful and attractive father-figure who seems to be there almost as a role-model to *help* him through the travails of adolescence. The discovery that even the trusted father-figure is irredeemably treacherous is something Jim has to learn as part of his own growth-process. However, though it is a lesson once learned, never forgotten, Silver will never be completely banished from the young man's mental impedimenta, nor even entirely from his affections. Had it been arranged otherwise, it would have suggested that the developing adolescent had completely vanquished the 'terrible father', whereas the symbolic figure of the father, with his quiver-full of prohibitions and anathemas, is a permanent fixture in psychic reality (as Stevenson's own life reveals all too clearly).

Stevenson has brilliantly sustained Silver's authenticity right to the end by mixing affectionate geniality with plentiful evidence of his capacity even for murder when his position is seriously under threat. When the 'son' defies him to his face he resorts to the full ferocity of the archetype, humiliating the rebellious adolescent by leading him on the end of a rope very possibly to his death. (The incident is a curious one, almost superfluous in fact, yet the intrinsically powerful image deployed in it graphically illustrates the savage and repressive discipline visited by the Stevensonian father-figure upon the son.) The authenticity is, however, further strengthened by having him not just escape but demonstrate his permanence by invading Jim's dreams as a mocking echo in the voice of the parrot.

The attractiveness of Silver's kind of power and freedom, though particularly magnetic for the late-adolescent, is universal, and were he to be extirpated the picture of the world left to us would be a false one. Silver may be primarily an authority-figure from the class of fathers, but, as has been shown, he is also an authority-figure from the class of Shakespearian villains. As such he is the reflection of that human desire for an unconstrained, amoral freedom coupled with – indeed premised on – an unachievable self-sufficiency:

'... I am I, Antonio,
By choice myself alone.'

Though the polychromatic Silver, so full of verbal panache, would never put the matter as baldly as Auden's Antonio, this is nonetheless the self-system at the root of all his actions.

It is a tribute to Jim's growing maturity that he recognises the ineradicability of Silver's appeal. To admit the attraction of such a figure is to recognise one's own limitations – or, rather, the limits within which one has elected to live – and at the same time to acknowledge one's secret desires. It is to admit that appearances are essentially deceptive and the drawing of moral distinctions hazardous. Jim does not seek to disown him, satisfied that the 'formidable seafaring man with one leg' has simply 'gone clean out of [his] life', but honest

enough to allow that he has not disappeared from his dreams. It is
the mature Jim, the author of the narrative, who tells us this, adding
that 'oxen and wain-ropes would not bring [him] back to that accursed
island'. As I said at the beginning such vehemence is initially
surprising, for the island could be thought of as the scene of his most
brilliant success; but then not everyone has Jim's – or Stevenson's –
difficulty in escaping the father's gravitational pull.

## Notes

1.  'Parables of Adventure: the Debatable Novels of Robert Louis Stevenson'
    in *Nineteenth Century Scottish Fiction*, ed. Campbell (1979), p. 111.
2.  'The Sea Cook' in *The Definition of Literature and Other Essays* (Cambridge,
    1984), p. 95.
3.  The words are Dianne Sadoff's in *Monsters of Affection: Dickens, Eliot and
    Bronte on Fatherhood* (Baltimore, 1982), p. 2.
4.  In *Son and Father: Before and Beyond the Oedipus Complex*, Peter Blos exam-
    ines the workings of the libidinal attraction between son and father.
    Discussing the boy's 'search for the loving and loved father' (so intense
    at times that it is often described as 'father-hunger'), he writes: 'This
    facet of the boy's father-complex assumes in adolescence a libidinal ascen-
    dancy that impinges on every aspect of the son's emotional life.' The
    resolution of the isogender complex during male adolescence occupies
    'the centre of the therapeutic stage on which the process of psychic restruc-
    turing is played out' (p. 33). This is when the adolescent boy faces the
    task 'of renouncing the libidinal bond that he had once formed and
    experienced in relation to the dyadic and triadic, i.e., preoedipal and
    oedipal, father' (p. 43).
        For an acute analysis of 'the most prohibited of the incest taboos' see
    Jean-Michel Rabaté's excellent essay, 'A Clown's Inquest into Paternity:
    Fathers Dead or Alive, in *Finnegans Wake*' in *The Fictional Father*, ed. Robert
    Con Davis, pp. 99ff.
5.  Leonard F. Manheim, 'The Law as "Father"', *American Imago*, Vol. 12,
    1955.
6.  Silver, having lost his own leg, is pulling the Squire's. Later Jim hears
    him telling his co-conspirators that he lost his leg in 'the same broad-
    side [where] old Pew lost his dead-lights'. And he adds the circumstantial
    detail that he was 'ampytated' by a surgeon —'out of college and all' —
    who 'was hanged like a dog, and sun-dried like the rest at Corso Castle'.
    The surgeon was one of Roberts' men, he tells us, and their collective
    misfortune was the result of changing their ship's name (66). Undoubtedly
    Silver is referring to Peter Scudamore, surgeon to Bartholomew Roberts,
    the pirate captain whose ship had been re-christened the *Royal Fortune*.
    After his capture, Scudamore tried to persuade other members of the
    crew to attempt an escape, arguing that the alternative was to submit to

being taken to Cape Corso 'and be hang'd like a dog, and be sun-dry'd'. They declined and Scudamore was sentenced to death at Corso Castle in March 1722, duly hanged and no doubt 'sun-dry'd'. (See Daniel Defoe's *A General History of the Robberies and Murders of the most Notorious Pyrates*, pp. 217ff.) Scudamore had been less than a year with Roberts so Silver's leg was 'ampytated' between October 1721 and March 1722! Further, unless he took up piracy at a precociously early age, Silver is also telling lies about his age when he takes occasion to tell his fellows that he is now fifty. Trelawney is clearly speaking *after* Quiberon Bay (1759) which means that Silver should indeed be concerned about his superannuation.

7. Or even Trelawney's perhaps: Edward John Trelawny's *Adventures of a Younger Son* (1831, 1835, 1856) had so much to do with piracy that Byron and Shelley took to calling its author 'The Pirate'. (I am indebted to Dr Robert Dingley for this reference.) After the publication of *Kidnapped*, Edmund Gosse wrote to Stevenson telling him that 'pages and pages might have come out of some lost book of Smollett's'. He adds: 'You are very close to the Smollett manner sometimes, but better, because you have none of Smollett's violence' (quoted by Frank McLynn, *Robert Louis Stevenson*, p. 268).

8. 14 July 1894 to Adelaide Boodle. Once again a parallel with Kafka suggests itself. Unlike Stevenson Kafka was deeply ashamed of his body, particularly when compared to his father's: 'I was, after all, depressed by your mere physical presence. I remember, for instance, how we often undressed together in the same bathing-hut. There was I, skinny, weakly, slight, you strong, tall, broad ... I was proud of my father's body'. *Letter to the Father*, pp. 163, 164.

9. Op. cit., p. 89.

10. Op. cit., p. 94.

11. Op. cit., p. 89.

12. Alastair Fowler, op. cit., p.111.

13. Ibid., p. 113.

14. Fowler suggests also the 'reprobate silver' of Jeremiah 6:30, the wicked being so called because 'God hath rejected them'.

15. In an essay published in 1951 but still of great value, David Daiches makes a highly perceptive remark which admirably pinpoints both the nature of the difference between *Treasure Island* and run-of-the-mill adventure stories and the source of the book's literary distinction: 'There are ways of blocking off overtones of meaning which certain kinds of popular artists use when they are writing *mere* adventure stories or mere romances; such writers pose only problems that are soluble, or apparently soluble, and the pretence is kept up throughout that the final resolution does indeed solve the problem .... How different from all this is *Treasure Island*! The characters for whom our sympathies are enlisted go off after hidden treasure out of casual greed, and when their adventure is over have really achieved very little except a modicum of self-knowledge. And Silver, magnificent and evil, disappears into the unknown, the moral ambiguities of his character presented but unexplained'. (*Stevenson and the Art of Fiction*, New York, 1951, pp. 10-11)

# 3

# Arabesque

A man may be reasoned into liking Wordsworth, but not into liking the 'Arabian Nights'.

Richard Garnett, Introduction to Beckford's *Vathek*

… certainly the arabesque is the oldest and most original form of human imagination.

Friedrich Schlegel

'Why must I think that almost all, no, all the methods and conventions of art today *are good for parody only?*'

Leverkühn in Thomas Mann's *Dr Faustus*

Invited to observe 'the very pathetic sight' of 'three futiles', Mr Godall, the tobacconist and sometime Prince of Bohemia, replies ironically that it is 'a character of this crowded age'. Crowded it seems to be, if *More New Arabian Nights* is anything to go by, but certainly not with futility; rather with a superabundance of creative activity which is forever opening up new prospects by challenging a range of intellectual and cultural assumptions and practices. Stevenson's *oeuvre* exemplifies this energy, some of it seeming to complement avant-garde thinking in new fields (*Strange Case of Dr Jekyll and Mr Hyde*, for instance, comes out in the same year as Krafft-Ebing's *Psychopathia Sexualis*), while other works appraise earlier models only to transform them into something so fresh and original that it will puzzle and offend many of his contemporaries and earn the title of 'un maître' from Mallarmé.

Stevenson shows his affinity with emerging Modernist sentiment by his restless, life-long experimentation and his refusal to have his aesthetic defined for him by 'the tradition'. He is, however, in very respectable Modernist company again when he declines to repudiate that tradition altogether. When Ezra Pound wrote

Tching prayed on the mountain and
wrote MAKE IT NEW

on his bath tub
   Day by day make it new

– he glossed the meaning of the Chinese characters for his imperative as 'Fresh, new; to renovate; to improve or renew the state of'.
He thus stresses *renovation* as well as innovation. Eliot picks this up
when, two years later, he declares in a lecture: 'The perpetual task
of poetry is to *make all things new*. Not necessarily to make new things.'[1]
Earlier, in his introduction to a selection of Pound's poems, he had
written 'True originality is merely development'; and that development can seem so inevitable that 'originality' may be denied the poet
for it will seem that '[he] simply did the next thing'.[2] In the same way
Eliot argues that Pound is often most original 'in the right sense'
when he is most 'archaeological', which helps to explain Robert
Adams' remark in 'What was Modernism?' that 'modernism gives
us a sense of an entire cultural heritage being ploughed up and
turned over'.[3]

That Stevenson should turn back to *The Thousand and One Nights*
to supply him with a form for a particularly iconoclastic literary
enterprise is, therefore, proof of something other than irresponsible
Celtic whimsy. Parody itself entails a recognition of the past and, in
its mixture of renovation and innovation (as well as in some other
respects to be discussed later), is quintessentially accessible as a
Modernist device.

In 1882 John Payne's nine-volume edition of the *Arabian Nights*
(the first complete English translation) had begun to appear and that
year also saw the publication in book form of Stevenson's *New Arabian
Nights*.[4] In 1885 his *More New Arabian Nights* was published and so
were the first volumes of Richard Burton's soon-to-be-acclaimed re-
working of *The Thousand and One Nights*. The concatenation of these
events might suggest either astute moves on the part of Stevenson
or his publishers, or a remarkable case of beginner's luck; but neither
explanation will suffice. What they do suggest is that J. C. Furnas's
dismissal of *New Arabian Nights* in his celebrated biography as 'a
spring-heeled freak' is itself freakish.

English literature had been assimilating tales from the *corpus* of
*The Thousand and One Nights* since Chaucer's time, though it was not
until the publication of a translation by the French orientalist Antoine
Galland in the early years of the eighteenth century that knowledge
of the tales became at all widespread.[5] In 1812 their influence was
greatly enhanced by the appearance of Henry Weber's *Tales of the
East: Comprising the most Popular Romances of Oriental Origin and Best*

*Imitations by European Authors,* remarkable both for its comprehensive scope and its long and scholarly introduction. In 1838 Henry Torrens published a translation of the first fifty tales which was followed by E. W. Lane's three-volume translation of a bowdlerised selection between 1839 and 1841. Three more editions came out in 1839 and new editions of Lane's translation appeared in 1853 and 1859.

From the time of Walter Scott onwards, the influence of the *Arabian Nights Entertainment* (as they came to be called) made itself increasingly felt in the development of the novel. The work of Thackeray, Dickens, Gaskell and Meredith, for example, all testified to the fascination the tales exerted in the period covered by Lane's and Burton's editions, when the leverage they exercised on the literary imagination was at its greatest. If one peak of this influence was to be seen in Meredith's *The Shaving of Shagpat,* published late in 1855, the next was surely Stevenson's successive volumes in 1882 and 1885.

Both Scott and Stevenson numbered the *Arabian Nights* among their favourite childhood reading, the former, while still a boy, having 'read them aloud to the family circle'.[6] Reviewers of Scott's works drew comparisons between *The Minstrelsy of the Scottish Border* (1802-3) and the Arabian tales, and suggested (still more surprisingly) that *Waverley* 'should be ranked in the same class with the *Arabian Nights*'.[7] A critic of our own time has, however, drawn attention to the fact that Scott's use of repetition and the tale-within-a-tale in, for example, *Redgauntlet,* is often explicitly related to the *Arabian Nights.*[8] Scott even precedes Stevenson in finding a place for Bedreddin Hassan's cream tarts in one of his novels (*The Heart of Midlothian,* no less). He might, of course, have been particularly susceptible to the *Arabian Nights* not just because of his childhood reading but because Henry Weber had been his amanuensis for some time nine years between 1804 and 1813.[9]

Stevenson's original attraction to the *Arabian Nights* was thus reinforced by their coming to him with the imprint of two writers he greatly admired, Scott and Meredith. With the first of these, Stevenson, of course, shared a native literary tradition where the digressive tale had long been established, but there is every indication that both writers exploited this device more fully and confidently because they knew that their readership's taste for tales-within-tales had been stimulated by contemporary publication of material from the *Arabian Nights.* Characteristically, however, Stevenson used it to confound expectation, to plough up and turn over his cultural heritage, in Robert Adams' words. Meredith's novel application of the tales in *The Shaving of Shagpat* was even more influential on Stevenson. This was in part the result of his intense admiration for Meredith whom he saw as a highly original talent ('out and away the greatest force in English letters'), [10] and also because *Shagpat* was shaped in something like the short-story form Stevenson was to find so congenial and do so much to establish.

The early years which saw the publication of *New Arabian Nights* (serialised between 1877 and 1880), *More New Arabian Nights* (1885), *Prince Otto* (1885), and *Strange Case of Dr Jekyll and Mr Hyde* (1886), bear powerful witness to the sustained interest the Arabian tales awoke in Stevenson. Setting aside for the moment the opportunity they presented him with for parody (itself highly germane to Stevenson's theory of fiction), he found them useful in a number of ways.

Not only did he adopt something of their style – which can be both ornate *and* cryptic – and, in a notably trans-gender manner, a modest amount of their sensuality, but, of far greater importance, their narrative strategies. Far from *New Arabian Nights* and *More New Arabian Nights* being freakish, they are, it could be argued, at the root of Stevenson's abiding interest in indeterminacy, the deferral of closure, reflexivity (often represented in the *mise-en-abyme* tale), multiple narratives, artistic self-exposure and the rehabilitation of art as game.

Writing of 'Modernism and Romanticism' Gabriel Josipovici has this to say:

> the modern rediscovery of the hieratic and stylised arts of other periods went hand in hand with the rehabilitation of forms of art which had not been considered serious enough to form part of the mainstream of post-Renaissance art in Europe: the puppet play, the shadow-play, children's games, street games and ballads were all used by Jarry, Stravinsky, Picasso and Eliot, and all helped them to forge their own individual styles. In these archaic and popular forms of art there is no pretence at illusion. Art is a game and its creation involves making something that will be of pleasure to others. [11]

It is not going too far to say that what the cluster of writings just adumbrated for the years 1882–86 have in common is their indebtedness to the *Arabian Nights* genre which Stevenson picks up and exploits in ways which realise and advance his own theoretic of fiction. A number of the devices employed in the oriental tale stand out as being particularly congenial to him and come to characterise a great deal of his narrative technique. Even in *Jekyll and Hyde* many of these are obvious: multiple narratives, arbitrary disjunctions, the deferral of closure, the fictionalising of 'the author', and all are manipulated in such a way that the authority of the text is enhanced to a point where it becomes the dominant reality.

So, not freakish then, either in terms of 'the tradition' or Stevenson's own *oeuvre*. That established, what remains to be said for the *New Arabian Nights*? Not much, according to Robert Kiely, always excepting the first forty pages where 'the satiric interest is clear and strong':

> unable to separate himself from the half-imaginary follies of his own characters – he retreats from satire into fantasy and from there blunders noisily into the protective excesses of farce and melo-drama.[12]

If this is so, what did that stern critic William Archer mean when he said (in 1895) that Stevenson 'never wrote anything more consummate in their kind than the *New Arabian Nights*' (adding that, nonetheless, 'one is glad that [they] came at the beginning of his career')?[13] Despite quoting this remark, Kiely does not attempt to reconcile it with his own observation – and rightly since the two are at considerable odds. Kiely is, in fact, still looking for that analysis and synthesis, that moral realism Archer had once – before he came to have greater sympathy for what Stevenson was about – accused Stevenson of flouting.[14] The view quoted by Kiely, however, while expressing relief that *New Arabian Nights* was not to be evaluated as a mature work, shows clear awareness of the mastery which Stevenson had begun to demonstrate in his highly individual literary technique. Reviewers of *New Arabian Nights* had reached the same verdict at the time of publication. George Saintsbury considered the tales to be (despite their faults) 'exceedingly good and original things in fiction' showing 'a much more original talent, and one much better worth cultivating than anything else that Stevenson has done'.[15] Another commented: 'Nothing in his previous work [could] lead us to expect fiction of such out-of-the-way originality.' The word 'original' appears frequently but he is also praised for his 'fertility of invention', 'audacity', 'boldness', and for producing work 'utterly unlike [any] fiction of the day'.[16] Many decades later, G.K. Chesterton was to endorse these opinions in his exceptionally perceptive study of Stevenson published in 1927: 'I will not say that the *New Arabian Nights* is the greatest of Stevenson's works; though a considerable case might be made for the challenge. But I will say that it is probably the most unique; there was nothing like it before, and, I think, nothing equal to it since.'

Archer's verdict is thus more in tune with the critical reception of the book than is Kiely's. To deplore Stevenson's failure to sustain his satire is to look for something that was never substantially there. And to say that he *retreats* into fantasy is to get the cart before the horse: the tales had never been anything else. Of course he pokes fun in a rather general way at the aesthetes – it was fashionable to do so, as the success of *Patience* in 1881 confirmed (after which it became even *more* fashionable); but there is considerably more 'satire' in Gilbert and Sullivan's operetta than in the whole of *New Arabian Nights*.

By Stevenson's time *The Thousand and One Nights* was widely recognised as a masterpiece in the art of storytelling, an art which Stevenson had been sedulously devoting himself to learning for many years before he produced his collection of 'Arabian' tales. The title was, of course, a characteristic piece of effrontery: multi-volume editions of the tales were thick as autumnal leaves in Vallombrosa and into their midst was slipped this conspicuously slim volume with its audacious title. What the tales offered him was a generic model within which, free from Archerian or Kielyvian expectations of high moral seriousness, he could pursue his own investigations into what should constitute the art of storytelling in his own time. The modes and stratagems discovered in the process will be found to inform a surprising amount of his later work though, true to the developing Modernist aesthetic, Stevenson would continue experimenting, and his theories about the art of fiction to evolve, to the end of his life. (Archer himself acknowledged Stevenson's 'many-sided critical doctrines'.)[17] Conspicuous among his debts to this genre, however, is the freedom and the confidence it gave him to defy contemporary demands for literary realism and to give the freest of reins to his instinct to justify art as game.

What Kiely perceives as faults in Stevenson are only so if his work is judged on a theory of fiction quite different from the one he, in fact, espoused at this time. Even more than his 'retreat' into fantasy does Kiely deplore Stevenson's addiction to what he describes as 'faking'; yet to many what Stevenson is doing when he incurs Kiely's displeasure is something for which Modernist and even Postmodernist writers receive praise. Stevenson, says Kiely,

> insists upon presenting an illusion, often a very compelling one and then turning to the reader and saying, 'This is a fraud. Not one word of it is true.' He is the magician who stops in the middle of his most convincing act to show his audience where the trap-door is....

Precisely, one might say, and a very calculated effect it is too; a fact of which some of his contemporaries were more acutely aware than Kiely. H. C. Bunner, a New York journalist, wrote:

> The new author has a power that is strongly akin to the dramatic. He juggles with his readers and with his characters. He dresses up a puppet and tells you it is a man, and you believe it, and hold your breath when the sword is at the puppet's breast. Then he holds up the stripped manikin and smiles maliciously.[18]

Bunner's review pleased Stevenson, who would have had no difficulty in reconciling himself with Kiely's view of him as a magician given to exposing his stage-machinery. Another reviewer (one or other of the Lathburys) writing in *The Spectator* employs a similar figure to 'place' him: 'He is the stage-manager skilfully directing his actors, while he never ceases to regard them from the point of view of pure art.' This is why, the Lathburys believe, though a comparison with Dumas strongly suggests itself, ultimately it doesn't suffice: 'We can imagine Dumas being himself in his characters, and believing in his stories, while Mr Stevenson gives us the impression of being outside both.'[19] All Stevenson's major fiction was yet to come, which makes the comment all the more perceptive. Even in those later novels where he might well seem to be losing himself in his characters and believing in his stories, somewhere in the structure of the narration there is always the hint of a disclaimer, a glimpse of the trap-door.

Kiely is even wider of the mark when he follows up his pejorative comparison with the magician who betrays his secrets, with another comparing the Stevenson of the *New Arabian Nights* to a faithless priest 'who announces at the moment of consecration that he does not believe in transubstantiation'. Stevenson, in fact, consecrates himself to his art with an almost exclusive devotion, imposing on himself a discipline so exacting that it came near to killing him – as well as winning the unqualified admiration of those who regarded the profession of letters as a sacred calling (most notably Henry James). So a priest he remains, albeit one who (appropriately enough for someone from a Calvinist background) never believed in transubstantiation in the first place.

The Modernist work, as is widely recognised, 'often wilfully reveals its own reality as a construction or an artifice thereby transforming much of art into a self-referential construct rather than a mirror of society'.[20] Unless one bears this in mind, it is difficult to see how a fair evaluation of *New Arabian Nights* can be arrived at; and one can see how perplexing many Victorian readers, brought up on very different literary principles, must have found it. The ending of the 'oriental' part of *New Arabian Nights* predictably caused much offence, and, in truth, it was nothing if not cavalier: 'As for the Prince, that sublime person, having now served his turn, may go, along with the *Arabian Author*, topsy-turvy into space.' However, for the reader 'who insists on more specific information', the further intelligence is supplied that Florizel because of his 'continued absence and edifying neglect of public business' has lost his throne and now keeps a cigar store in Rupert Street, still 'the handsomest tobacconist in London' (155).

W. H. Pollock, an exact contemporary of Stevenson's and editor of *The Saturday Review* from 1883 to 1894, reviewed the book and deeply regretted the fact that 'the author has not shrunk ... from pulling down the whole fabric of splendour and knightly valour which he has raised for our delight, and suddenly turning the dazzling figure from hero ... into the common type of foreign refugee with which we are only too familiar in the pages of many would-be comic writers'. And all, it seems, for the sake of 'an unwise imitation of Mr Gilbert's style of humour'.[21] H. C. Bunner was equally struck by what Pollock had called 'in the original sense of the word' this 'impertinent' ending, though he is also much less critical. The Prince, who 'is half Monte Cristo and half Haroun Al Raschid up to the last page', suddenly 'in an unexpected fashion ... leaves you laughing at him, laughing at yourself, and wondering how long his inventor has been laughing at you both'. And Bunner concludes:

This is the book on the face of it. But then, in fact, you cannot speak of the book on the face of it, for under the face is a fascinating depth of subtleties, of ingenuities, of satiric deviltries, of weird and elusive forms of humour, in which the analytic mind loses itself. [22]

What Stevenson is doing that so offends Pollock and Kiely is altogether characteristic of metafictional writing. Linda Hutcheon
describes the process succinctly in *Narcissistic Narrative*:

> By reminding the reader of the book's identity as artifice, the text
> parodies his expectations, his desire for verisimilitude, and forces
> him to an awareness of his role in creating the universe of fiction.[23]

Barry Menikoff makes a telling point when writing of the device of
the twin narrators which binds the tales together. (The two narrators
are the 'Arabian author' functioning 'as a traditional omniscient
narrator' and the outside or frame narrator 'who appears in italics
at the end of each story to remind us that what we have just read
was transmitted by the putative author of the new Arabian nights'.)
Menikoff writes:

> in the last story the outside narrator exacts his revenge, for in a
> final paragraph he dispenses altogether with the Arabian author,
> who is reduced to italics, while he completes the text in his own
> words, in full Roman type.

It is worth spelling out what is still only implicit in this critique –
namely that the omniscient narrator, as a device, is being jettisoned,
displaced by a capricious, playful, unreliable narrator who mocks
his reader. And one can go further, for this omniscient narrator is
the Arabian *author*; so it is the notion of the author which is thus
being 'sent up' and exposed as a fiction. To quote Menikoff again:

> When he reaches the end of the chain [of stories], [Stevenson] ...
> subverts the entire procedure by calling attention to the device
> and insisting upon its artificiality, indeed its spuriousness, and
> declaring in effect that *he*, the outside narrator, by the merest succes-
> sion of words and sentences can turn the Arabian author into an
> invention and the narrator into a reality or as much a reality as the
> reader cares to attribute to him. This play with narrative/linguistic
> technique is of course unsurprising to the reader of late twentieth-
> century fiction like Borges's *Ficciones*, for whom Stevenson's method
> would appear wonderfully postmodern.[24]

A word of caution here, however. Exposing the Arabian author
does not result in the endowment of the narrator with substantive
authorial powers. Certainly it reveals the fictionality of that author
and suggests the presence of a puppet-master; but it also makes the
reader suspicious of *any* author and all claims to authority. The

Arabian author having been exposed, the next to go is his usurper in a chain of replication comparable to that of the Arabian tales themselves.

The quality of *New Arabian Nights* – rather like its original – resides in an apparently unlimited inventiveness mediated through a virtuoso narrative technique. What holds everything together is the celebrated Stevensonian style so cleverly sustained in its chosen idiom and at its strenuous pitch that it makes sense when one hears the word 'inimitable' applied to it. 'Mr Stevenson', wrote the Lathburys, 'tells a story in a style so finished and so admirable, that it constitutes a distinct enjoyment in itself'; and they go on in their characteristically acute and well-phrased critique:

> The incidents are as strange and startling as in the best of Mr Wilkie Collins' stories, but improbable or impossible as they are, they do not seem so, because the actors in them behave with perfect consistency. The draft on our credulity is made once for all, and when it has been duly honoured, we are never reminded how large it was in the first instance.[25]

That narrative technique I have alluded to is, however, as far from being casual or unconsidered as it is possible to be, and despite the fact that he knows quite well that he is courting his readers' disfavour he persists with his 'freakish' experiments. Just how well he knew what he was about comes out in the comment by the frame narrator at the end of the tale. As the 'Arabian author' breaks off we are given this elaborate assurance:

> At this point, contrary to all the canons of his art, our Arabian author breaks off the STORY OF THE YOUNG MAN IN HOLY ORDERS. I regret and condemn such practices; but I must follow my original ... (118).

Such a truncation is, of course, contrary neither to the Arabian author's literary practice, nor to Stevenson's whose commitment to such a technique is signalled in the frame narrator's paraded abhorrence of it. As for the latter's obsequious deference towards his 'original' – that, too, is replete with irony coming, if indirectly, from someone who insisted so uncompromisingly throughout his career on finding his own voice.

To turn from technique to matter is to become aware of how difficult it is to draw apparently desirable distinctions. ('Pattern and argument live in each other', Stevenson had written in his essay 'On

Some Technical Elements of Style in Literature'.) Instead of incident being refined, amplified, rendered significant or even just organised by the discourse, all such hierarchies are dispensed with and content and form combine in an endless interweaving which is truly arabesque. The incident of the cream tarts at the beginning of 'The Suicide Club', for example, is high farce in a low pub and it marks a promising beginning. But it turns out to be an end, too, and disappears without trace into the rest of the fretwork: a momentary and outlandish piece of tipsy undergraduate humour with literary associations (it touches, as has been already indicated, on the tale of Bedreddin Hassan).

Lieutenant Brackenbury Rich in 'The Adventure of the Hansom Cabs' is another, equally blatant, example. The whole peculiar and entertaining selection-process in that tale is designed merely to provide two reliable seconds in a duel which, when it occurs, happens off-stage. The stratagem used to bring Frances Scrymgeour to the attention of Miss Vandeleur in 'The Rajah's Diamond' entails the non-meeting in the Comédie Française and though it is not as elaborate as the Brackenbury Rich affair, it is a highly-contrived incident also inflated far beyond all plot needs.

It is, however, precisely in 'the preposterous character of the incidents', as Saintsbury noted, that a great part of the story consists and from which most of the reader's pleasure derives – but only if we see this as an indissoluble part of his literary artistic strategy, which Saintsbury, by and large, does:

> The [reader's] pleasure (it is necessary to define it for the sake of some good people to whom the book will probably be a simple mystification) consists in the contrast of the fertility of extravagant incident, grim or amusing or simply bizarre, with the quiet play of the author's humour in the construction of character, the neatness of his phrase, the skill of his description, the thoroughly literary character of his apparently childish burlesque (108).

As Bunner noted, 'With [Stevenson] men and ideas are but literary properties, to be used as he sees fit, for this or that effect'. Even incident falls into the same category, for 'effect' is all-important and everything which conspires to limit its sovereignty is, according to Somerset at the end of More New Arabian Nights, 'the bitterness of the arts': 'you see a good effect, and some nonsense about sense continually intervenes' (202). Just as well, one might think, if the poetic effect being tried out at this point by the failed painter, failed detective and soon to be failed poet is anything to go by. Stevenson has not, however, let himself be too trammelled by the demands of sense in either of these volumes. Capriciously, provocatively and above all entertainingly, he has not so much put it to flight, perhaps, as played games with it, games which mock all such expectations in his readership. In the process, he claims a new freedom for the art of fiction which abrogates all existing contracts and asserts a volatile independence with the primary 'effect' of keeping its public guessing.

Despite this concentration on effect and his subversive deployment of parody and burlesque (in a way which even undercuts the pretensions of the text, so discouraging too-facile comparisons with *fin-de-siècle* writing), some themes do make a shy appearance in the interstices of the arabesques. These are, however, in my view, rather more tentative than Menikoff suggests in his essay. It is easy to agree with him that 'wealth and greed are the dominant motifs' in 'The Rajah's Diamond' but less so to share his opinion that 'by dramatizing the physical and spiritual corruption that drives the plots and the personages in these stories, Stevenson exposes the moral degradation of an entire culture'.[26] This is not only to confer on Stevenson something of that kind of 'constructive patience' Archer convincingly argues he does not possess, it also discovers a moral seriousness in these tales which simply does not exist. This is not to deny that the tales are positioned within the pale of Prince Florizel's moral authority. Indeed the Prince, either *in propria persona* or as T. Godall, plays the role of a fairly genial Providence and an appropriately extravagant deference is paid him: 'There is only one Godall' says Somerset in *The Dynamiter* (in rough imitation of *The Thousand and One Nights*), of whom he claims to be '*le fervent*' (203). Though the Prince is a compound of Haroun Al Raschid and Eugène Sue's Prince Rodolphe (who so impressed Stevenson that he took over his principality of Gerolstein for use in *Prince Otto*) he is rather more explicitly a figure of justice and a righter of wrongs than his two predecessors. But as a stand-in for a benevolent Providence he tends to act as a *deus ex machina*, dispensing justice with an Olympian condescension: 'go to Australia as a colonist, seek menial labour in the open air, and try to forget that you have ever been a clergyman' (149) is his advice to Father Rolles.

The generality of characters are rather more sceptical about distinctions between good and evil or in reaching moral judgements: 'Raise yourself', says Dr Noel grandly to the stricken Silas Q. Scuddamore, 'good and ill are a chimera; there is nought in life except destiny'

(43). The young members of the Suicide Club are also very careful not to make moral judgements. Somerset in *The Dynamiter,* after his acquaintance with the nihilist Zero, finds himself in a quandary. Having always prided himself on his scepticism, at the end of the tale he is confronted with the possibility of having to abandon his creed: 'I begin to doubt; I am losing faith in scepticism. Is it possible,' he cried in a kind of horror of himself – 'is it conceivable that I believe in right and wrong?' (199).

By the end of *New Arabian Nights,* Prince Florizel has lost his throne, but this is not to say that Providence has also been forced to abdicate – though at the point when the Prince is exposed as a mere device by the narrator (and the Arabian author is dismissed), Providence itself may seem a little less secure. Apparently adopting his *alias* as his permanent identity, the prince would seem to have, if anything, enhanced his moral ardour by calling himself *Theophilus Godall* (not Thomas as the sceptical Kiely would have it). As the Rupert Street tobacconist, he is the God-in-Everyman, or, at any rate, the God in every *flâneur.*

Questions of good and evil, having been lightly raised, are equally lightly dropped. So for some of the other themes that might be recognised as discernibly Stevensonian; one of which attracts attention, however, just because it is so uncharacteristic of the Arabian original. In *The Thousand and One Nights* family relationships are a crucial element, but in Stevenson's *New Arabian Nights* all the principal characters of 'The Suicide Club' and 'The Rajah's Diamond' are male and all of the numerous – and mostly very beautiful – young men are explicitly or implicitly parentless. On this striking fact there is, it would appear, a conspiracy of silence among the reviewers of the day (who were, of course, themselves mostly male).

Most of these fatherless young men also conform to that type of Stevensonian 'hero' who has difficulty emerging out of adolescence into adulthood. Surely the most striking thing about the members of the Suicide Club is their youth. There may be some diversity in the reason for their membership of the Club – some boast of their 'disgraceful actions' while another is there because he has had the misfortune to read Charles Darwin and 'could not bear to be descended from an ape' – but in all this gathering 'one type predominated: people in the prime of youth, with every show of intelligence and sensibility in their appearance, but with little promise of strength or the quality that makes success' (16). One assumes that the narrator means success in living adult lives in a competitive adult world. In fact, they are not even a success as suicides since they join the Club in order to be *killed*.

Silas Q. Scuddamore, 'a young American of a simple and harmless disposition', is one of those young men whose sexual maturity is more than once impugned: in truth, he is most at ease as a voyeur with his eye to the hole in the partition between his room and Madam Zéphyrine's – that is, until a wardrobe is dragged in front of it. When an exceedingly improbable assignation is offered him, his curiosity overcomes his timidity and he goes to keep the rendezvous at the Bullier Ball Rooms (no less). There he spies not only Madame Zéphyrine but a 'very handsome young fellow of small stature', and another 'strikingly handsome' man of a 'stately and handsome demeanour' who is seated at a table 'with another handsome young man, several years his junior'. Silas Q. Scuddamore clearly has problems; and these are not lessened when, on the brink of flight, he finds a hand laid upon his arm and discovers 'a lady cast in a very large mould' who arranges a second, more purposeful assignation. The lady does not keep it and Silas on returning to his hotel is confronted by the porter asking him if his visitor, 'the short, blond young man who came for his debt' has gone. Silas's denial of all knowledge of the young man doesn't convince the porter who behaves in a very knowing manner: '"I believe what I believe", returned the porter putting his tongue into his cheek with a most roguish air' (41). Silas dashes to his room 'assailed by the worst forebodings'. Groping his way in the darkness to a bedside table, he encounters the bed:

> He lowered his hand, but what it touched was not simply a counterpane – it was a counterpane with something underneath it like the outline of a human leg. Silas withdrew his arm and stood a moment petrified. 'What, what,' he thought, 'can this betoken?' (42)

If we had any doubts about Stevenson enjoying himself at this point, the second 'what' would dispel them. Silas's wild surmise is, of course, right: the leg belongs to the short, blond young man who had come to claim a debt, but it 'betokened' not whatever it was that Silas imagined, but a corpse. Silas is a born loser.

While it is not clear whether Silas is parentless or not, another even weaker young man, Harry Hartley in 'Story of the Bandbox', is explicitly an orphan. He, too, is 'a timid cavalier' although, it seems, a 'graceful' one: 'Blond and pink, with dove's eyes and a gentle smile, he had an air of agreeable tenderness and melancholy, and the most submissive and caressing manners' (78). At his best he is possessed of 'a sort of maiden dignity' (96) but his manhood has been fatally compromised by his ready adoption of the 'character of male lady's-maid and man milliner to Lady Vandeleur' (80). The inadequate young man's end is an ignoble one. Dismissed most cuttingly by his admired mistress – 'we are now persuaded that you equally lack manhood, sense and self-respect' (101) – he is dragged off to the police station and out of the story by an enraged General Vandeleur. A coda by the 'Arabian author' assures us, however, that, having inherited 'a sum of money from a maiden aunt in Worcestershire' (102) he begins 'a new and manlier life' with the capable Prudence in Bendigo or, just possibly, Trincomalee.

Young Mr Rolles the curate in the same tale is 'dark and strikingly handsome, with a look of mingled weakness and resolution' (96). To the extent that the latter quality gets considerable exercise in the aftermath of this theft of the Rajah's diamond – 'as long as I live,' cries the General's brutal sibling, the ex-Dictator of Paraguay, 'I will never hear another word against the cloth!' – Rolles is much less inadequate though, it would seem, equally bereft of family. He even shows a considerable flair for his new vocation: '"I do not wish to flatter you", says the Dictator, "but upon my word, you have an unusual disposition for a life of crime .... Cheer up, Mr Rolles, you are in the right profession at last!"' (117–18). Having rediscovered a conscience in consequence of losing the diamond, he is advised by the Prince to abandon the church and join the other delinquents heading for Australia.

Francis Scrymgeour of 'Story of the House with the Green Blinds' has lost his mother while young and discovers shortly after the story begins that he is not the son of the man he had believed to be his father. Francis, though 'of a docile and affectionate disposition', is not of the class of inadequates; nonetheless through him the pervasive Stevensonian concern with parent–child (particularly father–son) relationships gets its first real airing in the book. Learning from a 'well-known firm of Writers to the Signet' that Mr Scrymgeour senior is not his father, he also learns that a handsome annuity has been offered him on certain conditions, one of which is that his benefactor will be allowed to 'advise [him] absolutely in the choice of a wife'(120). Demurring at the mysterious and incredible circumstances of the affair, he seeks to find out who is at the bottom of it and receives the answer: 'Your father, and no-one else, is at the root of this apparently unnatural business' (121). It is where fathers are often to be found in Stevenson's work.

It needs only a very little reflection on Francis's part for him to make up his mind: 'His whole carnal man leaned irresistibly towards the five hundred a year, and the strange conditions with which it was burdened' (121). Eventually, following a labyrinthine procedure worthy of *The Thousand and One Nights*, he sets eyes on the chosen lady and his fantasies are fulfilled: 'A shock passed over his body, and he saw all the colours of the rainbow' (129). Various adventures have to occur before their wedding can be celebrated and on one of these occasions Stevenson combines his comic inventiveness with this theme of the problematic father–son relationship to great effect. Assuming that Jack Vandeleur, the ex-Dictator, is his father, he is horrified to discover him to be a 'dangerous and violent intriguer'. The 'hopeful tenderness' with which he has drawn near to overhear the conversation between him and Rolles is 'transformed into repulsion and despair' (124). Nonetheless, he decides to persevere and takes rooms overlooking the Dictator's garden. Beneath him is 'a very comely chestnut-tree with wide boughs' under which there are 'rustic tables'.

After some days, he observes the arrival of Mr Rolles to dine with the Dictator and his daughter and witnesses the drugging of the curate-turned-criminal. Vandeleur demands his daughter's help to drag Rolles into the house and this piquant exchange follows:

'It is a crime,' replied the girl.
'I am your father,' said Mr Vandeleur (136).

Not knowing whether Rolles is alive or dead, Francis recognises that 'a great calamity had fallen upon the inhabitants of the house with the green blinds'. To his surprise, however, Francis finds that his sympathies are more with the girl and the old man than their victim: 'A tide of generous feeling swept into his heart; he, too, would help his father against man and mankind, against fate and justice ' (136–7). Opening his window-shutters he launches himself into the air and lands in the top of the chestnut tree: 'Branch after branch slipped from his grasp or broke under his weight', but at last he finds one which will bear his weight and lets himself down to the ground. Entering the house he throws himself on his knees in front of Vandeleur:

'Father!' he cried. 'Let me too help you. I will do what you wish and ask no questions; I will obey you with my life; treat me as a son, and you will have a son's devotion.'

The response is far from encouraging:

> A deplorable explosion of oaths was the Dictator's first reply.
> 'Son and father?' he cried. 'Father and son? What d—d unnat-
> ural comedy is all this? ... And who, in God's name are you?' (137)

Francis, it turns out, has got the wrong Vandeleur: 'You are no son
of mine. You are my brother's bastard by a fishwife, if you want to
know'(138). Comic as the whole episode is, the Dictator's brutally-
worded repudiation of Francis draws attention to a theme that is
altogether serious and never far below the surface in Stevenson's
writing.

Implicit in the foregoing discussion of *New Arabian Nights* is another
theme which requires further consideration because ultimately it
throws significant light on the workings of Stevenson's fiction. I am
thinking of the remarkable incidence of gender-reversal. The confusion of male and female roles and attributes occurs so frequently that
it arrogates to itself a function well beyond that of any merely comic
device. Essentially it is a subversion of traditional narrative strategies where certain assumptions about gender are the bed-rock of
novelistic practice. That this happens in a text which purports to take
as its model an exceptionally erotic master-text, challenges all sorts
of notions of authority – textual, social and sexual – and its transmission. Conventional assumptions about the transmission of
authority in a male-authored text cannot but be jeopardised when
the sexual identity of some of its principal male characters is called
in question. The 'son' declines to play the role 'the male traditional'
assigns to him entailing the reproduction of the pre-scribed text, and
so would seem to flout literary canon-law at will.[27]

Thus while the proprieties would not be at all offended by a
simple 'bouleversement' *within* the gender – for example, a Persian
odalisque being transformed into a reasonably-virtuous London
chamber-maid called Prudence as happens in 'Story of the Bandbox'
– it is another matter when the Prince's Master of Horse is called
Colonel Geraldine. Moreover, much as is the case in *Jekyll and Hyde*,
we seem always to be on the brink of an even more scandalous
expression of gender-inversion. Precisely what *did* all these young
men kidnapped for 'Mr Morris's' party think when they found
themselves debouching in front of the brilliantly-lit villa in 'The
Adventure of the Hansom Cabs'? 'There is a gentleman's party in
this house', the uncommonly suave cabman tells Brackenbury Rich.

'I do not know whether the master be a stranger to London and without acquaintance of his own; or whether he is a man of odd notions. But certainly I was hired to kidnap single gentlemen in evening dress, as many as I pleased, but military officers by preference' (60). To give a remit of this sort to such an urbane cab-man seems to be asking for trouble; however, if the singular method of his recruitment didn't give a young man-of-the-world pause for reflection, then he is either much less worldly than he has any right to be or else he is in promiscuously questing mode. 'It is not a common way of collecting guests,' Brackenbury agrees cautiously, then immediately succumbs to the spirit of adventure, and enters.

He is ushered into the drawing-room where '[a] young man, slender and singularly handsome, came forward and greeted him with an air at once courtly and affectionate'. Brackenbury, 'unable to resist a sort of friendly attraction for Mr Morris's person and character', gazes round the room and sees some 16 men, 'few beyond the prime of life', engaged, amid 'a profusion of rare and beautiful flowering shrubs', in desultory gaming. 'I see', thought Brackenbury, 'I am in a private gambling saloon'; and we learn that '[h]is eye had embraced the details and his mind formed the conclusion, while his host was still holding him by the hand'. We have, of course, to remember that the lieutenant has been away fighting wars and making a name for himself on the Indian frontier but his equanimity is nonetheless impressive.

Mr Morris – who is, of course, none other than Colonel Geraldine – continues to cut what would have surely been regarded as an unusual figure for a Master of Horse:

> He went from group to group and from person to person with looks of the readiest sympathy and the most pertinent and pleasing talk; he was not so much like a host as like a hostess, and there was a feminine coquetry and condescension in his manner which charmed the hearts of all (65).

This *does* seem to make something of a meal of finding two reliable seconds for a duel. All things considered, it was quite an achievement for Mr Morris to have 'charmed the hearts' of all his captives.

However entertaining we find this apparent foolery to be, it shouldn't be allowed to obscure the seminal fact that what Stevenson is up to here is aiding and abetting the dismantling of polarised gender-systems. The notable fluidity of gender which often complicates his

characterisation is, in truth, part and parcel of his Modernist challenge to notions of fixity and hierarchy.

To cast aside settled assumptions about gender-identity based on
a clear dichotomy, to make gender itself contingent, has profound
ramifications: centrally it is 'to demonstrate that human identity is a
matter of self construction and presentation', and it is to 'challenge
the hierarchical arrangements of [society]'. These words are from
Jessica R. Feldman's exceptionally valuable study, *Gender on the Divide:
The Dandy in Modernist Literature*,[28] which, in analysing the French
dandy as an icon of Modernism, coincidentally sheds a great deal of
light on the nature of Stevenson's subversiveness.

Introducing her thesis, Feldman argues that writers 'on the divide'
are those 'who manage to escape, by the energies of genius, the
prison of dichotomous gender. They are able to reveal the authority
of patriarchal culture as neither monolith nor mirage, but a cultural
construction like any other.' The list of writers she selects – Gautier,
Barbey, Baudelaire, Cather, Stevens and Nabokov – could easily
have been extended to include Stevenson. (Her perceptive allusions
to his work and her account of Nabokov's debt to *Prince Otto* might
be construed as recognition of this.) The *need* to do so becomes clam-
orous when she goes on to observe that 'most men cannot write beyond
patriarchy' [i.e. because they are part of it], 'but some gifted artists
can, those who deliberately seek the new'. Only when she adds
'when they write beyond patriarchy – which is to say they display
patriarchy's fragmentation, its holes and contradictions, its concate-
nated nature – they often do so unconsciously, inadvertently' – only
then does one demur on Stevenson's behalf. For there is nothing
unconscious or inadvertent about Stevenson's exposure of the shortcomings of patriarchy as both the *Arabian Nights* tales and *Jekyll and
Hyde* – in their different ways – amply testify.

What usually goes with a deliberate confusion of gender in
Stevenson's work is a text which, from beginning to end, constantly
calls attention to itself: posing, impersonating, playing stylish tricks.
In a word, text, character and narrator in such works are all imbued
with the spirit of the dandy, that figure who, in Baudelaire's words
'cherche ce quelquechose qu'on nous permettra d'appeler la moder-
nité'. To Feldman the dandy 'impersonates some of the major struggles
of the modernist arena.... The figure who emerges not only rehearses
the thematics of modernity but also challenges "patriarchal thought".
He replaces the mythologies of "phallogocentrism" with something
else.'

The dandy is thus a disturbing figure who, in subverting the notion of dichotomous gender, casts doubt on 'the very binary oppositions by which his culture lives'. At the same time he offers that culture a signal *quid pro quo*:

> Paradoxically, dandies create a tradition by dismantling the notion of tradition as patriarchal line in which one writer inherits or wrests from another the sacred torch or sanctified pen. Rather, in courting the *coincidentia oppositorum*, dandies teach us of sudden metamorphoses, of 'a poetry not previously conceived of', of surprise and novelty which challenge orderly succession, neatly drawn lines, categorical exclusion and inclusion themselves.

Stevenson's *New Arabian Nights* and *More New Arabian Nights* illustrate the validity of Feldman's argument brilliantly. So much so that we might guess at his admiration of one of Feldman's subjects, Barbey d'Aurevilly, even if we didn't have proof of it in his letter to Colvin of June 1893. The extravagant posing going on in virtually every page of these two books, together with the constant metamorphosis of character, text and narrator ensures that nothing remains itself for long, that everything is translated into something else (as Feldman puts it *vis-à-vis* Pushkin's *Onegin*) through 'feint, sleight-of-hand, nuance, parody, travesty' so that 'direct meaning dissipates into texture'.

It is precisely through the same means that Stevenson secures very similar effects in these early stories. In particular, the transgression of gender boundaries is clearly a favourite device. Sometimes the objective is pursued with a wild extravagance of wit and humour suggesting a comparison with the Gautier story discussed by Feldman where the narrator's persona is 'one of manic wit, defying us to take anything in the story seriously'. In *More New Arabian Nights* we have a good example in Challoner's encounter with 'Miss Fonblanque'. Despatched to Glasgow by Asenath, alias Clara Luxmore, to deliver a letter to this lady, the faithful 'squire of dames' is greatly taken aback to be confronted at the specified address not by a woman but by 'a man of a very stalwart figure in his shirt-sleeves'. He is even more disconcerted when this figure impatiently attempts to reassure him in these words: '"I am Miss Fonblanque," he said; and then, perceiving the effect of his communication, "Good God!" he cried, "what are you staring at? I tell you, I am Miss Fonblanque"' (58).

Contrary to the argument advanced by Professor Kiely, *New Arabian Nights* certainly does not set out to be a satire, only relapsing into farce when it fails to sustain its aspirations. From start to finish it is a subversive burlesque which is so comprehensive that by the end no secure footing remains for anything – whether we are thinking of a traditional view of morality, the art of fiction or of gender-definition. Even what was perceived as the 'subtle humour' proved unnerving (to use Menikoff's word) to contemporary readers as they struggled to decide whether it was cold or mocking or both. Menikoff is altogether right when he argues that being 'unable to identify the function of the humour was undoubtedly more disturbing than its coldness'.[29] And they couldn't identify it because Stevenson left them no firm ground on which to stand to make their judgement. It is this practice which works against the book being considered as satire and it is the same factor which ensures that it cannot be simplistically written-off as *fin- de-siècle* self-indulgence, for its own paraded structures are ultimately not proof against the built-in subversion. Richard Poirier in *The Performing Self* describes parody as treating writing as performance rather than as a codification of significances, and he goes on from there to define a 'newly-developed' form: 'a literature of self-parody that makes fun of itself *as it goes along*' and which 'shapes itself around its own dissolvents':

> it calls into question not any particular literary structure so much as the enterprise, the activity itself of creating any literary form, of empowering an idea with a style. The literature of self-parody continues, then, the critical function that parody has always assumed, but with a difference. While parody has traditionally been anxious to suggest that life or history or reality has made certain literary styles outmoded, the literature of self-parody, quite unsure of the relevance of such standards, makes fun of the effort even to verify them by the act of writing.[30]

Stevenson parodies (or, more accurately, burlesques) his original so extravagantly that he ensures that no-one can be left in doubt that the cloud-capp'd palaces are anything other than the work of a conjurer obligingly ready at any moment to explain the success of his creation by demonstrating the gullibility of the audience. In the beginning is the signifier and most likely in the end too. Whether or not there's a signified depends upon your view of creation: the arabesque could well be all.

## Telling More Lies

Robert Kiely's response to Stevenson's *Arabian Nights* is a little like the Irish Bishop's to *Gulliver's Travels*. Writing of the tales in *More New Arabian Nights* (hereinafter called *The Dynamiter*), Kiely claims that 'we get the uncomfortable sense that Stevenson is almost compulsive about forcing his various narrators in these tales to plead guilty to telling lies'. Yet there is really no need to feel uncomfortable for Stevenson knows very well what he's doing, and Kiely himself provides the evidence. He goes on:

> Not only did most of the adventures not happen, but those who told them are posers and triflers. By repeating this pattern of deception followed by remorse, he implicitly casts aspersions on the validity of certain kinds of narrative art ... and on the integrity of artists like himself.[31]

But his integrity would suffer only if he were seriously espousing the 'certain kinds of narrative art' Kiely has in mind whereas Stevenson is experimenting with quite different strategies.

In the first part of this discussion, I held back one particularly interesting innovation effected by Stevenson. Into *his* version of the *Arabian Nights* he has introduced the figure of the urban detective. Virtually anyone in that volume is liable to turn detective at any moment – indeed it would seem that such a character is universal property, as we learn in 'Story of the Young Man in Holy Orders', where '[the] detective that there is in all of us awoke and became clamant in the bosom of Mr Rolles ... ' (104). Francis Scrymgeour and Lieutenant Brackenbury Rich both dabble in the trade in an amateurish way and Prince Florizel arrogates to himself something of the functions of a detective: 'rightly looked upon, a Prince and a detective serve in the same corps. We are both combatants against crime... . I had rather, strange as you may think it, be a detective of character and parts than a weak and ignoble sovereign' (152). The *real* detective to whom he is talking at this point is all but overwhelmed by the disclosure but the Prince is, in truth, almost a travesty of the detective. Such is his omniscience, ubiquitousness and status that he has but to be confronted by a mystery to bring about its solution.

When we come to *The Dynamiter*, however, it is to find that the book more or less begins with a paean to the detective, 'the only profession for a gentleman'. That Somerset is making a highly unusual claim is clear from Challoner's reaction: 'The proposition is perhaps

excessive,' said Challoner, 'for hitherto I own I have regarded it as
of all dirty, sneaking, and ungentlemanly trades, the least and
lowest' (6). Somerset is indignant – and histrionic: 'To defend society?
... to stake one's life for others? to deracinate occult and powerful
evil?' Moreover, one doesn't have to *do* anything to get started in this
career, which is a considerable advantage in the eyes of the three
well-nigh penniless 'futiles'. All they have to do is to wait for Chance
(which 'rules this terrestrial bustle') to deliver:

> Chance will continually drag before our careless eyes a thousand
> eloquent clues, not to this mystery only, but to the countless
> mysteries by which we live surrounded. Then comes the part of
> the man of the world, of the detective born and bred. This clue,
> which the whole town beholds without comprehension, swift as
> a cat, he leaps upon it, makes it his, follows it with craft and
> passion, and from one trifling circumstance divines a world (7).

The curious and unremarked thing about all this is that the detective in the modern sense which was just beginning to become
fashionable is altogether alien to the Arabian Nights genre, where
virtue often goes unrewarded while the wages of sin are quite
frequently more wages. The modern detective is the figure who
believes in 'the truth' and that it can be established by the empirical
method, not revealed by a Theophilus Godall, alias the sovereign
Prince of Bohemia, or by a djinn from a bottle.

Writing of 'the new figure of the urban detective', Raymond
Williams sees him as the literary response to the growth of the 'dark
side' of large metropolitan centres: an underside of inscrutable
mystery and danger only to be 'penetrated by an isolated rational
intelligence'.[32] Michael Holquist attributes to the detective a similar
character and traces his origins in Poe whom he regards as 'the
Columbus who lays open the world of radical rationality which is
where detectives have lived ever since'.[33]

It may be objected that Stevenson's would-be investigators are not
*quite* detectives 'in the modern sense' on the grounds that they are,
rather, half detective and half inquisitive *flâneur*. They are, of course,
all amateurs and compound what W. H. Auden, at least, regarded
as an unsatisfactory sub-species by brazenly advertising the role that
chance plays in their adventures. They also fail to meet Auden's criteria
for the true detective because their role does not conform to the strict
formula he lays down for the detective story. 'The vulgar definition,
"a Whodunnit", is correct. The basic formula is this: a murder occurs;

many are suspected; all but one suspect, who is the murderer, are eliminated; the murderer is arrested or dies.' From this definition Auden rigorously excludes 'Thrillers, spy stories, stories of master-crooks, etc., when the identification of the criminal is subordinate to the defeat of his criminal designs'.[34]

In fact, as in so much else, Stevenson burlesques the figure of the detective: inevitably so since the sort of penetrable truth that is virtual meat and drink to him is quite incompatible with Stevenson's own views of moral reality. As Auden rightly says, 'The interest in the thriller is the ethical and eristic conflict between good and evil',[35] but Stevenson spends a good deal of his time subverting the notion that the two can be satisfactorily distinguished. This is obvious in *Treasure Island*, *The Master of Ballantrae* and *Jekyll and Hyde* as well as *New Arabian Nights* where Dr Noel's view that 'good and evil are a chimera', though it may be an extreme version of Stevenson's recognition of moral ambiguity, is by no means an unfamiliar notion among his characters.

An investigator characterised by a penetrating rational intelligence is obviously redundant in an Arabian Nights world, if he is not, indeed, a contradiction in terms; for where tales never end (prolif-erating, instead, yet more tales in fruitful generation) and where the quality of their 'evidence' is measured not by their veracity but by their aesthetic impact, there can be nothing to detect. *Pace* Kiely, to 'fake' in this context, far from being a crime, is a condition of exis-tence, and not just for Scheherazade but – Stevenson would argue – for a healthy literary culture.

The timing of all this is quite extraordinary. The figure of the detective is just about to become a fashionable one and Stevenson (well-acquainted, of course, with Poe's Dupin as well as with the perhaps more hybrid types in Gaboriau, Sue, Dickens and Collins) is already exploiting and debunking him. He does so, however, because his own theoretical position requires him to. In burlesquing the detective he burlesques the whole idea that 'the truth' is a commodity a writer can trade in. It is as much a chimera as is the facile distinction of good and evil; every bit as unreal as the conven-tional means of representing it in fiction.

There is a splendid occasion when Stevenson links the world of the detective and the writer with a deftness of comic touch which helps to explain why Wilde admired him so much. When Mr Rolles, the clergyman who discovers in his own bosom 'the detective that there is in all of us' (104), gets his hands on the Rajah's diamond, the scales fall from his eyes and he decides that he urgently requires to extend his education: 'I ... am a recluse, a student, a creature of ink-bottles and patristic folios', he announces to a stranger in his club, 'and I desire to know more about life.' Then he is made to specify his need by means of a piece of Stevensonian playfulness at the expense of a novelist he had studied closely and owed a considerable debt to, William Makepeace Thackeray: 'By life ... I do not mean Thackeray's novels; but the crimes and secret possibilities of our society.' The sharp and double-pronged point that Rolles is made to serve in this Wildean sally is, of course, that Stevenson not only does *not* believe that 'real' life will be found in novels about the mores of society, but also that he is altogether of the opinion that no literary form can ever represent life or should ever arrogate to itself – however sardonically – a moral purpose in the manner of Thackeray's satire. (Thackeray insisted that 'the Art of Novels is to represent Nature; to convey as strongly as possible the sentiment of reality'.)[36] The club-member addressed by Father Rolles, who, predictably, turns out to be Prince Florizel, helpfully directs him to Gaboriau's works on crime and detection ('much studied by Prince Bismarck', he adds, which – though true – is a double-edged recommendation some seven years after the Franco-Prussian war). Dutifully the errant cler-gyman purchases some volumes on his way home but is disgusted to find out that what information they did have was 'scattered amongst romantic story-telling, instead of soberly set forth after the manner of a manual'; and he concludes that the writer 'was totally lacking in educational method' (107–8). Alas, no such life-manual exists and 'romantic story-telling' provides no very helpful compendium either.

The clergyman-detective is by the nature of his understanding disbarred from recognising what constitutes truth in modern story-telling since it is bound to fall outside the definition acceptable to either cleric or detective. Nonetheless, though he failed to find in Gaboriau what he wanted to know about life (which boiled down to how to cut the diamond he had purloined), he conceived a great admi-ration for detective Lecoq whom he measures by a very interesting · standard: 'He was truly a great creature', ruminated Mr Rolles. 'He knew the world as I know Paley's Evidences' (108). Paley was, of course, a noted utilitarian theologian who justified God by the design he perceived in natural phenomena. The *Arabian Nights*, ancient or modern, are well beyond Paley and all who immured themselves within his utilitarian doctrine. For Stevenson to plant Paley's Evidences in the middle of his arabesque is a jocular way of exalting the moral scepticism inherent in his form and realised in the tales over the facile assumptions of the 'Evidences'about the location of truth, so burlesquing both cleric and detective simultaneously. It is worth noting, too, perhaps, that in the encounter, Prince Florizel himself pointedly denies the usefulness and truthfulness of books:

'I confess I have no great notion of the use of books except to amuse a railway journey; although, I believe, there are some very exact treatises on astronomy, the use of the globes, agriculture, and the art of making paper flowers. Upon the less apparent provinces of life, I fear you will find nothing useful' (107).

It is all the more interesting, therefore, that in *The Dynamiter* we move from a position where truth becomes a plaything and is kicked around like a giant, multi-coloured beach-ball, to one where Somerset 'who had chosen the broad, daylit, unencumbered paths of universal scepticism', believing that 'right and wrong are but figments and shadows of a word' (138), comes to ask himself in melodramatic shock and horror, 'is it conceivable that I believe in right and wrong?' (199).

The *Dynamiter*, despite its generic title *More New Arabian Nights* and sharing some of the earlier collection's 'Arabian' devices like multiple tales-within-tales (though the 'Arabian author' becomes marginalised because, we are told, he is inclined to deal with matters 'too serious for this place' [6]), does have a skeletal argument chiefly centred on Somerset. To start with, his determination to 'deracinate occult and powerful evil' (6) is his hyperbolic way of dressing-up the proposed adventure – he is after all an exponent of 'universal scepticism' – and to provide the three 'futiles' with a *raison d'être*. When he harangues his companions with equal vivacity on the great opportunity that awaits them as detectives, the 'truth' he pursues is as neutral as jigsaw-making. Towards the end of the adventure, however, Somerset discovers that he does have some values after all and rejoices when at last Zero, the aptly named nihilist, is 'expunged'.

Between these occasions, Somerset and his friends show themselves to be utterly incompetent detectives – as incompetent in this trade as they have been (and are likely to be) in any other. Far from asserting that penetrating rational intelligence and seeing to the heart of the matter, they are repeatedly hoaxed. Chance, 'the blind Madonna of the Pagan', becomes an accessory after the fact and sees to it that each of the three young detectives encounters the same engaging arch-fictionaliser, Clara Luxmore. Thus the detective may attempt to insert himself into the *Arabian Nights'* world but his rational intelligence is completely routed by the storytelling genius of this Scheherazade, the anarchist and devoted follower of Zero.

Surely Stevenson should be credited with a distinctively Modernist achievement in this 1880s reconstruction of *The Thousand and One Nights*. To sustain at a constant level the idiom of his burlesque for the length of a substantial novel is in itself an extraordinary feat, with a humorous effect which not even Meredith could have bettered. Diverting as it is, however, what *The Dynamiter* demonstrates once again is Stevenson's conviction that the only 'truth' is the effectiveness of the tale; and that this effectiveness, this 'truth', depends, in part at least, on its self-replication, on the fact that it, like a true arabesque, is endless. When Challoner meets the young woman who had fled following the explosion in the lodging-house, the whole incident becomes outrageously literary. Despite having just been a party to some failed bomb-making which had come near to destroying the house if not the terrace, the young woman ignores Challoner's pleas for an explanation and has the effrontery instead to start reciting Wordsworth's 'Sonnet on Westminster Bridge'. This is followed by the equally histrionic dialogue:

> 'I perceive, Madam,' said [Challoner], 'you are a reader.'
> 'I am more than that,' she answered, with a sigh. 'I am a girl condemned to thoughts beyond her age … ' (14).

The absurdity of the whole episode, the extravagance of the sentiment is, of course, melodrama self-consciously parodying itself for comic effect, but the heightened performance which it calls for combines with a constant fictionalising to cut the tale off completely from the traditional strategies which had supplied it with its authority. For example, once upon a time a storyteller was presented as a reliable witness: a clear identity was conferred upon a text by an omniscient narrator or, collaboratively, between author and narrator, both tending to assume shared values with the reader and general agreement as to what constituted reality and realism. In *The Dynamiter*, however, Stevenson – though not the first to do so – plants his own explosive charge under that tradition and, in doing so, is considerably more successful than the hapless Zero. Not only does the tale acquire for itself quite new terms of reference, it ensures that these, too, will be continually subverted, since its only loyalty is to parody. Fictions are piled on fictions and then detonated as the extravagance of the parody ensures its betrayal; and the text discloses that the source of its new authority is its 'naturalisation' in constant movement and instability.

The detective, so out of his element, is quite obviously destined to become the sport of such fictional strategies and he is quickly suborned. In Challoner's case, all was, of course, lost the moment Clara seated him beside her on the park bench and 'began ... with the greatest appearance of enjoyment to narrate the story of her life' (17). The *ArabianNights* formula (with the addition of a characteristic Stevensonian grace-note) makes it very clear that we are a good deal nearer Baghdad than Regent's Park. At the close of Clara's preposterous story, Challoner, to his credit, recognises how thoroughly he has been vanquished, though he has succumbed, in part at least, because the penetrating rational intelligence of the detective has been seduced by aesthetic pleasure and not because of the truth of the tale:

> What with the lady's animated manner and dramatic conduct of her voice, Challoner had thrilled to every incident with genuine emotion. His fancy ... applauded both the matter and the style; but the more judicial functions of his mind refused assent. It was an excellent story; and it might be true, but he believed it was not (50).

Challoner has no idea how to deal with the situation (and is not helped by being 'a man averse to amorous adventures') and finds his spirits plummeting. He had never been convinced by Somerset's insistence that the detective's was a gentlemanly profession and, creature of convention as he is, he is consumed by embarrassment at the prospect of informing 'Miss Fonblanque' that he didn't believe a word of her story: ' it was doubtless possible for a lady to wander from the truth; but how was a gentleman to tell her so?' (50) For the sleuth so meekly to abandon his quest for the truth is to become an accomplice in deception. He whose new-found trade it is to fillet witnesses' stories for the truth, finds himself helpless when confronted by a blatantly mendacious storyteller whose artistry can dazzle even in a moral vacuum.

Somerset's experience with the lady of the superfluous mansion is not dissimilar. Mrs Luxmore has all the makings of a Wildean character; indeed, it is hard to believe that Wilde did not find in her a prototype Lady Bracknell. At any rate the latter, who was of the opinion that three addresses always inspire confidence ('even in tradesmen'), would have been deeply impressed by Mrs Luxmore's ownership of no fewer than eight mansions 'in the best neighbour-hoods in town'. Somerset had met Mrs Luxmore in extravagantly romantic circumstances while roaming London in search of the adven-ture which would prove his talent as a detective. The setting is promising for this is a very modern – even, to some extent, a Modernist – city, with its emphasis on crowds and an obscure secret life:

> In the continual stream of passers-by, on the sealed fronts of houses, on the posters that covered the hoardings, and in every lineament and throb of the great city he saw a mysterious and hopeful hiero-glyph .... Persons brimful of secrets, persons pining for affection, persons perishing for lack of help or counsel, he was sure he could perceive on every side; but by some contrariety of fortune, each passed upon his way without remarking the young gentleman ... To thousands he must have turned an appealing countenance, and yet no one regarded him.

Somerset allows his search to be interrupted by a Meredithian 'light dinner, eaten to the accompaniment of his impetuous aspira-tions' and then resumes his task; by which time:

> the lamps were already lighted, and the nocturnal crowd was dense upon the pavement. Before a certain restaurant, whose name will readily occur to any student of our Babylon, people were already packed so closely that passage had grown difficult; and Somerset, standing in the kennel, watched, with a hope that was beginning to grow somewhat weary, the faces and the manners of the crowd (66–7).

It is here that Somerset's adventure starts, for a brougham draws up and a white-gloved hand beckons him to get in. He does so and, confronted by the heavily-veiled lady, Somerset finds that all his care-fully rehearsed tactics for dealing with just such a romantic encounter fail him completely and he sits tongue-tied. In a desperate attempt to do *something* to 'dissolve the spell of his embarrassment', he pounces on the gloved hand. Alas, it is to no avail: 'he found himself no less incapable of speech or further progress; and with the lady's hand in his, sat helpless'. Worse still, he detects the sound of laughter begin-ning to rise behind the veil. Somerset has lost the initiative completely and can only sit in impotent discomfiture until the carriage draws up before 'a stately and severe mansion in a spacious square' (69).

This is not how either a detective or a man of the world should behave; and the extent of Somerset's mortification is heightened by the comparison that suggests itself between this carriage-ride and the notorious one taken by Léon and Mme Bovary some twenty years earlier. Nor is the *soi-disant* detective allowed to regain command of the situation. The lady, divesting herself 'of the lace in which she was enfolded', reveals (Somerset is *'relieved to find'*) white hair and a face 'lined with years' (69). More than that, *she* now asserts herself in the role Somerset had thought himself, as a man of the world, to be specially cut out for: ' I have a singular swiftness of decision, read my fellow men and women with a glance, and have acted throughout life on first impressions' (70). Having listened to Somerset's account of himself she concludes in a manner worthy of both Lady Bracknell and *The Thousand and One Nights*:

> You express yourself very well ... and are certainly a droll and curious young man. I should not care to affirm that you were sane, for I have never found anyone entirely so besides myself: but at least the nature of your madness entertains me, and I will reward you with some description of my character and life (70).[37]

The story which follows sustains both the comic invention and the same high key in its narration. At its end, Somerset, like Challoner, compliments the storyteller on her art, not on her veracity: '"Madam," said he, "your story is not only entertaining but instructive and you told it with infinite vivacity. I was very much affected towards the end ..."' (96). Mrs Luxmore's is far from an accurate description of her 'character and life' for she blatantly models truth in her own image. Rounding off her tale by giving Somerset tenancy of the mansion, she again discomfits the would-be detective. Instead of solving mysteries he seems to generate a series of bizarre and inexplicable events. Now he finds himself suddenly possessed of an exceptionally substantial house at the whim of a lady of boldly eccentric tendencies; and nothing really makes sense:

> Foursquare it stood, of an imposing frontage, and flanked on either side by family hatchments. His eye ... reposed on every feature of reality, and yet his own possession seemed as flimsy as a dream (99).

Mrs Luxmore, on the other hand, is perfectly self-possessed and is indeed every bit as radical a free spirit as her daughter who, like herself, had run away from home. ('Some whim about oppressed

nationalities – Ireland, Poland, and the like – has turned her brain'
[81].) Each is more than a match for the aspiring detective since neither
subscribes to the rules which govern the detective's world. They are
both untruthful, both equally likely to act on caprice rather than reason.
When Somerset, obeying his own rules, protests that she knows
nothing of the character of her new tenant, Mrs Luxmore brushes his
objections aside:

> 'It is in vain to reason. Such is the force of my character that, when
> I have one idea clearly in my head, I do not care two straws for
> any side considerations. It amuses me to do it, let that suffice. On
> your side, you may do what you please … , on my part, I promise
> you a full month's warning before I return, and I never fail reli-
> giously to keep my promises' (97).

Predictably, she turns up to reclaim her house (and, as she puts it,
to restore him to liberty) with no warning at all and is outraged at
the mess confronting her. In particular she takes violent objection to
Somerset's still-life arrangement – he has taken up painting with disastrous results – of, *inter alia*, 'a cabbage … relieved against a copper
kettle, and both contrasted with the mail of a boiled lobster' (107):

> 'My gracious goodness!' cried the lady of the house; and then,
> turning in wrath on the young man, 'From what rank in life are
> you sprung?' she demanded. 'You have the exterior of a gentleman;
> but from the astonishing evidences before me, I should say you
> can only be a green-grocer's man. Pray, gather up your vegetables,
> and let me see no more of you' (108).

She relents, of course, and departs (as she vaguely phrases it) 'for
the continent of Europe' (109). Mrs Luxmore is, in fact, a true restless denizen of the modern city. Though possessed of eight mansions,
she has a preference for lodging in hotels ('the life that I have always
preferred' [82]). Alternatively, she travels – and for an interesting
reason:

> I am a woman of the nomadic sort, and when I have no case before
> the courts, I make it a habit to visit the continental spas: not that
> I have ever been ill, but then I am no longer young and I am
> always happy in a crowd (97).

Frivolous and sketchy as this is, cumulatively it strengthens Barry
Menikoff's view that the urban settings of Stevenson's *Arabian Nights*

are 'a deft portrait of the modern city, the city we have come to associate with the late fiction of Henry James, the early poetry of T. S.
Eliot, and the short stories of James Joyce'. He quotes Lieutenant
Brackenbury Rich's thoughts on the subject and Colonel Geraldine's
more sombre reflections: '"They talk of war," he thought, "but this
is the great battlefield of mankind."'

What comes to Somerset with the property – Zero the nihilist and
his entourage of incompetent bombers – is, of course, also a modern
urban phenomenon. And they, too, are burlesqued – at times hilar-
iously so, as in 'Zero's Tale of the Explosive Bomb' which describes
McGuire's attempt to strike at the heart of English cultural imperi-
alism by blowing up the statue of William Shakespeare in Leicester
Square. (The Arabian author is allowed a voice at this point to tell
us that the inept dynamiter, anticipating an equally inept Inspector
Clouseau, has difficulty with the word 'bomb' which he pronounces
'boom'.)

Each of the adventures encountered by the three ineffectual detectives is linked to the nihilists (whose *provenance* is clear from their
occasional rhapsodic allusion to 'our green Erin') by Clara Luxmore
– another case of the 'blind Madonna of the Pagans' engaging herself
enthusiastically on the adventurers' behalf. The impossible symmetry
of these events is a further travestying of the mystery-tale, its villains
and investigator-heroes. Along with these popular shibboleths,
Stevenson is, of course, by his method, poking fun at, and further
subverting, the whole realist tradition which assumes shared social
values and a general willingness to rally in their defence.

It is a literary phenomenon of some interest that just as realism in
the novel appears to be losing its dominant role, the newly-emerging
detective story breathes new life into it, albeit 'life' of a somewhat
exiguous order. As Somerset's panegyric on the detective makes
very clear, the latter's function is to defend society and to 'deracinate occult and powerful evil', the definition of which is, of course,
dictated by 'society'. (Very properly W. H. Auden prefaces his essay
on detective fiction, 'The Guilty Vicarage' with an epigraph from
Romans VII, 7: 'I had not known sin, but by the law'. )[38] Rules have
been laid down; it is everyone's responsibility to regulate his or her
conduct by them. The detective-story also depends on traditionally-
sanctioned rules of evidence, rules of narrative, explanatory
dénouements and, for its characterisation, on 'the old stable *ego* of
the character' which D. H. Lawrence famously repudiated. It also
depends upon sustaining the illusion that what it deals with – its

milieu – is the real world, so that any questioning of the nature of the fictional process within the text (which does go on here) would be fatal to it.

All this Stevenson assails in his destructive burlesque: not for nothing does the title *The Dynamiter* always take title-page precedence over the generic title *More New Arabian Nights*. What is particularly remarkable is his great daring not just in choosing to deride canonical practice in the insouciant way he does (after all he was not the first, despite the frequency of the word 'original' in reviews), but even more so in applying his *Arabian Nights* treatment to a plot which, however insubstantial, would seem to clamour for realist treatment since it centres on the activities of the nihilists who are quite clearly lightly-disguised Fenians. These were the people who had perpetrated a number of bomb outrages in London during the so-called 'dynamite campaign' which lasted roughly from 1883 to 1887. (In the year of the publication of *The Dynamiter* bombs went off in the Tower of London, Westminster Hall and the House of Commons.) For a contemporary writer to deal with dynamiters with such levity was surely to risk provoking a hostile reaction from his public. Stevenson got away with it, however, and by a wide margin: published in April 1885, it was reprinted in May and July.

For all that, two pieces of evidence suggest that he was a little anxious lest he might be judged insensitive on such matters. The first is the unusually long dedication to two police officers who had distinguished themselves in dealing with a bombing attempt. In its uncharacteristically involuted prose, Stevenson seems to betray some uneasiness in having 'touched upon the ugly devil of crime' with such subversive jocularity. 'It were a waste of ink to do so in a serious spirit', he says without explaining why it should be so. This is followed by an admission that some criticism is due of 'ourselves, in that we have coquetted so long with political crime', but it is an admission which is more than a little disingenuous considering what he has just done in *The Dynamiter*.

The second piece of evidence is of a similar sort, and it, too, is located very prominently. In one of the few 'digressions' allowed him, the Arabian author is credited with encouraging the 'English people to remember with more gratitude the services of the police'. The 'translator' intervenes to cut short the encomium, however, on the grounds that the matter is 'too serious for this place' (6). Nonetheless, Stevenson's awareness of the need to forestall criticism does not lead to any significant moderation in his basic fictional method. True,

Somerset repudiates his earlier 'maudlin toleration' of Zero's character and he denounces his activities – but not to the police. In fact, he ends up paying Zero's fare to get him to leave the country, not for Australia this time but America, using up the last of his money to do so.

Zero and his nefarious occupation are still the source of considerable comic effect and make a continuing contribution to the fiction's reflexive character. Greatly demoralised by the failure of his many devices to explode, he takes farewell of his labours in Golden Square in a welter of quotations, several of them from the despised Shakespeare. ('It is strange how, at this supreme crisis of my life, I should be haunted by quotations from works of an inexact and even fanciful description' [194].) Not even the belated success of one of the bombs he leaves behind – which completely destroys the superfluous mansion – alters Somerset's decree, to Zero's surprise. He is inclined to attribute this sudden access of moral rectitude on the 'detective's' part to a momentary aberration, but Somerset is adamant – 'three days of you have transformed me to an ancient Roman' (200) – and he insists on supervising the 'Irish patriot's' departure. That, of course, is pretermitted by the fatal explosion which secures Zero's apotheosis as a Dynamiter Triumphant.

However, though Somerset does 'find in his heart a sort of peaceful exultation, a great content, a sense, as it were of divine presence and the kindliness of fate' now that Zero has been 'expunged', it is not only the continuation of the ironic note in his discovery which heads off that seriousness so repugnant to the 'translator'. When he returns, penniless, to Mr Godall, the anti-realist *Arabian Nights* mode with its accent on style rather than 'truth', is at once fully rehabilitated and his adventure with the nihilists becomes one more tale-within-a-tale in the continuous process which commenced with 'The Destroying Angel' and never concludes. '"Sit down, if you please," says Mr Godall, "suffer me to choose you a cigar of my own special brand, and reward me with a narrative in your best style."' (201) Experience *has* had its effect, however, and Somerset refuses a cigar and, in response to Godall's question 'I hope there is nothing wrong?', bursts into tears. Whether they are tears for his lost scepticism, the lost Miss Luxmore or his destitute state, we never learn. We do know that he, the 'total disbeliever not only in revealed religion, but in the data, method and conclusion of the whole of ethics' (137), ends up serving the 'one Godall' and acquiring a motto: *De Godall je suis le fervent'*; so perhaps Zero *had* robbed him of his youth after all, as he had feared when he began to suspect that his association with the dynamiter was leading him to moral seriousness and a belief in right and wrong.

*The Dynamiter* concludes with the 'Epilogue of the Cigar Divan', but as the venue might seem to hint we are more likely to be on the brink of more stories than we are of a clarifying postscript. It is true that Somerset, preoccupied with the composition of his appalling verse, espouses an aesthetic which helps to tug the magic carpet from under what has gone before, but Clara Luxmore, alias Miss Fonblanque, alias the Fair Cuban and now Mrs Desborough, is distinctly promising. When the Prince and Mrs Luxmore eavesdrop on her and the others in the Divan, it is to hear her say 'At that moment ... Mr Gladstone detected the features of his cowardly assailant. A cry rose to his lips: a cry of mingled triumph ... ' (210). And there her tale breaks off, interrupted by her mother demanding in Bracknellian tones (having just recognised one of the others), 'Mr Somerset, what have you done with my house-property?' Everyone adjourns to a 'collation' and, in the best *Arabian Nights* tradition, to hear an explanation. It is likely to be a lengthy one for, as Harry Desborough admiringly tells his friends (who need no reminding), 'She tells wonderful stories, too; better than a book.'

### The Incurable and Chimerical Hoax :
### *The Dynamiter* and *The Secret Agent*

Nine years after the publication of *The Dynamiter*, anarchists exploded a bomb in Greenwich Park. *The Times* headline for 16 February 1894 was restrained: 'Explosion in Greenwich Park'; that of *The Morning Leader* was sensational: 'Blown to Pieces!' This was followed by a sub-heading 'Victim an Anarchist(?)' and a melodramatic, self-parodying sentence: 'Was he a member of a gang who had fell designs on London's Safety?'

In fact, unlike Zero of whom 'no adequate remains were to be found', the bomber, Martial Bourdin, died later in hospital of his appalling injuries. Almost certainly he had been 'set-up' by his brother-in-law Samuels, a double agent, and the most likely explanation of his death was that the explosive mixture was every bit as unreliable as one of Zero's infernal machines (which was, incidentally, how *The Times* described Bourdin's explosive device).[39]

The attempt to blow up Greenwich Observatory – for so it was construed – was to become a central event in Conrad's *The Secret Agent*, and in early statements about his novel he freely acknowledged the link between the historical event and his plot. Some 17 years later when he was sent a contemporary pamphlet on the subject, he denied all knowledge of the 'Greenwich Bomb Outrages' except as a 'mere fact', claiming that he was abroad when it happened. He did, however, write to the donor to say how interested he had been 'to see how near actuality [he had] managed to come in a work of the imagination'.[40] Norman Sherry has clearly established that Conrad was *not* abroad but living in London at the time, and that the pamphlet was, in all probability, one of his source-books for the novel. From this, Sherry makes the reasonable assumption that his denial arose from a desire to conceal the extent of his indebtedness to the pamphlet.

This not uncharacteristic – though altogether unnecessary – attempt to conceal his borrowings shows a sensitivity in such matters which contrasts sharply with Stevenson's practice. Not only did the latter openly and unflatteringly declare himself to have played the sedulous ape – a coinage which did him no good at all – but he delighted in exposing a quite dense intertextuality in his work in pursuit of objectives which, we can now see, fit well with an aesthetic of Modernism already mutating towards Postmodernism.

Conrad's borrowings, I believe, went beyond newspaper articles, however, and may well have extended to include *The Dynamiter*. In fact, it is possible that Conrad was as disingenuous about his debt to Stevenson as he was in his response to the writer of the pamphlet. Discounting the possible migration of surnames such as Ransome from *Kidnapped* to *The Shadow-Line*, O'Brien from *Treasure Island* and Sebright from *The Wrecker* both to *Romance*, Jones from *The Dynamiter* to *Victory*, Singleton from *The Wrecker* to *The Nigger of the Narcissus* – discounting these coincidences it is quite clear from a reading of *The Ebb-Tide*, if of no other Stevenson text, that Conrad *was* to some degree influenced by Stevenson, yet his references to him are habitually slighting and dismissive. According to Richard Curle, he 'always spoke disparagingly and ... with aversion of Stevenson', calling him, among other things, a 'Virtuoso Cymbalist'.[41] The matter is worth pursuing primarily because to do so is to become clearer about Stevenson's place in the literary history of the nineteenth century: it is to recognise that a number of qualities which are thought of as representative of the Modernist character of Conrad's writing are to be found (partly where he, perhaps, found some of them) in Stevenson's work. At the same time it should be made clear that this is not intended to assert a parity of achievement for these writers.

With the foregoing discussion of *New Arabian Nights* and *The Dynamiter* in mind, it is worth reflecting on the fact that the central device sustaining Conrad's narrative in *The Secret Agent* – irony – is actually quite close kin to the virtuoso mix of light-hearted parody, irony and burlesque which sustains these *Arabian Nights* narratives. For all their appearance of being diametrically different, one only has to twitch the kaleidoscope slightly for the sparkle and apparent inconsequence of Stevenson's *Arabian Nights* to give way to the more sombre patterning of Conrad's world seen *sub specie ironiae*. Had *The Dynamiter* come after *The Secret Agent*, it would have been immediately recognised as a parody of it. The point deserves some emphasis since it helps to make clear that, in the discussion which follows of certain similarities between Stevenson and Conrad, the 'voice' of the latter is *not* being specially privileged. Most of Stevenson's texts are, to use Bakhtin's term, polyphonic, thus the Conradian is simply one among several 'voices' or, to speak more figuratively, one more hue to manifest itself in Stevenson's iridescent discourse. In order to provide evidence of the suggested connection, it is necessary to say something about the nature of the irony being practised.

D. C. Muecke, in the shorter account of irony derived from his admirable *The Compass of Irony*, suggests that *eironeia* as first used in Plato's *Republic* meant something like 'a smooth, low-down way of taking people in'.[42] Some of Stevenson's early readers might well have found that definition appropriate but it might be safer simply to say that dissimulation, or at least sleight of hand, is an essential component of irony. Allan Rodway could be cited in support: 'The sense of dissembling that is meant ... to be seen through must remain fundamental if the word [*eironeia*] is to have any consistent function' – which, as Muecke says, is acceptable so long as it is understood that the irony might not be seen through by the victim but only by the audience, and sometimes 'the sole audience is the ironist himself'.[43] What is clear is that in both Conrad and Stevenson the ironical element is of a distinctly late-nineteenth-century kind, going well beyond that rather limited sort of wit which led Mrs Slipslop to object to her passion being 'resulted and treated with ironing'.

In their use of irony both reflect important developments in late-nineteenth-century literary practice, but, as far as these categories can be separated, one does so *principally* in the field of aesthetics, the other ethics – or, to be 'pedantically exact,' as Mr Enfield would say, ethics *and* aesthetics. Stevenson fully exploits the potential in parody – with all its ironic shifts – for it to become a dialectical instrument in the aesthetic debate; in this case to pour scorn on the realist tradition and its defence of the integrity of artistic illusion. What Stevenson is doing is really to display his skill in writing parodistic metafiction, demonstrating the truth of Margaret Rose's dictum that 'some parody provides a 'mirror' to fiction, in the ironic form of the imitation of art in art'.[44] Parody is, however, hostile to other, more conventional forms of mimesis. In pointing out 'the role of modern parody in undermining the belief in art as imitation', Rose recruits the assistance of Terry Eagleton. Writing of Pierre Macherey's contribution to the debate on mimesis, Eagleton describes his position thus:

> For Macherey, the effect of literature is essentially to deform rather than to imitate. If the image corresponds wholly to the reality (as in a mirror), it becomes identical to it and ceases to be an image at all. The baroque style of art, which assumes that the more one distances oneself from the object the more one imitates it, is for Macherey a model of all artistic activity; literature is essentially *parodic*.[45]

It could be argued that there is nothing desperately new in Stevenson's parodistic metafictions in the way he presents art's awareness of itself as art: 'If this were played upon a stage now I could condemn it as an improbable fiction' says Fabian in *Twelfth Night*; and a host of other examples were available to Stevenson from Meredith, Thackeray and Sterne to Cervantes and beyond. He, however, is reviving it programmatically, so to speak, at a time when what had come to be seen as 'traditional' practices were fragmenting under all sorts of pressures for change, and new theories of fiction were coalescing to produce a body of work that would have sufficient common features to claim for itself an 'ism': Modernism. Chief among these features would be irony and – particularly with James Joyce and Thomas Mann in mind – parody.

Conrad's *The Secret Agent* (1907) is, of course, one of the great ironic masterpieces of the twentieth century. If we wanted to classify the book's dominant ironic mode it would fall into that category designated by Wayne Booth as 'the Discovery of the Abyss' where the author comes to recognise that the 'only final education' (as Booth puts it) is to be had in confronting emptiness, the abyss.[46] Conrad's irony is close kin to what Kierkegaard regards as essential irony or 'irony in the eminent sense' definable as such because it directs itself 'not against this or that particular existence but against the whole given actuality of a certain time and situation .... It is not this or that phenomenon but the totality of existence which it considers *sub specie ironiae.*'[47]

It might not seem that there is much connection between a cosmic irony of this sort which was first nature to Conrad, and Stevenson's parodistic arabesque. In fact, they have in common the fundamental processes of irony – principally as these are defined in the notion of *romantische Ironie* which Friedrich Schlegel (in particular), Adam Müller and Karl Solger began to formulate in the closing years of the eighteenth century.[48] As this ought to be seen to imply, in their instinctive and strong commitment to their individual versions of the ironic vision, both writers are definitive of central elements in Modernism.

I have spoken earlier of the discomfiture of some of Stevenson's reviewers, frustrated because they could not pin him down, were not sure where he stood or, worse still, where he had placed *them.* Were they up there sharing his ironic perspective from somewhere aloft or were they left behind, its hopelessly earth-bound victims? 'He juggles with his readers and with his characters', we may recall H. C. Bunner having said: 'He dresses up a puppet and tells you it is a man, and you believe it, and hold your breath when the sword is at the puppet's breast. Then he holds up the stripped manikin and smiles maliciously.'[49] He spends his inventive talents extravagantly in, say, the creation of Prince Florizel and his adventures, and then leaves W. H. Pollock and others like him deeply resentful when he capriciously 'pull[s] down the whole fabric of splendour and knightly valour which he had raised for our delight'.[50] In our own time, as we have seen, Professor Kiely has added his own plaintive note to the reproachful chorus.

What Stevenson is doing that these critics object to is simply availing himself of that detachment which is a principal characteristic of irony as a rhetorical method, a characteristic which, in Muecke's words, 'seems sometimes to reside in the ironist's pretended manner and sometimes in the real attitude of the ironist or the ironic observer'.[51] This detachment may manifest itself in a number of ways (Muecke lists, *inter alia,* distance, disengagement, freedom, serenity, 'play', and 'lightness') and in Stevenson it often does so in that celebrated lightness of touch which earned him a sharp rebuke from William Archer, the champion of moral realism, but praise from James, who in his *Partial Portraits* (1888), describes him as bringing to perfection in *The Dynamiter* a manner which is characterised by a 'kind of high-flown serenity in proportion as the incidents are more "steep". To just such a lightness of touch – which he explicitly links to the need for *Heiterkeit* (serenity) – Thomas Mann pays tribute in *Joseph and His Brothers*:

> Oh ... it is all too exciting and solemn for words! And just because it is so solemn it must be treated with a light touch. For lightness, my friend, flippancy, the artful jest, that is God's very best gift to man, the profoundest knowledge we have of that complex, questionable thing we call life. God gave it to humanity, that life's terribly serious face might be forced to wear a smile.[52]

What this serenity, lightness of touch or detachment really describes is a freedom on the part of the ironist to be everywhere and nowhere. In *New Arabian Nights* and *The Dynamiter* – and in many other places – Stevenson parades the presence of the artist to an extent even greater than parody necessitates (which illustrates the truth of Muecke's dictum that 'stylistically speaking irony is dandyism');[53] at the same time he ostentatiously fails to offer any commitment to character, idea or 'truth' which would give his creation a moral identity or any rationale other than the aesthetic. In comparing him with Dumas, the Lathburys had drawn attention to this: 'We can imagine Dumas losing himself in his characters and believing in his stories, while Mr Stevenson gives us the impression of being outside both. He is the stage-manager skilfully directing his actors, while he never ceases to regard them from the point of view of pure art.'[54]

In the Conrad of *The Secret Agent*, the same freedom (presented, however, as detachment or distance rather than lightness of touch) is what gives that remarkable text its immense authority, winning for it an apparent autonomy which seems to argue for a separate and superior reality from that of the world it depicts. It arrogates to itself a vantage-point so commanding that it even appears to give shape to anarchy. Obviously this is not the place for an extended discussion of the ironic vision and strategies of *The Secret Agent* or of the remarkable way our perspective is manipulated by them. As a sample of how Conrad utilises the freedom conferred on the ironist by his detachment one could, however, select his treatment of Winnie Verloc after the death of her husband. Despite the fact that she has murdered Verloc, all our sympathies engage themselves on Winnie's behalf. While these remain relatively intact, what the ironist manages to do at the same time from his Olympian distance is to extend our perspective in such a way that we are forced to observe the *degradation* of Winnie and the denigration of those human values which she embodies. The ironies clustering round her are of that savage sort which traditionally provide entertainment for the crueller gods. Heinrich Heine illustrates the point very well – and without recourse to lower-case pagan deities:

> Alas, the irony of God weighs heavily upon me. The great Author of the universe, the Aristophanes of heaven, wished to show me – the little, earthly, so-called German Aristophanes – as glaringly as possible what feeble little jests my most bitter sarcasms were in comparison with his own, and how inferior I was to Him in humour and in giant wit.[55]

Conveniently, this brings us to another link between the Stevenson of the *Arabian Nights* and the Conrad of *The Secret Agent*: for both writers, irony catches up and makes use of the absurd. Though it is fairly obvious that Conrad is a whole lot nearer to Camus than, say, to Edward Lear in the way he harnesses the notion of the absurd to his purpose, Stevenson's use of it is also forward- rather than backward-looking. However, both – ironically – could have found in Schlegel's concept of Romantic Irony encouragement to appropriate the absurd and apply it in their different ways and still be 'modern', for his theory allows for it to be exploited in a number of ways that anticipate its twentieth-century development. (Muecke sees that opportunity amply realised in Thomas Mann's novels which become a tribute to 'Schlegel's astonishing ability to see in Romanticism the seeds of Modernism'.)[56]

Writing of the distinction between satire and irony, Morton Gurewitch makes this apposite and felicitously-worded comment on the absurd:

> Perhaps the fundamental distinction between irony and satire, in the largest sense of each, is simply that irony deals with the absurd, whereas satire treats the ridiculous. The absurd may be taken to symbolize the incurable and chimerical hoax of things, while the ridiculous may be accepted as standing for life's corrigible deformities. This means that while the manners of men are the domain of the satirist, the morals of the universe are the preserve of the ironist.

Irony, unlike satire, does not work in the interests of stability. Irony entails hypersensitivity to a universe permanently out of joint and unfailingly grotesque. The ironist does not pretend to cure such a universe or to solve its mysteries. It is satire that solves. The images of vanity, for example, that litter the world's satire are always satisfactorily deflated in the end; but the vanity of vanities that informs the world's irony is beyond liquidation.[57]

While this distinction helps us to identify the particular quality of the irony which informs Conrad's work, Stevenson's treatment of his characters and his audience falls well within this definition of the absurd, for *New Arabian Nights* and its sequel can surely serve as an energetic expression of the incurable and chimerical hoax of things which is only superficially frivolous. With only a very little twist, they can also be seen to stand for life's *in*corrigible deformities as well.

A serious deployment of the absurd in ironic parody entails it being part of the demolition-process that is in hand. In Stevenson's case the intended victims are certain theories of fiction *and*, more daringly, the storyteller's readers. To play tricks with your readership like an 'Aristophanes of heaven' (or a magician) whereby you first win their confidence by carrying them aloft on a wonderfully-woven carpet and then desert them so that they find themselves abruptly back on an earth singularly bare of illusions, is really to say (and so it seemed to some) 'Lord, what fools these mortals be.' It is to perpetrate on them an unsettling joke in which they are cast as playthings in an unreliable and destabilised world. What it reveals is the true nature of that 'confidence-trick man plays upon himself' to reassure himself that a stable position in the world is possible. Muecke goes on from this remark to quote from Robert Musil: 'in fact the most important intellectual devices produced by mankind serve the preservation of a constant state of mind, and all the emotions, all the passions in the world are a mere nothing compared to the vast but utterly unconscious effort that mankind makes in order to maintain its exalted state of mind'.[58] Stevenson's aesthetic deliberately undermines that 'constant state of mind'. His ultimate objective is the one described by Linda Hutcheon in *Narcissistic Narrative*, that is, by making readers more self-conscious, to liberate them from the tyranny of habit and convention – from 'rank conformity' as Stevenson called it:

The unsettled reader is forced to scrutinize his concepts of art as well as his life values. Often he must revise his understanding of what he reads so frequently that he comes to question the very possibility of understanding. In doing so he might be freed from enslavement not only to the empirical, but also to his own set patterns of thought and imagination.[59]

The unstable, unpredictable nature of things will always be there, of course, visible, for example, in the potential in the absurd for the comic and the tragic to change places or even to overlap: as Muecke says, 'the history of irony is the history of both comic and tragic awareness'.[60] Thomas Mann in his preface to a German translation of *The Secret Agent*, writes that it is tragi-comedy which best represents the vision of modern art and thence the grotesque which is its most genuine style.

Hence that hybrid, black comedy, the deepest hues of which match with the divine sense of humour as we see in *The Secret Agent*; but the potential is there even in *New Arabian Nights* (which the Lathburys defined – 'strictly speaking' – as grotesque romances). The demented nonsense of 'The Young Man with the Cream Tarts', for example, is tragedy travestied as the 'Arabian Author' has observed: 'From the whole tone of the young man's statement, it was plain that he harboured very bitter and contemptuous thoughts about himself.... The farce of the cream tarts began to have very much the air of a tragedy in disguise' (7). The young man is at least half outside the histrionic mode set for him when he anticipates 'the last perfection' in this, 'the age of conveniences'. Now that we know 'that life is only a stage to play the fool upon for as long as the part amuses us', there is only 'one more convenience lacking to modern comfort: a decent, easy way to quit the stage' (9). Black comedy of a slightly more serious kind is there, too, in Zero's tale in *The Dynamiter*. It may be a hilarious farce about blowing up Shakespeare, but it is essential for the nihilist's plan that the bomb go off in a public place crowded with women and children. And this in a London where such bombings were a contemporary hazard.

The third element in the irony which is common to both Stevenson and Conrad in the books under discussion has already been briefly touched on: artistic self-consciousness. It is this element in Schlegel's Romantic Irony which most seems to me to justify Muecke's claim that '[t]o study Romantic Irony is to discover how modern Romanticism could be, or, if you like, how Romantic Modernism is'.[61] As I think has become obvious, this sort of artistic self-consciousness, where the creative mind turns in upon itself and examines its workings, is an identifying characteristic of Stevenson's writing and nowhere more so than in the *Arabian Nights* volumes. Add this to the Romantic awareness of the double nature of art – that it exists in the 'real' world as well as reflecting something *not* in the 'real' world but possibly being posed as an equally valid, or even superior, 'real' – and you get the opening Stevenson so fully exploits as an ironist. It is an opening whereby the self-conscious artist allows himself to revel in his power to bestride both worlds, a freedom which he exploits to enter his work at any moment of his choosing and, by pointing out that it *is* a work of fiction and not of the real world it purports to be, destroy – or at least expose – the artistic illusion at a stroke. The vantage-point this gives him allows him to deploy his irony with the freedom of a liberated Ariel so that it 'resembles a free flame which is the very spirit of agility and rises only towards the heavens'.[62]

Muecke sees Romantic Irony as 'the irony of the fully-conscious artist whose art is the ironical presentation of the ironic position of the fully-conscious artist'. In the impressive manner in which he ties irony and self-consciousness together, he goes a considerable way towards defining Conrad's *modus operandi* (though, regrettably, he never uses Conrad as an exemplar):

> The only possibility open for a real artist is to stand apart from his work and at the same time incorporate this awareness of his ironic position into the work itself and so create something which will, if a novel, not simply be a story but rather the telling of a story complete with the author and the narrating, the reader and the reading, the style and the choosing of the style, the fiction and its distance from fact, so that we shall regard it as being ambivalently both art and life.[63]

Conrad's world is built on this sort of awareness and mode of representation as we see not just in *The Secret Agent* but in all those works where, for example, his principal characters demonstrate their inability to find a language to describe their author's (Schlegelian) ironic vision because to find it would be to de-ironise it and discover order and harmony in the world. But the extract serves to describe Stevenson's *modus operandi* even better, given, in particular, his self-conscious preoccupation with 'process'. And if we are still worried, with William Archer, about his lightness of touch, we might comfort ourselves by recalling that Schlegel sometimes called his *romantische Ironie Witz* and sometimes *Arabeske*.[64]

## A Library of Possible Novels

I am anxious to make it clear that, in the foregoing argument, I am not seeking to represent *The Secret Agent* as *The Dynamiter* with a moral rinse through it to account for its darker hue. On the other hand, I do not find it difficult to envisage Conrad reflecting on *The Dynamiter's* unrealised potential and coming to the conclusion that all that was needed was for him to remove himself to the outermost point of the ironist's apogee where the comic could become the cosmic or be subsumed in cosmic irony. Stevenson might even be considered to have enticed him into doing so by allowing into *The Dynamiter* a tincture of moral concern prompted, perhaps, more by a wish not to offend his public politically as well as aesthetically than by any weakening of the aesthetic principles which inform and sustain his *Arabian Nights*.

This is not to imply that some of Conrad's comedy cannot still be surprisingly sub-lunary, however, and quite similar to Stevenson's, as we see if we listen to the Conradian narrator's animadversions on strayed houses or compare Vladimir's musings to Mr Verloc with Zero's tale. The latter opens with a description of Zero briefing his bomber: 'I dined with one of our most trusted agents, in a private chamber at St James's Hall' (121). It has been decided that the target will be the statue of Shakespeare in Leicester Square and Zero gives McGuire a 'little petard' complete with a new detonating device – which fills McGuire, well-knowing Zero's dismal record as an explosives expert, with great apprehension. Mr Verloc also has an appointment with *his* controller. Mr Vladimir talks to him, too, about a target for an attack and briefly considers 'art' as a possibility. 'Of course, there is art. A bomb in the National Gallery would make some noise. But it would not be serious enough. Art has never been their fetish.'[65] There is, however, science: 'Any imbecile that has got an income believes in that ... It is the sacrosanct fetish', says Vladimir with a contempt worthy of Somerset who tells *his* bomber: 'You are ignorant of everything but science, which I can never regard as being truly knowledge' (198). There is science, then, and in particular there is Greenwich Observatory, of which 'the whole civilized world has heard'. And Vladimir concludes his advice in a phrase that would not have been out of place in *The Dynamiter*: 'Go for the first meridian.'[66]

If one cared to, it would be easy, starting with Vladimir's command, to establish a strong case for Conrad's acute sense of comic absurdity being a principal source of nourishment for his irony. The interview just alluded to is full of it, witness Mr Verloc's demonstration of his vocal prowess upon the distant police-constable (who was at that moment 'watching idly the gorgeous perambulator of a wealthy baby being wheeled in state across the Square'). The sense of the comic is, however, made firmly subservient to his larger ironic purpose whereas in Stevenson it is quite frequently an end in itself. Yet, even then, perhaps not quite so frequently as we imagine, for it always tends to confirm the truth of one of Schlegel's insights into the nature of irony:

> There are ancient and modern poems which breathe, in their entirety, and in every detail, the divine breath of irony. In such poems there lives a real transcendental buffoonery. Their interior is permeated by the mood which surveys everything and rises infinitely above everything limited, even above the poet's own art, virtue and genius; and their exterior form by the histrionic style of an ordinary good Italian buffo.[67]

In fact, as I hope the earlier discussion has established, Stevenson's comedy has often a destructive intent, becoming the vehicle for challenging conventional assumptions about literary representation, and individual complacency about one's status in the order of things. In *The Dynamiter*, the iridescence of the comedy is enriched by the faint presence of a colour from the Conradian end of the spectrum: issues of moral being and moral consciousness are drawn into play and, however ironic the touch, they are there to the end.

It is all done very engagingly and with great sophistication, of course. Yet even while striking a Wildean pose which in a Conrad character would spell irretrievable degeneracy, Somerset can rouse in the mind of the reader versed in the later writer's work echoes which will suggest an affinity between the two authors. Thus the embryo detective sees himself as bogged down in futility and in need of that moral discipline and fidelity to a few simple ideas which Marlow is always talking about:

> here I stand, all London roaring by at the street's end, as impotent as any baby. I have a prodigious contempt for my maternal uncle; but without him, it is idle to deny it, I should simply resolve into my elements like an unstable mixture. I begin to perceive that it is necessary to know some one thing to the bottom – were it only literature (4–5).

These apparently frivolous sentiments have, in fact, a good deal in common with those which, in Conrad's characters, help to constitute an antidote to that hard-to-define, vaguely threatening moral surplusage (what Kristeva calls the 'abject') which undermines the possibility of stable identity.[68]

In fact, for all the stylistic arabesques Stevenson succeeds in infusing into his matter a thin haze of moral concern so that, very unobtrusively, it envelops his trio of 'adventurers' (like Conrad he uses the word in its various forms a lot) as well as, ultimately, his villains. Here and there, in an environment that bears considerable comparison with the London of *The Secret Agent*, he places an event or a figure that suddenly gives substance to the more serious reading. A distinctly Conradian policeman, for example, steps out of the dedication and into the tale, making frequent appearance as a solid, 'real', and authoritative emblem of moral order:

> So they continued to thread the maze of streets in silence with the speed of a guilty flight, and both thrilling with incommunicable terrors. In time, however, and above all by their quick pace of walking, the pair began to rise to firmer spirits; the lady ceased to peer about the corners; and Challoner, emboldened by the resonant tread and distant figure of a constable, returned to the charge with more of spirit and directness (13).

Though the reference may recall the policeman patrolling Brett Street in *The Secret Agent*, the juxtaposition of this significant and suggestive image, with the subversively frivolous cliché does, in reverse, what Conrad achieves with the deployment of his darker irony. The latter not only leaves that author's moral statement central and secure, it is also an essential means of enhancing it; whereas in Stevenson the embryonic statement is resolved into the ironic form and almost loses itself in the exaggeration of that form's playfulness. The same interesting comparison can be made in the following pair of extracts. In the first, Mr Verloc is 'going westward through a town without shadows in an atmosphere of powdered old gold'.

> He surveyed through the park railings the evidences of the town's opulence and luxury with an approving eye. All these people had to be protected. Protection is the first necessity of opulence and luxury ... Mr Verloc would have rubbed his hands with satisfaction had he not been constitutionally averse from every superfluous exertion. His idleness was not hygienic, but it suited him very

well. He was in a manner devoted to it with a sort of inert fanaticism, or perhaps rather with a fanatical inertness....Mr Verloc, steady like a rock – a soft kind of rock – marched now along a street which could with every propriety be described as private. In its breadth, emptiness, and extent it had the majesty of inorganic nature, of matter that never dies. The only reminder of mortality was a doctor's brougham arrested in august solitude close to the kerbstone. The polished knockers of the doors gleamed as far as the eye could reach, the clean windows shone with a dark opaque lustre. And all was still.... A guilty-looking cat issuing from under the stones ran for a while in front of Mr Verloc, then dived into another basement; and a thick police constable, looking a stranger to every emotion, as if he, too, were part of inorganic nature, surging apparently out of a lamp-post, took not the slightest notice of Mr Verloc.[69]

This passage from *The Secret Agent* is a well-known one and is characteristically packed with morally-allusive detail. Even so there is a tantalising evocation of it in this virtuoso display of Stevenson's talent:

[Edward Challoner] was a young man of portly habit; no lover of the exercises of the body; bland, sedentary, patient of delay, a prop of omnibuses. In happier days he would have chartered a cab; but these luxuries were now denied him; and with what courage he could muster he addressed himself to walk.

It was then the height of the season and the summer; the weather was serene and cloudless; and as he paced under the blinded houses and along the vacant streets, the chill of the dawn had fled, and some of the warmth and all the brightness of the July day already shone upon the city. He walked at first in a profound abstraction, bitterly reviewing and repenting his performances at whist; but as he advanced into the labyrinth of the south-west, his ear was gradually mastered by the silence. Street after street looked down upon his solitary figure, house after house echoed upon his passage with a ghostly jar, shop after shop displayed its shuttered front and its commercial legend; ...

Challoner takes the opportunity to marvel at the paradox of the city: 'Here, in broad day, the streets are secret as in the blackest night of January, and in the midst of some four million sleepers, solitary as the woods of Yucatan'.

He was still following these quaint and serious musings when he came into a street of more mingled ingredients than was common in the quarter. Here, on the one hand, framed in the walls and the green tops of trees, were several of those discreet, *bijou* residences on which propriety is apt to look askance. Here, too, were many of the brick-fronted barracks of the poor; ... Before one such house, that stood a little separate among walled gardens, a cat was playing with a straw, and Challoner paused a moment, looking on this sleek and solitary creature, who seemed an emblem of the neighbouring peace. With the cessation of the sound of his own steps the silence fell dead; the house stood smokeless; the blinds down, the whole machinery of life arrested; and it seemed to Challoner that he should hear the breathing of the sleepers.

As he so stood, he was startled by a dull and jarring detonation from within. This was followed by a monstrous hissing and simmering as from a kettle of the bigness of St Paul's; and at the same time from every chink of door and window spurted an ill-smelling vapour. The cat disappeared with a cry. Within the lodging-house feet pounded on the stairs; the door flew back emitting clouds of smoke; and two men and an elegantly dressed young lady tumbled forth into the street and fled without a word (9–10).

It is easy after reading this passage to agree with Edward Purcell, sometime editor of the *Westminster Gazette* and one of Stevenson's most perceptive early critics. Discussing its 'insolent prodigality of invention', he goes on to note that 'no modern English book contains such a profusion and superfluity of talent as this little *Dynamiter*'. He continues:

It is a masterpiece, upon which *Prince Otto* has not improved, and no novelist can read it without growing envy.... Mr Stevenson flushes a regular three volume covey of incident, pursues it for a while – for a chapter, a page, a few lines – and then gaily tosses it aside .... *The Dynamiter* contains a whole library of possible novels. Its charm lies in this wanton profusion of a spendthrift whose resources seem inexhaustible.[70]

'Wanton' is a good word in this context, for with our amusement comes some irritation at what Stevenson *seems* to be throwing away. Challoner's 'quaint and serious musings' are, potentially, at least as serious as quaint. There is enough in the passage quoted to convey

to us the atmosphere and expectation consonant with a moral statement of a vaguely Conradian kind, which we feel to be imminent in
the next line or paragraph. So much so that we meekly accept the
Wildean bathos of Challoner bitterly repenting his performance at –
whist! The growing conviction that a serious statement about, perhaps,
man's moral alienation, is immanent or imminent, is punctured by
a few words which I excised from the end of the second paragraph,
in the first part of the quotation, the last sentence of which reads '...
meanwhile he steered his course under day's effulgent dome and
through his encampment of diurnal sleepers, lonely as a ship'.
Nonetheless, into this baroque form a potential for serious moral statement has been absorbed like a dye, and as such, among all the other
rainbow colours, it remains.

The tantalising process goes on throughout the book. This apparently prosaic city is, actually, as the first line tells us 'the Baghdad of
the West', thus as mysterious and full of surprises as the more
conventional setting of the original *Arabian Nights*. The buildings,
streets and monuments seem to be possessed of as much animation
as they are in *The Secret Agent*, and they remain no less disconcertingly inscrutable. 'Street after street looked down upon [Challoner's]
solitary figure' we are told and we recall how the buildings had
stared down upon Comrade Ossipon: ' the towers of the Abbey saw
in their massive immobility the yellow bush of his hair passing
under the lamps. The lights of Victoria saw him, too, and Sloane
Square, and the railings of the park.' Sometimes a whole sentence
appears to come from Conrad – 'He looked east and west, but the
houses that looked down upon this interview remained inexorably
shut, and he saw himself, though in the full glare of the day's eye,
cut off from any human intervention.' (12) But the effect is again
deliberately undermined when we realise that the threat confronting
Challoner is nothing more than his bashfulness before the beautiful
young woman. Still, the sense of serious possibilities is kept teasingly alive in, for example, the silent, mourning appearance of the
streets (streets 'with the sense of city deserts') where the blinds are
down and 'the whole machinery of life arrested'. Conrad, of course,
found a more telling image in the doctor's brougham, 'arrested in
august solitude close to the kerbstone'. Both writers, however, occasionally use the *same* image to express the idea of mysterious life and
*apparent* – and fitful – solidity; for example, the cat and the constable,
and a 'garrulous' door-bell.

The Conradian analogue, and with it the possibilities of moral seriousness, are present again in the person of 'the redoubtable Zero' as 'Mr Jones' reveals himself to be.[71] Once more any prospect of seriousness is subverted by melodrama and farce. Mr Jones (Conrad would have appreciated the name and, indeed, uses it in *Victory*) or Zero reminds us a little of Mr Verloc but he has much more of the function of the professor in *The Secret Agent* and at times recalls him quite strongly – though the professor is a 'straight' version of Stevenson's burlesqued nihilist:

> Mine is an anonymous, infernal glory. By infamous means, I work towards my bright purpose .... I lead the existence of a hunted brute, work towards appalling ends and practise hell's dexterities (116).

Zero is an anarchist and he hails with evangelical fervour one of the inventions of the age as a messianic saviour: 'In this dark period of time, a star – the star of dynamite – has risen for the oppressed.' For all that, he is not particularly successful in his profession of a dynamiter, as Somerset politely calls it, beset as it is by so many unpredictable outcomes.

> I have toiled (let us say) for months, up early and down late; my bag is ready, my clock set; a daring agent has hurried with white face to deposit the instrument of ruin; we await the fall of England, the massacre of thousands, the yell of fear and execration; and lo! a snap like that of a child's pistol, an offensive smell, and the entire loss of so much time and plant! (118)

Comic as all this is (and much more is to follow) we might at the same time remind ourselves that there is, intentionally, a strong anti-heroic and even comic element in the behaviour of the anarchists of *The Secret Agent*; and the bathos of the explosion there – the blowing-up of a mentally-retarded youth instead of the first meridian and the citadel of Scientific Principle (otherwise Greenwich Observatory) – goes beyond irony and touches burlesque. Moreover, the professor also has to defend himself against a charge of incompetence, Ossipon provocatively suggesting that the death of their 'agent' at Greenwich might have been the result of the professor's variable success with detonators. The professor, too, can become almost as passionate as Zero on the subject of explosives: '"The detonator was connected with the screw top of the can. It was ingenious – a combination of time and shock. I explained the system to him. It was a thin tube of tin enclosing a –". Ossipon's attention had wandered'.[72]

Conrad's moral universe is, however, always easily identified, while the same could never be said about Stevenson's. This lack of a solid moral grounding for his narrative annoyed many of his contemporaries (just as it disqualifies him from being considered to be the same sort of ironist as Conrad). Returning to Edward Purcell, who was far from being either critically obtuse or insensitive to changes taking place around him, we find him complaining of a collection of essays (*Virginibus Puerisque*), published in 1881, that its 'bright thoughts and wise saws' are 'not bound together by any abiding principles of purpose and action firm enough to live by'. While the subjects of many of the essays are nothing if not serious, they are handled 'with playful dexterity and fantastic wantonness'. To many readers 'its confident maxims and playful audacity will seem to imply some background of solid opinion', but, in Purcell's view, they will be mistaken, for Stevenson, he claims, deals with even his serious subjects 'in no particular key'.[73]

Five years later the same critic reviewing *Prince Otto*, but having read what had been published in the interim (including *The Dynamiter*), is inclined to interpret these same signs more favourably. He now recognises that Stevenson will never have 'any new gospel of life to give us'. Nor will be ever be free of that ambivalence which had earlier disturbed him: 'There still ... remains that strange mixture of audacious candour and audacious reticence on the great issues of morality which attracted and distressed from the first.' And he goes on:

We have no right to demand his scheme of human life; but this is certain, that his puzzling enigmatic ethics, whether they be individual, or whether they are a true reflection of a present transitional state of society, are the real hindrance to his aim of producing a great romance worthy of his genius.

He then makes a telling comparison with Walter Scott:

Equal in imagination, the one is strengthened and disciplined to prolonged flights by his perfect assimilation of conventional principles; the other's course, rapid, erratic, and interrupted, displays far deeper insight, far keener perception, far bolder genius – a genius brilliant but seemingly troubled, because it ventures into a world ignored by Scott, where all is doubt and difficulty.[74]

## Bulls, Bicycles and 'the Play of Wit'

With the texts we have been discussing (primarily *The Dynamiter* and *The Secret Agent*) in mind, how truly can it be said that Stevenson and Conrad are brothers under the skin? And if they are, what does it signify? 'The work of pervasive modern irony', writes Malcolm Bradbury, 'has become more and more our kind of book, for very good reason. So has the serious melodrama, as a world that once seemed to belong to the exotic fringes of society seems much closer to its very centre.'[75] What Bradbury means by 'modern irony' is, I believe, very largely what Schlegel meant by Romantic Irony. For all their differences, these two books depend on just such an irony for both their form and substance. What drives the irony in each case is a sophisticated scepticism: scepticism about human nature, about the nature of reality and truth and about the conventional methods of their literary representation. They both share the awareness of Schlegel and the Romantic Ironists of the complex, paradoxical and contradictory nature of the world, but if this feeds their ironic vision it also shows them just how indispensable to their freedom as writers in the Modernist period is the ironic voice.

Though they utilise it in strikingly different ways, both writers take maximum advantage of that peculiar freedom which is the prerogative – or perhaps it is just the fate – of the ironist. Whether it manifests itself as distance, detachment, serenity or in some other form, the ironic mode separates these authors from their created world:

> From this [mimic] sphere [of his creating] ... he himself stands aloof. The eye with which he views his microcosm, and the creatures who move in it, will not be one of human friendship, nor of brotherly kindness, nor of parental love; it will be that with which he imagines that the invisible power who orders the destiny of man might regard the world and its doings.[76]

Thirlwall is writing here (in 1833) of the irony of Sophocles though the passage would also serve as a fair description of what Ford Madox Ford called (thinking particularly of Flaubert) the novel of Aloofness. It is in the importance to both our writers of aloofness, more precisely of the freedom inherent in the position of the ironist, that they are most alike. Distanced by their scepticism, they take up tenancy on a vantage-point well away from their 'mimic sphere', though in the case of Stevenson an artistic personality is allowed down from the mountain-top to play a sprightly game of pretended involvement with text and readers. Conrad is more austere: of the composition of *The Secret Agent*, he wrote in the Author's Note:

> Even the purely artistic purpose ... was formulated with deliber-
> ation and in the earnest belief that ironic treatment alone would
> enable me to say all I felt I would have to say in scorn as well as
> in pity.[77]

The last phrase betrays the moralist, of course; and it would be true to say that this points to a distinction between them: while Conrad's target is his reader's moral sensibility, Stevenson's is, *primarily*, his or her aesthetic. These are unsatisfactory and never exclusive cate-gories, but in both, moral and aesthetic, one might see that the object of attack is an undue deference to conventional attitudes and the superficial. The ironist's somewhat paraded aloofness from his created world – sometimes it seems simply 'the world' – signals to all who may be taken in by such attitudes and appearances that he is not. Parody rubs salt in the wound not only by accentuating art as game (instead of something which could encompass 'reality'), but also by stealing the very shape of surface appearances and exposing the arbitrariness of such shapes and their purely contingent relationship to so-called reality.

Irony, wrote Schlegel, very much in the modern manner, 'contains and inspires a sense of the unresolved conflict between the absolute and the contingent, between the impossibility and the necessity of full and complete communications'.[78] While it is a description which might be thought apt for *The Secret Agent*, when applied to Stevenson's *Arabian Nights* it would no doubt seem to some to illustrate what happens when a butterfly is made to walk the plank. Yet, as Conrad shows in *Lord Jim*, even *dead* butterflies can be quite sturdy creatures, and it only takes a few moments' reflection to see that both the form and the content of Stevenson's 'Arabeske' (so far as these are sepa-rable) subscribe to Schlegel's depiction of irony. In the form, it is there, for example, in the way he pays extravagant service to the Romance, appears to bow down before it (and Romance-lovers) and worship – then reveals that it is yet another masquerade, a clever convention merely, a beautiful cloak which conceals no valorising principle but simply emptiness. The critic who complained so tear-fully of Stevenson 'pulling down the whole fabric of splendour and knightly valour which he has raised for our delight ... turning the dazzling figure of a hero ... into the common type of foreign refugee '[79] bears eloquent testimony to the reader's investment in the convention and to his outrage when it is exposed as such.

As to that portion of content deemed separable from form in *The Dynamiter*, it could be argued that Somerset's adventure itself supports – albeit ironically – Schlegel's account of the conflict which helps to define irony. Somerset wants to defend both his notion of society, which includes a determination to deracinate 'occult and powerful evil', *and* his scepticism. This is not a happy position for a man who has just assumed – and with a great fanfare – the trade of detective. All comes to a predictably comic head when he instinctively saves the life of Zero, the unreconstructed idealist (otherwise the impenitent nihilist), who had all but fallen off the roof of the Superfluous Mansion. Zero sees the act as sealing 'a life and death' connection between them. Somerset, on the other hand, is horrified at the presumed complicity and, much to the sorrow of Zero ('I thought you were a good agnostic'), condemns him and all his works:

> 'Mr Jones,' said Somerset, 'it is in vain to argue. I boast myself a total disbeliever not only in revealed religion, but in the data, method, and conclusion of the whole of ethics. Well! what matters it? what signifies a form of words? I regard you as a reptile, whom I would rejoice, whom I long, to stamp under my heel. You would blow up others? Well then, understand: 'I want, with every circumstance of infamy and agony, to blow up you!' (137)

Mr Jones makes an appeal on the grounds of his friendship and is even more violently disowned, whereupon the nihilist, whose misanthropy is not proof against such shocks, bursts into tears. Such an outburst of emotion unsettles Somerset and doubt creeps in: 'Was he an agnostic? had he a right to act?' Moreover, if he handed Zero over to the police, would his honour not be compromised; but there again, as an agnostic and/or sceptic should honour matter?

> But honour! what was honour? A figment, which, in the hot pursuit of crime, he ought to dash aside. Ay, but crime? A figment, too, which his enfranchised intellect discarded. All day he wandered in the parks, a prey to whirling thoughts; all night, patrolled the city; and at the peep of day he sat down by the wayside in the neighbourhood of Peckham and bitterly wept. His gods had fallen. He who had chosen the broad, daylit, unencumbered paths of universal scepticism, found himself still the bondslave of honour. He who had accepted life from a point of view as lofty as the predatory eagle's, though with no design to prey; he who had clearly recog-

nised the common moral basis of war, of commercial competition, and of crime; he who was prepared to help the escaping murderer or to embrace the impenitent thief, found, to the overthrow of all his logic, that he objected to the use of dynamite. The dawn crept among the sleeping villas and over the smokeless fields of the city; and still the unfortunate sceptic sobbed over his fall from consistency (138).

Of its kind, this seems to me quite brilliant. Irony turned against itself gives a multi-dimensional rendering of this detective's predicament, and all is accomplished with a consistency of tone which itself argues the security of the ironist's vantage-point. Thus a parody of Psalm 137 can be incorporated and, far from imposing any stress, slips perfectly and meaningfully into its allocated place. Somerset *is* deracinated and 'lost', torn between the absolute and the contingent one might say; for though the substitution of inglorious, suburban Peckham for Babylon is amusing it still functions as a symbol of his alienation.

Though he still clings to his conviction that 'right and wrong are but figments and the shadow of a word', a pragmatic morality triumphs: 'for all that, there are certain things that I cannot do, and there are certain things that I will not stand' (138). When Challoner discovers him at the end, reconciled to minding the shop in Mr *Godall's* Cigar Divan (a significant activity for such a sceptic) he learns that he is 'going through a stage of socialism and poetry'. When asked about his fortunes as a detective, Somerset admits to having been an abysmal failure: 'There is more in that business, Challoner, than meets the eye', he says (thereby proving how unfitted he is for the profession). Then he adds 'there is more, in fact, in all businesses. You must believe in them or get up the belief that you believe' (203); a view which will later be echoed by Marlow in *Heart of Darkness* recommending the advantages of 'a deliberate belief'.

Stevenson and Conrad share the 'modern' view that art offers no moral solutions. Conrad's is perhaps the bleaker vision: '*The Secret Agent*', writes Malcolm Bradbury, 'is a paramount work of modern scepticism, which regards not just the instincts of anarchism but the aim of penetrating the meaning of life itself as a process leading either to madness or despair.'[80] Yet for all the ironic distance assumed in order to give him the freedom to promulgate his vision of a world without values, and to manipulate *our* perspective, Conrad is, in fact, much more involved than Stevenson is with *his* world. Humanity may, *sub specie ironiae*, be seen to be preying on itself like monsters of the deep, but what that portrayal has its source in is not contempt but a well-controlled moral rage. Though he can argue in a letter to Cunninghame Graham that an 'attitude of cold unconcern' is the only reasonable one to adopt when confronted by humanity's plight, such an attitude is wholly at odds with the inspiration which, in concert with an improbably commensurate artistry, makes of *The Secret Agent* one of the truly great literary achievements of the century.

If Stevenson's vision is less bleak it is so because he doesn't care as much. Confining ourselves to the evidence of the *Arabian Nights* volumes, Stevenson, it could be argued, is, in one respect, even more 'modern' than Conrad for his instinct is to ironise or, where that might seem to posit too firm a moral grounding, to burlesque *everything*. (If Somerset's 'moral crisis' survives this ironising, it does so by the slimmest of margins, having been all but knocked out by the comic burlesque.) His irony (unlike Conrad's) even deconstructs the text itself, though it would appear that the ironist himself lives to ironise another day in yet another form, emerging, with a change of identity, to tease and destabilise. Stevenson's subversive tactics are augmented by a provocative deployment of the ironist's personality (again something that is quite foreign to Conrad). Not for him the distant heights of a Conradian Olympus, which he has renounced, it would seem, in favour of the vaudeville stage and the prestidigitation of the magician. In truth, what Stevenson is doing here, in his own idiosyncratic way, is what Muecke (quoted on p. 125) says is the only possible thing for the real artist *to* do, namely, 'to stand apart from his work and at the same time incorporate this awareness of his ironic position into the work itself ...' Instead of veiling himself in remoteness, the ironist as artist-magician deliberately betrays himself at every turn as he betrays the expectations of his patrons. His style is flamboyantly self-advertising, his inventions have his extravagant imprint all over them, and there is the sort of relish in the execution of the victim which compares well with the gusto Lord Hermiston displays in pursuit of the same objective.

There can surely be no doubting the extent to which this attitude allies Stevenson with the Modernists. At its heart lies a quite different attitude to the notion of the authorial self from what has gone before. In the later nineteenth century what we find is a freeing of the artist from the magisterial, law-giving concept of the authorial self, monolithic and complacent in its inherited assumptions about its role as cultural commissar. Now the only self that matters for the 'modern' artist is the mercurial one expressed in his or her art. 'I *am* not but in my art', we may recall Stevenson saying, 'it is me; I am the body of it merely.' Josipovici sums up the change admirably:

Art, the making of an artefact, becomes the means whereby the artist frees himself from the shackles of the self without disintegrating into chaos. In this view the artist is no longer either thinker or prophet, looking inwards or upwards for the truth and then conveying it to a grateful multitude; rather, he is a gymnast, developing his potential with each new exercise successfully mastered. The analogy, like all such, is inadequate, but it will do. It suggests an image of human personality not as a stronghold but as a coiled spring.[81]

The description of artist as gymnast fits Stevenson quite remarkably well, something we can verify in the present instance by reflecting on the ironist-magician's cavalier attitude towards law. It is doubly useful to do so since it also shows that though he has come down from the mountain he has not, in fact, compromised his essential detachment: the ironist's eye, to quote Thirlwall again, is still not one of friendship or parental love. The crucial point is that, unlike Hermiston, this magician-artist upholds no commonly observed Law: to the contrary, the rules are his to make and break at will. Far from reassuring and stabilising his microcosm with *his* law, he infuses into it a *destabilising* arbitrariness. To do so is to make a mockery of the rules and the 'creatures' who are subject to them. Though it is tempting to take the matter further it cannot be done here without taking up a disproportionate amount of space. The questions left implicit are, however, of importance. For example, given this ironist's constant subversion of his own laws where, then, does Law – real, immutable Authority – reside? Anywhere? No firm point of origin is ever fully admitted. The ironist-magician, having exposed his trick, dons another disguise and moves on, deferring once again the manifestation of that 'final' authority, suggesting that the 'real' author is elsewhere, ironically engaged in pulling strings. And why should the series stop there? Further back still …. And is the unwillingness to concede a point of origin another example of Stevenson's difficulty with fathers and fatherhood? Is then his turning of law-giving into a game not making him a 'bad' (surrogate) father to the dependants he has created – his readers?

However we answer these questions, it is surely possible to argue that, in some ways, Stevenson shows signs of being more radically

Modernist than Conrad. Art is explicitly game but it is game which turns out to be without rules – *that* is its 'game'. The artist invites you to play, insists you follow his rules, then flagrantly and to his players' chagrin, reveals that the rules were a joke. 'Irony is a clear consciousness of an eternal agility', wrote Schlegel, and at times Stevenson seems to be the very embodiment of this aphorism.[82] He is forever the acrobat, but one who seems to have his very dwelling on the high wire; rarely coming down to *terra firma* for the very good reason that he is sceptical about just how firm it is. Stevenson revels in his artistry but he wants there to be no mystery about it: a master of illusion, he is also, and very deliberately, a master illusion-destroyer. 'What is important is not the finished product, but the process', says Gabriel Josipovici in 'Modernism and Romanticism', at that point talking about Picasso's sculpture of a bull's head made out of the seat and handlebars of a bicycle: 'Picasso wants us to be aware of the fact that what is in front of us is not a bull's head but a man-made object.' And he adds a sentence which seems to me to describe very well what Stevenson is up to: 'It is the play of wit which turns a universe we had taken for granted into a source of infinite possibilities.' But Picasso's bull signifies something else of great moment to the Modernist – something which helps to define Conrad and Stevenson as such – and that is the central importance to them of technique. What modern art claims to do, Josipovici argues, 'is to *recreate* within the willing listener or spectator the liberating experience of the artist himself as he makes the object'.[83] This focuses attention on *process*, something which Stevenson frequently does himself. In his celebrated response to Henry James's essay 'The Art of Fiction', for example, he makes this distinction: 'He spoke of the finished picture and its worth when done; I, of the brushes, the palette, and the northern light.'[84]

To some, of course, turning the universe into a source of infinite possibilities will be unwelcome for it will bring with it instability and anxiety; but to others it will be exhilarating and continuously creative (which is one reason why *The Thousand and One Nights* fits Stevenson's design so well). What Stevenson's design also accords very well with are those qualities of novelistic discourse which Bakhtin calls dialogic. Writing of the 'novelization of other genres', the latter describes the effect on these genres thus:

> they become dialogized, permeated with laughter, irony, humour, elements of self-parody and finally – this is the most important

thing – the novel inserts into these other genres an indeterminacy, a certain semantic open-endedness, a living contact with unfinished still-evolving contemporary reality....[85]

These are the elements which, to a considerable degree, constitute Stevenson's highly self-conscious aesthetic, infusing his texts with their polyphonic diversity, liberating them from the tyranny of 'the tradition', and providing Stevenson with the resources to, in Pound's phrase, 'make it new'.

## Notes

1. Quoted in Stanley Sultan, *Eliot, Joyce and Company* (Oxford, 1987), pp. 100, 101.
2. T. S. Eliot, *Introduction (1928), Ezra Pound. Selected Poems* (1959), p. 10.
3. Quoted in Sultan, ibid., p. 112.
4. Stevenson was well-acquainted with Payne's work. They were both admirers of Villon's poetry which Payne had translated (not always accurately in Stevenson's view); and in his preface to *Familiar Studies in Men and Books* Stevenson notes that Payne 'is now upon a longer venture, promising us at last that complete Arabian Nights to which we have all so long looked forward' (p. xxii).
5. The tales were serialised in the *London News* in 445 instalments between 1723 and 1726, and in 1785 the *Novelist Magazine* serialised the complete Galland translation (see *The* Arabian Nights *in English Literature: Studies in the Reception of* The Thousand and One Nights *into British Culture*, ed. Peter L. Caracciolo (1988), pp. 2–3.
6. Caracciolo (ed.), *The* Arabian Nights *in English Literature*, p. 11.
7. Ibid., pp. 11, 14.
8. Ibid., pp. 14-15.
9. Ibid., p. 2.
10. San Francisco *Daily Examiner* 24 June 1888. Quoted by Barry Menikoff, 'New Arabian Nights: Stevenson's Experiment in Fiction' in *Nineteenth Century Literature*, vol. 45, no. 3, 1990, p. 339.
11. Gabriel Josipovici, *The World and the Book* (1979), p. 196.
12. Robert Kiely, *Robert Louis Stevenson and the Fiction of Adventure* (Cambridge, Mass., 1964), p. 120.
13. Ibid., p. 114.
14. In an essay written in November 1885 and printed in Maixner, op. cit., pp. 160–9.
15. Maixner, op. cit., pp. 107, 108.
16. Quoted by Barry Menikoff, op. cit., p. 359.
17. Maixner, op. cit., p. 288.
18. H. C. Bunner in *Century Magazine*, printed in Maixner, p. 121.
19. Maixner, op. cit., p. 117.

20. David Harvey, *The Condition of Postmodernity: An Enquiry into the Origins of Cultural Change* (1989), p. 21. Harvey is at this point quoting from E. Lunn's *Marxism and Modernism*.
21. Maixner, op. cit., pp. 111, 110.
22. Ibid., p. 120.
23. Linda Hutcheon, *Narcissistic Narrative: The Metafictional Paradox* (1984), p. 39. My attention was drawn to Hutcheon's book by Wenche Ommundsen's interesting essay 'The Reader in Contemporary Metafiction' in *AUMLA*, No.74, November 1990, pp. 169–84.
24. Menikoff, op. cit., p. 343.
25. Maixner, p. 113.
26. Menikoff, op. cit., p. 347.
27. Edward Said, discussing certain textual conventions, describes one of these as being 'that unity, or integrity, of the text is maintained by a series of genealogical connections: author-text, beginning-middle-end, text-meaning, reader-interpretation and so on. Underneath all these is the imagery of succession, of paternity, of hierarchy' (p. 162).
28. Jessica R. Feldman, *Gender on the Divide: The Dandy in Modernist Literature* (Ithaca, 1993), pp. 13, 217. The quotations from this work which follow will be found on pp. 17, 5–6, 4, 270, 246, 28.
29. Op. cit., pp. 357, 358. William Hazlitt, when writing of Beckford's *Vathek: An Arabian Tale*, took strong exception to the 'diabolical levity of its contempt for mankind'. Stevenson was not guilty of contempt for mankind (condescension towards it maybe) but the levity in *New Arabian Nights* could well be seen as diabolical.
30. Richard Poirier, *The Performing Self* (Rutgers, 1992), pp. 27–8.
31. Robert Kiely, op. cit., p. 129.
32. 'The Metropolis and Modernism' in *Unreal City*, ed. Edward Timms and David Kelley (New York, 1985), p. 17.
33. Michael Holquist, 'Whodunnit and Other Questions' in *New Literary History*, 1971, vol. 3, no. 1, p. 141.
34. W. H. Auden, 'The Guilty Vicarage', in *The Dyer's Hand* (1963), p. 147.
35. Ibid., p. 147.
36. Letter to David Masson, quoted in Ioan Williams, *Thackeray* (1968), p. 68. What Stevenson could well have taken from Thackeray were some of his metafictional devices such as his mischievously intrusive, exhibitionist narrator and the idea of the narrator (or author) as a puppet-master.
37. If Lady Bracknell owes something to Mrs Luxmore, both may have common ancestors among some of Meredith's characters.

    Here is the Countess de Saldar cultivating her own high key: "You have your father's frown. You surpass him, for your delivery is more correct, and equally fluent. And if a woman is momentarily melted by softness in a man, she is forever subdued by boldness and bravery of mien". *Evan Harrington* (1889), p. 100.
38. Op. cit., p. 146.
39. See Norman Sherry's account in 'The Greenwich Bomb Outrage and *The Secret Agent*' in *Conrad: The Secret Agent* (1973), ed. Ian Watt.
40. Ibid., p. 203.
41. David Thorburn, *Conrad's Romanticism* (Yale, 1974), p. 176.

42. D. C. Muecke, *Irony* (1973), p. 14.
43. Op. cit., p.28
44. Margaret A. Rose, *Parody//Metafiction* (1979), p. 65.
45. Terry Eagleton, *Marxism and Literary Criticism* (1976), p. 51. Quoted by Rose, op. cit., p. 102.
46. Wayne Booth, *The Rhetoric of Irony* (Chicago, 1974), p. 210.
47. Søren Kierkegaard, *The Concept of Irony, with Constant Reference to Socrates* (1966), p. 271, quoted by D. C. Muecke, *The Compass of Irony* (1969), p. 120.
48. For an indispensable discussion of the nature of Romantic Irony, and its significance for the development of Modernism, see Chapter VII of Muecke's *The Compass of Irony*.
49. Maixner, op. cit., p. 21.
50. Ibid., p. 111.
51. *Irony*, p. 35.
52. Quoted in *Irony*, pp. 35–6.
53. *Irony*, p. 45.
54. Maixner, op. cit., p. 117.
55. Quoted in *Irony*, p. 39.
56. *The Compass of Irony*, p. 186.
57. Moreton Gurewitch, *European Romantic Irony* (Ann Arbor, 1962). Quoted in *The Compass of Irony*, p. 27.
58. *The Man Without Qualities*, quoted by Muecke, *Irony*, p. 71.
59. Linda Hutcheon, op. cit., p. 139.
60. *Irony*, p. 80.
61. *The Compass of Irony*, p. 182.
62. Jean Paul Richter, *Vorschule der Ästhetik*. Quoted by Muecke, *The Compass of Irony*, pp. 218–19.
63. *Irony*, p. 20.
64. Quoted in *The Compass of Irony*, p. 182.
65. *The Secret Agent*, The World's Classics (1983), p. 32.
66. Ibid., pp. 33, 35, 37.
67. Friedrich Schlegel, *Dialogue on Poetry and Literary Aphorisms*, trans. Behler and Struc (1968), p. 126.
68. The abject is, in the words of Elizabeth Grosz's study, *Sexual Subversions* (1989), p. 72, 'the underside of a stable subjective identity, an abyss at the borders of the subject's existence, a hole into which the subject may fall when its identity is put into question'.
69. *The Secret Agent*, pp. 12–15.
70. Maixner, op. cit., p. 196.
71. Stevenson's 'secret agent's' sign is O, Conrad's Mr Verloc's is Δ, or delta.
72. *The Secret Agent*, p. 76.
73. Maixner, op. cit., pp. 90, 91.
74. Maixner, op. cit., p.195.
75. Malcolm Bradbury, *The Modern World: Ten Great Writers* (1989), p. 99.
76. Connop Thirlwall, 'On the Irony of Sophocles'. Quoted by Muecke, *Irony*, p. 22.
77. 'Author's Note' to *The Secret Agent*, p. xxxvii.
78. Muecke, *The Compass of Irony*, p. 195.

79. Maixner, op. cit., p. 111.
80. Bradbury, op. cit., p. 96.
81. Gabriel Josipovici, *The Lessons of Modernism* (1987), p. x.
82. Friedrich Schlegel, op. cit., p. 155.
83. In *The World and the Book*, p. 193.
84. 'A Humble Remonstrance', in *Henry James and Robert Louis Stevenson* (1948), ed. Janet Adam Smith, p. 99.
85. M. M. Bakhtin, op. cit., p. 7.

# 4
# *Prince Otto*: To Write and Obliterate

All art, therefore, appeals primarily to the senses, and the artistic aim when expressing itself in written words must also make its appeal through the senses, if its high desire is to reach the secret spring of responsive emotions. It must strenuously aspire to the plasticity of sculpture, to the colour of painting, and to the magic suggestiveness of music – which is the art of arts. And it is only through complete, unswerving devotion to the perfect blending of form and substance; it is only through an unremitting never-discouraged care for the shape and ring of sentences that an approach can be made to plasticity, to colour, and that the light of magic suggestiveness may be brought to play for an evanescent instant over the commonplace surface of words: of the old, old words, worn thin, defaced by ages of careless usage.

Joseph Conrad

What *is Prince Otto*? Stevenson was himself unsure: 'the whole thing is not a romance, nor yet a comedy; nor yet a romantic comedy; but a kind of preparation of some of the elements of all three in a glass jar'.[1] He knows that its contrived and extravagant style is likely to be a problem for the public, perhaps even reminding it of the literary excesses of *New Arabian Nights*: 'It is all pitched pretty high and stilted; almost like the Arabs, at that.'[2] He insists, however, that this tale is 'not like these purposeless fables of today, but is, at least, intended to stand firm upon a base of philosophy – or morals – as you please'.[3] Whether he has achieved his aim or not 'only the brutal and licentious public, snouting in Mudie's wash trough, can return a dubious answer'.[4]

By and large the brutal and licentious public *didn't* like it and it is easy to see why. Histrionic and over-wrought, it was, wrote Edmund Gosse (a friend and admirer of Stevenson) 'a wilful and monstrous

145

sacrifice on the altar of George Meredith'. He has, of course a particular section – the flight of the princess – in mind:

> In this passage you inflate your chest and toss back your hair, and
> are, in fact, devilish brilliant and all that, by Gad. The reader that
> has followed you all entranced, and who has forgotten you entirely,
> in the excitement of the narrative, becomes conscious of you again,
> and is amazed to find you so offensively clever and original. And
> then back you go to the beautiful old simplicity that makes you so
> easily the master of us all.[5]

Gosse is justified in his complaint and Stevenson himself came to
believe that because of an 'unsteadiness of key' a dissonance had
grown up between the realism of some chapters and the idealism or
abstractness of others.[6] Sustaining the chosen key, he had long realised,
was both the problem and the secret of the success of writing such
as his. In 'the Arabs' he achieves this success brilliantly; not in *Prince
Otto*. 'Any story can be made *true* in its own key; any story can be
made *false* by the choice of a wrong key of detail or of style: *Otto* is
made to reel like a drunken – I was going to say man but let us
substitute cipher – by the variations of the key.'[7] Yet the book is very
far from being a failure, even though its achievement is of an unusual
sort, albeit anticipated in some respects by *New Arabian Nights*.

Stevenson devoted an enormous amount of time and care to *Prince
Otto*, rewriting it again and again: 'God help me, I bury a lot of
labour in that principality'; 'Prince Otto ... far my most difficult adventure up to now ... has long been gestated, and is wrought with care';
'For me, it is my chief o' works ... I strung myself hard to carry it
out'; 'My romance, which has so near butchered me'.[8] In the end he
was (initially at least) well pleased with the result and furious with
the reviewers who criticised it adversely.

There is no doubt that the treatment meted out by these reviews
was unfair, just as there is little doubt that Stevenson asked for it.
The book is, as his countrymen would say, neither fish, flesh nor
good red herring; but that could be said of very nearly all of his
longer fictional work and it reflects his extreme unwillingness to
subscribe to any one genre or any one style. To do so, in his view, is
to petrify and so to falsify; it is to subject the writer of the work to
unnatural constraints which constitute true artificiality. One could
argue strongly that the book is only a failure if its search for a style
is perceived as methodological confusion rather than an aesthetic
statement. Stevenson *wanted* the narrative and representational form

of *Prince Otto* to be multi-faceted: he was not interested in discovering *a* way of seeing but in exploring *ways* of seeing – often superimposing these ways one on top of the other in a single work. He is one of the relatively few writers of the period (in Britain at least) who, in his theoretical positions, implicitly subscribes to Gertrude Stein's declaration that 'nothing changes in people from one generation to another except the way of seeing and being seen'.[9] Invoking Stein's name here is apposite for in reading Stevenson one is continually tempted to draw parallels between the line of his restless experimentalism and developments in literature and painting taking place in France.

In *Prince Otto* he sought to combine elements of pastoral myth, philosophical romance and fairy-tale with elements of moral and even political realism at the same time as he questioned sceptically the value and viability of their embodying aesthetic forms. It is this last property which enables him to escape the self-indulgence of many *fin-de-siècle* artists and to transcend the limitations which such a classification normally signifies, leaving the way open for further developments. *Prince Otto*, turning appreciatively on its own axis, self-consciously appraises itself as a work of art, its multifarious style not a device but the object. The end is pessimistic, for the work is made to collapse in a number of different texts, themselves of strikingly different genres: poetry, diaries and memoirs, all treated with an irony bordering on derision. These heterogeneous fragments in the 'Bibliographical Postscript' (sub-titled 'To Complete The Story') represent the disintegration of *Prince Otto's* text or, rather, texts, so that, when Otto decamps for his father-in-law's court, there to become a name on a title-page of a volume of bad verse, a good deal more is involved than the end of a dynasty.

## The Romance of Space

In *New Arabian Nights* and *More New Arabian Nights* (alias *The Dynamiter*) we have seen how normal narrative sequence was airily set aside by Stevenson. Tales are interrupted by other tales, action stops in one place and starts in another, events apparently crucial to the narrative turn out to be fiction within a fiction. Discontinuity reigns, if that is not a contradiction in terms.

The *Arabian Nights* tales were still in Stevenson's mind when he wrote *Prince Otto*, which is not surprising since the latter appeared in 1885, the same year as *More New Arabian Nights* and 'had been long gestated'. Despite Chapter II being headed 'In which the Prince plays Haroun-al-Raschid', the structure of this 'not a romance' does not emulate that of the *Arabian Nights*, though the comparison of the Prince with the exotic Arabian does serve to emphasise the anti-realist nature of the work.

If discontinuity is not made part of the narrative technique in *Prince Otto* in the manner of *New Arabian Nights*, there is another sense in which it can be seen to be formally present, that is, in the quite remarkable 'spatialisation' of the book. To avoid misunderstanding it is necessary to say something about this term which, in the aftermath of Joseph Frank's influential essay 'Spatial Form in Modern Literature', has come to be seen as helping to characterise Modernist writing.

Edwin Muir was perhaps the first critic of the novel to talk about spatial construction, drawing what seems to be a rather suspect distinction between the dramatic and the character novel to do so:

> the imaginative world of the dramatic novel is in Time, the imaginative world of the character novel in Space. In the one, this roughly is the argument, Space is more or less given, and the action is built up in Time; in the other Time is assumed, and the action is a static pattern, continuously redistributed and reshuffled, in Space. It is the fixity and the circumference of the character plot that gives the parts their proportion and meaning; in the dramatic novel it is the progression and resolution of the action.[10]

Muir has a good deal more to say on the subject, particularly in regard to the 'almost mythical permanence' which the figures in spatial fiction display, and the 'spatial vitality' of novels of this sort which conveys 'a feeling of intensely-filled space as extraordinary in its way as the feeling of crowded time in the dramatic novel'.[11]

Joseph Frank carries the notion of spatial form on to a more sophisticated and complex level, approaching his subject through a discussion of Wilhelm Worringer's solution to the problem of why, throughout the history of the plastic arts, there has been a continual alternation between naturalistic and non-naturalistic styles. Worringer's conclusion was a very nineteenth-century one couched in terms that make the twentieth century nervous: that periods of naturalism always coincide with a time when an equilibrium has been reached between man and the cosmos. When, on the other hand, that relationship is characterised by disharmony and disequilibrium, 'we find that non-organic, linear-geometric styles are always produced'. The supervening non-naturalist form is characterised, in Frank's words, 'by an emphasis on linear-geometric patterns, on the disappearance of modelling and the attempt to capture the illusion of space, on the dominance of the plane in all types of plastic art'.

Frank goes on to point out that in the last quarter of the nineteenth century the pervasive insecurity, instability and uncertainty over the meaning and purpose of life amply provided it with all the characteristics of an age of disequilibrium and hence of non-naturalism. He has no difficulty at all in effecting the transition from the plastic arts to the art of literature:

Since literature is a time-art, we shall take our point of departure from Worringer's discussion of the disappearance of depth (and hence of the world in which time occurs) in non-naturalistic styles. 'It is precisely space', writes Worringer 'which, filled with atmospheric air, linking things together and destroying their individual closedness, gives things their temporal value and draws them into the cosmic interplay of phenomena'. Depth, the projection of three-dimensional space, gives objects a time-value because it places them in the real world in which events occur. Now time is the very condition of that flux and change from which, as we have seen, man wishes to escape when he is in a relation of disequilibrium with the cosmos; hence non-naturalistic styles shun the dimension of depth and prefer the plane ....

In a non-naturalistic style ... the inherent spatiality of the plastic arts is accentuated by the effort to remove all traces of time-value ... The significance of spatial form in modern literature now becomes clear; it is the exact complement in literature, on the level of aesthetic form, to the developments that have taken place in the plastic arts.... In both artistic mediums, one naturally spatial and the other naturally temporal, the evolution of aesthetic form in the twentieth century has been absolutely identical. For if the plastic arts from the Renaissance onward attempted to compete with literature by perfecting the means of narrative representation, then contemporary literature is now striving to rival the spatial apprehension of the plastic arts in a moment of time. Both contemporary art and literature have, each in its own way, attempted to overcome the time elements involved in their structures.[12]

Frank concludes that spatial form is the appropriate aesthetic expression of the common content of modern literature; and that 'common content', he believes, is the timeless world of myth:

> What has occurred, at least as far as literature is concerned, may be described as the transformation of the historical imagination into myth – an imagination for which historical time does not exist, and which sees the actions and events of a particular time, only as the bodying forth of eternal prototypes.[13]

There is a way in which Frank's views on spatial form can be seen to catch up what is aesthetically serious about the romance – which, as Gillian Beer has noted, 'has always flourished in periods of rapid change'[14] – for that, too, seems often to take place in suspended time, is ultimately inorganic rather than organic or organicist, and abandons depth and perspective. The past, too, is treated in a way that provides little or no causal progression towards the reader's present: history becomes ahistorical. As it develops, it is clear that the romance supplies a number of characteristics which have come to be seen as distinguishing features in Modernist writing, in particular its privileging of myth and its artistic self-consciousness.

The romance was, of course, traditionally hostile towards realism, something which deeply troubled Hawthorne in particular 'who perplexed himself frequently about the claims of a kind of fiction which he called the romance, which had in it much of the marvellous, the metaphysical, history as pastoral, and a bias towards symbolism and allegory, and the novel proper which was faithful to the probable and ordinary course of men's experience, history as process, and the denuded, untextured, fleeting present of the world'. Malcolm Bradbury, from whose book *Possibilities* this quotation is taken, goes on:

> Hawthorne's works are conducted in this frame of reference; he represented himself as constantly suspended between the claims of form and reality, form which was resonant but also coercive, in that it tended to transpose human agents and human matter into metaphor, and reality which was humanizing and progressive but had all the impoverishment of a history rushing into secular materialism and mechanism ....[15]

The development of the non-naturalistic phase through the last quarter of the nineteenth century is foreshadowed in Hawthorne's dilemma; and the attendant change in the novel does indeed register itself as a move away from realism. Bernard Bergonzi, in *The Situation of the Novel*, puts it like this:

> The tradition of nineteenth-century realism, which underlies most contemporary English fiction, depended on a degree of relative stability in three separate areas: the idea of reality; the nature of the fictional form; and the kind of relationship that might predictably exist between them.... It goes without saying that for many twentieth-century novelists and critics this assumption [of the reality of the world or the fictional form] is no longer credible.[16]

Malcolm Bradbury fills in this development in his chapter 'Phases of Modernism' in *Possibilities*. Discussing the critical consensus of a 'turn' in the novel in the closing years of the last century and the opening of the present one, he writes:

> The change has something to do with the fortunes of realism and liberalism in the novel. Both George Eliot and James merit the name of realists, but at different levels of comprehension of the term; George Eliot's is a realism of the middle distance, a realism in which the embodied life of society was both inescapable and a condition of personality and growth; James's, not so much a substantiation of reality as a questing for it, as if its substance were always provisional, so that all insight into it must be perspectivised, and the relation of those perspectives to the author himself managed with an utter care, intensely demanding on the logic of art itself.

This is well said, and he goes on to underline the link between this change and the modern novel:

> It is with this perspectivism that one essential aspect of the modern novel makes its presence felt. An essential feature of the twentieth-century novel is the presence of a new kind of self-awareness, an introversion of the novel to a degree unprecedented in its fortunes. This gave a stylistic milieu in which some practices which had been very close to the centre of fiction as a story-telling art were brought into question; it seemed that certain well-established types of narrative presentation, certain kinds and modes of realism, certain poised relationships between the story and its teller, certain forms of chronological ordering and particular views of character, even the belief that a form does not need to exceed the working needs immediately occasioning it, were being re-structured to fit the form of a new world.

Not only are we moving into a time of 'new intensities of technique', but now at least part of the focus of the novel 'becomes the process of its own making, which is what very articulately happens in much modernism, in which the making of the work becomes a theme shared between writer and reader, and a transcendent basis of the work's authority'.[17]

Modernism (or a phase of it) clearly pre-dates the twenties where it is often located:

> The emphasis on technique, or on the perceptual resources of the artist himself as a highly subjective consciousness; the emphasis on rendering, or the heightened resonance that might be attached to certain observed objects; the emphasis on tactics of presentation through the consciousness of characters rather than through an objective or a materialistic presentation of material; and the emphasis on the medium of art as the writer's essential subject-matter – these were all laid down before the First World War.[18]

Indeed they were, and in the work of Stevenson we can see the development not just forecast but, in fact, embarked upon. In *Prince Otto* , bowing his head over technique, as he had advised an aspiring writer to do first and last, he elaborates his art to the highest pitch, exposing the strenuous process in defiance of any doctrine of *ars celare artis*, and freezing the finished product by means of a markedly spatialised form which preserves the myth of the greenwood from the incursions of time. But of course he *has* given it a historical framework which shows Grünewald to be a vanished state and when a dispossessed prince and princess seek reassimilation in the greenwood dream he arranges a sardonic double-ending. The first leaves them restored to each other in the healing care of the pastoral order; the second shows them rudely awakened by a Bibliographical Postscript far more destructive than Thackeray's exhortation to the children to 'shut up the box and the puppets' at the end of *Vanity Fair*.

The romance is to be distinguished from other forms of fiction, according to Gillian Beer, 'by the relationship it imposes between reader and romance-world'. This relationship, she continues, 'liberates us but it also involves unusual dependency.... We have to depend entirely on the narrator of the romance: he makes the rules of what is possible, what impossible. Our enjoyment depends upon our willing surrender to his power.'[19] And the narrator in *Prince Otto*, very deliberately, violates this trust to reveal that art is game – the deconstructive game that we now associate with Postmodernism.

## Synaesthesia in the Park

Prince Otto has, of course, vanished before *Prince Otto* begins. The opening of the story is a good one: poised, slightly ironical, confident and succinct:

> You shall seek in vain upon the map of Europe for the bygone state of Grünewald. An independent principality, an infinitesimal member of the German Empire, she played, for several centuries, her part in the discord of Europe; and, at last, in the ripeness of time and at the spiriting of several bald diplomatists, vanished like a morning ghost. Less fortunate than Poland, she left not a regret behind her; and the very memory of her boundaries has faded (3).

The equally good description which follows, carefully-wrought with the care fully exposed, is therefore of a vanished pastoral whose reality has already been subsumed in texts. Thus we are told that on its south side the state of Grünewald (alias Greenwood) had marched with Seaboard Bohemia 'celebrated for its flowers and mountain bears, and inhabited by people of singular simplicity and tenderness of heart' (4). Prince Otto is linked by blood to this kingdom for he 'drew his descent through Perdita, the only daughter of King Florizel the First of Bohemia' (4). The world of *The Winter's Tale* is neatly evoked and at the same time equally neatly linked with its recent oriental variant in Stevenson's own *New Arabian Nights*.

The wide-lens view of the history of the vanished state is adroitly contracted to focus on the forest hillside where a hunt is drawing to an end. There is no question of realism here: the language is appropriately formal, evoking (without specifying) the iconography which has traditionally represented the hunt in art:

> In the wedge of forest hillside enclosed between the roads, the horns continued all day long to scatter tumult; and at length, as the sun began to draw near to the horizon of the plain, a rousing triumph announced the slaughter of the quarry (51).

As the description continues, the comprehensive filling-in of space is done in a manner which underlines its static and two-dimensional nature. As so often in the book, description is given in a marked vertical axis which in itself counters any naturalistic, linear, forward movement; instead we get detail, literally piled on top of detail leaving us with a highly spatial awareness of a scene where all is static, nothing has an organic relationship with anything else, no progress forward is perceptible, and time is thus removed from the picture:

> The first and second huntsmen had drawn somewhat aside, and from the summit of a knoll gazed down before them on the drooping shoulders of the hill and across the expanse of plain .... Through the confused tracery of many thousands of naked poplars, the smoke of so many houses, and the evening steam ascending from the fields, the sails of a windmill on a gentle eminence moved very conspicuously like a donkey's ears. And hard by, like an open gash, the imperial highroad ran straight sunward, an artery of travel (5).

Nor does the appearance of the highroad contradict what has just been said about the picture. True, it is certainly an act of violence on this static pastoral scene – it is 'like an open gash'. It does not, however, have the force needed seriously to upset the formal presentation and substitute a dynamic, linear mode. The main reason for this is that it is immediately enveloped in a dissolving perspective which ensures that it will register on our minds as a road to nowhere (or everywhere), an embodiment, not of purposeful, forward movement, but of the romance of journeys forever beckoning but never made:

> There is one of nature's spiritual ditties, that has not yet been set to words or human music: 'The Invitation to the Road'; an air continually sounding in the ears of gipsies, and to whose inspiration our nomadic fathers journeyed all their days. The hour, the season, and the scene were all in delicate accordance. The air was full of birds of passage, steering westward and northward over Grünewald, an army of specks to the uplooking eye. And below, the great practicable road was bound for the same quarter (5).

Again the movement is vertical: the eye is first directed to the birds flying high above and then, from this altitude, re-directed to a panoramic view of the contourless landscape beneath – which is partly in the mind's eye. Otto himself helps to underline the illusion and delusions associated with the road. As he, too, looks down upon it, he is fully aware of its romance:

> So it ran, league after league, still joining others, to the farthest ends of Europe, there skirting the sea-surge, here gleaming in the lights of cities; and the innumerable army of tramps and travellers moved upon it in all lands as by a common impulse, and were

now in all places drawing near the inn-door and the night's rest. The pictures swarmed and vanished in his brain, a surge of temptation, a beat of all his blood went over him, to set spur to the mare and to go on into the unknown for ever. And then it passed away; hunger and fatigue, and that habit of middling actions which we call common sense, resumed their empire ... (7).

The imagined army of travellers exists only as one of the pictures swarming in his brain, for the Grünewald section of the road remains effectively empty throughout the tale. When life does emerge upon it, it is solitary and fleeting and simply serves to accentuate its emptiness and loneliness:

The road lay all the way apart from towns and villages, which it left on either hand. Here and there, indeed, in the bottom of green glens, the Prince could spy a few congregated roofs, or perhaps above him, on a shoulder, the solitary cabin of a woodman. But the highway was an international undertaking, and with its face set for distant cities, scorned the little life of Grünewald. Hence it was exceeding solitary. Near the frontier Otto met a detachment of his own troops marching in the hot dust; and he was recognised and somewhat feebly cheered as he rode by. But from that time forth and for a long while he was alone with the great woods (29).

Stevenson's spatialisation of his text assists him in his stressing and heightening the formal, aesthetic properties of *Prince Otto*, the upshot of which appears to be an argument for the autonomy of art; for, if you like, the art of sensation to be given its due. Yet, though he goes further here in pursuit of this objective than has been generally recognised, recruiting all three of the sister arts to his cause, he is not recommending art for art's sake as a supreme value, and any idea that he might be is surely destroyed in the demolition that occurs in the 'Bibliographical Postscript'.

One in particular of the sister arts has been overlooked by those seeking to identify the formal modes which have influenced the structure of *Prince Otto*: the art of music. It has not, I believe, been generally noted that this romance (for want of any more stable name) is bracketed between two operas: *Der Freischütz*, and Handel's *Rinaldo*. Subsumed in the whole text is a third, Offenbach's *La Grande Duchesse de Gérolstein*, a satire on miniature courts and petty princelings which, when Bismarck saw it, convinced him both that the French military spirit was dead and that the petty German states deserved the fate he had already planned for them. *Prince Otto* is not, of course, the only text where Stevenson invokes musical forms to extend his reflexive reach – one thinks, for example, of *The Ebb Tide* which also makes clear the attraction which opera in particular exerted upon him. There is other evidence too. While in Frankfurt in August, 1872 he went to see Halévy's *La Juive* (a relatively new opera which had first been performed in 1835) and in a letter to his mother describing the experience, he reveals how directly opera engaged his feelings, despite all its conventions and formality. 'An opera is far more *real* than real life to me', he wrote, '... I wish that life was an opera. I should like to live in one.' For all that, he had had to leave the theatre before the end of the final act, unable to face the upsetting spectacle of Rachel's martyrdom in the boiling cauldron.

In *Prince Otto*, it could be argued, opera has more to do with structuring the text than had George Meredith who is so often quoted as having provided Stevenson with his model. Of course, Meredith did exert considerable influence here as elsewhere (particularly noticeable towards the end of the book), but it is mistaken to compare *Prince Otto* with *The Adventures of Harry Richmond* as though the latter were its matrix. Apart from a sylvan pocket-principality picturesquely described, a subordinate character called Prince Otto and a Princess called Ottilia, there is little specific connection. Meredith's is undoubtedly the greater achievement, concentrating largely on the father–son relationship which he explores with a subtlety and complexity which take it well beyond its romance ingredients and which Stevenson, for all his obsession with the same theme, never matched in intricacy. Preoccupied with this Meredithian paper-chase, these critics have given Weber no credit at all, failing to notice that Prince Otto, Killian the farmer, and Kuno the huntsman occupy a sizeable amount of space in the cast-list of *Der Freischütz*. (True, the Prince's name in the opera is Ottokar but the unusual ending shouldn't distract us any more than Weber's Killian having only one 'l' or his Kuno beginning with a 'C'. (In the opera 'the rich peasant' Kilian's daughter is, of course, called Agatha whereas Killian's is Ottilia.) *Der Freischütz* is set in Bohemia and is a romance of a distinctly Teutonic greenwood in which some baleful Gothic shadows are fairly easily dispelled.

Towards the end of *Prince Otto* the redoubtable Madame von Rosen gets to sing 'Lascia ch'io pianga' from *Rinaldo*, the oddity of the occasion making the intrusion of the opera all the more conspicuous. She sings it before the Felsenburg, the fortress where Prince

Otto is imprisoned. All sorts of irony and teasing are at work here. In the opera the aria is sung by Almirena bemoaning her unhappy lot since it is *she* who is imprisoned in the enchanted castle. Von Rosen is therefore having some mild fun at the expense of the occasionally effete and lachrymose Otto, sharpened by the fact that she has arrived at the Felsenburg with the means of freeing him from his bondage which she has obtained on her own courageous initiative. Before she can launch into her recital she has to persuade the Governor, Colonel Gordon (improbably, a deracinated Aberdonian) to allow her to announce her presence and her mission in this unusual way. The Governor, having a soft spot for the arts, makes little difficulty and conducts her to Otto's prison-suite. The *Baronne* prepares her entrance with care:

> 'Well,' she whispered, 'let me get my breath. No, no; wait. Have the door ready to open.' And the Countess, standing like one inspired, shook out her fine voice in 'Lascia ch'io pianga'; and when she had reached the proper point, and lyrically uttered forth her sighings after liberty, the door, at a sign, was flung wide open, and she swam into the Prince's sight, bright-eyed, and with her colour somewhat freshened by the exercise of singing. It was a great dramatic entrance, and to the somewhat doleful prisoner within the sight was sunshine (176).

The whole episode, one readily agrees, is pure comic opera. The two duly depart after the Prince has made a present of his verses to an appreciative Colonel Gordon ('Ha! ... Alexandrines, the tragic metre') who declares, after a careful perusal of the manuscript, that 'they remind [him] of Robbie Burns' (despite the fact that Burns was not particularly noted for his Alexandrines).

*Rinaldo* is, of course, poles removed from *Der Freischütz*, but it is still altogether relevant to *Prince Otto* as a reflexive form. It is a 'magic opera' with sorcerers, multitudes of supernatural beings and an enchanted palace with flaming battlements perched on top of an enormous mountain. But it mixes its wild fantasy with the realism of battles, hostage-taking, forced conversions and the like, sometimes making the transition with disconcerting abruptness. Everything combines to provide a vehicle for a number of beautiful arias often inappropriate to the dramatic occasion and frequently showing little connection with each other.

As well as appealing to musical forms to enlarge his reflexive practice and embedding – or embodying – them in his own text,

Stevenson calls, as I have already indicated, on another text quintessentially representative of the romance mode, namely *The Winter's
Tale*. But he also works very hard at involving the visual sense, too,
and here his reflexive form is, I would suggest, analogous to that of
the woodcut – an art-form Stevenson admired and practised.

The descriptions of the greenwood in *Prince Otto* are for the most
part strikingly two-dimensional and mostly without perspective.
Everything seems to appear on a vertical plane as an earlier quotation has shown: 'Here and there, indeed, in the bottom of green
glens, the Prince could spy a few congregated roofs, and perhaps
above him, on a shoulder, the solitary cabin of a woodman.' When
Seraphina flees into the forest she, too, appears in the middle of a
vertical plane: 'This lane of pine-trees ran very rapidly downhill and
wound among the woods; ... and now she looked up the hill and
saw the brook coming down to her in a series of cascades ...' (156).
Even the sun's ascent has its perpendicularity emphasised: 'up the
steep and solitary eastern heaven, the sun ... continued slowly and
royally to mount' (157). When the Princess gets down from Sir John's
coach she is still inscribed on the same plane: 'The place where they
had alighted was at a salient angle; a bold rock and some wind-
tortured pine-trees overhung it from above; far below the blue plains
lay forth and melted into heaven ... ' (167). The view from the coach
carrying Otto to prison had not been all that different:

> The carriage swung forth out of the valleys on that open balcony
> of high road that runs along the front of Grünewald, looking
> down on Gerolstein. Far below, a white waterfall was shining to
> the stars from the falling skirts of forest, and beyond that, the
> night stood naked above the plain (173).

Even Otto's palace manages to stack itself up like a Tibetan monastery:

> they mounted, one after another the various flights of stairs, snowed
> upon, as they went, with April blossoms, and marching in time to
> the great orchestra of birds. Nor did Otto pause till they had reached
> the highest terrace of the garden. Here was a gate into the park,
> and hard by, under a tuft of laurel, a marble garden seat. Hence
> they looked down on the green tops of many elm-trees, where the
> rooks were busy; and, beyond that, upon the palace roof, and the
> yellow banner flying in the blue (61).

This is a particularly jewelled and formalised print. (When carp
are found leaping as thick as bees we *know* we're in the realm of pure

art.) All of these tableaux, however, though static with a frozen discreteness as pronounced as that on the frieze of Keats's urn, are rich and expressive. The towering pine-woods and tumbling cascades have posed against their sombre green and frothing white the men and animals of the hunt, the Prince's carriage and military escort, the pastoral idyll of Killian in his River Farm, the Felsenburg and, finally, the Prince and Princess as babes in the wood (the title of the last chapter) wrapped in anything but a baby-like embrace.

Such 'prints' are marooned in space, for the dimensions they inhabit are spatial not temporal. They suggest nothing organic, no dynamic, no development. As much in an eddy as Prince Otto sees himself to be when contemplating the brook, and thus out of the stream of life, they can only add ornament to what is already given. Thus while they may have something of the vertiginous drama of an oriental landscape or the virtuosity of a Kandinsky woodcut, they have too little of the range of vibrant colours which suffuse the latter with energy and a similitude of life. What all of these attributes amount to is a depiction of the Prince's own situation. As marooned as the life in these prints in a world unsympathetic to his values, he can go neither forward nor back. In part his sense of futility is a reflection of his own character and as such partakes of that atrophy of the will which afflicts a number of Stevenson's adolescents on the threshold of manhood. Several times Otto's 'manliness' is called in question: by the people he meets when playing Haroun al Raschid, by Seraphina who is reported as saying that Otto was an amiable fellow 'except as a husband and a prince', and by himself when he admits at the end that he had 'no merit but a love, slavish and unerect' (188). The Princess's view of him is, of course, coloured by her political aspirations which convince her that she is capable of doing a better job in governing the country than this 'prince in Dresden china' as she unflatteringly calls him (78).

Otto does, however, occasionally defend himself and his lifestyle and questions what 'manliness' might mean: 'perhaps if all the kings in Europe were to confine themselves to innocent amusement, the subjects would be better off' (10). And Stevenson himself spoke up for him with unusual vehemence. Writing to Henley of a review which had pilloried Otto, Stevenson directs his attack squarely at the critic's assumptions about manliness: '... he is one of the large class of unmanly and ungenerous dogs who arrogate and defile the name of manly'.[20] In reply to another correspondent, Harriet Monroe, who had expressed a dislike of Otto, Stevenson defends him with some asperity, demanding 'what is man?' and going on: 'Think better of Otto, if my plea can influence you ... because, as men go in this world (and women too), you will not go far wrong if you light upon so fine a fellow; and to light upon one and not perceive his merits is a calamity. In the flesh, of course, I mean; in the book the fault, of course, is with my stumbling pen. Seraphina made a mistake about her Otto; it begins to swim before me dimly that you may have some traits of Seraphina.'[21]

## Bismarck in Bohemia

Otto is not really in the same case as those (much younger) Stevenson characters who seem unable to assume the adult male role. He is more nearly the man 'malade de sa différence avec son temps' who doesn't see anything worth fighting for in a world which has no place for him. In an age of Bismarcks he is, by contrast, a sensitive and humane man with something like a Hellenic system of values. His instinct is towards love and justice and the pastoral order; and he would prefer to see his court a reflector of those values rather than of political statecraft in the modern, Bismarckian sense. His world is dominated by personal and aesthetic ideals quite the opposite of those which would form the basis of a materialist regime such as is envisaged by the 'authoritarian' Roederer where political opportunity and advantage are relentlessly pursued in a ruthless search for power. Power does not interest Otto – 'There goes the government over the borders on a grey mare', the huntsman 'sneers'.

Explicitly, intermarriage with the pastoral kingdom of Bohemia has alienated the ruling family from its people. Its style and its values are passive and formal rather than 'manly':

> That these intermarriages had in some degree mitigated the rough, manly stock of the first Grünewalds, was an opinion widely held within the borders of the principality. The charcoal burner, the mountain sawyer, the wielder of the broad axe among the congregated pines of Grünewald, proud of their hard hands, proud of their shrewd ignorance and almost savage lore, looked with an unfeigned contempt on the soft character and manners of the sovereign race (4).

These views of the Grünewalders are not intended to compliment them: their value-system is crude, their horizons narrow and in both complacency is endemic. In every sense, it is the strong arm that these hewers of wood and burners of charcoal admire and are admired for: 'A man of Grünewald now,' says Killian of Gerolstein, 'will swing me an axe over his head that many a man of Gerolstein could hardly lift.' And, by strong implication, such forcefulness and physical energy are the qualities proper to the 'new age'. Fritz, old Killian's prospective son-in-law, has no doubts at all: passionately against princes in general and Otto in particular he regards the ruthless, scheming 'Baron' Gondremark as a hero. To Fritz, it is he who is 'the hope of Grünewald': 'He doesn't suit some of your high and dry, old, ancient ideas; but he's a downright modern man – a man of the new lights and the progress of the age' (4). Gondremark, 'a man from East Prussia' (15), is clearly intended to stand for Bismarck, 'the iron Chancellor', at the time aggressively engaged in unifying Germany under the Prussian crown, who makes a number of menacing appearances in Stevenson's work.

Even in the beautiful pastoral milieu of Book I, Otto is something of an outcast; so much so, indeed, that at one point he threatens to become the object of his own hunt:

'I do not see him, Kuno, ' said the first huntsman,'nowhere – not a trace, not a hair of the mare's tail! No, sir, he's off; broke cover and got away. Why, for twopence I would hunt him with the dogs!' (5)

And while he is with Killian in his River Farm he has to put up with a sustained attack on himself, full of calumny and ignorance. His host assails him with a biblical fervour, redolent of the Protestant ethic so familiar to Stevenson himself. 'Here is a man', says Killian, 'with great opportunities, and what does he do with them?'

'He hunts, and he dresses very prettily – which is a thing to be ashamed of in a man – and he acts plays; and if he does aught else, the news of it has not come here.'

'Yet these are all innocent,' said Otto. 'What would you have him do – make war?'

'No, sir,' replied the old man. 'But here it is; I have been fifty years upon this River Farm, and wrought in it, day in, day out; I have ploughed and sowed and reaped, and risen early, and waked late; and this is the upshot: that all these years it has supported me and my family; and been the best friend that ever I had, set aside my wife; and now, when my time comes, I leave it a better farm than when I found it. So it is, if a man works hearty in the order of nature, he gets bread and he receives comfort, and whatever he touches breeds. And it humbly appears to me, if that Prince was to labour on his throne, as I have laboured and wrought in my farm, he would find both an increase and a blessing' (10).

Measured against the activity of the materialist, workaday world (the story is full of references to mills, principally water-mills, many of which Otto now hears are standing idle as a result of 'his' high taxation policies), Otto sees himself and his kind as useless. His rather tentative view that states headed by princes who are passive, more interested in the arts than politics and happy enough to discharge their 'manly' feelings in the hunt rather than war, are to be approved of, is misunderstood by the boorish Fritz – even though Killian agrees with Otto that they have enjoyed 'a long peace – a peace of centuries'. 'I see that you are like me', says Fritz to the incognito Prince, 'a good patriot and an enemy to princes', and he accepts without demur the rumours of war that grow with the rumours of a republic.

The contrast between Fritz and Otto is a significant one, defining the new order against the old. When the Prince intervenes in the quarrel between Fritz and his future wife Ottilia (a quarrel originating in Fritz's baseless suspicions that she might be attracted to the Prince), and points out that 'if your own doings were so curiously examined, you might find it inconvenient to reply', Fritz's response is brutal: 'You know very well that a man is a man, and a woman only a woman. That holds good all over, up and down.' The Prince's rebuke is a comprehensive indictment of Fritz's values and judgement:

'When you have studied liberal doctrines somewhat deeper,' said the Prince, 'you will perhaps change your note. You are a man of false weights and measures, my young friend. You have one scale for women, another for men; one for princes, and one for farmer-folk. On the prince who neglects his wife you can be most severe. But what of the lover who insults his mistress? You use the name of love. I should think this lady might very fairly ask to be delivered from love of such a nature. For if I, a stranger, had been one-tenth part so gross and so discourteous, you would most righteously have broken my head. It would have been in your part, as lover, to protect her from such insolence. Protect her first, then, from yourself' (25).

Significantly, Otto refuses to be reconciled with Fritz, notwithstanding Killian's attempt to persuade him to relent.

To Otto as he sits by the stream 'dead in love with that sun-chequered echoing corner', his destiny appears bleak, given that Fritz's view of the future seems certain to prevail. War will take place with Gerolstein (for nothing: 'Geroll' means rubble and 'stein', rock) and the once timeless and enchanted world of the greenwood will disappear.[22] Already the marvellous pines, so much insisted on and, being drawn on the same formal plane as the Prince, blending with him to express that timeless, spatial world, are seen by old Killian in a sharply different light:

> Up and down, the road keeps right on from here to Mittwalden; and nothing all the way but the good green pine-trees, big and little, and water-power! water-power at every step, sir. We once sold a bit of forest, up there beside the high-road; and the sight of minted money that we got for it has set me ciphering ever since what all the pines in Grünewald would amount to (9).

The greenwood is no longer to be seen as manifestation of the harmonious vision of pastoral but as a cash crop. 'There must be more pines in that little state, sir,' says Killian enviously, 'than people in this whole big world' (9). Well might Otto, gazing down at the eddies in the stream, come to the conclusion that 'Eddy and Prince were alike useless, starkly useless in the cosmology of men' (18). And when Killian's daughter Ottilia upbraids him for not defending himself ('Come now, you know you are good') he replies, in a very Stevensonian accent, 'I am full of good ingredients, but the dish is worthless' (20).

On his way home, Otto encounters first a drunken miller who administers a few more unpleasant home-truths about Otto's reign – and that of his wife who is accused of immorality, responsibility for the excessive taxation, and for the re-arming going on. At the inn, however, he meets 'the licentiate Roederer' who proclaims himself an Authoritarian and an admirer of the Prince's cousin and Librarian, Gotthold Hohenstockwitz. He sees himself as being ahead of those republicans now plotting revolution against Otto's regime: 'I share none of those illusory, Utopian fancies with which empires blind themselves and exasperate the ignorant. The day of these ideas is, believe me, past, or at least passing' (33). Otto demurs but the authoritarian Roederer continues: 'in the laboratory of opinion, beside the studious lamp, we begin already to discard these figments. We begin to return to nature's order, to what I might call, if I were to borrow from the language of therapeutics, the expectant treatment of abuses'

(34). Roederer is clearly a prescient glimpse of the prototype Fascist.

Dr Gotthold, when we meet him in the palace, denies that he is an authoritarian when the Prince puts the question to him; but he does so in terms which discourage us from lending weight to anything he says or any ethical or moral position he may assume: 'I? God bless me no!... I am a red, dear child.' In fact, Gotthold is what he later accuses Otto of being, 'a born sceptic':

> 'All men, all, are fundamentally useless; nature tolerates, she does not need, she does not use them: sterile flowers! All – down to the fellow swinking in a byre, whom fools point out for the exception – all are useless; all weave ropes of sand; or like a child that has breathed on a window, write and obliterate, write and obliterate idle words! Talk of it no more. That way, I tell you, madness lies... Yes, dear child, we are not here to do battle with giants; we are here to be happy like the flowers, if we can be. It is because you could, that I have always secretly admired you. Cling to that trade; believe me, it is the right one. Be happy, be idle, be airy. To the devil with all casuistry! and leave the state to Gondremark, as heretofore' (44).

Otto's own ironic scepticism comes through quite clearly when he concedes that 'the whole thing, prince and principality, alike, is pure absurdity, a stroke of satire'. The rumour of hostilities with Gerolstein adds to the absurdity and irrationality of the situation – so ably compounded by the follies of those who make politics their trade: 'And war too, – I hear of war – war in this teapot! What a complication of absurdity and disgrace' (45).

Gondremark, 'the downright modern man', is at the very opposite pole from Otto. According to the touring English Radical, Sir John Crabtree, an extract from whose book, *Memoirs of a Visit to Various Courts of Europe*, characteristically forms a complete chapter of *Prince Otto*, Gondremark, 'using the lovesick princess for a tool and a mouthpiece, ... pursues a policy of arbitrary power and territorial aggrandisement'. Crabtree is very far from being an unbiased or even accurate observer: his estimate of Otto is, as he later admits, considerably at fault, and his view of the Princess's character equally so; but his portrayal of Gondremark's political power and ambition is not so wide of the mark. While one might think that only a Scotsman would conceive an English Baronet who is both a prototype gossip-columnist *and* a political radical, it is, in fact, Sir John's particular sort of radicalism which encourages a qualified admiration of Gondremark even though he recognises, in a very Conradian phrase, that what he is admiring is 'the audacity of the adventurer'. To construe his sympathies thus is not, I believe, to assume too much, for his appearance is surely also that of a 'downright modern man'. When he meets Otto he is described as 'a man of fifty, hard, uncompromising, able, with the eye and teeth of physical courage' who greets the prince 'with a sort of sneering ease' (59). He sees Otto as 'devoid of sterling qualities' and beneath the elegant exterior he detects only 'a deliquescence of the moral nature, a frivolity and inconsequence of purpose that mask the near perfect fruit of a decadent age' (53). Crabtree is, however, at the same time a supporter of 'the free lodges' which seek the overthrow of the state, and as such appears to classify himself as a liberal; but those lodges are Masonic which complicates matters further.

Gondremark, whose face was marked 'by capacity, temper, and a kind of bold, piratical honesty', has nothing but contempt for Otto. Playing on the Princess's ambition and infatuation with power, Gondremark has taken the reins of government into his own hands and plans the overthrow of the existing order. Against him, Otto is virtually helpless. It is not altogether, as the latter claims, that he is 'unfit by intellect and temper for a leading role [and] intended ... for a subaltern' (28); it is that the new order has no place for a Prince whose role is essentially one dedicated to art and a cultivation of the humaner passions, thus predicating all sorts of vanished or vanishing harmonies. Otto does have one passion still, however, and that is his love for the Princess. Blinded by her obsession with power, she does not recognise it for the value it represents, and spurns it and him to the extent, ultimately, of having him arrested and taken off to prison.

The Princess, however, is also near to her moment of truth when she is to discover how far Gondremark has been using and deceiving her. Reading the note Otto has written her before his arrest, the reality of her position comes home to her and she reacts in a way that reminds us a little of Gwendolen Harleth in *Daniel Deronda*:

She read with a great horror on her mind; that day, of which he wrote, was come. She was alone; she had been false, she had been cruel; remorse rolled in upon her; and then with a more piercing note, vanity bounded on the stage of consciousness. She a dupe! she helpless! she to have betrayed herself in seeking to betray her husband! she to have lived these years upon flattery, grossly swallowing the bolus, like a clown with sharpers! she – Seraphina! Her swift mind drank the consequences; she foresaw the coming fall, her public shame; she saw the odium, disgrace, and folly of her story flaunt through Europe. She recalled the scandal she had so royally braved; and alas! she had now no courage to confront it with. To be thought the mistress of that man: perhaps for that.... She closed her eyes on agonising vistas (143).

But she does not kill herself as she first intends; instead, in a scene which is again pure comic theatre – superbly done and characteristic of that heightened rendering which Stevenson delights in – she confronts the Baron. He, totally misunderstanding her angry and excited appearance, construes that she is infatuated with him and that the way to sovereign power is his for the taking. The effect of this catastrophic miscalculation on his *amour propre* makes for one of the book's most entertaining moments:

'Ah, madam!' he cried, plumping on his knees. 'Seraphina! Do you permit me? have you divined my secret? It is true – I put my life with joy into your power – I love you, love with ardour, as an equal, as a mistress, as a brother-in-arms, as an adored, desired, sweet-hearted woman. O Bride!' he cried, waxing dithyrambic, 'bride of my reason and my senses, have pity, have pity on my love!'

She heard him with wonder, rage, and then contempt. His words offended her to sickness; his appearance, as he grovelled bulkily upon the floor, moved her to such laughter as we laugh in nightmares.

'O shame!' she cried. 'Absurd and odious! What would the Countess say!'

That great Baron Gondremark, the excellent politician, remained for some little time upon his knees in a frame of mind which perhaps we are allowed to pity. His vanity, within his iron bosom, bled and raved. If he could have blotted all, if he could have withdrawn part, if he had not called her bride – with a roaring in his ears, he thus regretfully reviewed his declaration (145).

The scene ends as it had begun – in melodrama, with the Princess stabbing the Baron; not just melodrama, though, for there's parody, too, in that the knocking at the door turns the whole episode into an extract from a Ruritanian *Macbeth*.

Otto's own most powerful feeling is love, while even those who disparage him admit that he also has the courage to ignore what others would have him be and be himself. But now that Bohemian world of his, identified with the innocent arts (he sings like a child, says the imperceptive 'radical', Sir John, contemptuously), with the unexploitive pastoral order of the aptly-named Ottilia who was 'a plain, honest lass, healthy and happy and good and with that sort of beauty that comes from happiness and health' – that world is caught between the new, aggressive political opportunism of Gondremark and the sinister authoritarianism of 'the licentiate Roederer'.

In the middle there is the philosopher-librarian, Dr Gotthold. In his discussion with the Prince at the inn, Roederer, interestingly, sees him as a 'remarkable force of intellect' (which we do not) and, neither recognising the Prince nor understanding him, suggests that such a man as he perceives the Prince to be with such a man as Gotthold at his elbow 'would be, for all practical purposes, my ideal ruler', though he readily concedes that these 'would not be the ideas of the masses'. The number of unreliable observers or commentators which Stevenson puts before us in the book is of significance in itself. (Gondremark, Gotthold, Roederer, Crabtree, Seraphina – all misread the Prince's situation.) Roederer is also wrong – doubly so – about Gotthold. Not only is he *not* an Authoritarian, he professes himself to be a sceptic – that is, before his scepticism lapses. It is important to recognise that, whatever he may think himself, he is a poseur. Philosophically his shallow scepticism is of singularly little help to his Prince, as the Librarian freely admits: 'I am too sceptical to be an ethical adviser, and as for good resolutions, I believed in them when I was young' (42). Here in what is apparently the regime's cultural and ethical inner sanctum, all we find is a patronising, mannered evasiveness masquerading as scepticism, though not afraid to pass shallow judgements dressed with the appearance of worldly insight. Otto is mistaken enough to invite Gotthold's opinion on whether or not he is a popular sovereign. Gotthold adjudicates the matter pompously and then voices his malicious conclusion with a great deal of self-satisfaction:

'As a prince – well, you are in the wrong trade. It is perhaps philosophical to recognise it as you do.'
'Perhaps philosophical?' repeated Otto.
'Yes, perhaps. I would not be dogmatic,' answered Gotthold.
'Perhaps philosophical, and certainly not virtuous,' Otto resumed.
'Not of a Roman virtue,' chuckled the recluse.
Otto drew his chair nearer to the table, leaned upon it with his elbow, and looked his cousin squarely in the face. 'In short,' he asked 'not manly?'

'Well,' Gotthold hesitated, 'not manly, if you will.' And then, with a laugh, 'I did not know that you gave yourself out to be manly,' he added. 'It was one of the points that I inclined to like about you; inclined, I believe, to admire.... Without compromise you were yourself: a pretty sight. I have always said it: none so void of all pretence as Otto' (42).

It is not, in fact, within Gotthold's capacity to be philosophically objective about anything: he is not the shrewd, ascetic, scholarly, adviser Roederer sees him to be; in fact, he gets more comfort from his secret wine-bottle and a maudlin adoration of the Princess than he does from his philosophy. As for the Prince, at this point at least his situation is rendered very well in Jessica Feldman's study already referred to:

> To lose one's manliness, to have it degenerate into a soft effemi-
> nacy, describes both Otto's sexuality and his political authority
> and power. To lose one's manliness is to be unable to manage the
> affairs of state, to call down chaos upon the heads of his subjects
> precisely because the loss calls hierarchy itself into question.
> Otto's very fluidity, his decline from the state of manhood, compro-
> mises his ability to enforce hierarchy and category themselves.
> The peasant Fritz must remind a forgetful Otto that 'you know
> very well that a man is a man, and a woman only a woman' (37).
> Stevenson makes explicit the connection between Otto's sexual
> and political 'falls'.[23]

In fact Otto's concept of manliness challenges the need for hierarchy and category; but a prince who declines to exercise the authority vested in him has in effect already abdicated. Thus Otto is being quite logical when he refuses to accept the Countess von Rosen's advice to stand and fight: 'why should I resist ... I have no party, no policy; no pride, or anything to be proud of. For what benefit or prin-ciple under Heaven do you expect me to contend?' (129) For a greenwood Prince it is a noticeably clear-sighted, rational – and stubborn – argument and perhaps helps to explain Edmund Gosse's description of the Prince as 'delightfully exasperating and Scotch'.

At the centre of the royal government there is, on Otto's side, nothing but principled inertia to set against Gondremark's wholly unprinci-pled and subversive scheming. Interestingly, and by a device that offers a brilliant example of Stevenson's technique, Otto – the 'phantom of a prince', as Sir John predictably sees him – at the moment of almost his greatest physical reality, turns into a highly formal picture. Though alluded to earlier it is worth touching on again. Enraged (justly as it turns out) by Sir John Crabtree's scurrilous account of his wife's conduct, he is provoked into some uncharacteristically vigorous action and leads Sir John into the garden there to challenge him to a duel:

> So without more delay, the Prince leading, the pair proceeded down through the echoing stairway of the tower, and out through the grating, into the ample air and sunshine of the morning, and among the terraces and flower-beds of the garden. They crossed the fish-pond, where the carp were leaping as thick as bees; they mounted, one after another the various flights of stairs, snowed upon, as they went, with April blossoms, and marching in time to the great orchestra of birds. Nor did Otto pause till they had reached the highest terrace of the garden. Here was a gate into the park, and hard by, under a tuft of laurel, a marble garden seat. Hence they looked down on the green tops of many elm-trees, where the rooks were busy; and, beyond that, upon the palace roof, and the yellow banner flying in the blue. 'I pray you to be seated, sir,' said Otto (61).

It is as though one sees clear through the phantom Prince and finds his form blending with that of the garden. The spatialisation of the narrative at just the point where it might seem to be about to develop some sort of dynamic and describe an action both real and decisive (that is, the duel) is remarkable. Movement and action are at once slowed down, given relationships freeze, and all become objects, all existing simultaneously, defying time, on the same spatial plane. The duel, needless to say, does not take place. This spatialised narrative technique is the one which properly expresses the book, and which, as such, is inextricably part of the matter. The scenes in the palace are equally a matter of style and stylisation: a formal, mannered debate, with illustrations, about authority and the ethics of power, about culture and human values.

The ending of *Prince Otto* (by which I mean the end of Book III) is of a piece with the rest. There is no denouement in the sense of an unravelling of plot and an untying of knots, for the narrative has very little of that sort of sequence and forward movement; and most of what there is is rendered in a style so heightened that 'naturalising' tendencies are kept firmly at arm's length. The palace is stormed, the Princess flees and the new order is installed as we knew from the first that it would be. But something like a fifth of the novel is still to come and in it form becomes spatialised to an almost exclusive degree. The artificial style is sustained at an extravagant level and the internal references are to ideal worlds beyond mundane civilisations, where human beings dislimn:

> Sped by these dire sounds and voices, the Princess scaled the long garden, skimming like a bird the starlit stairways; crossed the Park, which was in that place narrow; and plunged upon the farther side into the rude shelter of the forest. So, at a bound, she left the discretion and the cheerful lamps of Palace evenings; ceased utterly to be a sovereign lady; and, falling from the whole height of civilisation, ran forth into the woods, a ragged Cinderella (153).

Princess Seraphina loses not only her sovereignty and Grünewald, but her substantial human reality as well: the life of the pines is more instinct with moral activity than she, and the phantom Prince gradually acquires a suitably phantom spouse:

> This lane of pine-trees ran very rapidly down-hill and wound among the woods; but it was a wider thoroughfare than the brook needed, and here and there were little dimpling lawns and coves of the forest, where the starshine slumbered. Such a lawn she paced, taking patience bravely; and now she looked up the hill and saw the brook coming down to her in a series of cascades; and now approached the margin, where it welled among the rushes silently; and now gazed at the great company of heaven with an enduring wonder. The early evening had fallen chill, but the night was now temperate; out of the recesses of the wood there came mild airs as from a deep and peaceful breathing; and the dew was heavy on the grass and the tight-shut daisies. This was the girl's first night under the naked heaven; and now that her fears were over-past, she was touched to the soul by its serene amenity and peace. Kindly the host of heaven blinked down upon that wandering Princess; and the honest brook had no words but to encourage her.
> At last she began to be aware of a wonderful revolution, compared to which the fire of Mittwalden Palace was but the crack and flash of a percussion-cap. The countenance with which the pines regarded her began insensibly to change; the grass too, short as it was, and the whole winding staircase of the brook's course, began to wear a solemn freshness of appearance. And this slow transfiguration reached her heart, and played upon it, and transpierced it with a

serious thrill. She looked all about; the whole face of nature looked back, brimful of meaning, finger on lip, leaking its glad secret (156).

This is only one of many such descriptions in Book III whose highly-wrought lyricism amounts to a sort of paean to a pastoral myth which – we must remember the opening – has vanished. Even the dispossessed Princess's sufferings as she wanders through the forest are composed into a picture, and one where, once again, all features and incidents appear upon a vertical plane:

Past ten in the forenoon, she struck a high-road, marching in that place uphill between two stately groves, a river of sunlight; and here, dead weary, careless of consequences, and taking some courage from the human and civilised neighbourhood of the road, she stretched herself on the green margin in the shadow of a tree. Sleep closed on her, at first with a horror of fainting, but when she ceased to struggle, kindly embracing her. So she was taken home for a little, from all her toils and sorrows, to her Father's arms. And there in the mean-while her body lay exposed by the highwayside, in tattered finery; and on either hand from the woods the birds came flying by and calling upon others, and debated in their own tongue this strange appearance (162).

Once more we get the effect of a skilfully-executed woodcut where the few simple but strongly delineated objects – the road, the trees, the recumbent body, the birds – are tiered one above the other in a densely-integrated filling-up of space. It is present again when, reunited with Otto, she descends once more through the trees:

A little below where they stood, a good-sized brook passed below the road, which overleapt it in a single arch. On one bank of that loquacious water a footpath descended a green dell. Here it was rocky and stony, and lay on the steep scarps of the ravine; here it was choked with brambles; and there, in fair haughs, it lay for a few paces evenly on the green turf. Like a sponge, the hillside oozed with well-water. The burn kept growing both in force and volume; at every leap it fell with heavier plunges and span more widely in the pool. Great had been the labours of that stream, and great and agreeable the changes it had wrought. It had cut through dykes of stubborn rock, and now, like a blowing dolphin, spouted through the orifice; along all its humble coasts, it had undermined and rafted-down the goodlier timber of the forest; and on these rough clearings it now set and tended primrose gardens, and planted woods of willow, and made a favourite of the silver birch. Through all these friendly features the path, its human acolyte, conducted our two wanderers downward, – Otto before, still pausing at the more difficult passages to lend assistance; the Princess following ... (184).

In these passages Stevenson clearly owes a debt to Meredith, though far more to *The Amazing Marriage* than *Harry Richmond* as the following passages, from different chapters, show. (We might note, incidentally, that Meredith also works on a vertical plane but his metonymic art-form is not the woodcut but, explicitly, a tapestry.)

The armies of the young sunrise in mountain-lands neighbouring the plains, vast shadows, were marching over woods and meads, black against the edge of golden; and great heights were cut with them, and bounding waters took the leap in a silvery radiance to gloom; the bright and dark-banded valleys were like night and morning taking hands down the sweep of their rivers.

The phantom ring of mist enclosing for miles the invariable low-sweeping dark spruce-fir kept her thoughts on them as close as the shroud. She walked fast, but scarcely felt that she was moving. Near midday the haunted circle widened; rocks were loosely folded in it, and heads of trees, whose round intervolving roots grasped the yellow roadside soil; the mists shook like a curtain, and partly opened and displayed a tapestry-landscape, roughly worked, of woollen crag and castle and suggested glen, threaded waters, very prominent foreground, Autumn flowers on banks; a predominant atmospheric greyness.[24]

It seems to me that Stevenson is not guilty of unacknowledged borrowings here; rather, he is overtly invoking Meredith's art in the same way that he invokes Shakespeare's, Weber's or Handel's so that he can weave them all into a tapestry which loudly proclaims its repudiation of the 'real' world. The ending of Book III confirms this repudiation with the re-integration of Otto and Seraphina into the pastoral world:

'Look round you at this glade,' she cried, 'and where the leaves are coming on young trees, and the flowers begin to blossom. This is where we meet, meet for the first time; it is so much better to forget and to be born again. O what a pit there is for sins – God's mercy, man's oblivion!'

'Seraphina,' he said, 'let it be so, indeed; let all that was be merely the abuse of dreaming; let me begin again, a stranger. I have dreamed, in a long dream, that I adored a girl unkind and beautiful; in all things my superior, but still cold, like ice. And again I dreamed, and thought she changed and melted, glowed and turned to me. And I – who had no merit but a love, slavish and unerect – lay close and durst not move for fear of waking.'

'Lie close,' she said, with a deep thrill of speech.

So they spake in the spring woods; and meanwhile, in Mittwalden Rath-haus, the Republic was declared (188).

Court intrigue, statecraft, ideological disputes are all an 'abuse of dreaming', and Otto and Seraphina return again to slumber in the sympathetic bosom of the timeless greenwood.

Had the story finished here what we would have been left with was a nostalgic reverie in which the squalid *Realpolitik* of late-nineteenth-century Europe was briefly illuminated by the residual glow from a more benevolent *Weltanschauung*, from Arcady itself. The idealised, enamelled beauty of the greenwood state exists out of time to satisfy all that is least physical, least time-bound in humankind: to remind it, indeed, that all that is best and enduring in it is abstract; from which comes its ability to challenge its own finitude in making music, in creating pictures which transcend their materials, and texts which, though inscribed in time, realise their significant being beyond it. The vision is a harmonious one and exists in the starkest contrast to the scheming, divided, competitive habitat of politicians.

All this has passed away before the story opens: it has, we are told, in the first paragraph, 'vanished like a morning ghost'. The last days of Grünewald and the last days of the last of its long line of princes reaching back to Perdita and Florizel of Bohemia, are indeed reconstructed but they are so only to show that Prince Otto's is a winter's tale without a spring. To this sad state of affairs, the text of *Prince Otto* brings the traditional consolation. All the carefully-wrought effects, the Meredithian arabesques, the scenes from the hunt in woodcut, the opera in the park, are there to demonstrate that, though no longer to be found in the maps of Europe, Grünewald, the greenwood state, lives on in art. What is more, Stevenson does extremely well, sometimes even brilliantly, all that he sets out to do to convince his readers of this. He couldn't be expected to know, after all, that Walt Disney would so comprehensively corrupt the notion of the pastoral that a late-twentieth-century readership would find it impossible to take its conventions seriously. But – and it is a huge 'but' – Stevenson did not leave it at this; that is, with Otto and Seraphina curled up together in a beautiful woodcut. In fact, despite being mercifully unaware of Walt Disney (there *are* consolations in dying young), he heads him off with a remarkable postscript; remarkable, because it alters our whole perspective on the book.

*Prince Otto* is, in fact, a book with two quite different endings: one I have talked about already where all the values associated with the pastoral order have withdrawn from the world and are to be found now only in art-forms like *Der Freischütz*, *Rinaldo* or Stevenson's literary equivalent of the woodcut. That comes to an end when Otto and Seraphina, recognising how far they have strayed, gladly surrender themselves again to dreaming.

The other is altogether characteristic of that side of Stevenson which so annoyed his less wary readers. Having sold them Arcadia, he proceeds to show them that it was simply one more of his 'performances'. Otto, we learn, has a great love of theatricals, but his originator cruelly reveals that the Prince, too, is a puppet. Such negating happens frequently in, for example, *New Arabian Nights* and again in *The Dynamiter*, but here it is at its most destructive. Having shown them that Arcadia is a fiction, he then proceeds to show them that there is no mysteriously creative power in art. Yet can he be believed? Will he not try the same trick again – and possibly succeed? It is a disturbing prospect but a real possibility for, unlike Prospero, he has *not* broken his staff.

Earlier writers who had exploited the romance genre occasionally discountenanced their colourful material: one prominent precursor of Stevenson even doing so in a playfully deprecatory postscript. Chapter 27 of *Waverley* is headed 'A Postscript, which should have been a Preface', and in it Scott maintains that the book is much more history than romance: 'Indeed, the most romantic parts of this narrative are precisely those which have a foundation in fact';[25] and he proceeds to pedestrianise a number of them. Stevenson goes much further than this, however and there is much irony in *his* sub-title to the 'Bibliographical Postscript' since what it does is not so much 'complete the story' as deconstruct it. Some nine publications are invented or alluded to in this short conclusion and their compilation clearly gave Stevenson a lot of pleasure; in particular, one would guess, the notion of Swinburne dedicating 'a rousing lyric and some vigorous sonnets to the memory of Gondremark' and the Naples diary of 'J[ames] Hogg Cotterill, Esq.', the nephew of Sir John Crabtree. (This far-flung namesake of the Ettrick Shepherd has also published

*Remarks on Sicily*.) There is, in fact, some evidence that Stevenson got rather carried away with the whole enterprise in that he has Roederer publish the memoirs of Herr Greisengesang, making 'a great figure of his hero'. But Roederer's great hero in the book was Dr Gotthold – the man whom he totally misread.

While the authoritarian Roederer's work is generously described as being 'able and complete', notwithstanding the giant misunderstanding at its core, Sir John Crabtree's 'famous *Memoirs on the Various Courts of Europe*' is credited with being 'bracing and vigorous', though it is recognised that Sir John 'who plays but a tooth-comb in the orchestra of this historical romance, blows in his own book the big bassoon' (189). One consequence of this is that he has attracted 'the sympathy of Landor [who] has countersigned the admiration of the public'; which rather suggests that he is represented in Landor's *Imaginary Conversations of Literary Men and Statesmen*, a nice reflexive touch to finish off the imaginary Sir John.

The allusion to the orchestra of the romance is also apt enough since throughout the whole composition up to the end of Book III, musical elements are arranged in ways which, with constant invocation of the visual and literary arts as well, provide the work with a structure that has its objective in the celebration of art. Orchestrated as they are, they bring the performance to a pitch of intensity where every manifestation from tinkling rivers to the song of birds and the jewelled beauty of the greenwood has its harmonious place.

To call it a *historical* romance is, however, self-evident nonsense: it is located outside time and has no link with the present or the past except, perhaps, as parable (though Andrew Lang denied it any such function, seeing it simply as 'free invention'). Any possibility of a physical or historical reality is subverted from the start with such names as the Greenwood State, with its capital of Middle Wood and its near-neighbour of Rubble-stone. On the other hand, its *aesthetic* reality is intense and it is in large part the product of that dense spatialisation of form which is rendered so brilliantly.

Even writers and critics of the day who were contemptuous of much 'traditional' contemporary writing were uneasy with this new offering of Stevenson's. W. E. Henley's review (which so wounded Stevenson) reveals him to be disconcerted by this book which was 'so plainly an essay in pure literature':

> It has none of the qualities of an ordinary novel. Means, atmosphere, character, effects – everything is peculiar. Mr. Stevenson has worked from beginning to end on a convention which is

hardly to be paralleled in modern literature. The ordinary material of the novel he throws aside; in half a dozen sentences gives
the results of a whole volume of realism; he goes straight to the
quick of things, and concerns himself with none but essentials....

But he concludes: 'in some respects ... it may be taken as a model by
anybody with an understanding of art in its severer and more rigid
sense, and a desire to excel in the higher ranges of literary achievement'.[26]

Other reviewers searched – sometimes rather desperately – for the
right word to describe this unusual book. Andrew Lang thought he
had found it: 'Iridescent is just the word to describe Mr. Stevenson's
fantasy in this its latest expression ... the colours flit and flash and
flow into each other, and will not bear enumeration, much less analysis
... If we were required to docket this book with Polonius-like accuracy we should call it a philosophical-humouristical-psychological
fantasy.'[27]

Both of these commentators have, however, simply ignored the
'Bibliographical Postscript' whose avowed purpose is 'To Complete
The Story'. And there, as book after non-existent book is reviewed
and, like the 'Arabian Author' and Prince Florizel of New Arabian
Nights, sent 'Topsy-turvy into space', we come on a peculiarly savage
dismissal of Otto and Seraphina. Book III had finished with them
touchingly reconciled and, deep in the greenwood, rejoicing in their
fortunate fall. (The section is sub-titled 'Fortunate Misfortune'.) But
the timeless dream they have reimmersed themselves in is rudely
interrupted by the author as he enters it to drag them out into the
'real' world, expose them to the unaesthetic ravages of time, and laugh
at how little they have to say for themselves – in this world so alien
to all they emblemised when we last saw them as babes in the wood
in the chapter of that name. Poésies par Frédéric et Amélie is Otto's
book which the narrator finds 'very dreary' and which the ever-self-
deprecating Otto has inscribed apologetically 'Le rime n'est pas
riche' (unlike the text from which he has just been so unceremoniously turfed out, we might say). Seraphina's contribution is singled
out for special derision: 'those pieces in which I seem to trace the
hand of the Princess are particularly dull and conscientious'.

The 'vulgar' description of the Prince and Princess 'ageing peace-
ably at the court of the wife's father, jingling French rhymes and
correcting joint proofs' is, of course, completely destructive of the
idyll that has preceded it; but it can also be taken as a declaration of
no confidence in the whole business of book-making – at least as

anything other than a frivolous enterprise. Having thrown out the baby, he then, quite sensibly, gets rid of the bathwater. If all book-making is as puerile as *Poésies par Frédéric et Amélie* or *The Diary of J. Hogg Cotterill, Esq.*, or *Memoirs on the Various Courts of Europe* (including the non-existent), why should anyone bother to practise the art of fiction? Unless it were as a game of blind-man's buff to while away a few idle hours until one got tired and removed the blindfold.

Once again Stevenson, having solemnly set certain rules for his fiction, deliberately violates them to show that all art, be it never so strenuously wrought, is, so to speak, a *Tempest* in a tea-cup. He has charmed his readers with cloud-capp'd towers and almost-gorgeous palaces, and now he tells them, as he did in *New Arabian Nights*, that the fabric of the vision is baseless. But Prospero had exercised his magic for a purpose: to get back his dukedom; and the achievement of his aim brings some degree of comfort. Stevenson, however, having expelled his faithful readers from the greenwood, offers them no Milan. He has apparently adopted Gotthold's view that the sum of human achievement is to 'write and obliterate'.

Prospero had, of course, entered a sort of postscript of his own when he reminded retired magicians, restored dukes and their diversity of creatures that all of them *à la fin des fins* – as Stevenson was fond of saying – are such stuff as dreams are made on and thus as insubstantial as his 'pageant'. That sobering truth is rendered a bit more palatable if, in the interim before the reality strikes home, you can have a good time in Milan or, alternatively, a quick fix of pastoral in the greenwood. But Stevenson offers no such palliatives. Because of the 'Bibliographical Postscript', there 'To Complete The Story', the most we get out of the beautiful, gentle romance of the greenwood is pleasure in the ingenious process by which we have been fooled – and a great fear that we shall get caught up in the spell-binding sleight-of-hand all over again.

**Notes**

1. Maixner, op. cit., p. 176.
2. Ibid., p. 176.
3. Ibid., p. 178.
4. Ibid., p. 178.
5. Ibid., p. 189.
6. Ibid., p. 194.
7. Ibid., p. 194.

8. Ibid., pp. 177–9.
9. Gertrude Stein, op. cit., p. 36.
10. Edwin Muir, *The Structure of the Novel* (1928), p. 63.
11. Ibid., p. 85.
12. Joseph Frank, *The Widening Gyre; Crisis and Mastery in Modern Literature* (New Brunswick, NJ, 1963), pp. 54, 56–7.
13. Ibid., p. 60.
14. Gillian Beer, *The Romance* (1970), p. 78.
15. Malcolm Bradbury, *Possibilities: Essays on the State of the Novel* (Oxford, 1973), p. 12.
16. Bernard Bergonzi, *The Situation of the Novel* (1979), pp. 188–9.
17. Malcolm Bradbury, op. cit., pp. 81–2.
18. Ibid., p. 85.
19. Gillian Beer, op.cit., p. 8.
20. Maixner, op. cit., p. 188.
21. Maixner, op. cit., p. 198.
22. As well as being home to a Grand Duchess, Gerolstein was also the principality of Sue's Prince Rodolphe in *The Mysteries of Paris* and he, of course, was the model for Prince Florizel in *New Arabian Nights*. Presumably Anna's Grand Duchy grew out of Rodolphe's principality.
23. Op. cit., p. 263.
24. George Meredith, *The Amazing Marriage* (1895), pp. 41, 47.
25. Walter Scott, *Waverley* (1972), p. 493.
26. Maixner, op. cit., p. 185.
27. Maixner, op. cit., p. 181.

# 5
# *Kidnapped* and *Catriona*: The Missing Storey

'... if the ghost of a man's own father cannot be allowed to claim his attention, what can, Sir?'

Joe Gargery in *Great Expectations*

'Maroon you! We are not living in a boy's adventure tale ...'

The Captain in Conrad's *The Secret Sharer*

David Balfour tells lies about his age. At least he does so in the first edition of *Kidnapped* and those subsequent editions which take it as their master text. In Chapter 1 he tells us that he is sixteen but in Chapter 27 he tells Rankeillor very precisely that he was born on the 12 March 1734, which makes him seventeen. A mere slip of the pen? Perhaps, but we have long been taught to regard such slips as significant.

Stevenson's late-adolescents are always telling us that they are unready for manhood, that they are mere lads, mere boys, even mere children; thus delaying a little longer the painful confrontations which will earn them their spurs. Of such is David Balfour. Though he may appear from the opening sentences to be precipitately ready to launch himself into the adult world, it is immediately obvious that such a translation for him is of a story-book kind – more accurately of a ballad-kind, for when he discovers the treachery of his uncle, he sees his own story to be 'like some ballad I had heard folk singing, of a poor lad that was a rightful heir and a wicked kinsman that tried to keep him from his own' (21). Much later he looks forward to knocking at Rankeillor's door to claim his inheritance 'like a hero in a ballad' (188). The simple fact is that David is altogether ignorant of what it is that distinguishes the adolescent from the adult male and has no idea of the complex psychological processes the change will entail.

*Kidnapped* opens with what appears to be the decisive shutting of a door. For a naive David Balfour, locking the door between himself and his dead father is a gratifying assertion of independence: 'I will begin the story of my adventures with a certain morning early in the month of June, the year of grace 1751, when I took the key for the last time out of the door of my father's house.' Despite the recent death of his parent, David's spirits are light as he takes his departure, apparently at one with the jocundity of his surroundings:

> The sun began to shine upon the summit of the hills as I went down the road; and by the time I had come as far as the manse, the blackbirds were whistling in the garden lilacs, and the mist that hung around the valley in the time of the dawn was beginning to arise and die away.

But the summit upon which the sun shines, though it may seem a hopeful symbol of David's aspirations, is just one of what will be many misleading signs, and a good deal of the protagonist's journey will take place on a vast and featureless moor whose desolation will bring him near to total demoralisation, if not, indeed, to death. For the blitheness of David's departure from the paternal home rests on a delusion, namely that he is fit and ready for the adult world; that displacing the father and assuming his role is as easy as turning a key in a lock and that it is an act he is capable of carrying through to its appropriate conclusion thereby achieving maturity and independence.

Complete as it is with the ritual blessing of the initiate by the minister (who escorts his youthful parishioner away from the father's home), David's start is nonetheless a false one. It is so because, in a sense, he believes he has already arrived, assuming that by the mere act of turning a key, he has acquired the necessary self-sufficiency to exercise the authority demitted by his father and so earned his place in the great world which lies beyond that of his Essendean childhood. 'When all you want to do is to arrive', says the tutor in *Emile*, 'you can dash in a post-chaise; but when you want to travel, you must go on foot.'[1] At this point, David has no idea of just how much travelling he has to do, nor of the true nature of the journey.

Bearing this out, Chapter 1 is optimistically entitled 'I set off upon my journey to the House of Shaws', and the heading of Chapter 2 is 'I come to my journey's end'. The latter turns out to be more than a little ironic, however: what he has arrived at is not a solid, prosperous family seat, sanctified by time and capable of confirming the authority and identity he has naively arrogated to himself, but appropriately enough, a half-built shell which appears to him to be 'a kind of ruin' (8). Access to this identity-confirming 'home' is not along a fine, long-established avenue, but by means of 'a little faint track in the grass ... very faint indeed to be the only way to a place of habitation' (9).

So much for his having 'arrived', but worse is to come. The gateway – the outer portal – consists only of stone uprights with a coat of arms on top and an unroofed lodge beside them, no fine gates enclosing his demesne to open at his command: 'A main entrance it was plainly meant to be, but never finished; instead of gates of wrought iron, a pair of hurdles were tied across with a straw rope...'. Direct access is effectively blocked by the hurdles and David has, ignominiously, to follow the path which skirts the pillars 'and [goes] wandering on towards the house'. His journey, begun with such complacency and self-confidence, peters out in this indeterminate, meandering track. The house itself, the object of his travels, is scarcely more formed: 'What should have been the inner end stood open on the upper floors, and showed against the sky with steps and stairs of uncompleted masonry. Many of the windows were unglazed, and bats flew in and out like doves out of a dovecote' (9).

At this first reversal, David's disappointment is acute: 'Was this the palace I had been coming to? Was it within these walls that I was to seek new friends and begin great fortunes?' (10). And the journey, which had started with him shutting and locking his father's door forever ends with him raining 'kicks and buffets' on that 'great piece of wood all studded with nails' which was to have admitted him to man's estate in general and the estate of Shaws in particular. When it does eventually open it allows David into a deeply hostile world which threatens to cut him off long before he achieves either estate. This is the *true* beginning of his journey.

Since doors or thresholds play a conspicuous part in Stevenson's fiction it is useful to remind ourselves of the significance Bakhtin ascribes to them in *The Dialogic Imagination*. There he coins the term 'chronotope' to define particularly resonant time–space intersections which certain images embody (and in doing so help to define '[a] literary work's artistic unity in relation to an actual reality'). He singles out three images, all of which carry a considerable burden of signification in *Kidnapped*. They are the road, the threshold and (less emphasised) the staircase. The chronotope of the road allows the spatial and temporal series defining human fates and lives [to] combine with one another in distinctive ways ... [it] is both a point of new departure and a place for events to find their denouement. Time, as it were, fuses together with space and flows in it (forming the road); this is the source of the rich metaphorical expansion on the image of the road as a course: 'the course of life', 'to set out on a new course' ... ; varied and multi-levelled are the ways in which road is turned into a metaphor, but its fundamental pivot is the flow of time.

Bakhtin then goes on to mention another chronotope, that of the threshold where he defines its 'most fundamental instance' as the 'chronotope of *crisis* and *break* in a life'. The word 'threshold', he notes, has already a metaphorical meaning in everyday usage but in literature 'the chronotope of the threshold is always metaphorical and symbolic'. In Dostoevsky, he points out, 'the threshold and related chronotopes – those of the staircase, the front hall and corridor ... are the main places of action in his works, places where crisis events occur ... decisions that determine the whole life of a man'.[2] *Kidnapped*, it is clear, is structured by two of these chronotopes – the threshold (or door) and the road – while a third, that of the staircase, provides us with the book's most vivid and indelible image which is also one of its most telling.

David Balfour's meeting with his uncle is the first of his major encounters (also a Bakhtinian chronotope) on his particular road. Ebenezer, the embodiment of generational hostility, is the first of several menacing father-figures whom David has to confront. By removing David's real father, a deceitful nature had apparently conducted its own by-pass surgery for the oedipal condition, leaving the adolescent to conclude that the arterial route to adulthood was straight and unobstructed. Extravagantly true to Freudian type, Ebenezer attempts to bring about David's death and chooses a method of doing so rich in appropriate symbolism. David, transfixed at the top of an unfinished staircase, the abyss into which he is about to step suddenly illuminated in a flash of lightning, provides a vivid image for his own incomplete development and the vulnerability accompanying it. Having been sent by his uncle (despite the darkness) to bring down a chest from a room at the top of the stairs, David discovers, when part-way up, that neither the tower nor the stairs has been completed:

This was the grand stair! I thought; and with the thought, a gust of a kind of angry courage came into my heart ...

The tower, I should have said, was square; and in every corner the step was made of a great stone of a different shape, to join the flights. Well, I had come close to one of these turns, when, feeling forward as usual, my hand slipped upon an edge and found nothing but emptiness beyond it. The stair had been carried no higher: to set a stranger mounting it in darkness was to send him straight to his death ... (25).

That his uncle should have devised such a premature ending for David is, of course, eloquent of *his* need to ensure that his nephew will never succeed in dispossessing the father-substitute. His failure precipitates just what he had feared: David now has his eyes opened to his uncle's enmity: 'there was no doubt I carried my life in my hand, and he would leave no stone unturned that he might compass my destruction' (28). The reflection brings a surge of confidence and a growing ambition: 'it would be a fine consummation to take the upper hand, and drive him like a herd of sheep ... I saw myself in fancy smell out his secrets one after another and grow to be that man's king and ruler' (28). A fine consummation indeed, with its hint of sexual dispossession or emasculation wrapped up in the son's undisguised lust for sovereign power over the father.[3] But dislodging and degrading the father-substitute is no easy matter.

It may be thought paradoxical to claim that what demonstrates conclusively the strength and urgency of David's need to assert himself in the ritual struggle between father and son is the unexpected appearance of another, much more dramatically unfinished being, Ransome, 'the half-grown boy in sea-clothes' whom David finds on the doorstep. The claim is, however, altogether defensible for no Stevenson character is sufficiently trustful of a benevolent Providence to say 'there, but for the grace of God, go I'. The grotesque, stunted figure capering on the doorstep is a terrifying reflection of what David fears might yet turn out to be the truth about himself.

Brief as his appearance is, Ransome, this half-grown boy, is one of the harshest indictments in all of Stevenson's work of the cruelty of the father-oppressors and of a religion which likes to claim that it has at its apex a Heavenly Father of infinite love and mercy. The image of Christ the ransomer is nowhere to be seen in the creature whose corrupted innocence is painfully displayed in a precocious and foolish worldliness. The only identity remaining to him is that of victim, any other human quality having been erased in his suffering and humiliation. When David opens the door to him, he gives no name, only a performance: 'He had no sooner seen me than he began to dance some steps of the sea-hornpipe ... snapping his fingers in the air and footing it right cleverly' (29). This is, in fact, his debased and degraded signature, for the performance is merely that, signifying nothing except the vacuous routine of the clown.

A few sentences earlier, David had been reminiscing about his own arrival at his uncle's door 'no better than a beggar and little more than a child'. Discounting 'child' – David is, as I have said, given to minimising his age – the characteristically self-pitying reflection helps to connect him with this 'half-grown' figure on the doorstep. David feels an intense compassion for Ransome: 'there was something in his face, a look between tears and laughter, that was highly pathetic and consisted ill with his gaiety of manner' (29). But the affinity goes deeper than humane compassion, for David recognises in him something in the nature of a *Doppelgänger*, and it is not at all surprising to learn that, long after the story ends, Ransome still 'comes about [him] in [his] dreams' (47). What he has done, in effect, is to confront David with a vivid image of one who has all too clearly been launched prematurely into an adult world – and has *not* developed though (worse still) he thinks he has. Strengthening the links between them, David takes him indoors and gives him the rest of his own breakfast which the boy devours, grimacing the while in a way which, David concludes, 'the poor soul considered manly'. Later he tells us that he tried 'to make something like a man, or rather I should say something like a boy of the poor creature, Ransome. But his mind was scarcely truly human' (46).

Predictably, Ransome is also fatherless, and also has difficulties with his age. He tells David that 'he had followed the sea since he was nine, but could not say how old he was as he had lost his reckoning' (31). He has cultivated an admiration for Captain Hoseason because he believes that the latter's brutal and unscrupulous character is 'something seamanlike and manly'. His appalling condition (the physical abuse he has suffered being illustrated, in David's words, by 'a great, raw, red wound that made my blood run cold'), his pathetic attempts to represent himself a man, move David profoundly: 'I have never felt such pity for anyone in this wide world as I did for that half-witted creature...' (32). But David is greatly given to *self*-pity and it is hard not to see him beginning to perceive something of his own predicament in this creature whose development has been so drastically stunted, whose father is also dead and his place taken by a brutal surrogate (in league, as it turns out, with David's own callous father-substitute) and whose premature pretensions to manhood have proved to be grossly incapable of substantiation.

It has already been hinted that there may be another dimension to Ransome which links him both to David and all fatherless – or even Fatherless – victims despised and rejected of men. Names are nearly always of more than passing significance in Stevenson's work and here especially so. The brig is called the *Covenant*, its captain, Hoseason, its cabin-boy, Ransome. The ship's name is a reference to one of the Scottish Covenants either of 1638 or 1643 (entered into by Scottish Presbyterians in defence of their religion) or to the covenant between God and the Israelites whereby God was to be worshipped as the one true God. More likely it is the latter for the captain's name is easily read as Hosea-son, and Hosea was the prophet whose oracles (as they are rendered in the Book of Hosea) consist of an account of the offence given to God by the Israelites and conclude with God's offering his covenant to them. What these names suggest is, of course, the duplicity of words and world: David has decided that 'the brig *Covenant* (for all her pious name) was little better than a hell upon the seas' (32); and Hoseason gives ample evidence of being remote from God's counsels even though he is Hosea's son. Ransome, we can see then, represents a travesty of Christian love not, as his name might signify (and does in Conrad's *The Shadow Line*), the finest expression of it. His corrupted innocence and bruised flesh are evidence of the inefficacy (or simply the brutalisation) of the Redeemer son, and of the absence of the Father.

The ironic ambiguities in all three names convey an image of the world as a deceitful place where acts, agencies, relationships and, above all, words seemingly descriptive of one thing – like a covenant with God – can come to stand for their very opposite. One's own relationship to the world is therefore far more uncertain and far more difficult to establish with any confidence as a 'true foundation' than David at first assumed. The Master of Ballantrae's derision for anyone naive enough to aspire to being *un homme de parole* seems likely to serve the voyager better than an uncritical trust in a prescribed and classified order of things. Emile's tutor might have added that reading signs aright is also an essential part of travelling successfully.

Ransome, who had 'lost his reckoning' and could not tell his age, knows virtually nothing about his father except, ironically, that he made clocks. David Balfour also, it seems, has known less about his father than he believed though enough to contradict the inn-keeper's confident assertion that he had been murdered. At least by the time he is kidnapped he has begun to suspect the truth: that his father was the elder brother and so the rightful heir to the estate of Shaws, but he has to wait until the very end of his adventure to have this confirmed. And like Ransome, he is more than a little inclined to see Hoseason as a father-substitute. Just before the latter has him knocked on the head and shanghaied, David notices him on the pier 'among his seamen, and speaking with some authority'. Observing him carry 'his fine, tall figure with a manly bearing', he wonders if Ransome's stories about him could be true, 'they fitted so ill with the man's looks'. The answer is a familiar Stevensonian one: 'in fact, he was two men, and left the better one behind as soon as he set foot on board his vessel' (38). Even then, however, he has an appeal for David despite his known duplicity so that when, after the fight in the round-house, he presents himself to David and Alan, he wins something more than compassion from David by impressing what might be called father-appeal on a bad filial conscience:

> A little after the captain came ... and stood there in the rain, with his arm in a sling, and looking stern and pale, and so old that my heart smote me for having fired upon him (72).

David will never condemn Hoseason outright any more than Jim Hawkins will excommunicate Long John Silver. However, in the immediately-following exchange with Alan Breck, Hoseason's affronted insistence that his word is his bond re-establishes his duplicitousness; and his effrontery is pounced upon by Alan:

> 'Captain ... I doubt your word is breakable. Last night ye haggled and argle-bargled like an apple-wife; and then passed me your word and gave me your hand to back it; and ye ken very weel what was the upshot. Be damned to your word!'(72)

Hoseason is *un homme de parole* only so far as it suits him, as Alan Breck makes clear, though less ready than James Durie to acknowledge it.

From this point it is now possible to review the nature of the tale Stevenson has presented to us, and to adjust our focus and our expectations. The opening is a clever feint for it is certainly not the beginning that it appears to be: at the end of that journey a door is shut fast against David and when it does open, it admits him not to a fine inheritance, a defined place in the world, in filial succession to a dead father, but to an unfinished building and a future, it seems, of interminable wandering, of innumerable departures and arrivals. David's brash assumption in Chapter 1 that his journey's end is virtually within sight is knocked on the head as effectively and expeditiously as he himself is soon to be on the *Covenant*. He has, in entering the House of Shaws, no more than put his foot on the first step of the staircase of his adult future when the problematic nature of that objective is graphically revealed in the transfixing flash of lightning. Our doubts about his ever reaching the top of the staircase are reinforced if we recall the author's own experience recounted in 'A Chapter on Dreams':

> while he was yet a student, there came to him a dream-adventure which he has no anxiety to repeat; he began, that is to say, to dream in sequence and thus to lead a double life. ... Well, in his dream-life, he passed a long day in the surgical theatre, his heart in his mouth, his teeth on edge, seeing monstrous malformations and the abhorred dexterity of surgeons. In a heavy, rainy, foggy evening he came forth into the South Bridge, turned up the High Street, and entered the door of a tall *land*, at the top of which he supposed himself to lodge. All night long, in his wet clothes, he climbed the stairs, stair after stair in endless series, and at every second flight a flaring lamp with a reflector. All night long, he brushed by single persons passing downward – beggarly women of the street, great, weary, muddy labourers, poor scarecrows of men, pale parodies of women – but all drowsy and weary like himself, and all single, and all brushing against him as they passed. In the end, out of a northern window, he would see day beginning to whiten over the Firth, give up the ascent, turn to descend, and in a breath be back again upon the streets, in his wet clothes, in the wet, haggard dawn, trudging to another day of monstrosities and operations.[4]

The passage goes some way to explaining the motif of the staircase which recurs in a number of Stevenson's works. Where a young man is concerned, the ascent is towards maturity and independence: an ascent which, the dream shows, he feels reluctantly compelled to make. The effort and loneliness entailed by the undertaking are vividly clear – 'all drowsy and weary like himself, and all single ...'. When we find Weir of Hermiston climbing 'the great bare staircase of his duty', he may be protected from much of the loneliness by his self-sufficiency, but the image is, just the same, one of isolated and endless endeavour. David Balfour is a fairly extreme projection of the 'dream-adventurer' whose progress up the staircase is going to be abruptly terminated by the 'bad father', Uncle Ebenezer, but even for Weir the ascent is going to end in a void, as we shall see in a later chapter.

From the start, David has, in fact, behaved in a way suggestive of a latent contest with the inhibiting influence of the father. The actual death of the latter is brushed aside with as little ceremony as Jim Hawkins shows towards the same event in *Treasure Island* and as little sense of bereavement. (The similarity is altogether striking.) And just as Hawkins has, in Billy Bones, a ready surrogate for whom he shows more affection, so David finds one in Mr Campbell the minister. From him he readily gets the love *and* the legitimising blessing which Stevenson's young men on the brink of manhood seem always to be deprived of by their natural fathers.

David's 'escape' from the house of his dead parent symbolised by his turning the key in the lock, is accompanied by a sense of relief which finds its correlative in the pleasure he gets from his new, extramural environment to which he reacts like a prisoner who has just been given his liberty ('I took the key for the last time out of the door of my father's house. The sun began to shine ...'). His eager readiness to lock the door between himself and his father forever is a clear invitation to see the episode in Freudian terms as the figurative murder of the father: that necessary event which allows the son to enter upon his inheritance, free to exert his own authority, social and sexual, as well as to become, in turn, author of the Law which, in Lacanian terms, sustains the symbolic structure. Yet, though the perspective is a valid one, David's act is not at all as decisive as this would make it appear. The fact remains that, for all the brisk confidence of his departure from his father's home, David has not actually *chosen* this course, which would have made the renunciation of the father, implicit in a young man's setting forth upon his travels, more telling; he really had no alternative. By dying unrenounced, as it were, this father has evicted his son, renounced *him*, one might say.

Nonetheless, David's response is to act as though he *had* taken the initiative, appearing to believe that he is fully capable of that self-sufficiency necessary to establish an *oikonomic*[5] of his own. Thus, precipitated though his departure may have been, the journey which he sets out upon is still a journey into manhood and a supersession of the father. His not having really taken the initiative, however, means that his development from adolescent to adult will be more than usually problematic. Stevenson's most perceptive illustrator, N. C. Wyeth, shrewdly represents David as a 'handsome brawny boy whose burly shoulders and well-developed muscular arms and legs seem too powerful for his sensitive and almost girlish face'.[6] Predictably, his way ahead will be thickly populated with menacing father-figures with whom he will not be able to escape confrontation.

All that said, the relished turning of the key *is* an important gesture involving repudiation. Freud himself stressed the possibility that the postulated first act of parricide might well have happened only within 'psychic reality'.[7] Subsequent to the turning of the lock in his father's door, David's travels are, of course, one long extended metaphor for a progress towards maturity and adulthood. There is nothing new in this; in fact it is something of a commonplace for journeyings of this sort to be seen as a rite of passage to manhood. Departing the family home, leaving the father (dead or alive) is clearly representable as a renunciation of the father, particularly if, like Robinson Crusoe or Charles Darwin, the son has been explicitly ordered *not* to travel. Teresa de Lauretis formalises this in a perception of the discourse of travel as a 'technology of gender', a set of 'techniques and discursive strategies' by which gender is constructed. Georges Van Den Abbeele in his book *Travel as Metaphor* (from which the de Lauretis quotation comes) locates the discourse of travel in relation to Freudian theory thus:

> The son can only succeed the father if he can establish a relation of resemblance between himself and his father. But this states the necessity for the son of making himself like the father, of *making* what distinguishes the father part of himself, of internalizing his fatherliness. Thus the institution of the law of the father in such a way that it makes the son worthy of succeeding him, that is, of becoming a father in his own turn. And yet, this metaphorical process of internalization or incorporation, this institutionaliza-tion of the father through such ceremonies as rites of passage and tests of lineage, must take place without the father.... Paradoxically, one must move away from the father in order to come near him, ... : just as one must turn oneself into one's home, so must one turn oneself into (the image of) one's father, but both of these transformations can only be effected by leaving home and father. The succession to fatherhood has the structure of a voyage (as the succession of places defining an itinerary to or from a home) insofar as the father becomes the point of reference (*oikos* or home) for the stabilization or domestication of family relationships.[8]

We would be mistaken, however, if we were to assume from the opening that what we were to get was a simple, Freudian-based

*Bildungsroman* which would show David Balfour developing from a callow, self-righteous youth into a man of considered judgement and mature self-awareness, ready to take his place in the adult world. In the event, he gets stuck halfway through the process, for though he loses his innocence of the world – having started off priding himself on his sixteen- (or is it seventeen-?) year-old worldliness – he never achieves, or feels that he achieves, maturity and independence. The whole tale, in fact, comes to reflect his anxiety on just this issue.

His early naiveté is well rendered near the start of his travels while he is on his way to the House of Shaws when he chances on a regiment of soldiers on the march: 'The pride of life seemed to mount into my brain at the sight of the red-coats and the hearing of that merry music' (6). By the time he has become not just a traveller but a hunted fugitive in direst peril from these same red-coats, his toytown view of soldiery will have undergone a dramatic change. As such it is symptomatic of a more significant shift in his view of himself and his relation to the world, in particular the abandonment of his complacency and illusory self-sufficiency.

Having had these assumptions radically challenged, David actually *regresses* and becomes more passive; self-pitying instead of self-assertive, and more dependent. So strongly does this regression – accompanied by a recurring paralysis of the will – colour the second half of the book that *Kidnapped* transcends the character-building adventure-tale to become a tormented story of arrested development. Images of desolation, anxiety and acute alienation predominate with virtually nothing to suggest a resolution to the problem thus exposed.

Though it is not, I believe, legitimate to elide the two books, it is true that in *Catriona*, written some six years later as a sequel to *Kidnapped*, David's education is taken further. Under Prestongrange's tutelage, he learns that honourable principles quickly become obfuscated in the *Realpolitik* of government. It is also true that he at length gets round to proposing to, and ultimately marrying, Catriona. But it is a near-run thing and to the end of that book David continues to bemoan his youth and his unreadiness for adulthood. The image which encapsulates the moment of his coming of age and remains most powerfully printed on our memories is that of a lachrymose hero, his suit just accepted, wrapping his arms round Catriona's knees and being cradled in the bosom of the woman who, as so often in Stevenson, is both lover and mother.

David's failure to develop is marked in another way, which is itself curious. Depending on which edition we use, he is sixteen or seventeen at the beginning of *Kidnapped* and for the next eight months or so he takes great care to keep us abreast of the calendar. It is early in June when he leaves his home, he tells us, and Chapter 21 begins: 'Early as day comes in the beginning of July ...'. Towards the end of his and Alan's flight when David is sufficiently convalescent to resume his travels, he takes the trouble to up-date events. Chapter 26 begins: 'The month as I've said, was not yet out, but it was already far through August, and beautiful warm weather with every sign of an early and great harvest ... '. Chapter 27 provides us, almost gratuitously, with another useful date: David's actual birthday. In reply to Rankeillor's question, 'Where were you born?', he replies 'in Essendean, sir, ... the year 1734, the 12th of March' (which, of course, make him seventeen). Though we are not told in *Kidnapped* the date on which the story closes, *Catriona*, its sequel, does. We leave David outside the British Linen Company bank and we discover him in *Catriona* emerging from it in the opening sentence on 'the 25th day of August, 1751, about two in the afternoon'.[9]

*Catriona*, in fact, demonstrates the same concern that we should follow a precise calendar of events. Chapter 5 opens: 'The next day, Sabbath, August 27th ... ', Chapter 8, 'The next day, August 29th ... ', and it also tells us that the trial of James Stewart 'is to be held in Inverary, Thursday, 21st *proximo*' (65). From these opening sentences we can deduce from the Writer Stewart's comment that 'Andie picks [Alan] up at Gillane sands tomorrow, Wednesday' (75), that this important event occurs on 30 August. Chapter 9 ends with the Writer (who is one of James Stewart's defence counsels) arranging to meet David on 16 September. But David, a key witness on behalf of James Stewart, is, of course, kidnapped and held captive on Bass Rock, his jailers' instructions being to release him on 23 September (124) by which time the trial is supposed to be over. Chapter 16 opens thus: 'On the seventeenth, the day I was trysted with the Writer, I had much rebellion against fate' (139). David is still a prisoner as he is on the next date of importance: 'The 21st, the day set for the trial, I passed in such a misery of mind as I can scarce recall to have endured ... ' (140). Early on the 23rd he is taken off the Rock and persuades Andie to land him near Stirling so allowing him to reach Inverary on the 24th – just too late to testify, even though the jury had not retired until the previous evening. On 25 November (188) David takes ship for Holland and we do not get any more calendar clues (not even Christmas) until p. 271 when David and Alan arrive in Dunkirk 'Near dark of a January day'.

One reason for the author's care in recording the passage of time with such fidelity is, obviously, to add to the excitement and tension: that so much can happen to David Balfour in such a short time (and in three different countries) undoubtedly adds pace to the narrative. There is, however, another reason which touches on the nature of *Kidnapped* and indeed of *Catriona*.

While *Waverley*-like elements continue to recur (particularly in the Highland scenes but also in the attitude of Edinburgh's professional classes), providing us with a perspective on the Highlanders and Jacobites which shows them swimming against the stream of history, this is not what these novels are 'about'. Neither, as has been noted, is either novel in any definitive sense a *Bildungsroman* or *Erziehungsroman* where the young hero undergoes a number of testing situations which result in the advancement of his moral education as he learns more about the world and himself. While there are elements of both these 'kinds', these are essentially novels about unfinished business, or interrupted development, strikingly emblemised in *Kidnapped* by the unfinished House of Shaws as well as by the stunted figure of poor Ransome. It is true that David tells us that he eventually embellishes the place much as he and Miss Grant had passed the time imagining when waiting for Prestongrange – but that is something which happens at some quite distant time, outside the book's action and, interestingly, even then appears to have had more to do with establishing 'plantations, parterres and a terrace' (182), rather surprisingly leaving us only to infer that the building of the mansion and its gatehouse (which symbolised so much in their unfinished state) has also been completed.

The real effect of accumulating these dates is the way it draws our attention to the fact that so much has happened but so little has changed, though some concessions have to be made in the case of *Catriona*. When David, Rankeillor and the others pass the Hawes Inn again towards the end of *Kidnapped*, David, having recognised the landlord, 'was amazed to see him look no older' (210). The reader is inclined to think the same of David, I would suggest. Thus, while the constant reference to the calendar registers the swift passage of time, it fails to chart equivalent progress in David towards manhood, as though, somehow, he were out of time, stranded in an invisible eddy.

The lack of development is reflected not just in the proliferation of departures and arrivals, but in the fact that the place David finally

arrives at – and where the narrative simply stops – is not intrinsically an end but a means (of further travel, among other things), that
is, the British Linen Company's bank. That David's journey should
end at a *point de départ* confuses arrivals and departures in such a
way as to suggest the impossibility of coming to any final destination and hence completing the story.[10]

As I have said, *Kidnapped* is a novel of arrested development. All
the extravagant evidence of hectic flight and travel testifies to the
intense desire to break out of a disabling adolescent imprisonment
into that fuller self-realisation deemed to lie on the other side of adolescence, and conventionally embodied in such concepts as maturity and
independence. It demonstrates the necessity for the son, described
by Van Den Abbeele, of 'making himself like the father, of making
what distinguishes the father part of himself, of internalizing his
fatherliness'. Despite the apparent resolution of the crisis at the end
of *Catriona*, it, too, conforms in very large measure, to the same paradigm, at times making more explicit aspects of that inhibited
maturation process which dominate the earlier novel.

It is in the aftermath of the shipwreck (appropriately enough) that
the extent of the crisis afflicting David reveals itself. Under the tutelage of Alan Breck, David may have indeed been blooded in the
defence of the roundhouse ('Let's make a bit of a soldier of ye,
David', says Alan [62]), but his initiation into the martial arts does
not prove to be a turning point. Far from it, in fact, as he finds
himself a particularly helpless castaway on the island of Earraid.

David, we cannot fail to notice, exhibits lamentably little ability to
take control of events, and he is far from being alert to seize his
chance should any accident offer him an advantage. Characteristically,
after Ransome's death he takes the latter's place as surrogate cabin-
boy with remarkable docility. It is instructive to compare his behaviour
when the ship founders with Alan Breck's when his small boat is run
down by the brig. Though 'encumbered with a frieze overcoat that
came below his knees', Alan had managed to kick free and grab the
brig's bowsprit which 'showed that he had luck and much agility
and unusual strength' (55). David, by contrast, when he lands in the
water becomes a passive victim and, once on Earraid, gives way to
despair, believing himself to be cut off from the mainland. Of course
Earraid is an island only at high tide, so that we are forced to see

David's reaction for what it is: as self-marooning on an island of aborted maturity. Thus, at precisely that moment where, following his display of manly resolve which allows him (in the best tradition of adventure-fiction) to execute several of his abductors, David might be thought to have begun to exercise some control over his destiny, the very opposite happens and he islands himself on Earraid.

In fact, the Earraid episode is carefully prepared and actually starts *before* the siege in the roundhouse about whose outcome David is pessimistic:

> I do not know if I was what you call afraid; but my heart beat like a bird's, both quick and little.... As for hope, I had none; but only a darkness of despair and a sort of anger against all the world that made me long to sell my life as dear as I was able (64).

This blackness of mood provides a stark contrast with the hero's *joie-de-vivre* of the opening paragraphs; the world, he is discovering, is not going to be his oyster (rather appropriately it proves, instead, to be his limpet – and makes him sick when he eats it!) and his earlier presumptuous self-confidence supplies him with no resources with which to meet this reversal of expectations. But it is David's lack of maturity and resolution which is at issue here, for such a reversal of expectation is everyone's experience though most come to this realisation without being shanghaied or marooned.

'The novel of pure adventure', writes Bakhtin in 'Discourse on the Novel'

> frequently reduces the potential of the novel as a genre to a minimum, but nevertheless a naked plot, brute adventure cannot in itself ever be the organizing force in a novel. On the contrary, we always uncover in any adventure the traces of some idea that had organized it earlier, some idea that had structured the body of the given plot and had animated it, as if it were its soul, but that in pure adventure novels has lost its ideological force, so the idea continues to flicker but only feebly.[11]

To the extent that there is much more than a trace of an organising idea in *Kidnapped*, it obviously exceeds the definition of a 'pure adventure story'. From the beginning, in fact, a well-modulated psychological realism, very much in tune with its period, has provided a substructure for the tale, though the rapid unfolding of events has emphasised the more superficial elements of the boy's adventure-story where realism of any sort seems only pigment deep. Now, in the aftermath of the foundering of the brig, what surfaces with David is a convincing moral realism as he begins to suffer the sort of existential crisis that can afflict the adolescent caught in the toils of the maturation process, cripplingly aware of the possibly too-exacting demands of adult self-realisation. Appropriately enough the limbo he is falling into, the expression of his growing self-alienation, is represented in his becoming a castaway on what seems to him to be the worst sort of desert island. Indeed, the word 'desert' becomes something of a *Leitmotiv* for the rest of David's travels – with all that that implies for the success of his journey to independence and manhood.

David's is a crisis, however, which we can see to have been forming since he closed his father's door with such premature and misplaced self-confidence. The journey towards self-resolution and adult inheritance, begun with such insouciance, had almost immediately run into the obstruction of Uncle Ebenezer, for the first time forcing an at least partial awareness on the protagonist of what such a journey as his would involve. But David, despite this revelation, was still complacent enough to be easily outwitted, underestimating the power and resourcefulness of the treacherous father to whom he lost the initiative. Instead of the bold voyager faring forth in tenacious pursuit of 'the internalization of the father through such ceremonies as rites of passage and tests of lineage', the very opposite happened. Falling easy victim to a blunt instrument, David had been carried away unconscious in the brig *Covenant*, destined for slavery in a West Indies plantation. Even to himself he seemed to be little more than an inert commodity, complaining that the 'dogs of thieves' of the *Covenant* 'had *stolen me* from my country' (60: my italics).

His complacency and naiveté had, however, at last been brought home to him: 'with the clear perception of my plight, there fell upon me a blackness of despair, a horror of remorse at my own folly, and a passion of anger at my uncle...' (41). Rounding Cape Wrath with a shipload of destroyed illusions would have been the beginning of wisdom for many a fictional traveller and the ensuing shipwreck an opportunity for a new start to his journey. But what happens? David's journey doesn't proceed anywhere, but instead turns into a giant eddy with the hero powerless, it seems, to break out of it and cross that last narrow channel on one side of which lies self-sequestration on an island of aborted maturity and on the other, adulthood.

The more superficial action of the boy's adventure-story is now held in abeyance, and at this pivotal point (almost literally the centre of the tale) David's state of mind becomes the focus of interest and its depiction, appropriately enough, draws on something like a surreal mode of representation. As the *Covenant* goes down, David quite literally floats free of everything and for a while is 'out of himself' as far as that self is identified with and through conventional time and place. Once in the sea David exerts little positive effort to save himself: he cannot swim and floats into the bay dog-paddling behind the spare yard-arm which, as he tells us, he had 'found' he was holding on to. True, once in calm waters beyond the tide-race in which he has so nearly drowned, David exerts himself 'in about an hour of kicking and splashing' until he can wade ashore. Stevenson is careful in preparing us for what is to follow: 'The sea here was quite quiet; there was no sound of any surf; the moon shone clear, and I thought in my heart I had never seen a place so desert and desolate' (89).

The draining-away of sound and colour, to be replaced by a sense of desolation, suggests a premonition of moral dislocation leaving an impression that the island is not what it seems (which indeed it isn't). Yet despite its centrality and the change of emphasis it embodies, the episode on Earraid has been curiously neglected by critics, and the rich symbolic pickings usually to be had from desert islands and maroonings have been in this case largely ignored. Even Wallace Robson in his excellent essay 'On *Kidnapped*' is dismissive of it, seeing it as sounding 'a comic note' and, perhaps, like some other incidents while David and Alan are parted, 'put in deliberately to relieve the tension'. Yet the same critic can observantly note 'how much emphasis there is in this part of *Kidnapped* on the state of mind which David calls 'horror'.[12] Robert Kiely is one of the few to see some of the potential in the situation referring to the episode as a miniature *Robinson Crusoe*, but David himself draws a sharp contrast between his position and Robinson Crusoe's:

> In all the books I have read of people cast away, they had either their pockets full of tools, or a chest of things would be thrown upon the beach with them, as if on purpose. My case was very different … and being inland bred, I was as much short of knowledge as of means (92).

David is acutely aware of his being utterly on his own with no providential assistance in the shape of tools or anything else. And his own insufficiency is brought home to him in the most unequivocal way. That he himself should regard this period as 'the most unhappy part of [his] adventures '– given all the vicissitudes he endures before he is brought by 'the hand of Providence' to the British Linen Bank – reinforces the obligation to take the episode seriously.

At the beginning of this strange chapter of his existence there is another of those odd dissonances we occasionally find in this book, and this one, too, has to do with the passage of time. 'It was half-past twelve in the morning', David tells us with precision and we cannot help wondering how he knew. Then the precision immediately dissolves:

> There was no sound of man or cattle; not a cock crew, though it was about the hour of their first waking; only the surf broke outside in the distance. ... To walk by the sea at that hour of the morning, and in a place so desert-like and lonesome, struck me with a kind of fear (90).

The reference to the time may have been a slip but 'a kind of fear' certainly isn't, for after its considerable airing in this, one of the longest chapters in the book, it recurs from now on with such frequency as to join the word 'desert' in becoming a *Leitmotiv*. Fear, or at least anxiety, dominates this hero whether scanning the sea for the vanished brig – 'I was afraid to think what had befallen my shipmates and afraid to look at so empty a scene' – or even when looking for rescue: 'I had become in no way used to the horrid solitude of the isle, but still looked round me (like a man that was hunted) between fear and hope that I might see some human creature coming' (93).

The terms in which Earraid oppressed him – 'The time I spent upon the island is still so horrible a thought to me, that I must pass it over lightly' (92) – make it clear that his fear and loneliness are existential. What heightens and at the same time helps to focus the moral crisis, however, is the fact that, unusually, it is an island where the rest of the world – and, therefore, salvation – is only just out of reach. It seems as though David can almost touch these symbols of a resolved life – spiritual and domestic – in the adult world:

> from a little up the hillside over the bay, I could catch a sight of the great, ancient church and the roofs of the people's houses in Iona. And on the other hand, over the low country of the Ross, I saw smoke go up, from morning and evening, as if from a homestead in a hollow of the land (93).

His tantalising nearness to solving his predicament is brought out again when he suddenly thinks of using the yard-arm to get himself across the narrow creek which separates him from the mainland. He finds it still floating in the bay and wades in to retrieve it. However, as the water rises to his face his attempt at self-rescue is again frustrated: 'at that depth my feet began to leave me and I durst venture in no further. As for the yard, I saw it bobbing very quietly some twenty feet in front of me' (92).

The most dramatic of these three 'trials' is the appearance of the fishing boat which passes so close to him that he can tell the colour of the crew's hair and distinguish their speech as Gaelic. But the fishermen ignore him. It is only when they return and David catches the word 'tide' when they shout to him that he guesses the truth, to wit that Earraid is an island only at high tide, and he realises that the depths of anguish and anxiety he has suffered (to say nothing of a fairly close brush with death) are entirely the result of his own failure to cope with the predicament he finds himself in. If there is anything comic in this, however, it is the comedy of the absurd where the human condition itself is a howling farce when viewed from an Olympian perspective.

Thus, from his brash self-confidence at the beginning which rested on spurious notions of self-sufficiency and maturity, David proceeds essentially to discover that he is far from having laid the paternal ghost. The unconfronted father, refusing to be so easily despatched by his callow son, jumps out at him again in the shape of the murderous uncle and, to a lesser degree, Captain Hoseason. Now, quite alone, he has to confront *himself* and face up to his own weakness. That this youth should suffer an acute existential crisis at an early stage in his wandering is therefore entirely authentic; and even without a knowledge of Jungian archetypes, we recognise that a barren islet supplies an ideal *mise-en-scène* for its exposure. Its appositeness is all the more patent given the specific nature of his crisis, rooted as that is in the adolescent's nightmare vision – so terrifyingly illustrated in Ransome – of a selfhood fatally arrested in mid-development, able to discern the adult mainland but separated from it by the unbridgeable gulf of his own immaturity and insufficiency. Burdened by that insufficiency – his inability to swim or to tell edible from poisonous shellfish, for example – he several times comes near to death. As he readily concedes, he has none of the resourcefulness of Robinson Crusoe and the mere raising of the analogy is enough to confirm that this character is Crusoe's exact opposite. To Defoe's hero, finding himself on a desert island is a challenge to establish his mastery over his environment, not to subordinate himself to it, far less to give way to self-pity and despair. In triumphantly meeting the challenge, Crusoe shows himself to have all the makings of the independent, self-reliant entrepreneur, which amounts to a catalogue of David's deficiencies. (Crusoe, one could argue, even acquires a son in Man Friday.)

Setting aside the metaphor of travel momentarily, David's journey should have been from Essendean to Shaws and then to Edinburgh where judicial process would have established the legitimacy of his claims to the estate of Shaws. Twice, however, David deviates from his prescribed path, once involuntarily and once quite deliberately after a serious debate with himself. When we reinstate the metaphoric and symbolic significance of travel, as *Kidnapped* quite clearly requires us to do, the importance of these deviations is obvious. Postponing arrival means postponing the sort of legitimisation alluded to in Van Den Abbeele's somewhat congested account of the imperatives of filial succession.

The indictment against David for the first deviation must be confined to criticism of his unreadiness for the challenges implicit in such a journey, an unreadiness compounded of ignorance, vanity and misplaced self-confidence. His second detour is altogether different, however, and his culpability is much greater. Explicitly he turns aside from the path which would lead to Edinburgh and an invocation of the law in his own interests, and allies himself with an *outlaw*. The text lingers on the choice confronting David, so magnifying its significance. Just before he is due to meet Alan Breck again he sits down by the wood of Lettermore to consider his position: 'Here I was not only troubled by a cloud of stinging midges, but far more by the doubts of my mind' (116). Remarkably often, at significant moments or when decisions have to be made, David confesses that his ears are troubled and his mind confounded by what is going on around him: 'I saw he was speaking but the roaring of the falls and the trouble in my mind prevented me from hearing...' (137). When he discovers his nightmarish predicament on the unfinished staircase, he tells us: 'my ears were now troubled and my mind confounded by a great stir of bats in the top part of the tower, and the foul beasts, flying downwards, sometimes beat about my face and body' (24). What he is now considering here in Lettermore is what he again calls the folly of his going to join 'an outlaw and a would-be murderer' instead of acting 'more like a man of sense' and tramping straight to Edinburgh to settle his own affairs.

David's concern with the law is not, it should be emphasised, of merely practical significance. He depends on it, of course, for the legitimisation of his inheritance but that in itself takes us straight to the fundamental significance of the law in the son's aspirations to take the place of the father and himself assume fatherhood. Freud's reading of earlier anthropological analyses of social structures convinced him that the authority of the father resided in his being the sole originator and guarantor of the law which gave structure to family and clan, manifesting itself particularly in the prohibition of incest. Following and extrapolating from Freud, Jacques Lacan argues that when the sons 'metaphorically murder the father, they bind themselves as subjects "for life to the Law", to certain symbolic structures, to the cultural prohibition against incest, to a positionality in the chain of signifiers that is culture and language'. [13] David's determination to invoke the law against Uncle Ebenezer is, therefore, a claim to a good deal more than the estate of Shaws. But though both *Kidnapped* and *Catriona* are crowded with lawyers, these men have a knack of turning into father-figures themselves and turning the law *against* David so that he seems forever to be denied access to that state where he can become the law-giver. Concomitant with this position is David's harping on his own unreadiness for this position – ultimately and quite explicitly the position of father – until it comes to seem that the fault lies altogether with him as it was shown to do on the island of Earraid.

Though understandable, it is too simple to read David's indecision as to whether he should go to Edinburgh as part of the romantic/realist debate, not least because David has strenuously insisted that he is immune to the 'romance' of the Jacobite or Highland cause. What induces this 'canny goer' (as his father had called him) to abandon, for the time being at least, his pursuit of legal redress and the substantiation of his title as the rightful laird of Shaws, is not Alan's cause but Alan himself. Instead of making a decisive move towards independence by *proving himself at law*, he binds himself to yet another father-substitute.

It has been noted earlier that David's boyish pleasure in the sight of redcoats when he was on his way to Shaws was a mark of his naiveté – particularly if one considers all that had happened to his country a mere five years before. Now, on his way across Loch Linnhe to meet Alan, he has his second sighting of the military and this time his reaction is quite different. It is noteworthy that he himself points the contrast when he learns what the 'little moving clump of scarlet' signifies when he glimpses it on the far side of the loch: 'it was a sad sight to me; and whether it was because of my thoughts of Alan, or from something prophetic in my bosom, although this was but the second time I had seen King George's troops, I had no good will to them' (115).

Prophetic or not, within the hour (or so it would seem), the Red Fox has been assassinated and David has become a fugitive, hunted by the same redcoats. Flight is now the only option, confirming David in his passive role, a victim of authority apparently no nearer exercising it despite his tentative arrogation to himself of the title 'laird of Shaws'. In the partnership with Alan, it is the latter who devises their escape strategy and all depends precisely on his local knowledge and survival skills – those commodities of which David had shown himself so bereft on Earraid. Despite his condescension towards Alan and his tendency to regard him from the elevation of his seventeen years 'as a mere child', David is completely dependent on him. The absent authority-figure is found in this man who never tires of telling us that he 'bears a king's name', and he sustains the role better than most in the book.

Where Stevenson shows both insight and consistency is in his portrayal of the tension between David and Alan, adding to the psychological authenticity by having the younger man the more dissatisfied, repeatedly saying that the two must 'twine' (part). David couldn't survive independently if he and Alan were to 'twine', yet resentment builds up in him to such a degree that this comes to be the end he seeks above all. The growing anger amounting at times almost to hatred is extremely well done, particularly in its mix of the justified and the spurious. In fact, David is actually making some progress in his own development here. Maturity, he is discovering, is not to be gained merely by locking your dead father's door behind you as you set out on your travels. In Alan Breck he finds a man, twice as old as he, who will guide him through a series of dangers, a man towards whom he will feel a powerful attraction which is not devoid of some libidinal element, and a man whom he will fear much as a child might fear its father: 'I saw Alan knitting his brows at me, and supposed it was in anger; and that gave me a pang of light-headed fear like what a child might have' (159). It is fear of Alan, David tells us plainly, which keeps him going (lending him 'a

false kind of courage') in the flight through the heather after he had
betrayed his trust (when his head 'was nearly turned with fear and
shame') by falling asleep during his watch (155, 154).

David's fear of Alan may seem a trifle extravagant but it is important to remember that he is continuing to experience the mental and
moral crisis figured in his sojourn on Earraid. His tendency to see
himself as victim is given dramatic reinforcement when he witnesses
Colin Campbell's murder and becomes a suspect but his response is
a dramatic and indulgent externalisation of that crisis in self-devel-
opment, the solution to which seems as far off as ever:

> So we sat again and ate and drank, in a place whence we could
> see the sun going down into a field of great, wild, and houseless
> mountains, such as I was now condemned to wander in with my
> companion (126).

Chapter 22, 'The Flight in the Heather: the Moor', is peppered with
references to 'desert land', to the country before them 'lying as waste
as the sea', and, of course, to despair. When the moor has at last been
safely traversed, David collapses; but the collapse is not entirely
physical, the general vacancy of things weighing heavily on him: 'a
sort of horror of despair set on my mind so that I could have wept
at my own helplessness' (159). The precise source of David's malaise
is never specified – to him it is 'a general black abiding horror' (66),
or 'a groundless horror and distress of mind' (162). Yet it is remarkably sustained for all that and the flight with Alan seems less a contrast
with the island experience than a continuation of it: indeed he remarks
on aspects of his physical distress being the same as the afflictions
he had experienced on the island (172).

If David rises to the challenge that Alan imposes, he does so with
every fibre of his body in revolt. Extreme weariness plays a part but
there is in these expressions a surplus of unexplained meaning, of
occult significance, which is never fully disclosed. When he tells us,
for example that 'anger would come upon me in a clap that I must
still drag myself in agony and eat the dust like a worm' (156), there
is surely a manifestation of that temper which would in the end
rather resign from life than sustain the endless demands and
confrontation which seem to be an essential part of getting even a
modicum of command over one's destiny.

David sees his suffering as unique, and his experiences on the
island and in the flight through the heather are linked by his appeal

to literature and literary history to validate the claim. 'My case was very different', he says, when comparing his predicament as a castaway with those other cases '[in] all the books I have read' (92). This time it is physical exhaustion and a growing conviction that the demands made upon him by the world are too great:

> By what I have read in books, I think few that have held a pen were ever really wearied, or they would write of it more strongly. I had no care of my life, neither past nor future, and I scarce remembered there was such a lad as David Balfour. I did not think of myself, but just of each fresh step which I was sure would be my last, with despair – and of Alan, who was the cause of it, with hatred. Alan was in the right trade as a soldier; this is the officer's part to make men continue to do things, they know not wherefore, and when, if the choice was offered, they would lie down where they were and be killed. And I dare say I would have made a good enough private; for in these last hours, it never occurred to me that I had any choice, but just to obey as long as I was able, and die obeying (156–7).

David's expatiation on his sufferings in this passage is of particular interest for it explicitly casts Alan in the role of authority and himself as the humble and submissive private soldier whose simple task it is to do or die. His supine conduct here ('it never occurred to me that I had any choice') leaves little room for optimism about his progress to maturity and independence.

Casting Alan as an authority-figure, David could be expected to get at odds with him: the absent father can, after all take many shapes. The quarrel when it comes is excellently realised but, predictably, it ends by David collapsing and being virtually carried by Alan who reproaches himself for not remembering that David was 'just a bairn' (178). And indeed when they reach Edinburgh and finally part, David, carrying his island on *his* back, feels once again 'lost and lonesome' and, he tells us, 'could have found it in my heart to sit down by the dyke and cry and weep like any baby' (223). He doesn't, of course, but sensibly carries on to the British Linen Company bank, though he leaves us with the teasing allusion to 'a cold gnawing in [his] inside like a remorse for something wrong' (223). We can only guess that his sense of guilt has something to do with his relationship to Alan and the way he had abused it. After all, the 'hatred' that he at times claims he feels for Alan is the obverse and the measure of that very deep affection that had drawn him to his side in the first place and then kept him there when he had a choice to do otherwise.

In her balanced and sagacious biography *RLS: A Life Study*, Jenni Calder remarks of the ending that it furnishes the book with a certain ironic symmetry framed as the tale now appears to be between the minister at one end and David's providential delivery at the bank on the other.[14] Though an attractive proposition, this would mean that the 'canny goer' has come into his own, albeit without much effort on his part since the last sentence is: 'The hand of Providence brought me *in my drifting* to the very door of the British Linen Company's bank'. I would argue that David, far from coming into his own, still doesn't know what his 'own' is (as the gnawing at his vitals might suggest). Symmetry there might well be but it could be constituted by the fact that this is no more a real ending than David's departure from Essendean was a real beginning. The abrupt conclusion to the tale in a single-sentence paragraph leaves the impression that the account is as unfinished as David himself. As such, it is not unusual in Stevenson's writing where endings are often inconclusive (as in *The Ebb-Tide*) or ambiguous (as in *The Master of Ballantrae*). It is worth reminding ourselves that when he finished *Kidnapped* Stevenson had no sequel actually planned – and it took many years for it to appear.

When David emerges from the British Linen Company six years later in *Catriona*, nothing has changed, except that he is now accompanied by a porter and 'a bag of money'. The year is still 1751, the date is 25 August and the question uppermost in the reader's mind as he or she opens the book is bound to be: is this where David finally grows up? Certainly he shows himself much more willing now to take the initiative. In fact, he takes on the whole system of justice in a Scotland still in political turmoil following the Jacobite rising and defeat, taking his stand on admirable principles but again being out-manoeuvred by those he would seek to best whose creed is pragmatism naked and unashamed. His objective may be a noble one but he remains a boy in a law-giver's world and one whose single-minded pursuit of principle is, in this tarnished context, doomed to failure. His retrospective view that politics is 'all bones and blackness' may have found a striking phrase, but it is, in fact, a somewhat facile expression of callow youth rather than a mature judgement. In truth, he delivers the remark with something like relief as he washes his hands of the whole sorry business and prepares to pursue his study of the law *outside* Scotland.

Making every allowance for David's worthiness of purpose, it cannot escape notice that what he is doing at the same time is submitting himself to a series of father-figures who have the power of life and death over him, perhaps, even, *because* they have that power. Thus while arrogating to himself (with no little self-righteousness) the right, even the duty, to make moral judgements, he shows simultaneously his *lack* of independence. The fact is actually emphasised by having this sententious teenager harangue the Lord Advocate on ethical practice at one moment and the next disarm criticism by reminding his interlocutors of his youth. Thus to Lord Prestongrange, the Lord Advocate: 'But for me, who am just a plain man – or scarce a man yet – the plain duties must suffice.' David has just been warned by the Advocate that James Stewart's death may be the price of staving-off civil war:

> 'To protect the life of this man Stewart – which is forfeit already on half a dozen different counts if not on this – do you propose to plunge your country into civil war, to jeopardise the faith of your fathers, and to expose the lives and fortunes of how many thousand innocent persons?' (38)

David sees no complications:'If the country has to fall, it has to fall.' Yet this is hardly the admirable repudiation of political pragmatism it might appear to be. Though seemingly preoccupied with standing firm on a principle of personal loyalty, even striking an attitude of uncompromising moral rectitude, he is always inclined to contextualise this with his own youthful unreadiness for a man's part which thus seems to be always there to account for – or even prepare the way for – failure. This image of youth which hasn't yet made the breakthrough into adulthood is always represented in these two ways: by David's own attraction towards the authority or father-figure, and by his harping on his own youth.

At least in this novel (unlike *Kidnapped*) there is a serious attempt by David to confront these figures, even to challenge them. Of his many skirmishes with them, his engagements with Lord Prestongrange, the Lord Advocate, offer the liveliest and most extensive evidence. What he gets from him is a lesson in *Realpolitik*. Prestongrange bluntly tells him that 'Patriotism is not always moral in the formal sense' (36) and defends the claims of political necessity: 'I regard in this matter my political duty first and my judicial duty only second' (37), and he takes his stand on the maxim *Salus populi suprema lex* (35). Despite his condescending to engage in argument with David, Prestongrange makes clear how completely the latter is in his power: 'I should tell you ... your fate lies with me singly. In such a matter ... I am more powerful than the King's Majesty ...' (33). He also makes it clear that he does not believe David has reached the years of discretion (32) and he redresses the balance between them in a way that reproves David and manoeuvres him into apparently playing the role of a presumptuous son under instruction:

> 'Tut! Tut! young gentleman', says he 'be not so pragmatical and suffer a man who might be your father (if I was nothing more) to employ his own imperfect language and express his own poor thoughts even when they have the misfortune not to coincide with Mr Balfour's' (36).

Though sensible of Prestongrange's forbearance and grateful for it, David is still not inclined to absolve him of duplicity:

> He smiled upon me like a father as we spoke, playing the while with a new pen; methought it was impossible there could be any shadow of deception in the man: yet when he drew to him a sheet of paper, dipped his pen amongst the ink, and began to address me, I was somehow not so certain, and fell instinctively into an attitude of guard (66).

David's final word on Prestongrange is surprising in the force with which it confirms this suspicion. Having admitted that 'this was a man that might have been my father, an able man, a great dignitary', (159) he concludes: 'He was kind to me as any father, yet I ever thought him as false as a cracked bell' (169). As elsewhere in Stevenson's work, fatherhood, threats and treachery seem to go naturally together in an alarmingly frequent coalition. When David encounters the unscrupulous Simon Fraser he learns that the great Duke of Argyll himself has heard of him and, presuming he takes the right decisions, will 'watch upon [him] with the affectionate disposition of a father' (49); and again there is the implied threat of serious consequences for the 'son' if he does not accept this surrogate father's benevolence.

There is yet another treacherous father to deal with and he, too, is willing to sacrifice David's life if it advantages his own case. This is

Catriona's father who ultimately becomes, if only for a short period before his death, David's father-in-law. From the start, David conceives an intense aversion towards James More and that start is an attempt by James to borrow money from the young man; the malice of his foes having, as he neatly puts it, 'quite sequestered my resources' (42). His suspicions of James are, however, more than justified, he thinks, when he hears that he has been summoned from prison to see the Lord Advocate and recalls Simon Fraser's reference to men in prison ready to 'redeem their lives by all extremities'. James, it seemed, would be persuaded to bear false witness, committing 'murder by the false oath', with David as the intended victim. At least, however, it strengthens the bond with Catriona: her cherished honour being aspersed in the father's behaviour at the same time as David's life is put at stake by James More 'bargaining his vile life for mine'. And in a sentence which brings them all closer together he adds: 'I saw her now in a sudden nearness of relation, as the daughter of my blood foe, and, I might say, my murderer' (55). By standing up to James it could be argued that in *Catriona* David *does* eventually confront the father and win his adult spurs. At the end, after besting the resilient James again (with the help of Alan), David and Catriona marry.

But to entertain some reservations is still in order. Catriona's aunt, the formidable Mrs Ogilvy, unquestionably has David's measure. Describing him as 'countryfeed' she ensures that the word not only signifies what is provincial in him but also his stiff-necked self-righteousness: 'ye'll have to soople your back-bone, and think a wee pickle less of your dainty self', she tells him and gives him some advice about his transactions with women: 'and ye'll have to try to find out that women folk are nae grenadiers. But that can never be. To your last day you'll ken no more of women-folk than what I do of sow-gelding' (59).

David's Mackellar-like response confirms Mrs Ogilvy's judgement: 'I had never been used with such expressions from a lady's tongue ... Mrs Campbell and my mother being most devout and particular women.' Observing his shock, Mrs Ogilvy follows up with another thrust which says something about the significance of the match between these two young people so very different in temperament:

'Keep me!' she cried struggling with her mirth, 'you have the finest timber-face – and you to marry the daughter of a Hieland cateran! Davie, my dear, I think ye'll have to make a match of it – if it was just to see the weans' (59).

There is, however, much more in David's relationship to Catriona than the laying of the groundwork for a symbolic union of prosaic Lowland canniness with Highland ardour and romance. Primarily there is the constant theme of his doubts about his readiness for adult commitment with its concomitant in his frequently-expressed loneliness in the midst of a desolate landscape, and his passivity. Mrs Ogilvy's somewhat risqué conversation now gives, as he says, his 'thoughts a boldness' when he thinks of Catriona:

> I let myself flow out to her in a happy weakness and looking all about, before and behind, saw the world like an undesirable desert, where men go as soldiers on a march, following their duty with what constancy they have and Catriona alone there to offer me some pleasure of my days. I wondered at myself that I could dwell on such considerations in that time of my peril and disgrace; and when I remembered my youth I was ashamed (59).

It is really all there: passivity struggling with a sense of duty requiring a more energetic reaction, selfishness – Catriona's role is to be nothing more than this weary young foot-soldier's consolation – and the refuge sought in a disclaimer of adulthood. 'A tall strong lad of about eighteen' is how he had been portrayed in the 'wanted' poster but his unwillingness to give up the status of a 'lad' is everywhere. 'I had yet to learn, and know and prove myself a man; and I had so much sense as to blush that should I be already tempted with these further on and holier delights and duties'. Reminding himself of his upbringing he concludes sternly: 'I knew that he was quite unfit to be a husband who was not prepared to be a father also; and for a boy like me to play the father was a mere derision' (60).

He has seriously entertained the thought only, it seems, to erect a barrier to its fulfilment in a somewhat exaggerated insistence on his youthfulness. He is alone in the world, he tells Catriona self-pity-ingly, destined to die a shameful death 'and me scarce a man' (62). She, in turn, tries to put some steel into him: 'Fy! this is no time to crouch. Look up! Do you not think that I will be admiring you like a great hero of the good – and you a boy not much older than myself' (64). The last remark is of interest since it provides the rather surprising – and telling – information that she who has always seemed older than David, is, in fact, younger; and he might very well be, as he says, 'but a child frightened by bogles', turning to this youthful companion for maternal comfort. Or is it *paternal* for she earns from David the description of 'a bloodthirsty maid' (54) and herself admits that 'I am made this way, I that should have been a man child. In my thoughts it is so I am always: ...' (84). She is impressed when she elicits from David the fact he has killed two men, but of course he spoils the effect for her by adding characteristically, 'and me still a lad that should be at college'(54). Whether it is welcome or not, Catriona endorses his opinion of himself when she concludes: 'You are true, you are brave; in time I think you will be more of a man yet. I will be proud to hear of that' (72). The matter, however, seems still in the balance as late as Chapter 25 when James More is of the opinion that 'we shall make a man of you yet, Mr David' (240).

There is a sense in which David is always on the verge of being 'islanded' all over again: his sense of acute loneliness in the middle of deserts and desolate wastes, his pessimistic view of the blackness of society, his self-centredness and self-preoccupation. And, of course, it happens. This time David is neither shipwrecked nor responsible for his own marooning. Prestongrange needs to get rid of an inconvenient witness determined, in spite of all threats and blandishments, to testify at James Stewart's trial. So David is kidnapped for a second time and carried off to the Bass Rock, an island some five miles from the Scottish mainland but well within sight of it. At first not knowing his destination when he is taken off in a fishing boat, he fears that he is once more on his way to a larger vessel and hence once again to the plantations, but this time, with 'no second Alan, no second shipwreck ... I saw myself hoe tobacco under the whip's lash' (118). In fact, matters are very different on the Rock from what they were on Earraid. For one thing, it is genuinely an island surrounded by a deep and turbulent sea, for another there is plenty of company, and finally there is the certainty that in due course, his sequestration will come to an end. David honestly admits all this: 'I should trifle with my conscience if I pretended that my stay upon the Bass was wholly disagreeable' (123).

David eventually arrives at Inverary just too late to give evidence on behalf of James Stewart. But though he has failed in his enterprise there is nowhere the feeling of near-collapse into total mental depression and paralysis which the desolate places of the Highlands threaten to bring David to in *Kidnapped* and the difference is very much summed up in the contrast offered by his two maroonings. In this case, in fact, he is so much more in command of the situation that he can maroon his captors, even describing them as 'our maroons' (144). The only time the Earraid distress is near to being replicated is when the 21st arrives – the day of the trial – and he realises that he has failed: 'I passed [the day] in such misery of mind as I can scarce recall to have endured, save perhaps upon Isle Earraid only' (140).

*Catriona* could well have ended with David turning his back on politics but he has still to make the break into adulthood, and winning Catriona is part of the process and virtually all of the evidence. Such a break could have been achieved easily enough had not Stevenson made David's problems with maturity an absolutely central concern in *Kidnapped* and its sequel. So there has to be a further 'proving-time' to see whether he will ever enter upon his inheritance as an adult male. The confrontation with the surrogate father James More is part of this proving process, but David's ability to leave adolescence behind him and cross the all-important threshold is in doubt right to the end and probably beyond. Only a prolonged sojourn in the company of Catriona offers any hope, it seems, and Stevenson submits him to it as to a course of hormone therapy.

So once again – and for not entirely dissimilar reasons – David sets out on an arduous journey. His criss-crossing of the Low Countries, though less dramatic than his flight through the heather with Alan, is a continuation of that journey. Alan, however, could not be both father and lover, though the curious blurring of the very large age gap ('about 18' to 'about 35' according to the poster) allows feeling to reach a pitch where some physical expression or manifestation seems to wait only on the hazard of time, chance and opportunity.

To the youth trapped in an adolescent time-warp there is nothing inauthentic in an equivocal libidinal element entering into the relationship between son and father. Nor is the fact that this aspect of the relationship has stalled at this subliminal level expressive of a repressed homosexuality. Quite the contrary, in fact. A sexual relationship will not be actualised precisely because David is *not* homosexual: there is no self-realisation for him that way, so he has either to get though the adolescent barrier and achieve a heterosexual masculine identity or ignominiously stick where he is at the rather-more-than-half-way point. And it is touch and go.

In Chapter 23 we find again that familiar voice, the wail of the not-yet-enfranchised youth. Struggling to work out what to do with the unworldly Catriona when she is rendered dependent on him in Holland by the desertion of her father (absent fathers don't only afflict sons) David is terrified of compromising Catriona, yet aware of the powerful feelings urging him to see that they stay together. (It never occurs to him, so *self*-engrossed is he, that he might employ a duenna.)

'You are a very young maid,' said I, 'and I am but a very young callant. This is a great piece of difficulty. What way are we to manage? Unless, indeed, you could pass to be my sister?'
'And what for no?' said she, 'if you would let me!'
'I wish you were so, indeed!' I cried. 'I would be a fine man if I had such a sister. But the rub is that you are Catriona Drummond.'
'And now I will be Catrine Balfour,' she said. 'And who is to ken? They are all strange folk here.'
'If you think that it would do,' says I. 'I own it troubles me. I would like it very ill, if I advised you at all wrong.'
'David, I have no friend here but you,' she said.
'The mere truth is, I am too young to be your friend,' said I. 'I am too young to advise you, or you to be advised. I see not what else we are to do, and yet I ought to warn you' (220).

David is, in fact, being set a fair trial. The dangerously innocent Catriona – 'I am cast upon your hands like a sack of barley meal, and have nothing else to think of but your pleasure' – has to be found shelter, but in sharing this shelter with her, David is too-nearly approaching that position of husband or lover which he continually doubts his readiness for. At the same time, ironically, by simply cohabiting with her he may well ruin her in the eyes of others. Nor can he leave her. The understatement in her words when she contemplates the possibility of his *not* looking after her ('– she turned and touched her hand upon my arm – "David I am afraid"') is expressive and moving, and really leaves David with very little choice.
So he and Catriona set up house as brother and sister and are there discovered by the far-from-unworldly James More. The latter instinctively sets about turning the situation to his own advantage, and aware of David's expectations, decides that he should marry Catriona regardless of her views on the matter; which helps to establish him as a false father. As usual his utterly selfish objectives are cloaked in fatherly concern:

'I am a careful parent, Mr Balfour; but I thank God, a patient and deleeberate man. There is many a father, sir, that would have hirsled you at once either to the altar or the field ...' (254).

When rebuked by David for shouting at him in his own chamber, he becomes apologetic, asking for the offence to be set down to 'the agitation of a parent' (254). Something more like the truth emerges in another exchange with David who is trying to find out how James comes by the money he believes him to be receiving. James professes outrage:

> 'I bid ye beware. I will stand no more baiting ... I am sick of her and you. What kind of a damned trade is this to be a parent! I have had expressions used to me –' There he broke off. 'Sir, this is the heart of a soldier and a parent,' he went on again, laying his hand on his bosom, 'outraged in both characters – and I bid you beware' (263–4).

James's hypocrisy and self-concern are there on and between every line. In David's view he was 'so false all through that he scarce knew when he was lying' (248). Yet when David also says that 'I saw him to be perfectly selfish with a perfect innocency in the same' (247), a bell surely rings and we are uncomfortably aware that while he can notice this quality in James he does not recognise its kinsman in himself.

To the end, then, even in *Catriona*, there is some doubt as to the success with which David surmounts the barrier between adolescence and maturity. The unfinished staircase which nearly brought about his death in *Kidnapped* is no doubt complete in the refurbished House of Shaws and now that he has the strong support of Catriona there is every chance that he will ascend it. Yet it sometimes looks as though he is going to have to be carried up and perhaps, in a certain sense, he was: when, after their marriage, David proposes going to see James More, Catriona's reply – 'If it is your pleasure' – is followed by David's rather dry comment: 'These were early days.' At all events, at the climactic moment of his proposal to her, he contrives to make his appeal so abject that it could only be directed at one who was perceived to be rather more mother than lover: '"Try to put up with me," I was saying, "try to bear with me a little."' And again (as she remains silent): '"Catriona" I cried ... "is it a mistake again? Am I quite lost?"' When Catriona accepts him, the tableau composed by the two figures is just what we should expect after two volumes crammed with what the detumescent hero perceives to be threats of emasculation: the adolescent-male, in a position half-way between couchant and rampant, embraces the knees of a young woman who is, madonna-like, bent over him cradling his head on her breast:

I kneeled down before her in the sand, and embraced her knees, and burst into that storm of weeping that I thought it must have broken me. All thought was wholly beaten from my mind by the vehemency of my discomposure. I knew not where I was, I had forgot why I was happy; only I knew she stooped, and I felt her cherish me to her face and bosom, and heard her words out of a whirl.

## Notes

1. Jean-Jacques Rousseau, *Emile*, trans. Allan Bloom (Penguin Classics, 1991), p. 412.
2. M. M. Bakhtin, op. cit., pp. 243–4, 248.
3. In his recent book *The Haunted Study*, Peter Keating gives considerable space to generational conflict. See, in particular, the important discussion of the subject in Chapter 3, 'Parents and Children', where he quotes Edwin apostrophising his father in Bennett's *Clayhanger*: '"When you're old and I've *got* you"–he clenched his fist and his teeth–"When I've *got* you and you can't help yourself, by God it'll be my turn!"' (p. 234). There is an element of the same exultation in David's relishing the power he thinks he has over Ebenezer.
4. 'A Chapter on Dreams' in *Further Memories*, pp. 43–4.
5. The usage is Georges Van Den Abbeele's in *Travel as Metaphor*, p. 100. Basing his remarks on Rousseau's article for the *Encyclopédie* on political economy ('The word Economy ... is derived from *oikos* a house, and *nomos*, law and meant originally only the wise and legitimate government of the house for the common good of the whole family'), he extrapolates from this that, in Rousseau, it is 'The father who defines the home' (p. 114).
6. Susan R. Cannon, 'The Illustrator as Interpreter: N. C. Wyeth's Illustrations for the Adventure Novels of Robert Louis Stevenson', in *Children's Literature* , vol. 19, 1991.
7. 'the mere impulses of hostility towards the father and the existence of the wish phantasy to kill and devour him may have sufficed to bring about the moral reaction which has created totemism and taboo.... The causal connection which stretches from that beginning to the present time, would not be impaired, for the psychic reality would be of sufficient importance to account for all those consequences. 'Totem and Taboo', in *The Basic Writings of Sigmund Freud*, ed. A. A. Brill (New York, 1938), p. 929.
8. Georges Van Den Abbeele, op. cit., p. 99.
9. Stevenson more than once shows himself wanting to push the age of his young protagonist beyond that which his young readers might expect or accept. Jim Hawkins started as 14 but appears to have had his age revised upwards like David Balfour's. The point is that they have to be old enough plausibly to experience that crisis in maturation which their

author wants to expose them to but still young enough to allow a young readership the opportunity of identifying with them.

10. Cf Van Den Abbeele's discussion of Rousseau's *Emile and Sophie* in *Travel as Metaphor*, p. 101.
11. M. M. Bakhtin, 'Discourse on the Novel', op. cit., p. 390.
12. Wallace Robson, op. cit., pp. 110, 115.
13. The formulation is Dianne Sadoff's in *Monsters of Affection*, p. 79.
14. Jenni Calder, *RLS: A Life Study* (1980), p. 189.

# 6

# *Jekyll and Hyde*: The Story of the Door

it will strike me myself as strange that the case histories I write should read like short stories.

Sigmund Freud

The double stands at the start of that cultivation of uncertainty by which the literature of the modern world has come to be distinguished.

Karl Miller

Today two things seem modern: the analysis of life and the flight from life.... One practises anatomy on the inner life of one's mind, or one dreams.

Hugo von Hofmannsthal

'The Sire de Malétroit's Door', one of Stevenson's earliest short stories, was published in 1878 and gives the first substantial indication of his interest in the symbolic potential of doors (stairs come later). In the story, the symbolism develops surprising ramifications: surprising, at any rate, given that Freud was at that time still an unpublished young man of twenty-two. The door has, of course, as much to do with domestic architecture as the china in *The Country Wife* has to do with household ornaments, Sir Willoughby Patterne's leg with walking or Mme Bovary's carriage-ride with sight-seeing in Rouen. So laden with sexual significance is it, in fact, that it's a wonder it stays on its hinges.

Eight years later come in quick succession *Jekyll and Hyde* and *Kidnapped*, and each of these major works starts with an allusion to a door. In *Kidnapped*, the resolute shutting of a door seems to promise David Balfour much, but instead of marking a new and crucial chapter in his life, it turns out to be an act of self-deception signalling a false beginning. Doors and deception, it would seem, go together.

215

In *Strange Case of Dr Jekyll and Mr Hyde*, the first chapter is given the title 'Story of the Door' and so also raises certain expectations: principally, that we shall be given access to what lies behind it. The deferral of the fulfilment of these expectations not only heightens our interest and desire to know, it also gradually focuses more and more interest on the story as story, the text as text. When, in the penultimate chapter, an inner door – this door's double so to speak, a 'red baize door' giving public access to the same space – is broken down by force, it discloses only the mute corpse of Edward Hyde; and another story, sealed in an enclosure. The owner of the 'place with the door', as it is several times called, and the author of the story has vanished. But he has left more than a rack behind; he has left a text. By cunningly allowing for all this, Stevenson has opened another door and it is one which leads straight into the twentieth century.*

Already, however, we get ahead of ourselves. In a narrative which is as over-determined as that in *Heart of Darkness*, and is, in fact, a mosaic of 'stories', the chapter-heading teases us with a question: is the door subject or object? Rummaging again in what lies beyond the first chapter (and slightly adapting what we find there) we could reply that if it could rightly be said to be either, it is only because it is radically both. And what could be more modernist?

In the chapter's fourth paragraph we are given a description of what will later be revealed as Dr Jekyll's home and, rather alarmingly, we are guided to it by doors – 'Two doors from one corner, on the left hand going east … ' – which seem to be in some danger of turning into mirrors. The house 'was two storeys high; showed no window, nothing but a door on the lower storey and a blind forehead of discoloured wall on the upper …' (30). Doors and narratively-inclined storeys cluster thickly here and the first of many significant references to faces also occurs in this paragraph. In the face depicted here the door is in the position of a mouth, and it is firmly shut; in this respect recalling Mr Utterson, to whom we have just been introduced and who, despite being called Gabriel John Utterson, is greatly given to silence and is prized by his friends precisely for his defiance of his baptismal encipherment.

How much we shall learn from this story-telling door is thus immediately put in doubt though our appetite may even have been whetted by the information that it is a door of the lower storey. The

---

* All references are to *Dr Jekyll and Mr Hyde and Other Stories* (Penguin Classics, 1979), ed. Jenni Calder.

paragraph is not quite finished, however; we have yet to discover that 'The door ... was blistered and distained', that tramps and children had left their mark upon it and that 'for close on a generation no-one had appeared to drive away these random visitors or to repair their ravages' (80). An aged door, even, to extrapolate from William Veeder's indispensable essay, 'Children of the Night: Stevenson and Patriarchy', a patriarch amongst doors, time's ravages being measured in the scale of human generations.[1]

There is yet more to be said about the door, for its age and significance can also be measured in *literary* generations. When we have done so it will be clear that Utterson, Jekyll and their tight-lipped friends move and have their being under a very dark cloud. At the beginning of Chapter 47 of Thackeray's *Vanity Fair* there is a description of the environs of Lord Steyne's 'town palace' situated in 'Gaunt Square' the original of which was Cavendish Square. It is already in decline from its aristocratic beginnings, however, and we are told that 'brass plates have already penetrated into the Square' belonging principally, it would seem, to doctors and Banks. As well, 'three sides are composed of mansions that have passed away into Dowagerism'. Dr Lanyon, of course, lives in Cavendish Square 'that citadel of medicine', and Dr Jekyll lives in an unnamed Square, 'round the corner from the by-street', full of handsome houses 'now for the most part decayed and let in flats and chambers to all sorts and conditions of men: map-engravers, architects, shady lawyers, and agents of obscure enterprises' (40).

Close by Thackeray's Gaunt Square there is Great Gaunt Street and New Gaunt Street; and it is through a doorway in the latter that the disreputable Lord Steyne admits his dissolute guests bent on pleasure. The door sounds a little familiar:

A few yards down New Gaunt Street, and leading into Gaunt Mews, indeed, is a little modest back door which you would not remark from that of any other of the stables. But many a little close carriage has stopped at that door, as my informant ... told me. 'The Prince and Perdita have been in and out of that door, sir,' he has often told me; 'Marianne Clarke has entered it with the Duke of —. It conducts to the famous petits appartements of Lord Steyne – one, sir fitted up all in ivory and white satin, another in ebony and black velvet ...'.

When we remember that the taciturn lawyer introduces himself to Hyde as 'Mr Utterson of Gaunt Street' (and Jekyll's dissecting-rooms are described as 'gaunt'), it is easy to accept that there is a link between the Jekyll milieu and that of the lecherous Lord Steyne. (It even encourages us to wonder about that curious description of Jekyll's door as 'distained'.)

Mature though Stevenson's door is, in one respect at least it is very unsatisfactory: it is a distinctly unhelpful witness and such testimony as its reticence allows it to give is unreliable. The figure of speech here is in no sense an extraneous one, for, as more than one critic has noticed, what we are given (one year before Sherlock Holmes solves his first crime in *A Study in Scarlet*) is an extraordinarily interesting and sophisticated detective-story. It is one with a superabundance of clues, a bewildered investigator constantly seeking for a sign which will provide an explanation, a *flâneur* who observes all, but ostentatiously declines to draw conclusions, a doctor who eventually learns the identity of the murderer but prefers to die rather than bear witness against a fellow-professional (partly because, in a roundabout way, it implicates himself).

In his excellent essay in Veeder's and Hirsch's collection, Ronald Thomas writes: 'The text [of *Jekyll and Hyde*] ends as a detective novel customarily begins – with the disappearance of a body and the appearance of an enigmatic text (a will clouded by incestuous intentions, disputed authenticity and an alteration of the name of the heir). The absent body, in this case, happens to be that of the text's author' (75). From the start, however, there is a clear invocation of the genre. The novella's title *Strange Case of Dr Jekyll and Mr Hyde* is, given the missing definite article, much more in the idiom of the detective's cryptic jottings (perhaps as these are translated in the newsboys' sensationalising placards mentioned in the story) than the distinguished medical specialist's writing up of a case-history; though the two types of cases will shortly be brought closer together in the investigative writings of Sigmund Freud.

The idiom is continued in the first chapter-heading, 'Story of the Door' (not, as Thomas has it, '*The* Story of the Door'); the second is 'Search for Mr Hyde'; another 'Incident of the Letter', and another 'Remarkable Incident of Dr Lanyon'. As the roll of these headings mounts, the newsboys' 'read all about it' cries sensationalise the detective's text while at the same time depriving it of context and limiting it in meaning. Only twice does the definite article make an appearance in these headings and its use on one of these occasions – 'The Carew Murder Case' – confirms the sequence as Holmesian rather than Aesculapian.[2]

It could be argued, however, that the significance of the absent definite article for the narrative structure of the novella goes beyond this. *Strange Case of Dr Jekyll and Mr Hyde* is not one story but ten enigmatic *stories* (composed, as Ronald Thomas has pointed out, of ten disparate 'documents') looking for an all-encompassing explanation. It never comes of course, because, as we are to learn, no story ever does get fully told. And does this not jog our memories? It should, for what is being allowed to influence the structure of the work is the genre Stevenson had been closely involved with shortly before the publication of *Jekyll and Hyde*: that of the *Arabian Nights*.

In *New Arabian Nights*, five out of the seven stories have no definite article in the heading ('Story of the Young Man with the Cream Tarts', 'Story of the Bandbox', etc.) while the remaining two are headed 'The Adventures of …'. What is heightened by the omission of the definite article is the sense of arbitrariness and endless sequence ('Story of …', 'Story of … ', 'Story of … '), in which indefiniteness and incompleteness are implicit concomitants. The authority of the story-telling text is consequently greatly enhanced until it achieves a sort of teasing autonomy – teasing because it appears to play with us. While it deigns to make us privy to certain goings-on, it keeps us guessing as to whether it will ever divulge their meaning. In the end just when it seems about to be forced into telling all in Henry Jekyll's 'Full Statement of the Case', it escapes again and makes of its teller its victim.

*The Thousand and One Nights* is an appropriate model (however hazily present), for both Scheherazade and King Shahryar are, in the end, the tales' victims; Scheherazade becoming so not just because (as Laurence Housman once pointed out) she had to sleep for one thousand and one nights with a homicidal maniac, but because the story, in saving her life, makes her its slave. Clearly the story is destined to go on forever: that the king gives in to the narrative onslaught after some three years is an arbitrarily-arranged interruption. One of Stevenson's mentors, Edgar Allan Poe, builds a splendid story on just such a presumption. His 'The Thousand and Second Tale' stoutly maintains that 'the literary world' has been duped into thinking that the sequence ends when Scheherazade secures her reprieve. What *really* happened was that Scheherazade then recalls that she hasn't told quite all of Sinbad's adventures and she sets about doing so. However, the king, waking up to an appalling future entirely dictated by narrative, declines to be a slave of the story any longer and, deciding that it's all a pack of lies, proceeds to have Scheherazade bow-strung after all. She, however,

derived ... great consolation (during the tightening of the bow-
string) from the reflection that much of the history remained still
untold, and that the petulance of her brute of a husband had
reaped for him a most righteous reward in depriving him of many
inconceivable adventures.

So, perhaps, the story wins in the end just as it does (as we shall see)
in *Jekyll and Hyde*.

I have said that, throughout 'Story of the Door', the door itself –
the mouth underneath the 'forehead of discoloured wall' – appears
to remain firmly shut. In Enfield's story the door does open, however,
when it admits the perpetrator of the act of violence witnessed by
Utterson's kinsman to get money to give to his victim's family. This
mystery man has a key, something to which particular emphasis is
given at the end of the chapter when Utterson presses Enfield on the
point: 'The fellow had a key; and what's more, he has it still' (34).
Several more references are made to the key but it never unlocks any
secrets for us. To the contrary, when it finally comes within Utterson's
grasp, it is lying on the floor, *inside* Jekyll's laboratory, broken in two
– thereby creating yet another secret.

The broken key has much the same function as the door which,
when broken down, reveals only the dead body of Hyde. Together
they play a similar role to the figure of Allegory in Mr Tulkinghorn's
chambers in *Bleak House*. Forever pointing and appearing to give the
eye directions, 'the Roman' only once does so meaningfully – and
then it is to the dead body of the lawyer. So in *Jekyll and Hyde*, where
a plethora of clues and promising 'openings' lead to a plethora of
dead ends, or rather into yet another aisle of the labyrinth. Doors
which don't open, keys which are found broken, enclosures which
contain other enclosures, utterers who won't speak. Well may Stephen
Heath claim in his important essay (to be ranked along with Veeder's
and Thomas's), 'Psychopathia Sexualis: Stevenson's Strange Case'
that 'the organising image for this narrative is the breaking down of
doors, learning the secret behind them'.[3] The only trouble is that we
never really do penetrate to all the secrets beyond the doors for there
is always another enclosure and another story.

Perhaps we should not really expect the doors to disclose secrets.
After all, the first reference to doors in the text (in the middle of the
very first paragraph) is to the doors of a theatre; and the last reference, in the last paragraph of 'The Last Night' is again to the theatre,
and, reflecting the chapter-heading, it is couched in a form which

suggests the end of a performance: 'They went out, locking the door of the theatre behind them' (73). True, this last theatre is 'old Dr Denman's surgical theatre' to which many allusions are made throughout the tale, but the conflation is not accidental and illustrates admirably the truth of Hofmannsthal's dictum which heads this chapter.[4]

Stevenson extracts maximum advantage from deploying the idea of theatre here and elsewhere. Virtually all his major works reflect his intense interest in theatre as *mise-en-scène*, as alternative reality, as space for play-acting or performance, as a prism through which other personalities or selves might be refracted.[5] To have his whole cast of characters, suddenly – even if only temporarily – seem to be set upon a stage, is part of that strong deconstructive tendency in Stevenson which ensures that the 'realism' he despised will never take hold and that his fiction will be recognised as the self-validating construct it is rather than as the fine distillation of truth which will teach society how it can best realise itself.

We can think of this as a determination not to hide from himself or others that the fabric of his vision was as baseless as Prospero's, and that the *process* of art is all. Alternatively, we can see it in more explicitly late-Modernist terms – nicely illustrated here by the theatre of illusion and the dissecting theatre – as the deliberate construction of a fictional illusion followed by the laying bare of that illusion; which is, in fact, Patricia Waugh's description of how the metafictional novel works.[6] It is a process which is encountered many times in reading Stevenson's fiction.

Behind the doors, then, there might lie the theatre of illusion and self-deception – or the surgical theatre, so that, despite their reticence, these doors have the capacity to tell two stories. But can they be trusted in telling either tale? Enfield calls 'the story of the door' a 'bad story'which is a pointedly odd way of saying that it is a bad business. The story can't in itself be 'bad' just because it taints one of their own with scandal: 'the person that drew the cheque is the very pink of the proprieties, celebrated too, and (what makes it worse) one of your fellows who do what they call good' (33). Calling it a 'bad' story, however, opens the way for readers to argue that it is so because, in Enfield's words, it is 'far from explaining all' (33). This is what Ronald Thomas does, entirely plausibly, and from that goes on to contend that most of the tale is of the same character, presenting 'a world of vain searches, unexplained disappearances, random incidents, and incomplete statements', all of which lead him

to the conclusion that the remainder of the text 'is merely a repetition of this "story" gone "bad"'.[7]

Bearing this in mind, it is not hard to see Stevenson as indulging
himself in what is a favourite pastime of his – metafictional game-
playing – when he has Jekyll write in his letter to Lanyon that 'if you
will punctually serve me, my troubles will roll away like a story that
is told' (75). As Stevenson knows only too well, no story ever does get
told; a conviction which is reflected in his own cavalier treatment of
endings exemplified in, for example, Kidnapped and The Ebb-Tide and
in his remark in a letter to Colvin in September 1891 that 'The dénouement of a long story is nothing; it is just a 'full close', which you may
approach and accompany as you please – it is a coda, not an essential
member of the rhythm ....'[8] So when he has Enfield remark ingenu-
ously 'Well ... that story's at an end, at least. We shall never see more
of Mr Hyde' (60), we are immediately confident of two things: that the
story is not ended and that we shall see a great deal more of Mr Hyde.

Returning to the back door in the by-street, we might recall a
significant omission in the façade which contains it: no windows are
mentioned. Above the mouth in this face – the mouth which stubbornly declines to 'utter' or disclose anything – there are no eyes. It
is a detail to which our attention is drawn by the 'forehead of
discoloured wall' being described as 'blind' (30). Away from the street,
however, three windows on the first floor, we are carefully told, give
on to the courtyard. In replication of Jekyll's experiment on the
'inner life of his mind' (to use Hofmannsthal's phrase again), the house
has turned its gaze inward. Exactly what goes on in its interior is,
however, difficult to establish because it is impossible to be sure –
again reflecting Jekyll's problem – what constitutes its individual
identity: 'the buildings are so packed together about that court, that
it's hard to say where one ends and another begins' (33).

The house, then, appears to be as self-preoccupied as its owner
and blind and indifferent to what is going on in the street. Tempting
as it is to see the building's demeanour as suggesting a contrast
between the introverted and the open, the hidden and the overt, it
would be a mistake. Virtually everything in Jekyll and Hyde is touched
with ambivalence and 'otherness' and the 'public' by-street is far
from being an exception.[9] In fact, Stevenson has a particular talent
for defamiliarising and he applies this to the streets of the city in a
manner which brings him closer to the manner of Conrad and other
Modernists than to, say, Poe's or Dickens's ways of depicting the
city.

Thus though the description of the by-street might seem initially to be simply of a thriving side-street frankly and innocently displaying its commercial wares, ambivalence and 'otherness' exist there too:

The inhabitants were all doing well, it seemed, and all emulously hoping to do better still, and laying out the surplus of their gains in coquetry; so that the shop fronts stood along that thoroughfare with an air of invitation, like rows of smiling saleswomen. Even on Sunday, when it veiled its more florid charms and lay comparatively empty of passage, the street shone out in contrast to its dingy neighbourhood, like a fire in a forest; and with its freshly painted shutters, well-polished brasses, and general cleanliness and gaiety of note, instantly caught and pleased the eye of the passenger (30).

If this description owes a little – a very little – to Dickens, whose buildings display an alarming propensity for developing personalities, it is hard to believe that Conrad does not, in turn, owe something to it. To compare the description of the side-street with that of Brett Street in *The Secret Agent* is to recognise an affinity; and even though Conrad has deepened the chiaroscuro to make his street more sombre and dingy, points of similarity remain. The unexpected and apparently alien simile of the forest-fire in Stevenson's description, for example, comes back to mind when we read in *The Secret Agent* of 'the glowing heaps of oranges and lemons' which, under the lamplight, 'made a violent blaze of colour' on the fruiterer's stall, and hear of the Assistant Commissioner of Police feeling 'as though he had been ambushed all alone in a jungle'.[10]

But Stevenson's description (including his image of the fire in the forest) is, as Heath's analysis confirms, also suggestive in a sense quite different from Conrad's. The respectability it exudes is only façade-deep. Beneath the prosperous and pleasing aspect of the thoroughfare where pride is taken in the cleanliness and decorousness of its frontages, lies another which suggests the opposite: a street that is far from respectable. The figurative language in the extract quoted and, in particular, the coherence of sexually significant terms, compel the reader to such a conclusion. In its context 'coquetry', for example, is initially a great surprise, but that (largely assumed) context immediately gives way to another where the word is perfectly at home. It might just have been possible to rescue the innocence of the shop-fronts' 'air of invitation' from contamination by 'coquetry' had no more been made of it; but that possibility disappears once the metaphor has been extended and the shops have been likened to 'rows of smiling saleswomen'.

To put it no more strongly, the invitation *we* have received is to consider that the source of the street's prosperity and the propriety of its commerce may be other than they seem. The subsequent reference to the street's 'florid charms' being 'veiled' on a Sunday seems calculated to tease as much as please the eye of the (male) passer-by.[11] And what of the word 'gaiety' – a word that makes a remarkable number of appearances in this tale – if it has no other significance than that of 'cheerfulness'? While I am not persuaded by William Veeder's implicit acceptance that the word 'gay' had, in all likelihood, acquired a homosexual meaning for the *cognoscenti*, at least, in 1886,[12] it certainly had become widely associated with promiscuity and loose morals. The word was specifically applied to fallen women but it was widely used to signify a certain sort of entertainment illustrated in this verse which was written after the dissenters in Parliament had succeeded in closing the Chelsea pleasure-gardens:

Who now remembers gay Cremorne
And all its jaunty jills
And those wild whirling figures born
Of Jullien's wild quadrilles?[13]

From this inspection of the by-street, it is clear that Jekyll's is not the only house to enjoy a hidden life; the streets of the city, too, have their secrets, their deceptive 'faces' and hidden depths. In the way he represents this activity Stevenson has gone well beyond Dickens both in the sophistication of his metafictional narrative and in his exploitation of what would become familiar as Freudian themes and imagery, strengthening his claim to being considered a harbinger of Modernism.

## The Unreal City

To those aspects of Stevenson's writing which give it its Modernist cast, there should be added his representation of the city in *Jekyll and Hyde*. His subject, of course, dictated that his location should be the city but his *treatment* of that subject dictated it too. As has already been suggested, its 'doubleness' – the contrast between façade and interior, its capacity to sustain a complex secret life, the contrast between its day- and night-time existence, the multifariousness of its

aspects which can change from being one moment concretely physical to disconcertingly surreal the next – all these dualities and
ambivalences contribute to the working-out of his dominant pluralist
vision. 'Modernism', writes Malcolm Bradbury,

> seems ... to substitute for the 'real' city ... the 'unreal' city, the
> theatre of licence and fantasy, strange selfhoods in strange juxta-
> positions that Dostoyevsky and Baudelaire, Conrad and Eliot,
> Biely and Dos Passos convey as an unresolved and plural impres-
> sion ... Realism humanizes, naturalism scientizes but Modernism
> pluralizes, and surrealizes.[14]

Ira Bruce Nadel describes the 'movement from fact to the "innermost secret", from a brilliant surface to an underlying force' as
something which 'is part of the Victorian aesthetic emerging in the
1860s and 70s'.[15] Even the apparently solid realism of Gustave Doré
reveals this process at work. Nadel describes it particularly well:

> The reality of the city for Doré is dualistic – at once detailed and
> imagined, identifiable and illusory. Doré revealed the urban world
> of Victorian London as one of depth and multiplicity, and the success
> of *London: A Pilgrimage* resides in its ability to take the city and its
> inhabitants and transform them into the surface and symbol of
> Victorian life.[16]

*London: A Pilgrimage* appeared in 1872. The author of the text,
Blanchard Jerrold, published his *Life of Doré* in 1897 and in it he
continues to exhort others to plumb the depths of the city's dualism.
'The true innermost secret of the mighty fact of London must be
sought', he urged.[17] In between these two publications had come a
number of fictional works doing just that, including *Jekyll and Hyde*.
Not that Doré's work necessarily influenced Stevenson in any way,
since he was already an admirer of Poe, Dickens, Eugène Sue and
Baudelaire who had all explored the same urban dualism considerably earlier.

The treatment of the by-street behind Jekyll's house goes some
way to show how Stevenson exploited the city's capacity to suggest
discordances and 'strange selfhoods', characterised as it is by double
standards, a lascivious and disorderly subterranean life, and by the
preoccupation with façades and frontages. As for the by-street, so
for the city as a whole – which plays a bigger role in the novella than
is usually recognised.

The principal characters, each with his own shady 'otherness', are the product of the city, professional élitism of the sort they represent being an urban phenomenon.[18] It is, of course, the increasingly powerful *haute bourgeoisie* which, busily engaged in setting-up and refining its own hierarchies, has accorded these men eminent status and appointed them *doyens* of sub-aristocratic society. The legal and medical professions were perhaps the most highly-regarded and rewarded of all: the first for the most obvious reason that they were there to defend the privileges (hence the status) of their peers, as Utterson makes very clear in his conversation with Jekyll ('I am a man to be trusted'); and the second because new diagnoses, new technology and new treatments coincided with a great deal of new money, much of it concentrated in cities. Add to that 'the stress of urban living', which covered everything from gout to syphilis, and the status of the medical profession was assured. Fashionable Cavendish Square where Dr Lanyon had his house 'and received his crowding patients' is quite correctly described by Stevenson as 'that citadel of medicine' (36).

As it appears in *Jekyll and Hyde*, the city of London has all the material solidity and prosperity such a society postulates and it is set before us here in considerable variety – Cavendish Square, Soho, Regent's Park, labyrinthine by-streets. As the earlier discussion on the by-street suggested, however, the city is far from being mere background to the tale: to the contrary, it is a very active presence – or *presences* for it has multiple voices and shapes, some of them altogether menacing. While Utterson is keeping vigil for Hyde, for example, he hears 'the low growl of London from all around' (38). As he and Poole wait for the servants to get to their posts before they begin their assault on the door to Jekyll's cabinet, all round 'that deep well of building' where they are waiting, 'London hummed solemnly' (68). Sometimes the footsteps of a single person are counter-pointed – marvellingly – against the 'vast hum and clatter of the city' which ought to swamp the sound they make but somehow don't. Utterson describes this unexpected audibility, this individuation, as a 'quaint effect' he has often noticed (38). As a result of these allusions, we find ourselves listening attentively – even uneasily – for the voice of the city. So much so that when a chapter opens with 'London was startled by a crime of singular ferocity' (46) the lively and momentarily convincing anthropomorphism startles *us*.

At other times – and particularly at night – this chameleon city can take on a quite different character; its voices are silent and from the darkness beyond the street-lamps it becomes watchful. Enfield feels this very strongly as he makes his way home at 'about three o'clock of a black winter morning':

> my way lay through a part of town where there was literally nothing to be seen but lamps. Street after street, and all the folk asleep – street after street, all lighted up as if for a procession, and all as empty as a church – till at last I got into that state of mind when a man listens and listens and begins to long for the sight of a policeman (31).

Conrad may well have had this scene in mind when he came to describe Comrade Ossipon's journey across London in the penultimate chapter of *The Secret Agent* (though he might also have been thinking of *The Dynamiter*). There is the same endless perspective of silent streets, empty of people and defined not by their houses but by the street-lamps illuminating nothing but themselves.[19] Compared with Conrad's (which are explicitly gas-lamps) there is nothing mellow about the street-lighting here: it, too, is moving towards the twentieth century. The processional route 'all lighted up' suggests something of the bright fluorescence of the new electric lighting which was already being installed in some of London's processional routes and which Stevenson himself described in an early essay as 'unearthly ... a lamp for a nightmare'. This new light is, in fact, to illuminate a particularly Modernist nightmare which Stevenson seems to anticipate: 'Such a light as this should shine only on murders and public crime, or along the corridors of lunatic asylums, a horror to heighten horror.'[20] It is through 'labyrinths of lighted city' that Utterson sees Hyde speeding in his dream (37) and it is 'through the lamp-lit streets' that Hyde runs in a 'divided ecstasy of mind' (91) after he has murdered Sir Danvers Carew.

The streets through which Enfield is travelling are not only empty of people, they are made to appear spiritually empty, by the surprising simile of the empty church, so alien to both period and place.[21] The darkness held at bay by the lights, the expectancy inherent in the empty processional route and now the suggestion of moral vacuity make it quite understandable that Enfield should get into 'that state of mind where a man listens and listens and begins to long for the sight of a policeman'. What he catches sight of, however, is not the morally reassuring figure of the policeman but Edward Hyde and his victim. It is they who fill the empty space.

Much the same scene occurs again when Utterson is keeping watch for Hyde though the metaphor this time is a secular one and the lighting less intense: 'It was a fine dry night, frost in the air; the streets as clean as a ball-room floor; the lamps unshaken by any wind, drawing a regular pattern of light and shadow. By ten o'clock, when the shops were closed, the by-street was very silent and ... very solitary' (38). The ball-room also is empty and when, after a succession of references to 'an odd light footstep', 'the foot-falls of a single person', 'the steps ... [which] swelled out suddenly louder' (38), someone does take the deserted floor, that person is, once again, Edward Hyde. The image evoked on these two occasions is of a dream city on the edge of nightmare.[22] True to the pluralising habit of this tale, however, another image is visible behind the first and it is one which posits the city as theatre. The curtain has gone up on a well-lit theatrical set – without its cast of day-time characters. The fact that it is Utterson and Enfield as well as Hyde who emerge out of the darkness to play their roles under the lights (unequivocally gas-lights here) makes night-stalkers of all three and is another example of the blurring of the edges between presumed good and evil entities which characterises *Jekyll and Hyde*.

The tension created in these scenes – heightened by the ambiguities in Enfield's and Utterson's roles – is proof that there is nothing relaxed or peaceful about the deserted city: to the contrary, violence is liable to erupt upon its stage at any moment. Reinforcement for this view is to be found in the fact that Enfield's longing to come across a policeman is endorsed by Utterson a short time later when he goes out on 'a wild, cold, seasonable night of March':

> The wind made talking difficult, and flecked the blood into the face. It seemed to have swept the streets unusually bare of passengers, besides; for Mr Utterson thought he had never seen that part of London so deserted. He could have wished it otherwise; never in his life had he been conscious of so sharp a wish to see and touch his fellow-creatures; for, struggle as he might, there was borne in upon his mind a crushing anticipation of calamity (63).

Though the city is often presented with much of the character of a nocturne, its outlines obscured and indistinct, it is noteworthy that it can, even more disconcertingly, adopt just such an appearance in day-time. Thus, if at night it provides a labyrinth for Hyde (or even a Labyrinth since Hyde, who is several times described as ape-like, has something in common with the half-human, half-beast Minotaur), in day-time it can still be associated with the unconscious, as Utterson shows when he likens Soho wrapped in dense fog to 'some city in a nightmare' (48). The passage is worth quoting in full, not least because of the way it carries Dickens forward, foreshadowing Conrad's moral impressionism and disclosing an affinity with Eliot's 'Unreal City/Under the brown fog of a winter noon':

> It was by this time about nine in the morning, and the first fog of the season. A great chocolate-coloured pall lowered over heaven, but the wind was continually charging and routing these embattled vapours; so that as the cab crawled from street to street, Mr Utterson beheld a marvellous number of degrees and hues of twilight; for here it would be dark like the back-end of evening; and there would be a glow of a rich, lurid brown, like the light of some strange conflagration; and here, for a moment, the fog would be quite broken up, and a haggard shaft of daylight would glance in between the swirling wreaths. The dismal quarter of Soho seen under these changing glimpses, with its muddy ways, and slatternly passengers, and its lamps, which had never been extinguished or had been kindled afresh to combat this mournful reinvasion of darkness, seemed, in the lawyer's eyes, like a district of some city in a nightmare.

Daylight is at best no more than haggard and the swirling fog and sombre hues combine to form a murkiness that bespeaks disorientation and moral confusion. Like Conrad's Assistant Commissioner, Utterson might well be a member of the criminal classes as, sealed in his cab, he journeys through this opacity, glancing apprehensively at his companion, the police-officer, 'conscious of some touch of that terror of the law which may at times assail the most honest' (48). Utterson's thoughts which are described as being of the 'gloomiest dye' (as well they might be since he has just come from the scene of Carew's murder where evidence has been discovered which implicates Jekyll in the crime and underlines his own association with both Jekyll and Carew) merge with the drab colours which surround him. The fog is 'as brown as umber' and the futile attempts of the sun to shine through it only succeed in making the time look like twilight, creating 'a glow of rich, lurid brown like the light of some strange conflagration'.

The fog is exploited to provide another metaphor which links the city with the exploration of the unconscious and, in particular, the repression of desire. Allusions to hidden depths are everywhere – Utterson, for example, feels an impulse 'to dive at once to the bottom of these mysteries' (59) while Jekyll savours to the full his new-found capacity as Hyde to 'spring headlong into the sea of liberty' (86). It is not surprising, therefore, for the city to be called on to provide an image of the same ulteriority:

> The fog still slept on the wing above the drowned city, where the lamps glimmered like carbuncles; and through the muffle and smother of these fallen clouds, the procession of the town's life was still rolling in through the great arteries with a sound as of a mighty wind (53–4).

Like a sea-bird which needs no land to rest on, the fog floats over the city, and the ubiquitous street-lamps of dream or nightmare are transformed into rich red jewels glowing in the watery depths. The sound of the city is still to be heard but, appropriately enough, it is now a wind blowing over the world's oceans.

That cities have an underside which embodies 'darker' realities unacknowledged in their public façades is a trope which exerts an increasing fascination for writers as the nineteenth century progresses. One literary product of this is described by Raymond Williams:

> The 'dark London' of the late nineteenth-century, and particularly the East End, were often seen as warrens of crime, and one important literary response to this was the new figure of the urban detective. In Conan Doyle's Sherlock Holmes stories there is a recurrent image of the penetration by an isolated rational intelligence of a dark area of crime which is to be found in the otherwise ... impenetrable city.[23]

The 'doubleness' now perceived in the city is something of a paradox for it coincides with the *destruction* of the dark places of the old medieval city and their replacement (in Paris for example) by grand boulevards, elegant buildings – and, eventually, electric street-lighting. For the urban historian these great European cities represented, as Edward Timms says, 'one of the highest levels of metropolitan civilization'.[24] But it was precisely the extravagant claims being made – more *visibly* to more people than ever before – that nurtured perceptions of doubleness. The more the public face of cities proclaimed the inexorable march of progress and civilisation, the greater the perceived disparity between public face and ulterior reality. It was not only on the sensibility of the great social and political reformers that this reality registered. To a new generation of artists and intellectuals, more interested than ever before in the 'underside' of their own consciousness, the double image of the city was a trope for their time.

Stevenson's 'unreal city', with its hidden or submerged life, is thus clearly very much of its period. It is doubly so by having close links to the continent of Europe, particularly France, where Baudelaire (much admired by Stevenson) could be said to have lived in the 'doubleness' of his *cité pleine de rêves*. Walter Benjamin, in fact, stresses the 'chthonic' elements in Baudelaire's verse (which go beyond the topographical) and notes that the Paris of his poems 'is a sunken city, and more submarine than subterranean'.[25]

## *Flâneurs* by Gaslight

There is another link between Stevenson's city and Baudelaire's: both have their *flâneur*, though in *Jekyll and Hyde* he is described as 'a man-about-town'. Richard Enfield, Utterson's kinsman, is one of the most enigmatic – and far from the least important – characters in Stevenson's novella and the ways in which he is and isn't like Baudelaire's *flâneur* are instructive in trying to define his role.

Baudelaire's *flâneur* is 'l'homme des foules' – a man of crowds, where Enfield appears to be a more solitary figure. As a man-about-town, however, Enfield must also be (at least in his day-time activities) part of the crowd and we wonder if, like the central figure in Poe's 'The Man of the Crowd' (whom Baudelaire saw as a *flâneur*), he is not, in fact, asocial – a man-about-town who goes with the crowd but in no way loses his identity. It is at any rate curious that Stevenson very deliberately creates Enfield a man-about-town, an essentially gregarious figure, and then, on the occasions he actually presents him to us, he renders him as a solitary who nevertheless, as Benjamin says of Poe's character, 'does not feel comfortable in his own company'.[26] To such an extent is this the case that his periodic ambulations with the uncommunicative Utterson are regarded as the 'chief jewel' of his week, though no one can see that the two men have anything whatever in common.

Enfield, like Baudelaire's *flâneur* – the observer who, while preserving his own secrets, studies closely the lives of those who come under his gaze – has something in common with the detective. For

Baudelaire this is not accidental: when he writes that 'An observer is a *prince* who is everywhere in possession of his incognito'[27], he may well have arrived at this insight via the work of Poe whose detective-stories he introduced to France in his translations and whose method he adopted (though he was never likely to have written detective stories himself since according to Benjamin, 'it was impossible for him to identify with the detective').[28] But these observers-liable-to-turn-detective have about them a moral ambiguity. The paradox that Poe noticed – that your *flâneur* can at the same time be asocial – gives him a dangerous freedom in his world of crowds which is also the haunt and the refuge of the criminal with whom he therefore shares common ground. As Benjamin points out, the notion that the urban masses 'appear as the asylum that shields an asocial person from his persecutors'[29] is not a new idea. However, Stevenson gives it an ironic twist when he has Jekyll realise that Hyde regards him simply as 'a city of refuge', able to bury his criminal evil in the decorous facade of the city's *professional* classes.

Enfield *does* have something of the detective in him; he is a keen observer, well aware of human foibles and frailties, curious, quite able to draw conclusions – but, interestingly, not at all willing to push his 'investigations' to a dénouement, which would mean sheeting home moral responsibility: 'I feel very strongly about putting questions, it partakes too much of the style of the day of judgement' (33). No more than Baudelaire is he on the side of the detective. Moreover, as William Veeder points out, there are a number of factors which link Enfield and Hyde, from the fact that they are both cane-carrying nightstalkers to (as he sees it) 'an unconscious [on Enfield's part] inclination to free Hyde'. Also, in his role as narrator, says Veeder, 'Enfield reveals a complicity in Hyde's first act of night violence that colours the scene significantly.'[30]

Enfield has, in fact, to be seen as separate from the patriarchy in a way Veeder does not allow for. The doubling that is evident everywhere in *Jekyll and Hyde* is there too, though lightly sketched, in Utterson-and-Enfield. Though Enfield is described as a 'young man' (34) the bond between the two is exceptionally and – this is emphasised – *inexplicably* strong. But just as Hyde seems to be the complete antithesis of Jekyll, so, though represented in a more reticent and decorous way, is Enfield *vis-à-vis* Utterson. Most prominently, Enfield is emphatically not of the professional class (Veeder wrongly lumps him in with the others), being a man-about-town, that is, an idler. The man-about-town has, of course, something of the dandy in him and it is easy to see in Enfield what contemporary French writers regarded as *un homme du monde*. Two of those writers whom Stevenson admired, Barbey d'Aurevilly and Baudelaire, had written at length about the dandy in just such terms. To Barbey he was 'un homme du monde' who could be, like Enfield, 'grave et intellectuel', while Baudelaire saw him as someone who could be both in and outside society, 'trop *homme du monde* pour ne pas mépriser le monde',[31] a description which helps to fill out Enfield's sardonic reference to the man whose name was on Hyde's cheque as 'one of your fellows who do what they call good' (33).

In fact, the dualism inherent in the representation of the city in the later nineteenth century, the dark secrets hidden beneath the 'mighty fact' of London (as Jerrold saw it), ensures that vestiges of moral obliquity cling to the city's creature, the man-about-town. In 1886 the latter term is of too recent invention for a reader to be altogether sure of its moral weight. Dickens appears to have been the first to use it in something like its modern sense in *Martin Chuzzlewit* (1844) though the OED's next identification of it in 1889 (in Robert's *History of English Bookselling*) is more convincing. What is clear is that in the previous century a 'man of the town' was associated with lewdness and debauchery while a 'fellow-about-town' was a term current late in that century to describe a rake.

Stevenson has made sure that Enfield's ways remain mysterious and inscrutable. At the very least, a man-about-town is assumed to lead a very public existence, yet Enfield is matter-of-fact about his returning home, *on foot*, at 3 a.m. 'from some place at the end of the world'. Why this flaunting of his nocturnal habits, and why be so teasingly reticent about telling his kinsman where he'd been? The idiom he uses, as so often in the text, is just sufficiently unusual to draw attention to itself. Why 'at the end of the world' when the received idiom is 'the ends of the earth'? Is Stevenson having a little joke, telling us in code that Enfield has been to Chelsea, part of which was (and is) called World's End? (Not so much of a joke, perhaps, if we recall the unsavoury reputation of Chelsea Gardens after dark.) The questions are not altogether inconsequential for where Enfield is 'coming from' is important in establishing his relationship to Hyde and the latter's cruel abuse of the child.

In fact, it is almost impossible to plot the course followed by the three people involved in that scene in a way that accords with Enfield's account of events. Hyde, we are told carefully, 'was stumping along eastward at a good walk'; the girl was running down an intersecting street. Somehow both were visible to bird's-eye Enfield. A principal point in his description of the collision is that Hyde neither pauses nor deviates from his course which means that he carries on eastwards. Enfield then sets off in pursuit so he, too, must have been travelling in roughly the same direction when he first sighted Hyde. Even more odd is his giving a 'view halloa' as he goes after his quarry: Enfield is a 'man-about-town' not a country-squire given to fox-hunting. And why, asks William Veeder pertinently, should he describe the pursuit with the idiom 'I ... took to my heels' which is an expression normally assumed to mean 'to flee from'?[32] Veeder's explanation that the usage reflects an unconscious desire to free Hyde which cohabits with his conscious wish to capture him, and so 'marks the patriarchy's uncomfortable implication in what it officially condemns', is less than convincing since, as has been said, Enfield is quite distinct from the patriarchy of Utterson, Jekyll and Lanyon.

An alternative and simpler answer is that Stevenson *wants* Enfield's (moral) position *vis-à-vis* the act of violence to remain ambiguous. Not only does the direction he is travelling in suggest that he may have come from notorious Chelsea, but his name, as Veeder argues, may also be meant to link him to violence, in that Enfield was not just the site of the Royal Small Arms Factory but had given its name to the 'Enfield Riflemen' and the 'Enfield skirmishers' which were 'important components of the British Infantry' (158). These names were quite possibly known to Stevenson who had a life-long passion for toy-soldiers and for playing large-scale war-games with them. Enfield could, however, suggest a number of other associations. Some ten miles from the centre of London, Enfield was, in the 1880s still partly rural (Enfield Chase still exists) which would make Richard Enfield (with his 'view halloa') a deracinated country gentleman – and so even further removed from the professional class.[33]

There is yet another and quite different possibility. Henry Enfield was a minor painter of the era and a friend of both Robert Louis Stevenson and his cousin Bob. Richard Enfield could, therefore, be seen as a figure of the artist, observing, non-committal and with a shifting perspective on events. In Paris the growth of the city with its new glassed-over arcades, its even newer boulevards, railways and gas street-lighting, had incited the writer 'to desert his study and go into the street as a *flâneur* ... and journalist'.[34] It was a model Stevenson would have been well-acquainted with; and Enfield is, if not the author, at least the narrator of the door's story.

## A Man to be Trusted

There is surely little doubt that the text invites the reader to find the close friendship between Utterson and his *distant* kinsman as puzzling as those other observers do who cannot understand what the two have in common. They make an incongruous pair. Mr Utterson is an eminent, middle-aged lawyer of notable dourness, as formal in manner as the ubiquitous honorific 'Mr' would suggest, very conscious of his professional and social position. Yet his chief pleasure (alluded to almost sensuously as 'the chief jewel of each week') is his Sunday walk with his kinsman.

Enfield, by contrast, has no profession, is young and is a well-known man-about-town who, presumably, dresses like one and who, if he were true-to-type, would be bonhomous and not too particular about his company: all of which sounds a trifle *outré* in the companion of Mr Utterson. True, the lawyer is known to his intimates for his good influence on 'down-going' men which, while it says something unexpected about the breadth of his acquaintanceship, has a sufficiently Gladstonian ring about it to encourage us, if only for a moment, to speculate both on his innocence and on the security of young Enfield's footing.

Nothing can be gleaned from their scanty exchanges about the nature of their relationship – except perhaps once, when the dialogue strikes another of those odd notes which so often alert the reader of this book to ulterior significance. On this occasion Utterson addresses Enfield with a sternness which has more than a little of the paternal in it: 'You see, Richard, your tale has gone home. If you have been inexact in any point, you had better correct it.' And Enfield replies like a son rebuked for venturing beyond his depth: '"I think you might have warned me", returned the other with a touch of sullenness. "But I have been pedantically exact as you call it"' (34).

'Sons' who set themselves up as authors or narrators in Stevenson usually have (or have had) a hard time from 'fathers', and Enfield seems to encounter some such antagonism here. Still, at least he shows his resentment in his sullenness and even underlines his right to tell his story by the barbed choice of the word *pedantically*. Even this quotation, however, can be used to illustrate what is by far the most striking thing about Utterson and Enfield, separately and in relationship with each other, that is, the absence of explanation and the lack of clues. Thus, while it may seem to mirror the Jekyll-and-Hyde relationship in its general contours, there is absolutely no sign of holograph wills, keys to inscrutable doors, murderous walking-canes or any of the rest of the plethora of clues which gossip about Jekyll and *his* protegé.

It is an absence characterised by (defended by?) an almost provocative reticence. If any part of anthropomorphised London 'was startled to see' the soberly-clad lawyer on his Sunday constitutional with the young and presumably fashionably-dressed man-about-town, the pair offer no sign which would restore metropolitan eyebrows to the level. Those who reported seeing them noted 'that they said nothing' (30) and when on the (unobserved) occasion when Enfield actually gets round to telling his 'very odd story', he expresses regret at having done so: 'Here is another lesson to say nothing ... I am ashamed of my long tongue. Let us make a bargain never to refer to this again.' Utterson replies, 'With all my heart' (34). Enfield takes his own advice, too, and despite being as shaken by the later revelation of Jekyll's terror as Utterson, his response to the latter's opaquely meaningful exclamation 'God forgive us! God forgive us!' is a mute one: 'But Mr Enfield only nodded his head very seriously, and walked on once more in silence' (61).

Reticent Utterson may be on a subject which would seem to him to require no commentary, but, in pointed contrast, he speculates furiously, almost obsessively, on the relationship between Jekyll and Hyde (though for the most part he keeps these speculations to himself). One consequence of his preoccupation with this issue is that it inevitably reflects back on his own puzzling relationship with Enfield and his contrasting reticence about *it*. Which prompts the question: is it Utterson's reticence (and Enfield's perhaps) which is all that stands between him and the full realisation of his Jekyll and Hyde potential? The possibility suggests a closer examination of Utterson.

*Gabriel John* Utterson would appear to have a direct line to God. Both Gabriel and John proclaimed the coming of Christ, yet the lawyer conspicuously utters (presents) no son. The 'birth' which he has responsibility for disclosing (*after* the event – and to the police) may be by parthenogenesis but it is the distillation of man's evil not of redemptive good. As a man who professes the law with great distinction, Utterson has an exalted position in the *cénacle* of authority – or father-figures. He is the confidant of other professional men of great eminence whose most sensitive affairs can be safely consigned to his discreet keeping. Jekyll, Lanyon and Carew are all clients of his and all attest to his discretion by conveying to him mysterious, sealed communications. These four distinguished men, at the apex of their professions

(Carew can be included if we concede that being a Member of Parliament is a profession which in 1886 might well have been disputed) consti- tute a representative patriarchy of the privileged and powerful *haute bourgeoisie*, owing their position not to birth but to their intellect and specialist skills in medicine and the law, both of which being intimately concerned with maintaining the constitutional health of their society. The imbrication of these two professions is deliberate, Dr Jekyll being entitled to put not just 'M.D.' after his name but 'D.C.L.' and 'LL.D.' as well.

There is something both substantial and shadowy about the élite to which these men belong. It is marked by the sort of excessive discretion and exclusivity more appropriate to Freemasons or an upper-class homosexual sub-culture than a legal and medical frater- nity. They show a high-minded determination to cover for each other, and they do not dine out but give exclusively male dinner parties in each other's homes. When Utterson presses Jekyll to let him help him, believing that some piece of scandalous behaviour in the doctor's past has led him to his present distress, he does so in a manner which indicates his ability to manipulate his society's ordinances or salvage its broken taboos in the interest of his confrères:

'Jekyll,' said Utterson, 'you know me: I am a man to be trusted. Make a clean breast of this in confidence; and I make no doubt I can get you out of it' (44).

But *is* Utterson a man to be trusted?[35] If he is, it would seem to be by no more than his fellow *cénaclistes* perhaps (who seem to feed on as well as off each other). And is there not something both fraudu- lent and sterile about this great proclaimer whose name promises so much (in terms of father/son or Father/Son generation) and who delivers so microscopically little? With such an emphasis on the prophetic word, the discovery that the chosen vessel's chief charac- teristic is reticence and an inability to 'see' presents a paradox which clamours for attention.[36] To all intents and purposes, the story-telling door keeps its 'mouth' (in the by-street façade) firmly shut; Mr Utterson is valued by his friends for his 'rich silence'. Does this uniform taci- turnity – extending to a man-about-town for whom it is surely not normal stock-in-trade – signify a recognition that words cannot articulate the deeper levels of consciousness, or a fear that they might? Is it Conradian helplessness in the face of the inarticulable or Freudian repression of what is demanding freedom of expression?

From the opening sentences of *Jekyll and Hyde* we have been made very much aware that those hidden depths, which are to become such a familiar trope, mark Mr Utterson's character too. Described as unsmiling, he is also 'odd, scanty and embarrassed in discourse; backward in sentiment; lean, long, dusty, dreary, and yet somehow lovable' (29). Impossible, one might say of this last, and doubly so to a young man-about-town. What can there possibly be to love about such a character – unless it is his subconscious? And maybe this is it for, in friendly company and relaxed by wine 'something eminently human beaconed from his eye'. 'Beaconed' or 'beckoned', either way it is an interesting word, dictated by the fact that the 'something' alluded to 'never found its way into his talk' but instead 'spoke ... in these silent symbols of the after-dinner face'. But what are we really being told in this elliptical fashion? Could it be that Mr Utterson becomes roguish in his cups – mutely roguish, that is? What *are* these silent symbols of the after-dinner face?

If the light in Utterson's eye indicates that there is warmth within, he seems to be mortally afraid to give it oxygen lest it should become a consuming blaze. To his preference for silence there is added self-imposed austerity in his pleasures: he 'drank gin when he was alone to mortify a taste for vintages; and though he enjoyed the theatre, had not crossed the doors of one for twenty years' (29). We might recall, too, that despite an alleged adherence to Cain's heresy, he was frequently 'the last reputable acquaintance and the last influence in the lives of down-going men' (29). Put all this together and there is certainly more to Utterson than is allowed to meet the eye. Why *should* he mortify himself in this way? Why *should* he concern himself with 'down-going men', or they with him? He tells us he subscribes to Cain's heresy yet in what sense can he be a good influence if he isn't, to some degree, acting as his brother's keeper? Could it be that there is yet another text underlying all the others – 'There but for the grace of God, go I'?

Later the narrator ventures to read Utterson's mind in which Jekyll figures as an 'inscrutable recluse' (59), but Utterson is equally inscrutable and even the narrator doesn't get very far. At least, however, the latter lets us see that the lawyer's inscrutability and reticence are achieved at a cost. Giving little away on the surface, Utterson nonetheless clearly exerts on himself a repressive force which bespeaks energies and drives very different from those which find expression in his professional life. These buried longings peep out in the envious wonder he expresses at 'the high pressure of spirits' involved in the 'misdeeds' of those who exercise less restraint than he.

More significantly, there seems to exist in him an ingrained level
of anxiety like a low-grade fever which never quite disappears. In
the main it seems related to an abiding concern that he might find,
in peering into his own past or beneath the surface of his actions and
responses, something that will make him a secret sharer in 'poor
Jekyll's' iniquity:

> 'Poor Harry Jekyll', he thought, 'my mind misgives me he is in
> deep waters ... the ghost of some old sin, the cancer of some
> concealed disgrace; punishment coming, *pede claudo*, years after
> memory has forgotten and self-love condoned the fault.' And the
> lawyer, scared by the thought, brooded awhile on his own past,
> groping in all the corners of memory, lest by chance some Jack-in-
> the-Box of an old iniquity should leap to light there (41–2).

His train of thought is interesting and not quite so obvious as it
might seem at first glance. His swift *reprise* of his own past is not just
to ensure that his conscience is clear – it is also to reassure himself
that he could never be subject to the same blackmail he thinks is
being applied to Jekyll. Immediately he gains such reassurance he
thinks of turning the tables on Hyde, finding out *his* secrets and
blackmailing him: 'This Master Hyde, if he were studied ... must
have secrets of his own: black secrets, by the look of him; secrets
compared to which poor Jekyll's worst would be like sunshine' (42).
Secrets would appear to exercise an unhealthy fascination upon
Utterson.

When Enfield tells him of his encounter with Hyde, his interest is
immediately caught. As he admits, prior to Enfield's account the
problem of Hyde 'had touched him on the intellectual side alone'
(37). There was a will, an unknown beneficiary and a most unusual
set of provisions. Now there is more than a name, for Mr Hyde has
materialised 'clothed upon with detestable attributes', and Utterson's
imagination can take over: 'out of the shifting, insubstantial mists
that had so long baffled his eyes, there leaped up the sudden, definite presentiment of a fiend' (36). Not only has his imagination become
engaged, it is, he admits, 'enslaved' (37), ample evidence for which
is provided by the way in which the incident at the centre of Enfield's
tale invades Utterson's dreams.

The passage in which Utterson's nightmare (for such it is) is
described is of great importance in establishing his role. It has an
interesting brief preamble: 'Six o'clock struck on the bells of the church
that was so conveniently near to Mr Utterson's dwelling ...' (37).

'Conveniently' indicates that the lawyer is a churchgoer but, given its morally ambiguous context, the church joins Utterson's battery of defences against unworthy inclinations, which includes his reticence, his inoculation with the company of down-going men, his chaste Sunday walks with Mr Enfield. Even then, the church's efficacy has already been undermined in Enfield's allusion to moral vacuity in his casually-dropped simile of the empty church.

Utterson's dream is dominated not by the act of violence on the child but by its perpetrator – and his association with Dr Jekyll. While Enfield's account 'went by before his mind in a scroll of lighted pictures', what colours Utterson's dreaming most vividly is something like an imagined assault upon Jekyll:

> He would see a room in a rich house, where his friend lay asleep, dreaming and smiling at his dreams: and then the door of that room would be opened, the curtains of the bed plucked apart, the sleeper recalled, and, lo! there would stand by his side a figure to whom power was given, and even at that dead hour he must rise and do its bidding (37).

Here is a dream-door that *does* open and is, in fact, the first of three acts of violation involving forcible entry. (Dr Jekyll's 'cabinet' will twice have its door forced, once with great violence.) As much as the act itself, however, what focuses Utterson's attention, in what seems to be a sort of waking dream, is the person of the violator, this figure 'to whom power was given'.

He sees, then, not one but two 'assaults' and it is the figure 'in these two phases', we are told, which haunts him all night. What seems to disturb him most of all about the figure is that it is *faceless*. When he 'dozed over' it was to see this intruder 'glide more stealthily through sleeping houses or move the more swiftly ... through wider labyrinths of lamp-lighted city'. But 'still the figure had no face by which he might know it; even in his dreams it had no face, or one that baffled him and melted before his eyes ...' (37–8). It has already been made clear that façades and what might lie behind them are an important motif in *Jekyll and Hyde*. Utterson contributes to it in an important way for he shows himself to be intensely concerned with the face of things, almost desperately clutching at the hope that he will be able to confine himself to the surface and read there the answers to the riddles which beset him. As the erotic character of his nightmare would suggest, however, he is deceiving himself.

At one point his attributed repetition of the word 'face' seems to amount to an attempt at exorcism, though whether the demon is in him or Jekyll is a moot point:

> thus it was there sprang up and grew apace in the lawyer's mind a singularly strong, almost an inordinate, curiosity to behold the features of the real Mr Hyde. If he could but once set eyes on him, he thought the mystery would lighten and perhaps roll altogether away, as was the habit of mysterious things when well examined. He might see a reason for his friend's strange preference or bondage (call it which you please), and even for the startling clauses of the will. And at least it would be a face worth seeing: the face of a man who was without bowels of mercy: a face which had but to show itself to raise up, in the mind of the unimpressionable Enfield, a spirit of enduring hatred (38).

Twice in this quite dense paragraph, Utterson's profession as lawyer is conspicuously alluded to (the figure 'haunted the lawyer', there 'grew apace in the lawyer's mind ...') and in neither case does the allusion reflect that dispassionate and deliberate habit of mind which might normally be expected in a literary representation of the legal mind (such as is found in Rankeillor's characterisation in *Kidnapped*, for example, or in the Writer Stewart's in *Catriona*). Instead, that mind seems to be invaded by disordered images, unacknowledged compulsions and ulterior desires.

From being haunted, Utterson now furtively starts to 'haunt the door in the by-street of shops' (38), keeping his vigil at all hours of the day and night:

> In the morning before office hours, at noon when business was plenty and time scarce, at night under the face of the fogged city moon, by all lights and at all hours of solitude or concourse, the lawyer was to be found on his chosen post (38).

'If he shall be Mr Hyde ... I shall be Mr Seek' he tells us, oblivious to (or sub-consciously aware of?) the fact that when the seeker finds the hider, they exchange roles. Tormented by the impenetrability of the conundrum Jekyll has set him and unwilling or unable to admit that his investigation is doomed to frustration when the founding imperative of all such enquiries – *nosce teipsum* – is ignored, he is wrapped in a fog of ignorance and repression every bit as dense as the one that turns morning in Soho into twilight.

When at last he succeeds in intercepting Hyde he eagerly asks to see his face. It doesn't help: 'The lawyer stood awhile when Mr Hyde had left him, the picture of disquietude' (40). Having seen Hyde and stared into his face, he cannot find words to describe what he has seen. Hyde 'gave the impression of deformity without any nameable malformation' but that doesn't fully account for the 'hitherto unknown disgust, loathing *and fear*' (my italics) which now assail Utterson: '"There must be something else", said the perplexed gentleman. "There *is* something more if I could only find a name for it."'

But he can't, of course, because Hyde is an unacknowledged construct of his own, the product of the dark and complex workings of human underconsciousness and is no more 'nameable' than is, say, the power which Marlow in Conrad's *Lord Jim* is called upon to explain to Jewel who sees it as possessing Jim. So Utterson falls back on a traditional theory of possession and on the wishful thinking that such powers obligingly autograph their victims' faces: 'O my poor old Harry Jekyll, if ever I read Satan's signature upon a face, it is on that of your new friend' (40). It must take a considerable effort, one might think, for Mr Seek to conceal from himself the fact that he, possessed of the same underconsciousness, is also Mr Hyde; and that the face he is searching for – and failing to recognise – is his own.

The next time Utterson gazes upon the face of Mr Hyde he is given another chance to reflect upon what they might have in common. Having battered down the door into Jekyll's cabinet he and Poole find lying beyond it a dead body and a profusion of ironies: 'They drew near on tip-toe, turned it on its back and beheld the face of Edward Hyde' (70). When, after so many references to doors – usually shut except where they occur in dreams – a door is finally broken open, it discloses no solution to the mysteries Utterson seeks to unravel: to the contrary, the *dead* face of Hyde is going to tell him nothing he didn't know before. Far from advancing his knowledge, the lawyer almost comically fails in his interpretation of what he *does* see: he 'knew', he says, that he was 'looking on the body of a self-destroyer'. What he was actually looking on was himself; and perhaps he is saved by his ignorance. Lanyon, by contrast, who has likewise (in Veeder's words) 'never had to face the Hyde hidden within us all, succumbs to the epiphany which is self-revelation'. Whatever is destroyed when Hyde kills himself, it is not *simply* Hyde, not simply *a* self. Jekyll had, after all, knowingly taken a drug which he was well aware would shake 'the very fortress of identity' (83) and release one or more of those denizens that dwell within the human polity. Perhaps the most telling irony, however, lies in the fact that Utterson, in company with the reflecting Poole (the *bon mot* is Veeder's), *enacts* what has evaded his comprehension. Stevenson achieves this by his deft juxtaposition of two tableaux.

The first of these has already been mentioned and consists of two faces peering down at the not entirely immobile features of the dead Hyde, who therefore seems to be staring back at them ('... the cords of his face still moved with a semblance of life ...' [70]). A page later we learn that 'the searchers came to the cheval-glass, into whose depths they looked with an involuntary horror'. What do they expect to find in it that they look in with 'horror'? More secrets, presumably, and they are, of course, again disappointed.

For one thing, the mirror was so turned that it did not even reflect the dead Hyde; instead it reflected a scene of great domestic 'ordinariness' and warmth, 'the rosy glow playing on the roof, the fire sparkling in a hundred repetitions along the glazed front of the presses' (71). Only at the end of this cunningly-worked sentence which, as Veeder rightly points out, is designed to mislead us momentarily into thinking that this domestic scene is *all* we are going to see, do we get the materialisation to which their horror then becomes related – 'their own pale and fearful countenances stooping to look in'. Thus, from seeing them stooping over the uncommunicative face of the dead Hyde, we are switched to their stooping over the cheval-glass where they find first the very opposite of the horror they anticipate – cosy domesticity – and then, unwillingly perhaps, their own faces. There is irony in this *coup de théâtre*. All Utterson's attempts to read secrets from faces or to discover solutions to mysteries behind closed doors or inside one of the many enclosures which come his way are doomed to failure; the answer lies all the time within himself, behind his own face, deep in his own subconscious.

This suggests another possible dimension to the 'Hyde hidden within us all' explanation. In one obvious sense, Hyde is the son of Henry Jekyll and in being sired in the way he was he becomes available as 'the *son* within us all' to the middle-aged bachelors in this austere, apparently self-denying *cénacle*. What these men have denied themselves above all is children – specifically sons who might ultimately challenge the privileges, authority and powers of the patriarchate. Thus, one could argue, what they find monstrous in Hyde is, *au fond*, his sonship. However, sons, like Nemesis, will not be denied, and in finding his own in looking for Hyde's face, Utterson makes the most unwelcome discovery of all – himself as father. Recognising this helps us to understand the lawyer's relationship to Enfield which was such a puzzle to everyone, and the significance of the pairing of Utterson/Enfield with Jekyll/Hyde. Enfield, with his slight hints of the mysterious and the disreputable, is a prophylactic foster-son: he is, to pursue the risky metaphor, the vaccine Utterson innoculates himself with to prevent himself contracting a Hyde. The same explanation would account for the lawyer's unexpected relish for the company of 'down-going men'.

Questions remain. Why, for example, do Poole and Utterson attack the red baize door with such savagery? Why is the description so extended, the door so stubborn and so nearly imbued with life? If the syntax in the passage describing the mirror is designed to mislead initially, here it also encourages us to adopt an interim reading which runs counter to the one the whole paragraph eventually demands:

> Poole swung the axe over his shoulder; the blow shook the building and the red baize door leaped against the lock and hinges. A dismal screech, as of mere animal terror, rang from the cabinet. Up went the axe again, and again the panels crashed and the frame bounded; four times the blow fell; but the wood was tough and the fittings were of excellent workmanship; and it was not until the fifth that the lock burst in sunder, and the wreck of the door fell inwards on the carpet (69).

When we read 'the red baize door leaped against the lock and hinges. A dismal screech ... .' we recognise another piece of syntactical sleight-of-hand which has the effect of making it impossible for us not to think of the door as a living thing giving voice to pain. Yet the next paragraph begins 'The besiegers ... ', which makes Utterson and Poole sound like an army besieging a fortress rather than the brute murderers that their hacking at the screeching door suggests. What lies beyond the door is Dr Jekyll's inner sanctum and since he is, as Veeder rightly says, 'the very embodiment of patriarchy' (qualified, as he is, in both medicine *and* law) his room is the very fortress of the patriarchy's identity. So why does Utterson (or rather Poole) come to attack it, and with such ferocity? After all a crow-bar would have done a better job than an axe. Or, to put the question another way, who is the door?

Veeder claims it is Jekyll but to justify his position he has to mount the awkward (though, given the amount of doubling in the text, not altogether indefensible) argument that 'Jekyll is father at this moment'; that he can be at once 'oedipal father to Utterson and oedipal son in his own fantasy life' (135). Thus Utterson, through Poole, in assaulting the door is 'directing against Jekyll the oedipal "vengeance" that Jekyll directed against Carew through Hyde' (136). Here, I believe, this very ingenious critic is practising his own sleight-of-hand, causing the fact that, in the text, 'vengeance' is tied firmly to the rights of *patriarchy* to disappear.

The first part of 'The Last Night', culminating in the conversation between Utterson and Poole before the assault on the door, is both very dense and very important. For the first time the patriarchs (I include the 'elderly' Poole here since he is an integral part of the sub-structure of patriarchy) invoke the aid of the Supreme Patriarch and it is assuredly not invoked against the terrestrial *doyen* of the fathers.

Both Poole and Utterson suddenly turn pious on page 63. Then, 'Bless God! it's Mr Utterson', cries the cook on page 64, intrepidly running forward 'as if to take him in her arms'. On page 65 Poole delivers a threnodial lament pitched somewhere between Mistress Quickly and the Hound of Heaven:

'No, sir; master's made away with; he was made away with eight days ago, when we heard him cry upon the name of God; and *who's* in there instead of him, and *why* it stays there, is a thing that cries to Heaven, Mr Utterson!'

On page 66 God's help is invoked by both Jekyll and Utterson while on page 67 Poole gives up altogether on human reasoning (on which Utterson had set such store): 'No, Sir, that thing in the mask was never Dr Jekyll – God knows what it was ...'. On page 68 he draws a distinction between legal and biblical texts and audaciously chooses to put his faith in the inner light rather than the Inner Temple: 'O I know it's not evidence, Mr Utterson; I'm book-learned enough for that; but a man has his feelings; and I give you my bible-word it was Mr Hyde.' On the same page Utterson concedes that 'God alone can tell' and then proceeds to take Him over with 'Well, let our name be vengeance' – before descending rather abruptly from the transcendental to appeal for help from a distinctly lower-level cherubim: 'Call Bradshaw.' Intriguingly, what triggers the assault is Hyde appealing to Utterson to have mercy in the name of God. '"... that's not Jekyll's voice – it's Hyde's", cried Utterson. "Down with the door, Poole"' (69).

There seems to me to be no way of reconciling this sequence of allusions and events with the notion of Utterson oedipally raging against father Jekyll. As the solidarity of the patriarchs dissolves in death and disappearance, those remaining have to reach out beyond themselves and press into service the sanctions of a greater Patriarch (but one who can be confidently depended on to side with the fathers); and the object of their combined wrath is, of course, *the usurping son* – 'a thing that cries to Heaven'.

The ferocity of the attack on the red baize door has, I would suggest, a good deal to do with the unaccommodating reticence of the scarred one which gives on to the by-street; the door which remains shut except when young Mr Hyde, in privileged possession of a key, opens it. It was a door which, in admitting Hyde, shut out the rest of the patriarchy from Jekyll's confidence. At this time it was the red baize door which had provided the 'official' entrance to the inner sanctum of this hierarch whom Enfield had described as 'the very pink of the proprieties'; and when an attack upon it would have been an attack on Jekyll and all he stood for. It promised direct access to the innermost recesses of his – and thence the patriarchy's – being and could only be approached (like the documents in Mr Utterson's safe) through enclosure after enclosure. When Utterson makes his last visit, he goes first into the house then through it into the courtyard, then 'into the laboratory building and through the surgical theatre' (64) until he reaches the stairs leading to the door of the cabinet.

Now everything has changed: the Holy of Holies has not just been invaded by Hyde; he has *displaced* Jekyll and usurped his quarters. This is what most outrages Poole, the servant of the patriarchy, as a total inversion of the moral order governing his universe. In another reversal of affairs symptomatic of the demoralisation of the West End patriarchate, it is the servant Poole who stiffens Utterson's sinews and it is *his* ageing muscle which finally breaks down the door to get at the hated Hyde.

Once convinced of Jekyll's death – "I believe poor Harry is killed" (68) – Utterson is nothing loath to spearhead the assault. He has long shown himself to be curious, disapproving and partly jealous of young Hyde's special relationship with Jekyll: 'Your master seems to repose a great deal of trust in that young man, Poole', he says to Jekyll's servant, playing the *faux naif*. In his sensual dreaming he sees Hyde as a potent figure, one 'to whom power was given' and he perceives him to dominate the very embodiment of patriarchy, Henry Jekyll.

Those who want to pursue the homoerotic line could quote what is surely the most visibly 'camp' remark of the novella when Utterson, under pressure from Jekyll to look after Hyde should he, his protector, die, responds (almost tearfully, it seems), 'I can't pretend that I shall ever like him' (44).

The whole episode of the assault upon the door teeters on the brink of absurdist farce. These two men, well-advanced in years, set about planning the operation with a military briskness that is almost convincing. 'We give you ten minutes to get to your stations' (68), General Utterson tells his forces (consisting of a foot-man and a knife-boy), and a *candle* is set in place 'to light them to the attack' (69). All culminates in Utterson's command (to the butler) 'Down with the door, Poole!' (69) and, though not without a prodigious effort, the red baize door duly collapses.

No doubt Veeder is right in seeing significance for patrilinear succession in Jekyll having purchased 'old Dr Denman's surgical theatre'. No doubt, either, that 'Denman is the primal father, the absent origin' (121); and it is interesting to learn that 'cabinet' – the name always used in referring to Jekyll's private laboratory – can mean 'the den of the beast'. All this confers profound symbolic significance on the patriarchal incumbent. The trouble is that when the door crashes down what the somewhat disconcerted 'besiegers' are confronted by is neither a raging beast nor a profaned shrine but the total antithesis of such expectations: what appears, at first glance at least, to be a scene of archetypal Victorian domesticity. Well may they stand 'appalled by their own riot', contrasted as it is with 'the stillness that has succeeded' (69).

Veeder would have it that the whole tableau constitutes 'a kind of parlour primal scene' (136) with Jekyll/Hyde as father/mother and Utterson/Poole as the observing child. But, one is inclined to object, the kettle is singing on the hob, the tea-things are laid out; this is London, the capital of England and heart of the Empire, and father Jekyll and mother Hyde are going to have tea, not sex, before the eyes of their affronted (and bifurcated) child. Or they would if they were there, but father is nowhere to be seen and mother lies dead (but twitching) on the carpet.

The chamber is described as 'the quietest room ... and but for the glazed presses full of chemicals, the most commonplace that night in London' (70). The glazed presses *and* 'the body of a man sorely contorted and still twitching' one would like to add; plus, perhaps the slight oddity of the absent 'embodiment of patriarchy' spirited away (we are told again) while about to engage in the most innocent of homely activities: 'the easy chair was drawn cosily up, and the tea-things stood ready to the sitter's elbow, the very sugar in the cup' (71).[37]

The fact is that the screech from the door is the patriarchy's *dernier cri*. Lanyon and Carew are both dead, Jekyll has likewise gone forever and now the focus of the survivors' antagonism, young Mr Hyde, the 'ugly idol in the glass' as his begetter calls him, the embodiment of anti-patriarchy, is also beyond their reach. 'Hyde is gone to his account', says Utterson, 'sternly' proving that, like Lord Weir, he can be stern and gratified simultaneously.

The triumph is, however, hollow and for two reasons, the first of which has already been touched on. The power and standing of the patriarchy have been irretrievably forfeited: their clay feet of hypocrisy and appalling lack of self-knowledge have given way under them. 'The Last Night' of the chapter-heading signals the end of the patriarchal collective not just the demise of its *doyen*. Scandal and exposure, which Utterson has throughout laboured to prevent, are inevitable.[38]

Secondly, the discovery of the quiet chamber beyond the door, devoid of any raving monster, confronts them with the unwelcome reality that the threat to the patriarchy had *never* been external. The only secret that lay behind the door (indeed behind all the many doors) was their own unruly and unacknowledged (save, ultimately, by Jekyll) underconsciousness, whose workings expose the inauthenticity in their assumption of patriarchy. These men have all ingeniously evaded the necessary confrontations which would have ensured their maturity and justified their aspirations at least to paternity if not patriarchy. They have done so, it would seem, by secretly partitioning themselves into unsinkable compartments behind stout bulkheads with watertight doors. But Jekyll, in his desire to leap into the sea of liberty, had crossed one of these thresholds with the aid of a drug which 'shook the doors of the prison-house of [his] disposition' (85).

Utterson, on the other hand, battens down all hatches, though not without some effort, as his nightmare shows. As a result, not even the emptiness of the chamber beyond the red baize door or coming face to face with himself in the cheval-glass, brings home to him the truth of what experience is trying to tell him. Face-to-face for him will, alas, always mean *I-to-I*: he will never get beyond that construct to the *alter idem*. Characteristically, he retires to his house clutching his 'enclosures', still determined to find an external explanation; which is why he is not only the last but, in some ways, the most dangerous of the patriarchs.

## Sons and Lovers or Disgusting Phoenix?

In a useful reference to the Vienna–Edinburgh axis, Veeder writes that

> [n]ot only are Freud and Stevenson both products of late-nine-teenth-century European culture, they share the more particular fact of personal concern with and anxiety about professionalism, fathers and Fathers. Still more important, they envision the psyche, experience, and art as each multi-levelled and occlusive.

As this study has attempted to establish, nearly all of Stevenson's major fictional works deal, obliquely or frontally, with complexly hostile father/son relations.[39] Most often the focus is on that critical phase in oedipal development when the son's progress to maturity has been arrested either by a paralysis of his will or by a perceived antagonism of the real or symbolic father (which may, of course, be the same thing). In *Jekyll and Hyde* a large part of the alterity the patriarchs deny and repress is that of their youthfully independent selves, including that self-indulgence which sets them at odds with authority. The worst of his faults, says Henry Jekyll, 'was a certain gaiety of disposition, such as has made the happiness of many' and he who was 'fond of the respect of the wise and the good' found it hard to reconcile these instincts with his 'imperious desire to carry [his] head high ... before the public' (81).

*Jekyll and Hyde* is the most complex of all the texts dealt with in this study, part of that complexity being signalled in Jekyll's explicit recognition 'that man is not truly one, but truly two' and in his knowledgeable forecast that 'man will be ultimately known for a mere polity of multifarious, incongruous and independent denizens' (82). Jekyll's perception here makes it clear that the sort of complexity confronting us results from what a critic has called that radical probing of the nature of selfhood which is a central characteristic of modernist writing. Dennis Brown in his book *The Modernist Self* writes of the divided self as helping to prepare the way for the fragmentary self but he sees Browning as the harbinger of this latter notion rather than Hogg, Wordsworth or Stevenson, since he was able to suggest 'both the plurality and the relativity of selfhood, without any passage through the paradoxicality of the Double'. He quotes Hillis Miller in support of his view of Browning as a ground-breaking pioneer:

> in Browning's day and in England, the idea of the indeterminacy of selfhood was a scandalous notion, contrary to the traditional British conviction that each man has a substantial inner core of self.[40]

The idea was not at all scandalous to Stevenson, however, to whom Brown devotes only one line, and Ronald Thomas's account seems to me to 'place' him (as the author of *Jekyll and Hyde*) much more satisfactorily. Advancing the view that the novel 'is no longer the scene of self-possession; it has become a sign of the self's dissolution', Thomas goes on to argue his case that

> *Jekyll and Hyde* announces this development by launching an elaborate assault on the ideals of the individual personality and the cult of character that dominated the nineteenth century, striking at the heart of that ideology: the life story. Moreover, this case is in its narrative form as well as its content at the beginning of a tradition subversive to conventional self-narration, a tradition that can be traced through the central modernist English writers of fictional autobiography – Conrad, Joyce, and, most prominently, Beckett. A further claim is that *Jekyll and Hyde* is ultimately concerned with fundamental questions about the authority of texts and the power of language to represent human life – the very questions that preoccupy much of modern fiction and criticism as well.[41]

This Modernist reading of the significance of *Jekyll and Hyde* is in no way diluted if we observe that the multifariousness Jekyll speaks of does not just exist on a linear, horizontal plane: fathers and sons still form a competing hierarchy though in keeping with the emerging Freudian age they have now a capacity to substitute for each other in a way that will perpetuate all sorts of relational ambivalences.

The patriarchs of the novella are all to a greater or lesser degree hypocrites; but it is not enough simply to quote Stevenson himself ('The harm was in Jekyll, because he was a hypocrite – not because he was fond of women.... The hypocrite let out the beast Hyde...'.[42]) and to leave it at that. Even a hypocrite has to have a 'real' or stable character to be false to, and these men do not have such a thing as a 'real' self or even a stable polity of selves. While they may conform to the image of the patriarch dictated by their society, their qualifications are professional ones, not psycho-biological. They have missed a phase of oedipal development and become old without ever having become mature. As a result they are not sure whether to treat the young as sons, sibling rivals or lovers. It we take Jekyll as the model, they end up by treating them as all three.

Too inhibited, repressed or immature to sire sons, these men find them by creating unencumbered alter egos; younger versions of themselves, in fact, whom they can love with more than narcissistic fervour, yet without actually committing incest. Thus Jekyll can dote upon the liberated Hyde and Utterson upon Enfield the urban nomad. Of course, for these men to do this is to turn the oedipal cross-roads into a by-pass. No father will ever get killed; no mother will become the object of her offspring's desire; and no son will ever grow up.

The story of the door has a parallel text though we became aware of it only retrospectively. The effect is of an inadequately cleaned parchment or *palimpsestus* where the first text is still faintly – or not-so-faintly – legible under the second. Thus by the time we get that text in Henry Jekyll's 'full Statement of the Case' all sorts of speculations have been inscribed which will not be erased by Jekyll's explanatory statement – which is, into the bargain, anything but full.

The opening words of the novella set complacently before us a world of upper-middle-class professionals, closely-knit, self-regarding, secure in their society's approbation: 'Mr Utterson the lawyer ...'; the definite article says it all. 'Everybody' in society knows who Mr Utterson is: he is one of their own anointed. So for his friends: 'the great Dr Lanyon' has his home in Cavendish Square 'that citadel of medicine', the two have been 'old mates both at school and college' and both are 'thorough respecters of themselves and each other' (36). Dr Jekyll's is a name 'very well known and often printed' (32). Nothing could be more stable it would seem and yet within a few pages not only Utterson but Jekyll, Lanyon and Enfield, too, will have large question-marks over them and this male world will begin to seem very *unstable* in its representatives. Perhaps Lanyon shows best just how fragile it is when, ambushed by the war in *his* members, instead of looking into the abyss, he turns his face to the wall.

Writing of the negation of male sexuality in *Jekyll and Hyde* – 'taken for granted and repressed in the one operation' – as something which 'goes along with the exclusion of a woman', Stephen Heath concludes with this remark: 'Excluding women, Stevenson loses the

key to the stable representation of men ... the result is the fascination with the double, men as unstable, something else ...'.[43] While I
agree that there *is* a connection, to say Stevenson *loses* the key is to
make it sound as culpably reprehensible as being found in a hand-
bag was to Lady Bracknell. Stevenson is surely postulating what
happens when the key has been lost, thrown away, never found or
never looked for.

What draws attention to the instability is the imbalance between
their social and professional eminence, which requires of them the
sobriety and *gravitas* of patriarchs, and their personal and domestic
lives, celibate and childless. As a consequence, their insisted-upon
solidarity takes on the character of a clique with an obscure vested
interest in bachelorhood. The substitution of the barren formalities
of the master/male servant relationship for the family hierarchy of
father and son reinforces the introverted character of their relationship to each other.

The impression these men leave is of a defensive masonic sodality
displacing family relationships. In the privacy of their homes they
are seen to be notably isolated figures – an isolation which is, if
anything, accentuated by their giving each other all-male dinner
parties. (Sometimes dinner is for a meagre two only as, for example,
when Utterson has his clerk, the anonymously-named Mr Guest, in
to dine with him.) After one sociable evening, when Jekyll had
entertained to dinner 'some five or six old cronies, all intelligent
reputable men' (43), Utterson remains behind. This 'was no new
arrangement,' we are told, since tired hosts 'loved to detain the dry
lawyer' so that they could 'sit awhile in his unobtrusive company,
*practising for solitude,* [my italics] sobering their minds in the man's
rich silence, after the expense and strain of gaiety' (43). The paragraph is a dense one, tantalising in the way it dangles before us
inscrutable possibilities. There is an irresistible suggestion that these
men are practising to resume their masks of impassivity, preparing,
'after the expense and strain of gaiety', to seek refuge in discreet
silence, husbanding themselves, one might say. The sheer incongruity
of the phrase 'the expense and strain of gaiety' also demands our
interrogation, it being so utterly at odds with the image we have of
Jekyll and his 'cronies'. What expense, we want to know? Not finan-
cial, obviously, since they are all rich enough not to notice it. What
strain – and, above all, what *gaiety*? It, too, begins to take on an occult
significance, a surmise which is strengthened when the word occurs
again (as 'gaily') a mere nine lines later. As has already been

mentioned, the word has by this time (1886) acquired insalubrious connotations with prostitution. William Veeder, quoting studies by John Boswell and Eve Kosofsky Sedgwick, and his own research in Anglo-American gothic fiction between 1885 and 1914, goes further, writing that he has 'no doubt that the use of 'gay' and 'queer' in the homoerotic sense was widespread in the years before 1900'.[44] It should also be noted that 1885, the year in which *Jekyll and Hyde* was written was, in the words of Jeffrey Weeks, 'an *annus mirabilis* of sexual politics'. Stevenson could not but have been aware of the intense debate which went on about sexual morality, sometimes very publicly. In August of that year there was a huge demonstration in Hyde Park with one speaker holding forth on the theme that 'our public men shall be pure', the sort of demand that Jekyll would have us believe drove him to create Hyde. Shortly after this rally, the Criminal Laws Amendment Act was passed dealing with, *inter alia*, prostitution, the age of consent and male homosexual behaviour. It was on to this measure that the notorious Labouchère Amendment was grafted, bringing within the law *all* forms of male homosexual activity whether conducted in public or in private.[45] Such a context as this furore provides, makes the reticence and furtiveness of Utterson and his circle seem even more suggestive.

It may be, however, that our attention is simply being drawn to the fact that what binds these men together is not their commitment to the public good, but deeply personal concerns which cannot be overtly expressed or acknowledged. There can be no doubt that their private 'gaiety' – excessive enough to be fatiguing, if we give due regard to 'expense' and 'strain' – is quite at odds with their public *personae*. Just as these men have, collectively, a private world which lies beyond our scrutiny (let me repeat, they dine at each other's homes, not, as you'd expect from men of their prominence and wealth, in clubs), so individually they keep us at arm's length, an effect due precisely to that impenetrable 'otherness' with which each is invested. Thus Utterson is 'cold', 'scanty and embarrassed in discourse, and backward in sentiment' (29). He is also given to mortifying the flesh, drinking gin instead of his preferred wine and depriving himself of visits to the theatre despite his love of it. Jekyll is described as having 'something of a slyish cast' (43); while Lanyon expresses a geniality which is 'somewhat theatrical to the eye' though it 'reposed upon a genuine feeling' (36). Obviously, these men are anything but open books. Utterson's unsmiling reticence conceals an unidentified anxiety which surfaces as nightmares, apprehensive soul-searching and self-mortification. Jekyll's slyness and Lanyon's falseness (his 'theatrical' gestures are contrasted with 'genuine feeling') are both important qualifications of their public *personae*.

It is particularly noteworthy that though all three men have a high degree of what in Sir Danver Carew's case is called 'well-founded self-content', they all share a common fear of exposure. Utterson worries about this continually on behalf of Jekyll, and his concern is heightened by the possibility of his being 'sucked down in the eddy of the scandal' of Carew's murder. It is curious to find the word 'scandal' applied to the brutal murder of the Member of Parliament and quite enough to revive speculation as to just why the 'aged and beautiful gentleman' had found himself accosting a young stranger, 'with a very pretty manner of politeness', in a moonlit lane not far from the river, when all he'd gone out to do, apparently, was post a letter. On his part, one of the most important of Jekyll's reasons for creating Hyde was so that he should 'no longer [be] exposed to disgrace and penitence' (87). Lanyon who *does* suffer a vicarious exposure of himself when Hyde reveals who and what he is, recognises that he, too, is (as Jekyll twice calls him) 'hide-bound', and the truth kills him.

The secretiveness, which distinguishes this exclusive coterie, the other side of these very public figures whom 'everybody' knows, is well reflected in so much apparently going on behind closed doors. Their communications, too, testify to the same preference for concealment, as enclosures are wrapped in enclosures ending, more often than not, enclosed in Mr Utterson's safe. Thus Lanyon's letter to the lawyer is sealed with his seal which, when broken, discloses another enclosure, also sealed, which Utterson, despite the temptation to break it, too, and (he hopes) get straight to the heart of the matter, places as requested in 'the *inmost corner* of his *private* safe' (my italics). When Utterson and Poole search Jekyll's cabinet, they discover a sealed envelope and open it. Predictably, 'several enclosures fell to the floor', one of which is another 'considerable packet' sealed in several places. Taking it, the lawyer 'encloses' it in his pocket and, enjoining Poole to 'say nothing of this paper', encloses it in silence.

When Hyde's true origins are revealed in the last chapter, he at once provides a focus for all those alterities which have shadowed the patriarchs throughout the novella. In Jekyll's surprisingly conventional description he is 'the lower elements in my soul' (83).⁴⁶ At the risk of appearing presumptuous, we can, I think, do a bit better than this. Hyde is the product of patriarchal apprehensions, inhibitions, hypocrisy, self-deception and self-indulgence – to name but a few elements in his paternity suite, as one might call it.

Long before Jekyll's experiments had begun to 'suggest the most naked possibility of such a miracle', he had 'with pleasure' indulged himself 'as in a beloved day-dream' by imagining the delightful conse-quences of being able to house his two natures 'in separate entities'. The introverted sensuality that colours this description hints at the intensity of 'the perennial war among [the] members' (82) which his scientific studies chance to illuminate. It makes all the more urgent and attractive the prospect of being able to separate the just and the unjust, so that the former need no longer live in fear of being disgraced by his reprobate twin.

Jekyll makes great play with the fact that the pleasures he had indulged in and concealed were not of any great iniquity but suffi-cient to get in the way of his 'imperious desire' to hold his head high in society. Some men, he claims, would have 'blazoned such irregu-larities' but given the expectations of his peers and his own ambitions, he 'hid them with an almost morbid sense of shame' (81). Commenting on this 'duplicity of life', Stephen Heath quotes appositely from Freud's essay '"Civilized" sexual morality and modern nervous illness':

> All who wish to be more noble-minded than their constitution allows fall victim to neurosis; they would have been more healthy if it could have been possible for them to be less good.⁴⁷

Jekyll thinks he has found a way of circumventing such a problem by dividing his two natures into different entities and disclaiming all responsibility for what his 'second self' gets up to. He comes to learn, of course, that 'the doom and burden of our life is bound forever on man's shoulders' which leads him straight to the analyst's couch: 'when the attempt is made to cast it off, it but returns upon us with more familiar and more awful pressure' (83).

The creation of Hyde, with all its horrifying risks, is proof enough of the strength of Jekyll's desire to escape from the constraints and demands of patriarchy; but that desire is compounded of different elements. Among these, however, Jekyll does *not* number disinter-ested scientific enquiry or idealism: 'Had I approached my discovery in a more noble spirit, had I risked the experiment while under the

empire of generous and pious aspirations ... I had come forth an
angel instead of a fiend' (85). What does seem central in his compulsion to create Hyde is the drive to achieve a sensual gratification of
a limitless kind which allows aspects of the self to enjoy an infinite
degree of freedom. This, he is honest enough to admit, predicates
youth for which he clearly still has a hankering. Indeed, the latter
may have been something of a trigger:

> I would still be merrily disposed at times; and as my pleasures
> were (to say the least) undignified, and I was not only well-known
> and highly considered, but growing towards the elderly man, this
> incoherency of my life was daily growing more unwelcome.

And he adds (my italics): 'It was *on this side* that my new power
tempted me until I fell into slavery. I had but to drink the cup, to
doff at once the body of the noted professor and to assume, like a
thick cloak, that of Edward Hyde' (85–6).

In 'A Chapter on Dreams', Stevenson paid generous tribute to the
role of the 'Brownies' in the conception of *Jekyll and Hyde* but he
makes clear that the 'meaning of the tale' is his alone and 'had long
pre-existed in my garden of Adonis, and tried one body after another
in vain' (52). One such 'body' is Asenath's tale, 'The Destroying Angel'
in *The Dynamiter* (published in the previous year) where Dr Grierson's
experiments have quite a lot in common with Dr Jekyll's. Explicitly
the object of his scientific investigations is his own rejuvenation.
Having persuaded Asenath that she should marry his son (whom
she had never seen) he then reveals that that son is himself:'when I
offered you a son of mine I did so in a figure. That son – that husband,
Asenath, is myself – not as you now behold me, but restored to the
first energy of youth. You think me mad? When you behold me puri-
fied, invigorated, renewed, re-stamped in the original image ... I
shall be able to laugh with a better grace at your passing and natural
incredulity' (45). Unfortunately there has been a little hitch: 'A difficulty unforeseen – the impossibility of obtaining a certain drug in its
full purity – has forced me to resort to London unprepared' (44). He
believes he has solved the problem of the impure element (unlike Dr
Jekyll) and is confident of the outcome: 'I have succeeded in proving
that the singularly unstable equilibrium of the elixir, at the moment
of projection, is due rather to the impurity than to the nature of the
ingredients; and as all are now of an equal and exquisite nicety, I
have little fear for the result' (47). Of course, this being burlesque,
we do not share Dr Grierson's optimism and are justified when he

duly blows himself up. However, the links with *Jekyll and Hyde* are clear and in many respects (though certainly not all) Hyde is just such a 'figure' of Jekyll when young.

If, among Jekyll's strongest temptations, was the possibility of renewing his youth and re-experiencing the novelty of things, the effect of drinking the potion was all he could have wished for: 'There was something strange in my sensations, something indescribably new and, for its novelty, incredibly sweet. I felt younger, lighter, happier in body.' Appropriately enough the feeling is accompanied by the dissolution of his sense of responsibility and the release of a powerful sexual energy: 'I was conscious of a heady recklessness, a current of disordered sensual images running like a mill-race in my fancy, a solution of the bonds of obligation, an unknown but not an innocent freedom of the soul' (83).

Later, as he sees his 'original and better self' losing ground to Hyde, he makes a strenuous effort to reassert the old Jekyll with all his divided impulses – and his years:

> Yes, I preferred the elderly and discontented doctor surrounded by friends and cherishing honest hopes and bade a resolute farewell to the liberty, the comparative youth, the light step, leaping pulses and secret pleasures that I had enjoyed in the disguise of Hyde (90).

Before he suffers his change of heart and tries to 'embrac[e] anew the restriction of natural life' (91) he exults in his new-found ability one minute 'to plod in the public eye with a load of genial responsibility', and the next 'like a schoolboy, [to] strip off these lendings and spring headlong into the sea of liberty' (86). But Jekyll's immersion in this sea is far from the innocence his simile would suggest. In fact, all those hidden depths, guarded Pooles and deep wells are fed by this sea of liberty which is a whole lot closer to Baudelaire's 'mer monstrueuse et sans bords' than it is to a schoolboy's summer delight.

Another ambition nourished by his research which goes into the making of Hyde is the pursuit of knowledge into Faustian realms traditionally disastrous for man and having to do with the dissection or 'dethronement' of 'the powers that [make] up [the] spirit'. ('I thus drew steadily nearer to that truth by whose partial discovery I have been doomed to such a dreadful shipwreck' [82]). It is notable that when Hyde tempts Lanyon (successfully), he does so by offering the satanic inducement of access to hidden knowledge verified by means of a miraculous epiphany – 'your sight shall be blasted by a prodigy to stagger the unbelief of Satan' (79). As Veeder puts it, 'Lanyon, who has never had to face the Hyde hidden within us all, succumbs to the epiphany which is self-revelation.'[48]

Implicit in this ambition to penetrate arcane mysteries is an urge on Jekyll's part to – as a later writer was to say – 'make it new', to transcend the accepted professional rituals and fields of enquiry authorised by his conservative peers, and explore 'a *new* province of knowledge', '*new* avenues to fame and power' (79: my italics). And Jekyll relishes the role, as the heady sequence 'I was the first ... I was the first' (86) testifies. As reckless as Baudelaire's voyager who welcomes death itself as an opportunity 'To find something *new* in the depth of the Unknown',[49] he realises his ambition to the full.

So far, considerable space has been devoted to the 'why' of Hyde. (Stevenson is Freudian in his express wish 'to know ... not what people did, but why they did it – or rather, why they *thought* they did it'.)[50] Now, though the categories are far from exclusive, some attention can be given to the 'what'. It is clear that what Jekyll's friends fear and suspect is a sexual scandal, and it is easy to understand why. There are only three plausible explanations for the doctor's unlikely liaison: Hyde is either his son, a lover, or a blackmailer who knows of some indiscretions in Jekyll's private life. This last explanation is the one preferred by Enfield who sees Jekyll as 'an honest man paying through the nose for the capers of his youth' (33), and he confers the name 'Blackmail House' on the place with the door.

Enfield, however, has patently opted for the least damaging explanation and the others must be entertained. Though one might have some reservations about Elaine Showalter's assertion that, to contemporary readers, 'the term blackmail would have immediately suggested homosexual liaisons',[51] it is hard to dispute the view, given the nuances in the narrative, that this is the direction which the reader is being invited to follow. In the visit Utterson pays to Jekyll after hearing Enfield's story his insinuating and disingenuous interrogation of Poole (already referred to) comes near to endorsing this option. The dialogue between the two in the doctor's hall concludes with an altogether significant exchange:

'I do not think I ever met Mr Hyde?' asked Utterson.
'O dear no, sir. He never *dines* here,' replied the butler (41).

Poole's 'O dear no' speaks volumes and the emphasising of 'dines' is almost equally eloquent. Well may Utterson say to himself as he heads homewards, 'Poor Harry Jekyll ... my mind misgives me he is in deep waters.' In fact, in an earlier draft he says considerably more. After 'waters' Stevenson had continued, 'That could never be the face of his son, never in this world. No there is a secret at the root of it ...'.[52]

Jekyll's own behaviour at times seems almost calculated to confirm his friend's suspicions. 'It isn't what you fancy', he tells Utterson, 'it is not so bad as that ...' but then goes on to solicit the lawyer's interest on behalf of Hyde with an obliqueness of manner which is needlessly suggestive:

> 'I do sincerely take a great, a very great interest in that young man; and if I am taken away, Utterson, I wish you to promise me that you will bear with him and get his rights for him. I think you would, if you knew all; and it would be a weight off my mind if you would promise' (44).

The appeal, complete with the cajoling pressure of the hand on the arm of the reluctant (but, of course, ultimately amenable) confidant suggests that the relationship is something other than that between father and illegitimate son. Nor is his the sort of intercession one would make for even the most captivating of blackmailers. As the recipient of Jekyll's will inscribed to his 'friend and benefactor Edward Hyde', Utterson has never been given much room for doubt, such a description fitting neither son nor blackmailer.

The consequence of all these speculations and nuances is that long before we hear of Jekyll's metamorphosing draught, Hyde has been constructed for the reader in the fears and hypotheses of other members of the coterie – and, perhaps, of ourselves. We know him to be the underside, the sub-text of these worthies' lives and though he may be generalised into the product of all sorts of villainous tendencies, he has his real matrix in aberrant sexual energies, sexual inhibitions and social hypocrisy.

The release of the first two and the circumvention of the third, liberate another of those hidden compulsions in Jekyll: his drive to power. Lanyon, Jekyll and Utterson are members of an élite, which confers on them wealth, privilege and power. However, that power which they would appear to be honouring in their clandestine onanistic social rituals is a surrogate for the creative energies of full sexual expression which they all, in one way or another, dream about but only Jekyll releases in the form of Hyde. To them Hyde *is* power. Utterson dreams of this figure 'to whom power was given' dominating Jekyll; Poole tells the lawyer 'we have all orders to obey him', and Lanyon, when offered 'fame and power' by Hyde beyond his imagining, accepts while protesting his disbelief.

What then does Jekyll create or turn himself into? 'Unable to pair off with either a woman or another man,' writes Elaine Showalter, 'Jekyll divides himself, and finds his only mate in his double, Edward Hyde.'[53] Certainly there is self-love and perhaps more in Jekyll's reaction to his first sight of Hyde:

> yet when I looked upon that ugly idol in the glass, I was conscious of no repugnance, rather a leap of welcome. This, too, was myself. It seemed natural and human. In my eyes it bore a livelier image of the spirit, it seemed more express and single, than the imperfect and divided countenance I had hitherto accustomed to call mine (84–5).

Why 'idol', one might ask (rather than, say, 'image') if Jekyll doesn't want to suggest admiration, even veneration? There is more than a hint of Ovid's story of Narcissus here, perhaps mediated through that of Eve discovering her own reflection in the pool in Book IV of *Paradise Lost*. She, of course, had to be told it was herself but the same voice assures her:

> And I will bring thee where no shadow stays
> Thy coming, or thy soft embraces, he
> Whose image thou art, him thou shall enjoy
> Inseparably thine.

Milton's incomparable verse brilliantly unites two beings though one derives from the other and each is separate enough to possess the other and to enjoy possessing the other as though each were the only possessor. They are two but no space remains between them, desire being consummated. In creating Hyde from himself Jekyll has left enough space to allow for desire – an incestuous desire, however, for by a process of mitosis Jekyll has 'fathered' (and 'mothered') Hyde. Thus Hyde is a figure of both the son and the lover, something which is brought out well in this passage:

> This was the shocking thing ... that that insurgent horror was knit to him closer than a wife, closer than an eye; lay caged in his flesh, where he heard it mutter and felt it struggle to be born ....' (95)

In a way Jekyll has left too much space between himself and his creation, allowing him to savour altogether pruriently the excesses of the son:

> My two natures had memory in common, but all other faculties were most unequally shared between them. Jekyll (who was a composite) now with the most sensitive apprehensions, now with a greedy gusto, projected and shared in the pleasures and adventures of Hyde ... (89).

What the gap also allows for, however, is the son's expression of his antagonism towards the father. The sentence 'Jekyll had more than a father's interest; Hyde had more than a son's indifference' (89) is significant in its reticence. It has already been suggested in what way Jekyll's interest exceeds that of a father; William Veeder accounts well for Hyde having more than a son's indifference by arguing that he has a son's oedipal rage. If this is so, does Jekyll, who shared in Hyde's pleasures and adventures, share in his rage against the father(s)?

That Hyde is an antagonist of the father is, I think, quite clear, and an important alteration Stevenson made to his draft would seem to confirm it. Originally, the character who later became Carew was 'a youngish man about twenty-eight' called, rather obviously, Lemsome: 'obviously' because, from his characteristics, he is to be one of Stevenson's inadequate young men, the 'paradigm failed son' to borrow one of Veeder's phrases.[54] Deleting him meant that the much older man, Carew, could then become one of the patriarchs and Hyde's victim; his murder then becomes the paradigm parricide. Hyde cannot, therefore, be seen simply as Jekyll's evil 'second self': he is, crucially, a figure of the son also. Liberating the son in the father so that the latter can participate in 'the pleasures and adventures' of the son is only half the story: what Jekyll fails to realise is that, by the same token, it will expose the father to the son's parricidal fury.

There is some irony in the fact that the celibate Jekyll who appears never to have experienced the oedipal conflict in himself, should have concocted the whole Freudian drama in a graduated glass (an essential element coming from *Maws* the chemist) in his laboratory.[55] Creating Hyde at once son, self and lover might have seemed a sure way of avoiding such dangerous animosities but compounding him out of undiluted evil left no room for warmer feelings; merely ensuring, instead, the intensification of filial rage: 'This familiar that I called out of my own soul, and sent forth alone to do his good pleasure, was a being inherently malign and villainous; his every act and thought centred on self' (86). Hyde gives vent to that rage in a way that leaves no doubt about its source by destroying Jekyll's father's portrait and letters in another act of symbolic parricide.[56] But if this son, this 'child of Hell', demonstrates a taste for parricide he can also, rather more unusually, become the father of himself by, so to speak, fathering the father. Such an idea is not, however, altogether foreign to Stevenson as a later chapter will demonstrate. Veeder reminds us, too, that after editing his father's presidential address to the Royal Society of Edinburgh, Stevenson remarked that it left him 'feeling quite proud of the paper, as if it had been mine'. Rather more seminal is the same critic's observation that Louis occasionally used 'the profession of writer to appropriate the father-figure himself, turning the patriarch into the son whom Louis can then dominate' (124). The example he gives is a good one[57] but a better would have been Jim Hawkins who, from being the adolescent surrounded by a wilderness of fathers, becomes the author and so arrogates to himself the responsibility for constructing them.

In Hyde, then, the child is father to the man in a way not dreamt of by Wordsworth. Charles Baudelaire, however, *did* dream of something similar in 'Le Sept Vieillards' when, confronted by the possibly endless self-replication of the baleful old cripple, he describes him as 'Dégoûtant phénix, fils et père de lui-même'.

### '... like a tale that is told'

Baudelaire's wanderer of the streets (surely too soul-weary to be described as a *flâneur*) recoils from the 'cortège infernal',[58] doubting whether he could survive seeing yet further replication:

> Aurais-je, sans mourir, contemplé le huitième,
> Sosie inexorable, ironique et fatal.... [59]

What troubles him most is that these seven monsters have about them the air of eternity. ('Ces sept monstres hideux aient l'air éternel!') It was, one could argue, a glimpse of the eighth that killed Dr Lanyon – always somewhat precipitate in his envisaging, as his theatrical behaviour and Christian name ('Hastie') would confirm. Jekyll is not so fortunate: as he finishes his 'confession' he accepts that in a very short time he will 'again and *for ever* reindue that hated personality'

(97: my italics). He cannot know how, when or even if Hyde's life will end.

As *we* know, of course, Hyde kills himself in one of the less convincing actions in the novella. This is the Hyde whose 'love of life was screwed to the topmost peg' when he gratifies his 'lust of evil' (91) and of whom Jekyll tells us 'his love of life is wonderful'. Interestingly it is this which seems to weigh with Jekyll when he addresses the obvious question: why not kill himself and rid himself of Hyde forever:

> I who sicken and freeze at the mere thought of him, when I recall the abjection and the passion of this attachment, and when I know how he fears my power to cut him off by suicide, I find it in my heart to pity him (96).

He does not, however, kill himself. What he does is much more interesting: he writes himself out of the story at a point which is some distance from the end of the tale's narration. Jekyll now survives only in or as the text, he himself having disappeared.

Writing of all the allusions to the doctor's death or disappearance in, for example, his will, in Lanyon's instructions to Utterson, and in the note accompanying his final statement, Ronald Thomas concludes: 'Inscribed in each of Jekyll's texts, then, is the impending disappearance of its author, along with the implication that the author is not so much represented by his text as he is replaced – and victimized – by it'. He quotes Foucault's observation that 'If we wish to know the writer in our day, it will be through the singularity of his absence and in his link to death, which has transformed him into a victim of his own writing.' And Thomas goes on:

> The void left by this 'disappearance or death of the author' is filled by 'the concept of the work', the autonomous existence of the text itself. I have argued that this is precisely what *Jekyll and Hyde* has enacted.... The life is a function of the pen that writes it. Here, the text of the 'confession' remains and the life of Jekyll ends, 'sealed up' in the text itself, and the corpse of Hyde remains as a sign of the author's sacrifice of his life to the body of his work.[60]

As it happens, Thomas could, in fact, have taken *his* text from Stevenson's own life which the latter was, in any case, inclined to see as a literary artefact. In a letter written to Edmund Gosse two days before his death he engineers his own authorial disappearance as effectively as Dr Jekyll had done, allowing the text (and Gosse's dedication in which the word 'vanished' had appeared) to displace him and to convey more than he had inscribed in it when it was eventually read by Gosse many weeks later: 'Well, my dear Gosse, here's wishing you all health and prosperity.... May you live long, since it seems as if you would continue to enjoy life. May you write many more books as good as this one – only there is one thing impossible, you can never write another dedication that can give the same pleasure to the vanished *Tusitala*.'

The pen wielded by Henry Jekyll is, it seems, mightier than the cyanide pill. Not only does it call Hyde into being in the formula despatched to the chemist (albeit with the help of chance), it can cause its author to vanish.[61] Jekyll has been de-faced by the pen as surely as Hyde's usurpation 'severed [him] from [his] own face and nature' (96).

At times it seems to be the pen which gives Jekyll life rather than the other way round: 'as I lay down the pen ... I bring the life of that unhappy Henry Jekyll to an end' (97). The doctor unhooks himself from the pen as from a life-support system: it is as though his life has been coterminous with, perhaps inseparable from or even dependent on, a literary *Life* which the instrument has been busily inscribing almost of its own volition.

From very early in the novella we have been aware of mysterious inscriptions which seem to be in some way sufficiently at odds with their source to cause anxiety or very great surprise in the person reading them. There is, for example, the rogue inscription in the first will (which Utterson calls 'the mad will'). This inscription arbitrarily disappears and is succeeded by another, sealed in an enclosure, which, when the lawyer has broken the seal, causes him 'indescribable amazement'. What Utterson is looking at is his own name: he has been unaccountably substituted for Hyde. His discomfort at the association is palpable: 'He looked at Poole, and then back at the papers, and last of all at the dead malefactor stretched upon the carpet – "'My head goes round," he said' (72). It has; the writing has deformed him, changing him into Hyde.

Between these two confrontations has come another when Utterson receives an envelope from Lanyon inscribed with strange directions. Breaking the seal, he finds inside another enclosure with yet another inscriptions on *its* envelope (which is also sealed). So strange is this inscription that Utterson 'could not trust his eyes'. What he does is to hide it, or, rather, put it to bed: 'the packet slept in the inmost corner of his private safe' (58–9). The figure of speech is not inappropriate for this is another orphaned – or is it parricidal – text which replaces its dead author. So for that matter does the sealed envelope addressed to Utterson found on Carew's dead body and apparently responsible for his death. The seemingly endless repetition of inscription which only ever points to yet another enclosure ('real' or metaphorical) culminates in Jekyll's text – which, in fact, *discloses* nothing but itself in a Barthesian affirmation of its being the only reality. No fathers and no sons at the cessation; only the text.

The novella ceases on the word 'end', but it is *an* end not *the* end. We may think that we have already been privileged to see the real thing and that it lies elsewhere. But, of course, we haven't, for among the many things we don't know or haven't seen is Utterson's reaction for he, too, has disappeared. As Stevenson shows with consummate skill, the end is never where it seems to be – which means that we'll never know if we've reached it. Clearly, as Scheherezade realised and Richard Enfield didn't, stories go on forever: there's no such certifiable thing as 'a story that's been told'.

## Notes

1. Veeder's essay is to be found in *Dr Jekyll and Mr Hyde after One Hundred Years*, ed. William Veeder and Gordon Hirsch (Chicago, 1988). There are two particularly valuable essays in this outstanding collection, Veeder's own long and very detailed contribution and Ronald Thomas's 'The Strange Voices in the Strange Case: Dr Jekyll, Mr Hyde, and the Voices of Modern Fiction' which, among other things, draws an illuminating comparison between *Jekyll and Hyde* and the prose works of Samuel Beckett. My belated discovery of this book has inevitably resulted in some overlapping between these essays and this chapter. They have also, to adapt a Conradian phrase, made me 'see', where I have been blind.
2. That Stevenson should exploit some of the conventions and devices of detective fiction is not surprising. He admired Poe, Dickens and Wilkie Collins, for example, and may have been influenced by all three. In Collins's *The Moonstone*, Sergeant Cuff, the detective, is ably assisted by the steward, Gabriel Betteredge (who, as better-edge, is worth comparing with utter-son). Collins also makes something of a speciality of disabled or deformed characters.
3. In *Critical Quarterly*, vol. 28, nos 1 and 2, p. 95.
4. It is quoted in James McFarlane's essay 'The Mind of Modernism' in *Modernism 1890–1930*, ed. Malcolm Bradbury and James McFarlane, p. 71.
5. The interest began early. His splendid essay 'A Penny Plain, Twopence Coloured' describes well the near-delirium which could be induced in him by Skelt's Juvenile Drama which could be purchased in flat sheets, painted and cut out and made into a 'working theatre'.

6. Patricia Waugh, *Metafiction: The Theory and Practice of Self-Conscious Fiction* (1984), p. 6.
7. Op. cit., p. 76.
8. In *Letters*, vol. 4, p. 95. It is important to remember that Stevenson is here drawing a sharp distinction between the long and the short story.
9. I doubt, however, if one needs to go as far as Veeder who associates 'by-street' with bisexual, holding that 'side-street' would have 'sufficed mimetically'. (Op. cit., p. 159). It is, in fact, a widely used term in the period and not least by one of Stevenson's mentors, Edgar Allan Poe, in, for example, 'The Man of the Crowd'.
10. *The Secret Agent*, p. 126. Stephen Heath describes the image of the forest fire as having 'the presence of one of the dream symbols Freud was to analyse a few years later – in Dora's second dream, for example ...' (op. cit. , p. 94).
11. For Steven Heath the suggestiveness doesn't stop here (op. cit., p. 94).
12. Op. cit., pp. 159–60. Even John Boswell, on whose *Christianity, Social Tolerance, and Homosexuality* Veeder draws, only claims that the word 'gay' had become common in the homosexual sub-culture from 'the early twentieth century'.
13. Quoted in Cyril Pearl, *The Girl with the Swansdown Seat* (New York, 1980), p. 191.
14. Op. cit., p. 99.
15. Ira Bruce Nadel, 'Gustave Doré: English Art and London Life' in *Victorian Artists and the City*, ed. I. B. Nadel and F. S. Schwarzbach (New York, 1980), p. 161.
16. Ibid., p. 153.
17. Ibid., p. 161.
18. The growth of the professions coincides with the spectacular growth of the cities in the nineteenth century. Veeder quotes the findings of Magali Sarfatti Larson's study (*The Rise of Professionalism*) which noted that 'In England, of the thirteen contemporary professions ... ten acquired an association of national scope between 1825 and 1880' (op. cit., p. 110). A national association, is not, however, the measure of all things and Larson's study, in concentrating heavily on America and to a lesser extent on England appears not to distinguish Scotland from the latter. There the professions were in a dominant position long before 1825. The profession of the law, for example, had an enormous influence in the government of eighteenth-century Scotland, as even a cursory reading of *Kidnapped* and *Catriona* would confirm.
19. Cf *The Secret Agent*: 'His robust form was seen that night in distant parts of the enormous town.... It was seen crossing the streets without life and sound, or diminishing in the interminable straight perspectives of shadowy houses bordering empty roadways lined by strings of gas-lamps' (p. 300).
20. 'A Plea for Gas Lamps' in *Virginibus Puerisque and other Essays in Belles Lettres*, p. 132. A little earlier we find this:

    A sedate electrician somewhere in a back office touches a spring – and behold! from one end to another of the city, from east to west, from the Alexandra to the Crystal Palace, there is light! *Fiat Lux*, says the sedate electrician. What a spectacle, on some clear, dark nightfall, from the edge of Hampstead Hill, when in a moment, in the twinkling of an eye, the design of the monstrous city flashes into vision – a glittering hieroglyph many square miles in extent ....

In *New Arabian Nights* the Place de l'Opéra is described as being 'lit up like day with electric lights' (142), and in *The Dynamiter* there is even a working electric chair.

21. Enfield's choice of this figure could also be intended as an indictment of him.
22. It is quite likely that Stevenson was drawing on James Thomson's very well known 'The City of Dreadful Night' for some of these descriptions. Street-lighting was a powerful stimulus for both writers' imagination, it would seem:

> The street lamps always burn; but scarce a casement
> In house or palace front from roof to basement
>      Doth glow or gleam athwart the mirk air cast.
>      The street-lamps burn amidst the baleful glooms,
>      Amidst the soundless solitudes immense
> Of rangéd mansions dark and still as tombs.

It was, of course, the spread of gas street-lighting which, as Dolf Sternberger notes in *Panorama of the 19th Century* (Oxford, 1977), was responsible for the 'opening up of the city night', otherwise the introduction of city night-life in its modern sense. Accordingly, illumination became 'one of the most intrinsic motifs of the century' (pp. 176, 177).
23. 'The Metropolis and the Emergence of Modernism' in *Unreal City*, p. 17.
24. Ibid., Introduction, p. 2.
25. Walter Benjamin, *Charles Baudelaire: A Lyric Poet in the Era of High Capitalism*, trans. Harry Zohn (1985), p. 171.
26. Ibid., p. 48.
27. Ibid., p. 40.
28. Ibid., p. 41.
29. Ibid., p. 40.
30. Op. cit., p. 117 and cf p. 119.
31. 'Too man of the world not to despise the world'. See Jessica Feldman, op. cit., pp. 63, 128.
32. Veeder, op. cit., p. 119.
33. The only other reference to the country is curiously prominent and unexpected. The entrance-hall of Dr Jekyll's house is described as being 'a large low-roofed comfortable hall, paved with flags, warmed (after the fashion of a country house) by a bright, open fire, and furnished with costly cabinets of oak' (p. 41).
34. Peter Collier, 'Nineteenth-century Paris: Vision and nightmare', in *Unreal City*, p. 26.
35. See Veeder, op. cit., note 1, p. 156 for a summary of Utterson's critical friends and foes.

36. Cf Veeder, op. cit., note 17, p. 159: 'No annunciation is voiced by this Gabriel who generates neither progeny nor ample insight; little light is divided from darkness by this John for whom the notion of "in the beginning was the word" signifies an ironic imprisonment of the word.'
37. This is another example of the remarkable stress on orality which Veeder shows to pervade the text.
38. Stevenson's indictment of the fathers extends, Veeder argues, to Victorian patriarchy in general, its decline 'reflecting the widely recognized "autumnal" quality of late-Victorian life' (116). While I am dubious about this, I am wholly unconvinced that such an indictment includes professionalism as Veeder also maintains.
39. It is excessively simplistic (and surprising in such an insightful study) for Karl Miller to dismiss Stevenson's 'dualistic' fictions as 'images of disobedience dreamed by a loyal son'. *Doubles: Studies in Literary History* (Oxford, 1985), p. 213.
40. Dennis Brown, *The Modernist Self in Twentieth Century English Literature* (1989), pp. 1, 5.
41. Op. cit., p. 74.
42. Letter to Bocock quoted Maixner, op. cit., p. 231.
43. Op. cit., p. 100.
44. Ibid., p. 160, Note 21. This is a very long note worth examining in full.
45. Jeffrey Weeks, *Sex, Politics and Society* (1984), pp. 87, 91, 102.
46. Stevenson was insistent that Hyde was not to be seen simply as a figure of unbridled licentiousness. He was not 'a mere voluptuary' and it is only the fact that 'people are so filled full of folly and inverted lust that they can think of nothing but sexuality' that makes him so. What he is, is 'the essence of cruelty and malice, and selfishness and cowardice; and these are the diabolic in man – not this poor wish to have a woman'. (Letter to Bocock, Maixner, op. cit., p. 231).
47. Op. cit., p. 97.
48. Ibid., p. 153. Stevenson's reference to staggering the unbelief of Satan is, in fact, more than a little opaque. It could hardly mean that Hyde's revelation is of an order to convert Satan to a belief in God or in Christ the Son: that would elevate Hyde's creator to divine status. Perhaps it refers to Satan's disbelief in being created rather than being 'self-begot' in *Paradise Lost*, Bk V.
49.     Plonger au fond du gouffre, Enfer ou Ciel, qu'importe?
        Au fond de l'Inconnu pour trouver du *nouveau*.
                                                ('Le Voyageur')
50. *Letters*, vol. 1, pp. 35–6. Of this statement Veeder remarks that, though the words are Stevenson's, 'this fascination with the workings of the psyche is eminently characteristic of Freud' (p. 115).
51. Elaine Showalter, *Sexual Anarchy: Gender and Culture at the Fin de Siècle* (1992), p. 112.
52. William Veeder, 'The Texts in Question' in *Jekyll and Hyde after One Hundred Years*, p. 23.
53. Op. cit., p. 109.
54. Op. cit., p. 113.

55. The only reference we get to Jekyll's own father relates, perhaps significantly, to the time when Jekyll was in pre-oedipal phase ('I followed it up from the days of childhood when I had walked with my father's hand' [91]).
56. For Hyde to appear to jump a generation is not, I think, of particular significance. Jekyll *père* is, after all, the only *real* father around. For Hyde to destroy Jekyll's own portrait could be seen as an act of self-destruction rather than symbolic parricide.
57. 'When I have beaten Burns, I am driven at once, by my parental feelings, to console him with a sugar plum' (p. 124). Stevenson talks in a similar vein of his essay *Charles of Orleans*: 'I shall finish Charles of Orleans (who is in a good way, about the fifth month, I should think, and promises to be a fine, healthy child ...)'. *Letters*, vol. 2, p. 11.
58. '... hellish procession'.
59. 'Could I face the eighth without succumbing, face this unrelenting double, this fatal irony.'
60. Op. cit., p. 80.
61. To say, as Thomas does, that 'Hyde is from the outset the product of Jekyll's pen' is not, in fact, wholly true. Hyde could not have come into existence without the chemical formula; but neither could he have done so had that text not been 'misinterpreted' in the sense that Jekyll had not prescribed (or 'inscribed') the missing ingredient which accidentally appears in the salt. By implication, Thomas admits this when he writes of Jekyll trying to rid himself of Hyde 'by appealing to the authority of his original text of himself' – and finding it 'impure' in the sense that no text is ever 'a perfect representation of what it seeks to represent' (79). While this last is undoubtedly true, it does not fully acknowledge the huge gap which exists in this case between the text and the reality it invokes, a gap which is filled by wholly non-textual chance. It is a corrupt text with a missing causal link. In general, however, this part of my account parallels Thomas's, though he takes the argument much further to the greater benefit of all readers of Stevenson's text.

# 7

# 'No Other Father':
# Title Deeds in *The Master*
# *of Ballantrae*

'Hast thou but one blessing, my father? Bless me, even me also, O my father.'

Genesis 27: 38

Undecidability is not a weakness, but a structural condition of narration ... : in an utterance, several codes, several voices are there, without priority.

Roland Barthes

It is of some importance to start with the title, for the Master of Ballantrae, to all intents and purposes, isn't. Whether or not we choose to theorise this as a striking example of the absent centre, the peculiar fact remains that, throughout Mackellar's tale, the Master of Ballantrae is a title to which no one is entitled, a sign without a referent, a bonnet without a laird.

Among other things this releases James Durie from being any one thing: he can be a pirate (with strong if anachronistic links to Penzance), a courtier in France, a soldier-adventurer in India, a Government spy, a role-player in Genesis and, to crown it all, a literary consumer, for we are told in anything but a throwaway line that among the many other things he has taken from his father is 'a love of serious reading'.

From the time of Mackellar's first acquaintance with the family of the House of Durrisdeer whose misadventures he is to record, the title of Master of Ballantrae – a courtesy-title conferred upon the heir to the barony – has been forfeit. James, the erstwhile Master, is a proscribed rebel for his part in 'riding out' with Charles Edward Stuart in the '45; and though his younger brother could, in such circumstances, become the heir and assume the title, it would be almost impossible for him to do so without offending public sentiment and his own conscience, to say nothing of the law of primogeniture which proscription might set aside but never erase from the mind of a race so suffused with biblical tradition. As one would expect, Henry Durie declines to adopt the title, tartly correcting Colonel Burke when he addresses him as Master ('I have never taken that name' [25]). James Durie, liberated from his birthright, now adopts the name of 'Mr Bally' and wears his new 'title' with relish, no doubt revelling all the more in his own authorship because he is such a reader.

That Stevenson should take as the title of this book a title which is devoid of signification speaks volumes (one might say) about the nature of the text he has constructed and his attitude to it. Subverting the metonymic function of the title *vis-à-vis* the text is immediately to undermine any presumption of 'reality' or 'truth' the latter may traditionally be thought to embody. However, not only does Stevenson enjoy exposing the fictionality of his fictions and their deficiencies as vehicles of truth or 'theological' meaning, but he does so far more frequently and comprehensively than has ever been acknowledged. In *The Master of Ballantrae*, he sows the seeds of deconstruction with his opening words and, as this chapter will show, continues to manipulate a variety of disconcerting perspectives on his work quite literally to the last word. Nor – it must be said at once in view of the accusations of frivolity which have so long been levelled at him – was he doing all this for the pleasure of exercising his literary ingenuity, for he was, as Henry James and others recognised, a serious theorist in the art of fiction whose concerns are very modern.

From what has already been said, questions about the nature of fiction and representation, about discrepancies between word and thing, about legitimacy, about authorship and authority, float to the surface of the tale immediately and engage the attention of those who mimic the erstwhile Master in being lovers of serious reading (or who are mimicked by him). The fact that the Master is a great reader involves him in the process which we are engaged in, suggesting (however subliminally) that he may be reading his own story. In turn this strengthens the impression that *everything* is textual.

The alleged author's own role and reality are themselves far from sacrosanct. The preface is boldly declared to be by one 'Robert Louis Stevenson', who may or may not be the editor referred to in the opening sentence. Teasingly, the third-person attributions to the editor (and to 'the other') in the dialogue which follows are gradually displaced by the first person, so either 'Robert Louis Stevenson' is the editor or the editor has invented him. Unless, of course, they are both Mr Johnstone Thomson W. S., into whose hands the manuscript has been committed. At any rate the editor declines to do what Mr Thomson suggests, which is to fictionalise the Durrisdeer family history contained in these papers. ('Here ... is a novel ready to your hand: all you have to do is to work up the scenery, develop the characters, and improve the style'.) Instead, he resolves that it 'shall be published as it stands'.

'But it's so bald', objected Mr Thomson.

'I believe there is nothing so noble as baldness' replied I, 'and I am sure that there is nothing so interesting. I would have all literature bald, and all authors (if you like) but one'.

As we shall see (and as this playful confusion of fact and fiction would suggest), the story will be anything but bald.

'As it stands', then, it is a tale about the House of Durrisdeer, and it challengingly opens with Mackellar the steward promising us to divulge 'the truth', and not just that but 'the full truth of this odd matter', for it is 'what the world has long been looking for'. Further, 'the truth is a debt I owe to my lord's memory'. Mackellar's notion of the world, however, is circumscribed and parochial – even solipsistic – governed as it is by events in the House of Durrisdeer which are themselves largely determined, and altogether interpreted, by him. Thus we are warned that his notion of the truth may be similarly circumscribed.

In 1745, when 'the foundations of this tragedy were laid', the 'House' consisted of four people, the first-mentioned 'old lord, eighth of the name' whom Mackellar represents as 'not old in years' but as 'suffering prematurely from the disabilities of age'. His place, apparently, is 'at the chimney-side; there he sat reading ... .' (2). Then there is the Master, his brother Henry, and Alison Graeme, a kinswoman and an orphan destined to be the Master's wife since her inheritance is essential for the survival of the impoverished House. Mackellar pieces together this and the events surrounding the Master's role in the Rising from various accounts for he did not arrive until three years later, from when, he tells us, he takes up the history of these events 'as they befell under my own observation, like a witness in court' (12). The ramifications of this remark immediately alert us to the dimension Stevenson is invoking and make Mackellar sound more like *The Good Soldier* than the family steward.

Appropriately enough in a text suffused with self-consciousness, Mackellar discovers the 'old lord' in the chimney-corner reading his Livy – a work again appropriate to a pretended history. Henry has married a reluctant Alison Graeme who is now expecting their first child. But the shadow of the absent Master (at this stage presumed dead) hangs over the family and Mackellar quickly perceives that James is in everything Henry's rival. It is Mackellar, therefore, who, through his alert, not to say obsessive, reading of signs, discovers the Manichean dualism polarised in the two brothers though he arrives at his conclusion by, among other means, listening to and observing two old servants each of whom is a partisan defender of the brother most *unlike* himself, thus multiplying perspectives and refracting 'truth' through a bewildering number of prisms.

James Hogg had already given powerful expression to the idea of two siblings who, in defiance of consanguinity, are such polar opposites in their moral nature that they become types of good and evil. The satanic Robert Wringhim is no less implacable in his hatred of his brother than is James Durie, and eventually kills him. James, of course, also attempts to kill Henry but in a more-or-less fair duel. Despite the similarities (Hogg also uses the device of an 'editor' who presents his readers 'with an original document of a most singular nature' upon which he 'offers no remarks ... and makes as few additions... '), there is a crucial difference, namely Mackellar, with his insatiable interest in the Durrisdeer family as, it would appear, an extension of himself.

To review what we are presented with, then. First, we have an author inclined from the start to subvert his own authority even to the point of hinting that he himself may be a literary invention. At the same time, we have a text whose given title is a title going begging, a declared fiction, a delegitimised cipher. The text concerns itself with a House or family whose head, the father, has apparently abdicated his authority, where the elder son is not in a position to step in and exercise it because, in fact, he does not officially exist having been proscribed by the country's Government (whose own legitimacy has just been called in question, albeit unsuccessfully, by Charles Edward Stuart). This leaves the younger son, an uncharismatic 'manager' of the family's estates, who, though he may marry his brother's betrothed, will never fill his shoes *nor* win his father's fullest blessing. Eventually he does succeed his father and assumes the title of Lord Durrisdeer, but the final dénouement is precipitated by news (embodied in a pamphlet which, we are told, while purporting to be fact is a work of fiction by a Whig trouble-maker) that James was to be pardoned and reinstated, thus (in the normal course of events) disinheriting Henry's children. To prevent this, Henry arranges to have his brother murdered. Lastly, we are given a tale which, through the sensibility and perception of Ephraim Mackellar – the same Mackellar who attempts to murder James Durie for the most godly of motives – discovers the Manichean nature of the universe in the moral temper of the two brothers. It is this last which is always deemed to supply the text with its true texture, the tale with its substance.

Before further venturing into this arena where Stevenson subtly and sophisticatedly 'plays' with metafictional processes and the deconstructive effects of absent or illegitimate authority, some basic questions need to be asked. To what extent, for example, are such concerns in conflict with the emphasis given to an at times acute psychological or moral realism? And what is the relationship of the latter to the adventure-tale? For the extravagances of such a form are always liable to erupt in a way that undermines any assumption on the reader's part that moral realism alone supplies the formula with which the effect and worth of the story can be measured. The lengthy account of Mr Bally's and Colonel Burke's highly successful career as pirates (in the company of the Gilbertian Captain Teach who, despite his name, is easily outwitted, deprived of his authority and re-named Captain Learn) is as implausible as Colonel Burke himself. It certainly does not conform to the formula being offered to us through Mackellar's discriminating account of family relationships in the House of Durrisdeer. In fact, it reads suspiciously like a burlesque of another text, Defoe's *A General History of the Pyrates* which Stevenson certainly had read since, as I have already indicated in Chapter 2, this is where he found Israel Hands and the surgeon to amputate Long John Silver's leg.

The truth is that Stevenson makes no attempt to reconcile these forms, happy for them to coexist in the one text, regardless of implicit contradictions (between, for example, what might loosely be called the deconstructive and the moral realist). Hybridity, one might say, is a characteristic of his writing, witness the difficulty encountered by contemporary reviewers in trying to catalogue works like *New Arabian Nights*, *Prince Otto* and *Jekyll and Hyde* (all of which differ dramatically from each other). In *The Ebb-Tide* the experimentation with forms is foregrounded to such an extent that not just the nature of representation but its very possibility is debated, becoming and

remaining a principal concern throughout the text, properly inseparable from any other 'subject'.

A formal plurality almost seems to amount to a structural principle in Stevenson's compositions, though some critics would more
readily describe it as a destructive principle. (One thinks, for example,
of Robert Kiely's reactions to New Arabian Nights discussed in Chapter
3.) Though this formal diversity may not amount to what Frank
Kermode has described as the 'formal desperation' of Modernist
writers, it nonetheless implicitly calls in question certain assumptions about form: whether, for example, an artist's expressive needs
can be adequately met by reliance on only one, monofaceted form.
The idea of form itself may not be challenged (though, as I have indicated, some such question hangs over The Ebb-Tide) but Stevenson's
dissatisfaction with inherited forms and formal procedures and his
innovations in this area strongly suggest an affinity with what Ihab
Hassan regards as one of Modernism's characteristics – its 'assault
on forms', which he sees as without exact parallel in literary history
because it is 'at once more various, reckless, and equivocal than its
precedents'.[1]

Returning to The Master of Ballantrae, it is possible to argue that
Stevenson helps the different – even disparate – formal elements to
coexist by introducing another, umbrella mode: one which gets early
and specific mention in the lawyer's attempt to interest the 'editor'
in the manuscript. Not only is the manuscript 'a mystery', it is also
'highly genteel, for it treats of a titled family' and 'it ought to be
melodramatic for (according to the superscription) it is concerned
with death' (xx). It is, in fact, a melodrama in many more senses than
this and in addition to the provision of some of the form's hallmarks
– the various tableaux, for example, such as the duel in the moon-
light, or Secundra Dass exhuming his master – we are not infrequently
reminded of the fact by references to 'the plot', to performance and
to the theatre:

> He sang it well, even as a song; but he did better yet as a performer.
> I have heard famous actors, when there was not a dry eye in the
> Edinburgh theatre; a great wonder to behold; but no more
> wonderful than how the Master played upon that little ballad, and
> on those who heard him, like an instrument... (83).

The Master is a consummate 'performer' partly as a result of his
proscription but more, it seems, because of a natural instinct for it.
His double act while at Durrisdeer, where he presents one aspect of

himself to his father and Alison and a totally different one when they are absent, is performed with relish as well as skill. Nonetheless, while the element of exaggeration or extravagance is always on the verge of pulling the rug from under melodrama as serious exposition, this does not necessarily mean the repudiation of the truths about the human condition with which melodrama engages, or that it fails to deal seriously with them. Because it is a mode which Stevenson has quite clearly in mind when writing *The Master of Ballantrae,* and one which finds embodiment in important aspects of the text, it is worth considering it in some detail; but it is also worth pursuing because the process will reveal that, just like the moral realism formula, melodrama will also fail to provide a full description of the activity going on in this text.

Peter Brooks in his important study *The Melodramatic Imagination* decides that the term 'melodrama' is useful 'even necessary' because 'it points as no other word quite does, to a mode of high emotionalism and stark ethical conflict that is neither comic nor tragic in persons, structure, intent, effect'.[2] He adds: 'At its most ambitious, the melodramatic mode of conception and representation may appear to be the very process of reaching a fundamental drama of the moral life and finding the terms to express it.' This seems to me to describe very well an extremely important dimension of *The Master of Ballantrae* as well as accounting for a considerable degree of its impact upon the reader.

Reviewing the emergence of 'classical' melodrama in France at the beginning of the nineteenth century, Brooks notes that 'we find there an intense emotional drama based on the manichaeistic struggle of good and evil, a world where what one lives for and by is seen in terms of, and as determined by, the most fundamental psychic relations and cosmic ethical forces'. What follows is worth quoting in full since it enhances our critical perspective on what is a prominent strand in a great deal of Stevenson's writing:

> The polarization of good and evil works towards revealing their presence and operation as real forces in the world. This conflict suggests the need to recognise and confront evil, to combat and expel it, to purge the social order. Man is seen to be, and must recognise himself to be, playing on a theatre that is the point of

juncture, and of clash, of imperatives beyond himself that are non-mediated and irreducible. This is what is most real in the universe.[3]

While conceding that melodrama may well be considered 'a constant of the imagination and a constant among literary modes', Brooks argues that, as we need the term – 'as it demonstrates its usefulness' – it is 'a peculiarly modern form'.[4] The genre labelled melodrama coming into being in the specific historical context of the French Revolution, it is, Brooks postulates, this 'epistemological moment which it illustrates and to which it contributes'. This is the moment that

> symbolically, and really, marks the final liquidation of the traditional Sacred and its representative institutions (Church and Monarch), the shattering of the myth of Christendom, the dissolution of an organic and hierarchically cohesive society, and the invalidation of literary forms – tragedy, comedy of manners – that depended on such a society. Melodrama does not simply represent a 'fall' from tragedy, but a response to the loss of the tragic vision. It comes into being in a world where the traditional imperatives of truth and ethics have been violently thrown into question, yet where the promulgation of truth and ethics, their instauration as a way of life, is of immediate, daily, political concern ... we may legitimately claim that melodrama becomes the principal mode for uncovering, demonstrating, and making operative the essential moral universe in a post-sacred era.[5]

Stevenson's writings go a considerable way to validating Brooks' interpretation of the mode's relationship to this moment and its aftermath. His work is shot through with all the uncertainties, moral, ethical, social and aesthetic, subsumed in the analysis in a way which carries that word 'modern' across the threshold of 'modernist'. It is hoped that, as the evidence advanced by this study accumulates, such a conclusion will seem increasingly persuasive, not least in the way Stevenson both uses and abuses or, more justly, exploits and transcends the melodramatic mode.

We can now turn again to Stevenson's tale and see how far it functions within that representational mode which, in Brooks' words, will suggest 'the very process of reaching a fundamental drama of the moral life and finding the terms to express it'. Central to such an investigation is the sensibility of Ephraim Mackellar whose acute perception of the nuances of character and relationships uncovers to us dense substrata of meaning and moral significance. That perception is, however, anything but an objective instrument: not only does Mackellar, as he readily admits, quickly become a partisan in the conflicts which are destroying the House of Durrisdeer, but his very perception must be suspect since, as a deeply committed Presbyterian, his particular theology will present him with a dualistic universe where salvation will depend upon his recognising the speciousness of surface appearances and penetrating to the truly significant moral substance which lies beneath. In both a theological and a linguistic sense, he is a (particularly blinkered) seeker after signs: so much so, that the intensity of his investigation seems to turn mankind itself into (to borrow a phrase from Brooks) 'a kind of theatre of the sign'. Consequently the objects of his perception are deprived of something of their substantial reality and possible complexity. Mackellar confesses, for example, that there are moments when he thinks of the Master 'as a man of paste-board – as though, if one should strike smartly through the buckram of his countenance, there would be found a mere vacuity within' (163). At such moments he is imbued with a sense of horror (his word) 'and would draw away as though from something partly spectral'. His reaction is, in fact, extreme: 'I began to feel something shiver within me on his drawing near; I had at times a longing to cry out; there were days when I thought I could have struck him' (163).

Mackellar's 'nightmare' offers us a valuable insight into his mental processes and moral condition. Given his inability to fit the Master into the constricted universe prescribed by his dogmatic vision – the only world he wants to know – Mackellar is left with no alternative habitat in which to pigeon hole him, no other known world, no alternative reality. Consequently, the Master comes to inhabit an unknown dimension outside anything Mackellar can (or, perhaps, wishes to) conceive, which, while it may make his reality more spectral, gives him, ghost-like, more shapes with which to haunt the steward.

What Mackellar is actually being haunted by is, of course, his own claustrophobic creed in whose repressive articles he has long concealed his deficiencies and desires; which is another way of saying that he is haunted by his own larger, unacknowledged self. Predictably, he had initially tried to solve the problem by invoking that creed: the Master must be the Devil; but he found him too attractive, which left him no other option except, in moments of weakness like these, to admit, through his waking nightmare, that the creed by which he has rigorously disciplined himself is inadequate when put to the test. Well might he then describe the Master as infecting

him with 'a fever of resentment' (163) for the diabolical James Durie
is a disease in the steward's own flesh.

The specific occasion for this turmoil in Mackellar's underconsciousness is his being forced to recognise once more the deceit
and 'doubleness' in the Master's behaviour. While the latter can
display (and simulate) fine feelings in the most convincing manner,
these coexist (in Mackellar's perception) with a nullifying obduracy
which drains them of any moral referent. 'This outer sensibility and
inner toughness set me against him; it seemed of a piece with that
impudent grossness which I knew to underlie the veneer of his good
manners' (162). To Mackellar such a mode of behaviour calls in question the foundations of his own moral universe which he likes to
think he lives by; for, to apply the analogue of that later novelist who
owed much to Stevenson, the Master's subversive 'doubleness'
represents something of the same threat to Mackellar that Lord Jim's
apparent desecration of the merchant marine code does to Brierly
(and to Marlow). Mackellar remains, however, a few feet further
back from the precipice than Marlow with his gaze riveted upon the
self-inscribed Rock of Ages rather than on the abyss. Nonetheless, as
we see from his reaction here, he is near enough to get rather more
than a twinge of the Marlovian horrors.

What adds particular piquancy to this episode (and hints at the
way in which Stevenson transcends the melodrama formula) is the
recognition that its origins are literary and textual. When the Master
and Mackellar set out on their transatlantic voyage each sensibly
equips himself with adequate reading-matter. Mackellar's,
predictably, is the Bible; the Master's, however, is *Clarissa*.
Occasionally the Master reads aloud to his companion and is particularly good on 'the pathetic portions'. Mackellar responds by reading
passages from the Bible which, to his great annoyance, the Master
'tasted ... like the connoisseur he was'. Worse still, the latter would
occasionally take Mackellar's Bible and (showing that he was fully
conversant with its contents) with fine declamation, would give a
Roland for his Oliver, as Mackellar allusively puts it. But here's the
rub: the Master provocatively chooses to make no distinction between
the texts:

> Lovelace and Clarissa, the tales of David's generosity, the psalms
> of his penitence, the solemn questions of the book of Job, the
> touching poetry of Isaiah – they were to him a source of enter-
> tainment only, like the scraping of a fiddle in a change-house
> (162).

It is rather remarkable that Stevenson's *tour de force* here has gone unrecognised. That the duel between the Master and his brother is a brilliant piece of theatre has often been acknowledged but there are, in fact, not one but *two* duels and the second is only a little less vivid than the first. Of greater significance than its visual impact, however, is the fact that this duel is a battle of the books; yet it is no less life-threatening, for Mackellar is driven to try to kill the reader who prefers *Clarissa* – because such a preference fundamentally challenges *his* text-based value-system.

Once again in his dismissal of *Clarissa* as mere entertainment and the Master's taste for the book as evidence of moral delinquency, Mackellar shows himself to be the victim of his limited moral sensibility. Thus while he records (with some chagrin) the master's thorough familiarity with the Bible, he sees in the latter's ability to read with great feeling (he uses the word 'potency') from *both* texts, proof of the Master's levity and obduracy. Yet there were many eighteenth-century clerics (not Presbyterians, however) who preached that a reader could get almost as much edification from reading one of Richardson's novels as from the Bible.

From the start Mackellar is presented as a man of contrasting qualities. What initially seems to define him is his efficiency as steward, his pleasure in rigorous book-keeping, his tendency to pride himself on his commonsense materialism and his eschewal of aesthetics. When he first catches sight of Durrisdeer he notes that the house is 'commodiously built' and that its architecture derives from France or Italy, explaining his inability to distinguish between the styles by adding (with a certain complacency) 'I have no skill in these arts.' He is, however, highly impressed by the gardens and shrubberies – but by their cost rather than their beauty it would seem: 'The money sunk here *unproductively* would have quite restored the family; but as it was, it cost a revenue to keep up' (13: my italics). With this narrowness of sensibility there goes a prim and priggish temper so that it comes as a considerable surprise when he also shows himself to be quite remarkably penetrating in sifting people's natures and relationships. His ability to read the sub-text of people's lives, to interpret the sign-system of what Brooks calls the 'moral occult' (that is 'the domain of operative spiritual values which is both indicated within and masked by the surface of reality' [5]), may owe something to his Presbyterian indoctrination, as well as being significantly constricted by it, but it is an exceptionally well-honed faculty.

Probing with an eager intensity and a quick and penetrating comprehension into the occulted regions of the moral lives of those around him, Mackellar creates a powerful image of a divided self: the pedantic, timid, book-keeping steward contrasted with a monomaniac possessed of an at times 'fevered' drive to invade the moral space of others and root out false idols. In the course of his inquisition he displays a near uncanny insight into the motives and desires which fuel certain kinds of human action. It is precisely the quality which he fears in the Master.

In fact, Mackellar and the Master are engaged in a game of dice, the prize being possession of the House of Durrisdeer. But the game is really between the left and right hand of Ephraim Mackellar, for however much he tries to differentiate and objectify him as a satanic presence, the Master is his alter ego. And the Master recognises how much they have in common by deriding Mackellar's sermonising, dismissing it as self-serving verbiage through which he seeks to appropriate truth exclusively to his own moral discourse and so legitimise his claim to be *un homme de parole*:

> 'Oh! there are double words for everything: the word that swells, the word that belittles; you cannot fight me with a word!' said he. 'You said the other day that I relied on your conscience: were I in your humour of detraction, I might say I built upon your vanity. It is your pretension to be *un homme de parole*; 'tis mine not to accept defeat. Call it vanity, call it virtue, call it greatness of soul – what signifies the expression? But recognise in each of us a common strain: that we both live for an idea' (175).

Language provides no stable referent: words are intrinsically 'double', so *un homme de parole* is a contradiction in terms, offering no moral definition. It is in formulating engagements or exchanges like these in the deconstructive way he does that Stevenson forces us to recognise his Modernist connections.

Let us now look more closely at what appears to be happening within and to the House of Durrisdeer. Three areas, all briefly touched on already, seem to me to be particularly worth concentrating on: Stevenson's interest in, and mode of, representing and articulating the 'moral occult'; his concern with authority in a broad sense; and his attitude to his text.

It might seem a little extravagant to claim that, in his exploration and representation of the moral occult, Stevenson achieves effects that can claim kinship with James's and Conrad's writing. True, these effects are far from being as sustained as they are in his more celebrated contemporaries' usage where virtually everything hangs on the subtlety and sophistication of their representation. That James and Stevenson both drew substantially on the melodrama tradition – Jacques Barzun described its influence on James as long ago as 1945 in his essay 'Henry James, Melodramatist' – need not in itself signify much. However, both exploit what Brooks, defining melodrama, calls 'the expressionism of the moral imagination' – James to the full, Stevenson more fitfully – and both clearly regard the product of this exploitation as, in itself, an adventure-story. When George Moore described *The Master of Ballantrae* as an adventure-story with the story left out, he appears to have overlooked this dimension. Such a simplification is rebuked if we consider James's description in the Preface to *A Portrait of a Lady* of Isabel Archer's long review of all that has led to her becoming Gilbert Osmond's wife. James writes: 'It is a representation simply of her motionlessly *seeing*, and an attempt withal to make the mere still lucidity of her act as "interesting" as the surprise of a caravan or the identification of a pirate.'

Peter Brooks, commenting on this remark, again finds a formulation which in helping to define melodrama also felicitously defines the link between James and Stevenson: 'The terms of reference in the adventure story are mocked; yet they remain the terms of reference: moral consciousness must be our adventure, its recognition must be the stuff of heightened drama.'[6] Stevenson, of course, is far from mocking the terms of reference of the adventure-story but a great deal of the adventure expresses itself through the moral consciousness of his characters and so constitutes the story – and some of his best writing. George Moore missed this; Joseph Conrad, I believe, did not.

I have said that a game of dice is being played out by the Master and Mackellar with the House of Durrisdeer as prize. At a later stage in the book Mackellar comes to see the Master as disturbingly spectral, but from the beginning he has been something of a phantom in that, in the early stages at least, no one is sure that he has survived the battle of Culloden, and later, as a proscribed rebel, he has no official existence. His reliance at times on two familiars – Colonel Burke and Secundra Dass – does nothing to strengthen his physical reality but, in its suggestion of a power to possess others and speak through them, extends the idea of 'evil' and enhances the menace he poses. Certainly for Mackellar he is proof that there are limits to *his* power to make the world over in his own repressed image: that the moral order he represents and seeks to impose is *not* the only one, and that there are other forms of moral life outside his system which lie beyond his control.

Alarmed at such a prospect, this steward of the apparently impoverished sensibility, the ace of book-keepers, develops an almost manic compulsion to defeat the enemy, bustling about Durrisdeer (which is, of course, 'the world' for him), sifting prejudice, motive and heretical tendencies with the perspicacity and the single-minded tenacity of an inquisitor. And the target for both him and the Master is the same: Henry Durie.

James's antagonism to his brother is almost pathological: 'I have hated you all my life', he tells him before the duel in which he seeks, by foul as well as fair means, to kill him. Seeing Henry married to the woman who was destined for him, and taking *his* place in Durrisdeer, confirms the Master in his determination to destroy Henry. Mackellar, on the other hand, is more insidious and insinuating. From early in their acquaintance he identifies himself with Henry but this is but a prelude to identifying Henry with himself: for if the Master is a notable fiction (or a figment, for whatever reality he has is defined by Mackellar), Mackellar's take-over of Henry is so complete as to render him a mere cypher. He possesses him so completely as to play the role he thinks Henry should have played in defence of the House of Durrisdeer.

Mackellar, we should note, comes from nowhere, Edinburgh University being inadequate as a *provenance*. There is even a conspicuous allusion to an absent father when, in the course of telling us that he 'never had much tolerance for the female sex', he admits that 'my own mother was certainly one of the salt of the earth, and my Aunt Dickson, who paid my fees at University, a very notable woman' (67). In passing we might note that Mackellar will never inaugurate a House of his own either, for he adds (of the female sex), 'being far from a bold man, I have ever shunned their company. Not only do I see no cause to regret this diffidence in myself, but have invariably remarked that most unhappy consequences follow those who were less wise' (67).

Mackellar, who 'never had much natural sympathy for the passion of love' short-circuits the process of inheriting and begetting by 'possessing' Henry, his House – and his wife. That he *may* be unconscious of his usurpation is no mitigation: quite the contrary, in fact, for it again reveals the blindness which attends on his sort of egotistical self-righteousness. Though he may take ostentatious occasion to refer to himself as a servant or steward, in his heart of hearts he no more sees himself as a subordinate than does Malvolio. There is the same obdurate complacency in each and all their policy works towards their own self-aggrandisement and the substitution of their authority for their master's.

Stevenson's cumulative exposure of this driving-force in Mackellar is brilliantly done. Even Mackellar's first interview with his employer, the old Lord Durrisdeer, though ostensibly an account of the latter's kindness and courtesy, is turned to the gratification of Mackellar's self-esteem:

> He had many questions to ask me, I remember, of Edinburgh College, where I had just received my mastership of arts, and of the various professors, with whom and their proficiency he seemed well acquainted; and thus, talking of things that I knew, I soon got liberty of speech in my new home (14).

Very soon he had liberty of the accounts, too, in his new 'home' (the word is a pointer): 'for much of my service at Durrisdeer, I have transacted everything at my own time, and to my own fancy, and never a farthing challenged' (14–15). The phrase 'to my own fancy' is another indicator of the true extent of the 'liberty' Mackellar seeks and acquires. Later he tells Alison 'I belong to Durrisdeer as if I had been born there', which is less the expression of loyalty that it might seem to be and more a claim to proprietorship.

It is significant that the character in the tale whom Mackellar most frequently assails (after the Master, that is) is Henry's wife, Alison. The reason is twofold: it is she who puts up the most spirited defence against Mackellar's take-over bid and it is she who, being still deeply in love with the Master, greatly assists in thwarting Mackellar's determination to isolate and disempower the latter. Moreover, she (along with the Master) at times treats Mackellar with condescension: something which rankles deeply. At their first meeting, he notes that 'she used me with more condescension than the rest; so that, upon all accounts, I kept her in the third place in my esteem' (14). Later when Alison discovers how far he has gone in upbraiding her husband for being a bad father (which results in another seizure) her outburst is charged with resentment at Mackellar's arrogating to himself such 'liberties'. 'What have you done to my husband? Will nothing teach you your position in this house? Will you never cease from making and meddling?' (131)

It is, of course, Mackellar who lets us know of Alison's outrage, partly because he himself sees his harshness towards Henry as 'a blunder' deserving of censure. But he adds that he 'meant it for the best', and after having told her all 'with ingenuity, even as it is written here' he waits for Alison to reflect and to see his action in a more favourable light. He is duly rewarded, seeing 'her animosity fall': '''Yes,' she said, 'you meant well indeed. I have had the same thoughts myself, or the same temptation rather, which makes me pardon you''' (131).

Mackellar is, in fact, greatly given to telling his readers of the approbation he receives, often with a high degree of *dis*ingenuous self-effacement. 'Mr Mackellar is a gentleman I value', Henry tells the Master in front of him, 'and you must continue, so long as you are under this roof, to bring yourself into no more collisions with one whom I will support at any possible cost to me and mine.' When Lord Durrisdeer objects to strangers being present when they are discussing another shady transaction affecting the estate to help the Master, Henry replies, 'There is no one but Mackellar here, and he is my friend.' And when Henry receives from Mackellar proof of the fact that the Master is a Government agent he compliments him thus (*Mackellar tells us*): 'This is the best you have done for me yet Mackellar.' 'Thank God, Mackellar, I have you to lean upon', says Alison at another moment of crisis in New York. Earlier, when Mackellar, the Unco' Guid Angel of the House of Durrisdeer, has succeeded in effecting yet another reconciliation, he describes the scene in gratified detail:

> When I brought [Alison] in, my lord took a hand of each of us and laid them both upon his bosom. 'I have had two friends in my life .... All the comfort ever I had, it came from one or other .... Do what you please with me: God knows I love and honour ye' (193).

The truth is that Mackellar has done what he pleases with *him* for a very long time and, as the House of Durrisdeer passes more and more under his control (he is even appointed the family's avenger, with Alison telling him on the eve of her flight to America, 'I bequeath it to you to take our vengeance' [141]), he exercises his authority openly and with relish.

Predictably, it is the Master on whom he now visits his particular revenge. He it was who had used him 'with the extreme of family condescension'; but we should note its occasion. While the dissembling Master was dazzling his father and Alison with his role-playing as an affectionate brother when the family were all gathered together, he did not extend his pretence to include Mackellar whom he continued to 'condescend' to. To Mackellar, so eager to be wholly of the family, this was indeed an 'insult indescribable': 'That he should leave me out in his dissimulation, as though even my testimony were too despicable to be considered, galled me to the blood' (77). Though he quickly (and unconvincingly) adds, 'what it was to me is not worth notice. I make but memorandum of it here', he exacts a full revenge later when he is left in charge of Durrisdeer after the flight of the family to America, and takes over the role of head of the House. Though he doesn't get things altogether his own way – '"Sit down, Mr Mackellar, if you please" says the Master, taking, as he spoke, the head of the table, which I had designed to occupy myself ... ' (152) – his objective is clear: the subordination of the Master to his own hegemony over the House of Durrisdeer. In response to the Master's request for an allowance ('Have I to keep well with my good friend Mackellar for my pocket-money also? This is a pleasing return to the principles of boyhood' [153]), Mackellar tells him that though he has no instructions in the matter, he will take it on himself to see that he is supplied 'in moderation': '"In moderation," he repeated. "And you will take it on yourself?" He drew himself up, and looked about the hall at the dark rows of portraits. "In the name of my ancestors, I thank you"' (153). The sparring makes it clear that they are both very conscious of what they are contending for. The Master is explicit when his anger at his treatment bursts out shortly after this exchange: 'I will find out where these fools are fled to ... and when I have run my quarry to ground, I will drive a wedge into that family that shall once more burst it into shivers' (154). While James would destroy the family, Mackellar would simply control it, and at this point he is high in the ascendant.

But in seeking paramount authority over the House of Durrisdeer, what is he really after? He knows perfectly well that there is nothing substantial about it: in that sense it is pure illusion:

Now that all the living members of the family were plunged in irremediable sorrow, it was strange how we turned to that conjoint abstraction of the family itself and sought to bolster up the airy nothing of its reputation: not the Duries only; but the hired steward himself (107).

The answer must be that the 'House' firstly defines a space, a 'theatre', for the playing of 'authority' roles and secondly, posits a gratifyingly vulnerable moral order, the legitimacy of whose value-system is grounded on nothing more than the historical continuum as embodied in the laws of inheritance. When that House has two sons contending for their father's authority that is quite enough for a partisan third party to define an evil 'other' and to take upon himself the task of purging from the world the evil that has just been discovered.

Had Mackellar not found himself in just such a House, he would have had to invent it – and very probably did so. This man who shrinks from sword-play and women is utterly ruthless in his prosecution of the war against his satanic enemy. The Master shows himself well aware of this in his apparently flippant aside when complaining about the lack of spirit in his brother's card-playing; 'Even Square-toes has a certain vivacity when his stake is imperilled' he says (93). James Durie, in punning on the word 'stake', shows that he under-stands very well the nature and depth of the steward's interest in the House of Durrisdeer, and he will later learn just how far Mackellar, the inheritor of the Puritans, is prepared to go in defence of that stake when the latter tries to kill him on the way to America.

Mackellar and the Master may not seem to speak the same language, but it is made abundantly clear that they can communicate very well. I have said that Stevenson demonstrates this with a deftness which puts us in mind of those masters at signifying the 'moral occult', James and Conrad. And he is quite well aware of what he's doing, even introducing it reflexively in this tale:

> The poor gentleman sat for days in my room, so great a picture of distress that I could never venture to address him; yet it is to be thought he found some comfort even in my presence and the knowl-edge of my sympathy. There were times, too, when we talked, and a strange manner of talk it was; there was never a person named, nor an individual circumstance referred to; yet we had the same matter in our minds; and we were each aware of it. It is a strange art that can thus be practised; to talk for hours of a thing, and never name nor yet so much as hint at it. And I remember I wondered if it was by some such natural skill that the Master made love to Mrs Henry all day long (as he manifestly did) without startling her into reserve (89–90).

A great deal of use is made of eloquent silence and wordless gesture, though occasionally it is a single phrase that reminds the reader of a Conradian moral allusiveness. When, for example, Mackellar tries to deal with the drunken Jessie Brown (whom the Master had 'ruined' at a precocious age) he reports the meeting thus: 'all the time she carried on in a light-headed, reckless way – now aping the manners of a lady, now breaking into unseemly mirth, now making coquettish advances *that oppressed me to the ground*' (19: my italics). Stevenson doesn't *need* to have Mackellar explain the phrase: we understand what it is he seeks to evoke through the seeming opacity.

Perhaps the best-sustained example of Stevenson's ability to evoke depths of meaning and comprehension which the language of ordinary discourse seems inadequate to express occurs in the exchange between Mackellar and Alison in the aftermath of the duel. (That between Mackellar and old Lord Durrisdeer runs it a close second.) Up to that point he has been unremitting in his hostility towards Alison, not, primarily, because of her earlier 'condescension', but because he is convinced of her continuing devotion to the Master. Though Mackellar explains the strength of his antagonism by his outrage at the humiliations suffered by *his* master, Henry, what really gives his assault the vehemence it has is his recognition that he has been unable to eradicate the Master from Alison's – or old Lord Durrisdeer's – heart. To an imperially-minded Mackellar for whom the Manichean universe is – literally – a Godsend, no moral space can be conceded to the Adversary. There is only one God and Mackellar is his prophet: to love the Master is to worship at heathen altars. And, despite being informed of the Master's ruinous demands upon the estate, Alison continues, to Mackellar's mortification, to do just this: 'would not anyone have thought that my disclosure must have rooted up that idol?' he asks in amazement and dismay. But he knows that Alison has not ceased to care for his opponent, for so his acute ability to interpret the unspoken (which he never doubts) assures him:

> It is wonderful how a private thought leaks out: it is wonderful to me now how we should all have followed the current of her sentiments; and though she bore herself quietly, and had a very even disposition, yet we should have known whenever her fancy ran to Paris (67).

The duel brings everything to a head. What is more, in doing so it shows very clearly that the *underlying* duel which Mackellar has been conducting from the moment he realised that 'there were two parties in the house' is the one which is the true expression of the 'moral occult'. Appropriately, its expression is a matter of nuances, gestures and ellipses, for much of the 'moral occult' is inarticulable.

Though terrified of the naked sword (and derided by the Master for his timidity), Mackellar swiftly takes charge when the duel is over and the Master vanquished. Henry, believing that he has killed his brother, reveals his inability to assume any authority over events. Totally unmanned, his nerve is not to be restored by Mackellar plying him with brandy, but Mackellar is more than equal to the occasion: 'sit there', he instructs his 'master', 'and leave all to me'.

Interestingly, it is not to old Lord Durrisdeer that he goes first, but to Alison, ostensibly to get her to look after Henry and help preserve the secret of the night's events from leaking out to the servants and thence to the local community. This is only part of the explanation, however, for Mackellar is also vengefully bent on the final extirpation of the Master's presence in Alison's affections. And it is to be no gentle exorcism. The self-righteous moral fervour with which Mackellar is imbued ensures that there will be no quarter for the disciple even though the devil has himself apparently been conquered.

The impressive scene between him and Alison starts as he means it to continue: 'It was no hour for scruples, and I opened my lady's door without so much as a knock and passed boldly in' (98). When she has dressed, he tells her of the duel which had come about as the result of the Master's persecution of her husband – a persecution she had been blind to, according to Mackellar perhaps wilfully blind to:

> 'Things have been borne so long, things of which you know nothing, which you would not believe if I should tell. But tonight it went too far, and when he insulted you –'
> 'Stop' said she, 'He? Who?'
> 'Oh! madam,' cried I, my bitterness breaking forth, 'do you ask me such a question? Indeed, then, I may go elsewhere for help; there is none here!'

Alison does not, or will not understand: 'I do not know in what I have offended you …. Forgive me; put me out of this suspense' (99).

Mackellar's response to this, opaque as it may initially seem to be to the point of constituting a *non sequitur*, nonetheless indicates both his singleness of mind and the strength of the subterranean stream that feeds his moral purpose: 'But I dared not tell her yet; I felt not sure of her; and at the doubt, and under the sense of impotence with it, I turned on the poor woman with something near to anger' (99). At this point, Mackellar is, Marlow-like, uncertain of his ability to root out the corruption planted there by the Master, uncertain of his mastery over his own moral universe. A little like Kurtz's 'Intended', Alison, equally pure, has been unwilling to see what Mackellar sees. To her, as she said shortly before this confrontation, the Master may have been 'always of a thoughtless nature;' but 'his heart is excellent; he is the soul of generosity' (66).

Thus when Mackellar turns upon Alison he does so not with 'something near to anger' but with something like ferocity:

> 'Madam,' said I, 'we are speaking of two men; one of them insulted you, and you ask me which. I will help you to the answer. With one of these men you have spent all your hours: has the other reproached you? To one you have been always kind; to the other, as God sees me and judges between us two, I think not always: has his love ever failed you? To-night one of these two men told the other, in my hearing – the hearing of a hired stranger – that you were in love with him. Before I say one word, you shall answer your own question: Which was it? Nay, madam, you shall answer me another: If it has come to this dreadful end, whose fault is it?'
>
> She stared at me like one dazzled. 'Good God!' she said once, in a kind of bursting exclamation; and then a second time in a whisper to herself: 'Great God! – In the name of mercy, Mackellar, what is wrong?' she cried. 'I am made up; I can hear all.'
>
> You are not fit to hear,' said I. 'Whatever it was, you shall say first it was your fault' (99).

Just how far from sense and justice Mackellar has been carried by his obsession is well-summarised in the gross unfairness and extravagance of that last sentence.

Alison's reply is one of bewilderment: '"Oh!"she cried, with a gesture of wringing her hands, "this man will drive me mad! Can you not put *me* out of your thoughts."' It is a response which suggests that she still does not realise the extent to which Mackellar sees her as a rival (or an obstacle). He seeks complete ascendancy over Henry whom he needs to be sure of if he is to prosecute successfully his war against James; but he can't win while Alison has Henry's heart and the Master has hers. Alison's knowledge is only partial: and her bewilderment is the result of not knowing to whom or what she is a threat. She hasn't sounded the depths of Mackellar's polarisation of himself and the Master, nor the extent of Mackellar's colonisation of her husband, despite his so blatantly acting as an outraged surrogate.

By the end of Mackellar's harangue, her bewilderment has been to some extent reduced and her consciousness of Mackellar as the avenging angel (albeit self-appointed) considerably heightened. When it occurs to her that someone will need to tell old Lord Durrisdeer of the night's happenings, Mackellar assures her 'That shall be my part', to which she replies: 'You will not speak to him as you have to me?' It is a question to which she receives in answer nothing more than 'Leave my Lord to me' (101). There is no trace of the 'hired stranger' in his brutal humiliation of her. In the end she is dismissed to go and tend to her husband: 'Go to him now, where he sits in the hall; ... give him your hand; say, "I know all;" – if God gives you grace enough, say, "Forgive me"' (101). Alison's reply is now more comprehending, more aware of the authority Mackellar is wielding so savagely, and tinged with bitterness at being forced to see herself through the eyes of this uncompromising avenger so utterly impervious to all her charitable and loving ardour for the man whom he unwaveringly perceives to be the incarnation of the false god. The final exchange is loaded with occult significance:

> 'God strengthen you, and make you merciful,' said she. 'I will go to my husband.'
> 'Let me light you there,' said I, taking up the candle.
> 'I will find my way in the dark,' she said, with a shudder, and I think the shudder was at me (101).

She can scarcely be blamed for preferring the dark to Mackellar's 'light', and the eloquence of that shudder is one of the most telling moments in the book (gaining, of course, in density and resonance by the fact that Mackellar chooses to record it – the 'I think' being as teasing as it is impenetrable).

Mackellar's ensuing 'enlightenment' of Lord Durrisdeer is only slightly less harsh than his treatment of Alison. Again it is worth remarking that his simple task of informing him about the duel is not uppermost in his mind. Nor is he expatiating on the persecution suffered by Henry merely to soften the father's wrath at the presumed killing of his favourite son, though this is a factor. He is not, in his mixture of pleading with and hectoring the old man, simply redressing the balance by demonstrating the overlooked virtues of that 'dear, generous, ill-fated, noble heart', his 'unfortunate patron' (103). Once more he is out to eradicate completely any love for the Master in his father's heart: a love which the old man stubbornly refuses to renounce:

> 'Henry has been ever dear to me, very dear. James (I do not deny it, Mr Mackellar) James is perhaps dearer; you have not seen my James in quite a favourable light; he has suffered under his misfortunes.... And even now his is the more affectionate nature. But I will not speak of him' (103).

Partial Lord Durrisdeer may be, but nothing in this can justify Mackellar's extreme position in attempting to deny the Master the birthright of his filiality: '"You know how [Henry] has met your other – met your wishes," I corrected myself, stumbling at the name of son.' (102) Denying Lord Durrisdeer's admission that he has been weak ('and what is worse ... dull') though he knows it is true, Mackellar launches out on his mission of destruction in the face of the father's protest:

> 'You have not been weak; you have been abused by a devilish dissembler. You saw yourself how he had deceived you in the matter of his danger; he has deceived you throughout in every step of his career. *I wish to pluck him from your heart*: I wish to force your eyes upon your other son; ah, you have a son there!'
> 'No, no', said he, 'two sons – I have two sons' (103).

The violence in the sentence which I have italicised (with its echo of the death of Cinna at the hands of the mob in *Julius Caesar* – 'Pluck but his name out of his heart, and set him going'), completes the picture we have of the absolutism inherent in Mackellar's fanatical determination to wipe out every trace of his 'devilish' enemy. On the other hand, Lord Durrisdeer's protest wrung from him under such duress must not be overlooked, for it is altogether noteworthy. Weak as the protest is, it shows him attempting to reassert the unity of his family and the brotherhood of his sons in stark contrast to his steward whose moral identity depends on division and who constantly seeks not just to polarise the brothers but to ensure that the one with whom he apparently identifies should erase the other from the hearts and minds of everyone. What complicates matters, however, is that Mackellar also *needs* the Master!

Vivid as this whole scene has been – Mackellar leaning over the old man sitting up in bed and three times forcibly preventing him from getting out of it – the real drama is going on under the surface; in the occult sources of Mackellar's obsession often not fully articulated, in the interplay of his consciousness with that of the other characters. Characteristically of *this* sort of melodrama, the central characters are all highly perceptive, well aware of the undertow of meaning and significance and skilful in 'reading' it. Significantly, Lord Durrisdeer sees his failure in perception as a more serious defect than his weakness. Several times Mackellar reveals to us that Lord Durrisdeer is a good reader of signs (though he may choose to pretend otherwise at times), and, in the course of trying to account to himself for the latter's blindness towards the Master's conduct, he pays him a compliment in a currency which is clearly common to them both: 'And my old lord, too – that very watchful gentleman – where was all his observation?' (78) Alison's credulity, too, is a matter for surprise on Mackellar's part and he voices it in a way which once more strengthens the reflexive tenor of so much in this novel: 'And yet I think again, and I think always, Mrs Henry might have read between the lines: she might have had more knowledge of her husband's nature; after all these years of marriage she might have commanded or captured his confidence' (77–8). But then he reminds himself that the Master is so skilled in deceit that he could have 'gulled an angel' (78). The threat that comes from the abyss – exemplified for Mackellar in the Master's strategy in persecuting Henry, 'so perfidious, so simple, so impossible to combat' (77) – finds expression in a language which Conrad was to develop and make a hallmark of his writing.

The picture of *all* of the book's four principals leading a double life or, more precisely, living their lives on several moral planes simultaneously so that they all nurture secret animosities, desires and objectives, is remarkably well-drawn. It is this which provides the 'story' which George Moore felt was left out, *and* the real adventure. For Mackellar they are all on the edge of a moral abyss (the danger never more acute for him personally than when he feels he is struggling with a phantom, a thing of buckram). Unless he can tear the scales from the eyes of the deluded ('blinded by old ingrained predilections') he is convinced that the world they inhabit will be destroyed. Repeatedly in his arguments with Alison and Lord Durrisdeer after the duel he refers to the certain destruction that awaits the House of Durrisdeer if they *will not see things his way* and assist him.

The drama of the moral life which provides the real tension of *The Master of Ballantrae* depends entirely for its animation on the consciousness of Ephraim Mackellar, at first glance so prosaic, complacent, narrow-minded and self-righteous. That all his imagination should be concentrated on – and expressed through – the drama of the occult moral life is, however, not at all a contradiction. For centuries the Scottish fundamentalist had known that this was the stratum that mattered, since in it there lurked all the terrors and desires that marked out humankind for damnation. The conviction that the drama of the inner life was an open book to the All-Seeing Eye authorised repression (which in turn spawned hypocrisy and moral humbug), rendered appealing the idea of a Manichean universe as a way of shifting some of the weight off one's shoulders, and greatly stimulated a morbid imagination as a way of putting it back on.

Stevenson understood the psycho-pathology of this condition very well, not only through being the child of fundamentalist Presbyterians but from the lurid tales and superstitious admonitions of his nurse 'Cummy'. Ephraim Mackellar is well-educated and capable of presenting to the world a demeanour which appears to be one of composed, pedestrian self-sufficiency. Beneath that surface, however, there is an obsessive passion to rid the world of evil, for the securing of which end almost any means is justified. He vehemently assures his 'dear patron' of his utter devotion to his interests – 'For you I would obey in any point whatever – even to Sin, God pardon me!' (81) – and, of course, he *does* commit an extremely serious sin in his attempt to take the Master's life on board ship. But in doing so, what imperative is he driven by?

It is in the intensity of the scenes with Alison and Lord Durrisdeer that he comes nearest to showing his true colours and one might conclude this section by drawing particular attention to the character of the two different roles he plays so extravagantly there. The ferocity of his verbal attack on Alison for her perceived moral defects is charged with an implicit sexual violence. The improper and presumptuous liberty he takes in entering her room – 'I opened my lady's door without so much as a knock and passed boldly in' – is compounded by the tart familiarity of his command (before he has even explained to her what has happened) 'do you get as quickly as you can into your clothes. There is much to be done' (98).

Yet there is an obverse to this masterful performance in which he *appears* to play the role of surrogate (and violent) husband: he is driven as much by his fear of impotence as his hope of victory: 'But I dared not tell her yet; I felt not sure of her; and at the doubt, and under the sense of impotence it brought with it, I turned on the poor woman with something near to anger' (95). Of course what Mackellar is about is, as I've argued, the deletion of the Master from Alison's affections – and this makes Alison (for Mackellar) something of a surrogate too. Mackellar readily acknowledges that he finds the Master physically attractive. (When Henry strikes the blow that leads to the duel the Master 'sprang to his feet like one transfigured; I had never seen the man so beautiful' [94].) And the context for this, we must remember, is the repeated allusions to Mackellar's unmanly nature. Quite apart from the portrayal of his abject fear when confronted by physical violence, he is described by others as womanish in his behaviour. It is true that after the attempted murder, the Master somewhat revises his opinion of Mackellar, deciding that 'the old wife has blood in his body after all!' rather than being 'magnetised by the Ten Commandments' as he had believed (172). Alison's comment is the more considered and perhaps structured more tellingly, eliciting an interesting reaction from Mackellar:

'but when it came to the point, I have to suppose your courage failed you; for what you said was said cruelly.' She paused, looking at me; then suddenly smiled a little and said a singular thing: 'Do you know what you are, Mr Mackellar? You are an old maid' (131–2).

'Singular' is another of these opaque words frequently deployed by Stevenson at crucial moments in his characters' self-revelation. While it isn't explained, the plurality of possible meanings imbues Alison's descriptive phrase with a significance which arrests our attention. But Mackellar often focuses our minds on the same area more directly and explicitly. When, for example, he prays fervently for the ship in which he and the Master are travelling to America to founder in the storm so bringing about the Master's 'deletion from this world', he sees himself as expendable: 'I was already old; I had never been young, I was not formed for the world's pleasures, I had few affections.' The terms of his self-deprecation are filled out when he gets down on his knees to pray: '"O God!" I cried, "I would be liker a man if I rose and struck this creature down"' (165). These words from his 'prayer' return to him when the opportunity occurs to bring about the Master's death and directly precipitate his attack (171).

The dominating figure Mackellar's imagination has conceived the Master to be – he is 'the Satan of the *Paradise Lost*', the 'false idol' – also possesses the power to emasculate his creator/interpreter, it seems, and, in a clever device, Stevenson has the Master tease him on the subject. Well aware of Mackellar's extreme aversion to him, the Master tells him a parable which is also a lesson in how to go

about getting rid of your enemy. Mackellar sees the tale as the
Master giving in to what is for him an irresistible temptation: 'He
must tell me a tale, and show me at the same time how clever he was
and how wicked' (167), but Mackellar is engaged in doing something very similar: priding himself greatly on his acumen and skill
in defending the House of Durrisdeer, and he is in process of deciding
to try to kill the Master.

At the outset of the tale the Master instructs Mackellar on 'the first
principle of vengeance' which is to keep secret his intention to seek
revenge, and even the grounds for the enmity – for 'hatred betrayed
is hatred impotent' (167). Mackellar *has* betrayed his hatred, most
recently in the prayer for the ship to go down which has been over-
heard by Secundra Dass. Fixated on the 'deletion' of the Master from
the earth (and that word normally meaning the removal of something written or printed is of particular interest), Mackellar has
repeatedly felt himself to be impotent, made so, arguably, by the
character he has created, written down, and *cannot* delete. The Count
of the tale (whom Mackellar clearly believes to be the Master) *also*
considers himself to be an artist (he was 'a man of curious, searching
mind; he had something of the artist' [167]). Since Stevenson often
uses 'artist' and 'writer' interchangeably, complex questions are raised
of just who is authoring whom. What the 'Count' demonstrates in
his tale is that if you understand human nature well enough you can
bring about your enemy's destruction simply by playing on his human
weakness, notably his vanity and egotism; and the Master compliments 'my excellent Mackellar' for *his* knowledge of human nature
(169).

In some ways the telling of this 'parable' is the point where the
two characters are most densely interfused, least identifiable individually. And it is given a very specific, even bizarre context which
further confounds any attempt to see them distinctly as morally-
contrasted entities. The ship is rolling excessively and, given their
relative position 'at the break of the poop', they take over each
other's position every time the ship wallows from one side to the
other:

> I had continually before my eyes a measure of our evolutions in
> the person of the Master .... Now his head would be in the zenith
> and his shadow fall quite beyond the Nonesuch on the farther
> side; and now he would swing down until he was underneath my
> feet, and the line of the sea leaped above him like the ceiling of a
> room. I looked on upon this with a growing fascination, as birds

are said to look upon snakes. My mind, besides, was troubled with an astonishing diversity of noises… (166–7).

The last sentence alone would confirm Stevenson's objective of depicting a scene of *moral* confusion which bears the same clear import as did Lear's inversion of the justice and the thief: 'change places, and, handy-dandy, which is the justice, which is the thief?' Or, one might even say, which is the author, which the character?

Stevenson illustrates in the character of Mackellar the hectic activity of a consciousness trapped in a self-system several sizes too small for it. But saying this doesn't do anything like justice to his achievement, which is as multi-layered as his character's consciousness. In Mackellar he has created a character who is apparently rational to the point of emotional aridity but who soon reveals to us that he lives his true moral existence on a quite different plane. On that level he exhibits a vigorous creative energy which is nonetheless doomed to continual frustration because it is grounded in an obsession in whose convolutions self and other are hopelessly entangled.

Stevenson doesn't simply leave matters there, however. The monstrous product of this energy is Mackellar's figuration of the Master, but it becomes monstrous, paradoxically, only because his originator cannot or will not accept paternity, that is, *that he has created him*. In his rational mode (which is by no means totally disconnected from the more seminal stratum) Mackellar goes out of his way to let us know that he has no interest in procreation, has never been young and has 'few affections'. At crucial moments he finds himself unable to act because of a sense of impotence, and the only time he behaves 'liker [to] a man' (165) is when he attempts to delete, rub out, the issue of his, in truth, fertile imagination. (Ironically, part of the explanation for his attempting to do so is that *his* character – the Master – shows a preference for Richardson as 'father' rather than Mackellar's biblical Author of authors whom Mackellar, after the manner of religious zealots, has actually made his surrogate.)

Despite his ostentatious disavowal of any inclination towards biological paternity (with all the obligations to others which that entails), Mackellar has brought into the world an embodiment of what is, *au fond*, the darker side of himself – those forces, whose presence he then advances as proof of the world's evil. As confident as Dr Jekyll is with his creature (the parallel is quite close), Mackellar believes that *his* can be controlled with 'the brilliancy of [their] discourse' (155), that the Master has, thereby, become 'quite impotent for any evil'

(156). But this text has taught us to be wary about putting our trust in words and Mackellar's complacency is shown to be altogether unjustified. Having sired this character, however, he drees his weird (as Scots would say) when the character becomes the author (and teller of tales) and emasculates his begetter.

The complex tensions between the begotten and the begetter is a – possibly *the* – central theme in Stevenson's *oeuvre*. As a later chapter will substantiate, the biological and psychological are only two of its operative constituents for it is also, more interestingly to a Modernist or Postmodernist readership, expressed through the problematisation of traditional/patriarchal forms of textual authority and narrative processes. Before leaving this novel I should like to explore the father–son relationship a little further.

The scene in which Mackellar violently upbraids Alison (whom he always refers to as 'Mrs Henry') shows clearly enough that his aggression is linked to his sense of impotence. His playing the role of surrogate husband is thus compromised by the undertow of doubt about his own virility. The following scene with Lord Durrisdeer is therefore all the more interesting for in it he plays a quite different role. 'You will not speak to him as you have to me?', we may recall Alison entreating him and he certainly does not for, in great contrast to the previous confrontation, he plays the role of surrogate *son*, at the end of the interview, on his knees before his 'father' abjectly pleading for his understanding and forgiveness.

I have said that he identifies himself with Henry progressively from the start until he has, so to speak, fully colonised him. Just how fully comes out in this scene when it is difficult to believe that Mackellar is speaking on someone else's behalf, so imbued is his appeal with the anguish of the son denied his father's blessing. (It could, of course, be argued that he is not speaking exclusively on Henry's behalf, his own fatherless state having earlier been brought to our attention in his rather pointed reference only to female carers.) Of Lord Durrisdeer's blindness to the Master's persecution of Henry he says:

'All this my dear, unfortunate patron has endured without help or countenance. Your own best word, my lord, was only gratitude. Oh, but he was your son too! He had no other father' (103).

The significance of these last two intense sentences must not be under-estimated. They are the vicarious embodiment of that afflicted cry of accusation and appeal which resounds throughout Stevenson's work and which the 'son' directs at the 'father' perceived by him as hostile and repressive (or just absent). The first demands that the father acknowledges his paternity (' ... he was your son too!'), while the second is redolent of the son's almost tormented recognition of his dependence on the father, there being absolutely no other source for that liberating blessing which will legitimise his entry into manhood.[7]

Lord Durrisdeer – 'that watchful man' – refuses to see what it is Mackellar is trying to tell him – that Henry has (he thinks) killed his brother, and the steward flings himself on his knees at the bed-side.

> ' Oh, my lord,' cried I, 'think on him you have left; think of this poor sinner whom you begot, whom your wife bore to you, whom we have none of us strengthened as we could; think of him, not of yourself; he is the other sufferer – think of him! That is the door for sorrow – Christ's door, God's door: oh! it stands open. Think of him even as he thought of you. *'Who is to tell the old man?'* – these were his words. It was for that I came; that is why I am here pleading at your feet' (104).

Lord Durrisdeer's reply to this does not, however, give much away: '"Let me get up," he cried, thrusting me aside, and was on his feet before myself ... "Here is too much speech," said he, "Where was it?"'

As Mackellar has taken over more and more of Henry – it is worth noting that every depredation, every increase in persecution by the Master, results in an extension of Mackellar's authority – Henry has become more of a shell, until Mackellar can at times react to him with an impatience apparently devoid of respect: '"For God's sake, for all our sakes, be more courageous!" said I. "What must we do?" He showed me his face with the same stupid stare. "Do?" says he."' (97) Progressively he treats his 'dear patron' like a child, adminis-tering what he hopes will be a restorative brandy with parental exasperation: '"Drink that," said I, "drink it down." I forced him to swallow it like a child.' (98) And as Mackellar recounts the events, Henry himself does seem to regress to childhood though even that is not sufficient to secure the blessing he seeks from his father. The latter, after investigating the scene of the duel, goes to talk to Henry: 'My old lord walked very steadily to where his son was sitting; he

had a steady countenance, too, but methought a little cold' (102).
When he calls out 'My son', the acknowledgement galvanises Henry:

> With a broken, strangled cry, Mr Henry leaped up and fell on his
> father's neck, crying and weeping, the most pitiful sight that ever
> a man witnessed. 'Oh! father,' he cried, 'you know I loved him;
> you know I loved him in the beginning; I could have died for him
> – you know that! I would have given my life for him and you. Oh!
> say you know that. Oh! say you can forgive me. O father, father,
> what have I done – what have I done. And we used to be bairns
> together!' and wept and sobbed, and fondled the old man, and
> clutched him about the neck, with the passion of a child in terror
> (108).

Though the echoes from the parable of the prodigal son may be
present only faintly here (Henry does see himself as having sinned
and in need of his father's forgiveness), there is a crucial inversion.
In the parable, it is the father who 'had compassion, and ran, and fell
on his neck and kissed him'. Here no such response is forthcoming
and Stevenson's description of his composure – *and detachment* – while
his son clings to him babbling hysterically is extremely telling:

> Throughout all this my laird was like a cold, kind spectator with
> his wits about him. At the first cry, which was indeed enough to
> call the house about us, he had said to me over his shoulder, 'Close
> the door' (108).

It should come as no surprise to find this son, with whom Mackellar
so closely identifies, again disavowing his manhood following the
duel, this time before his wife:

> 'And O my lass, ... you must forgive me too! Not your husband
> – I have only been the ruin of your life. But you knew me when I
> was a lad; there was no harm in Henry Durie then .... It's him –
> it's the old bairn that played with you – oh, can ye never, never
> forgive him?' (108)

Increasingly Henry, Mackellar notes, regresses to childhood in his
relations with his wife: 'He turned to her with all his emotions, like
a child to its mother, and seemed secure of sympathy' (119), and
though this is presented as an aspect of his mental deterioration,
Mackellar with his usual shrewdness observes that it had been an

element in their relationship from the beginning. Recognising that her love – even passion – had been directed to the Master, he speculates that 'her sentiment to my lord, as it had been founded from the first in pity, was that rather of a mother than a wife; perhaps it pleased her – if I may so say – to behold her two children so happy in each other' (128). The two children here are her son Alexander and her husband.

These hints that Henry's reversion to childhood is not altogether at odds with aspects of his character detectable much earlier, coalesce with the reasons given for the depression that Mackellar has noticed from the start of their acquaintance. Chief of these is his acute consciousness that his father's countenance does not truly shine on him, that his blessing is reserved for the Master. The need for the unequivocal expression of his father's love is such that its denial (and bestowal on his undeserving elder brother) means that he never convinces himself that he can enter fully into his title of manhood. The fully-endowed, fully-legitimised elder brother, basking in his father's unstinting approval, emasculates and eclipses him. In contrast, when it is James who claims to be the prodigal son, the father's response is different. Says the devious Master:

'you must not be downcast because your brother has come home. All's yours, that's sure enough, and little I grudge it you. Neither must you grudge me my place beside my father's fire.'

'And that is too true, Henry,' says my old lord with a little frown, a thing rare with him. 'You have been the elder brother of the parable in the good sense; you must be careful of the other' (76).

But, of course, Henry is neither the younger son who 'wasted his substance with riotous living' nor the elder brother who, in the parable, expressed his indignation at having served his father and obeyed him in all things yet never having been offered even 'a kid wherewith to make merry with my friends'.[8] Henry's feeble protest – 'I am easily put in the wrong' – is unceremoniously dismissed by his father:

'Who puts you in the wrong?' cried my lord, I thought very tartly for so mild a man. 'You have earned my gratitude and your brother's many thousand times: you may count on its endurance; and let that suffice' (76).

Needless to say, it does not suffice and the inversion of responsibility proclaimed in the parable points up the injustice in the father's reproof. Being the elder son 'in the good sense' is small consolation, deprived as Henry is of all authority (deriving from primogeniture and the traditional paternal blessing) and so conspicuously of his father's love. Lord Durrisdeer's 'let that suffice' is almost brutal in the humiliation it inflicts on his younger son. It is another step in his emasculation and helps to precipitate Henry's demoralisation.

Mackellar told us early in his account that soon after taking up the stewardship 'I had begun to find my heart go out to Mr Henry ... he was a man so palpably unhappy'. It did not take him long to discern the reason:

> Dead or alive ... that man [the Master] was his brother's rival: his rival abroad where there was never a good word for Mr Henry ... and his rival at home, not only with his father and his wife, but with the very servants (15).

Later Henry himself confirms his moral disinheritance: 'Nothing is mine, nothing ... I have only the name and shadow of things – only the shadow' (60). The Master has, in fact, played upon the theme of unjust inheritance from the moment he reappears in a way calculated to put Henry in the wrong and, so to speak, permanently maim him. He does so by conferring on his brother (usually when out of their father's and Alison's earshot) the name of Jacob, and the Jacob/Esau analogue (false though it is) keeps the theme of inheritance and legitimacy, confirmed by paternal benediction, at the forefront of the book's patterning.

The analogy *is* false and unjust, of course, since Jacob the younger brother, cheats to get the father's blessing due to the elder by taking advantage of Isaac's blindness and pretending to be Esau. Such a blessing once made could not be withdrawn and, as Isaac admits to an indignant Esau, it has 'made him thy lord', since the blessing imparts the paternal authority to the recipient.[9] Esau is not pleased:

> Is not he rightly called Jacob? for he hath supplanted me these two times: he took away my birthright, and, behold, now he hath taken away my blessing.[10]

Esau is not being altogether fair to Jacob, however, even though the latter is – one might risk saying – a bare-faced opportunist. As we all know, he *bought* his brother's birthright for a mess of pottage when Esau was about to die of starvation. But the Bible does not approve of Esau's part in the transaction and the episode concludes: 'thus Esau despised his birthright'.[11]

Wounding as all this is for Henry (who has, from the moment the Master wins the toss of the coin and rides out for the Stuart cause, realised that 'if the expedition fails', he will be 'neither fish nor flesh' [41]), it is all the more insupportable in that he, unlike Jacob, does *not* gain his father's blessing. Esau, we may recall, 'was a cunning hunter, a man of the field', whereas Jacob 'was a plain man dwelling in tents'[12], and the old man's preference is clearly for the son who is a man of the field. He admits James is his favourite and when Henry openly alludes to the fact before his father, he is not contradicted.

The absence of his father's love and blessing, which he so craves, saps Henry's self-esteem. Characteristically, he declines to do what Mackellar urges and go to his father to complain about his brother's persecution. Understandable as this is in itself, the terms of his objection show that he is driven, first, by a fear that he would fall still further in his father's regard and, second, by a defeatism so abject that, as he tells Mackellar, he begins to despise himself. 'You do not see the weakness of my position', he protests to the steward:

> 'I can carry no such base thoughts to anyone – to my father least of all; that would be to fall into the bottom of his scorn. The weakness of my ground,' he continued, 'lies in myself, that I am not one who engages love. I have their gratitude, they all tell me that; I have a rich estate of it! But I am not present in their minds; they are moved neither to think with me nor to think for me. There is my loss' (90).

He carries this doleful acceptance of his being 'not one who engages love' to an extreme that comes near to allowing the Master to undermine his standing with his wife in a way that is the ultimate in humiliation. Of her increasingly 'tender familiarity' with the Master, Mackellar gives (for a man unacquainted with the passion of love) a sensitive, perceptive, and, of course, self-deprecating account:

> even to so dull an observer as myself, it was plain that her kindness was of a more moving nature than the sisterly. The tones of her voice appeared more numerous; she had a light and softness in her eye; she was more gentle with all of us, even with Mr Henry, even with myself: methought she breathed of some quiet, melancholy happiness. To look on this, what a torment it was for Mr Henry (84).

If Henry seems almost to abdicate his position (though it has to be noted that it is on precisely this subject that he does finally rebel when the Master goes too far in asserting his greater power to attract women), it is worth noting that his father frequently, by some act or comment, seems to assist in his mortification. When Henry accuses him of not objecting to the presence of 'strangers' (i.e. Mackellar) when it comes to visiting 'frequent blame' upon him (85), his father makes no attempt to propitiate him. In truth, earlier in the scene, when Henry has protested against breaking the entail on the estate to provide money for the Master, pointing out that it would be 'an injustice to my son, if ever I have one', his father responds with a remark capable of hurting his son deeply: '"But that you are not likely to have," said my lord.' There is no elaboration and the bald, wounding statement stands on its own.

Yet Lord Durrisdeer is not altogether unaware of James's faults. Sometimes this is turned to the latter's advantage: 'while he lived we were all very proud, all very proud. If he was not all that he should have been in some ways, well, perhaps we loved him better' (17). He believes James to be dead at this point, however, and at other times, he is almost shocked at his own partiality and well aware that the Master's shortcomings are far from insignificant: '"I think you are a devil of a son to me," cried his father, "you that have always been the favourite, to my shame be it spoken. Never a good hour have I gotten of you, since you were born, no, never one good hour," and repeated it again the third time.' (5) The outburst is interesting in that it shows Lord Durrisdeer fully acknowledging paternity, and accepting that what he has created and loved is deeply flawed as a human being. For his father to call James a 'devil' – however innocently – is grist to Mackellar's mill.

Durrisdeer surrenders much of his moral authority, however, in his stubborn partiality for James and that authority is further eroded as the turmoil in the House of Durrisdeer increases following the return of the Master. When the evidence proving that the latter is a Government spy is about to be brought home to James, his father intervenes to extricate him. Mackellar's description is perceptive and (as usual) couched in the sort of language which is capable of exposing the 'moral occult':

> it was not so much love, which should be an active quality, as an apathy and torpor of his other powers; and forgiveness (so to misapply a noble word) flowed from him in sheer weakness, like the tears of senility (89).

It is, I think, clear from the foregoing discussion that Stevenson has placed at the core of this book a set of powerful – indeed seminal – contradictions. Leaving aside the elusive phantom created by its title which no one can call his own, this House of Durrisdeer proves to be a domain where *no-one's* writ really runs. Where one would expect the patriarch to be in charge, we find that this father is as absent as Sir Thomas Bertram in *Mansfield Park*. While he allows his younger son to act in his stead in running the estate he studiously avoids conferring on him that blessing which will invest him with full authority and, indeed, maturity. That favour he reserves for the Master, a proscribed rebel, who can never succeed his father or act in his name, or any other since he *has* no name now.

All of the authority-figures, actual and potential, are neutralised, cancelled out, by one means or another. The Jacob/Esau theme (which, like the parable of the prodigal son, has its moral hierarchies inverted) keeps before us questions of legitimacy and wrongful inheritance. 'I love order', says Henry almost parenthetically while preparing to meet the Master's ruinous demands (60). But he is building on sand: in reality, *dis*order has invaded the House of Durrisdeer which is doomed to extinction, as we know. And among the agents of destruction are Henry and the steward.

Mackellar, in fact, does attribute to Henry (as well as to James) some responsibility for the dissolution of authority and the decline of the House. Having earlier painted a vivid picture of the persecution suffered by Henry (which his father had compounded) and of Lord Durrisdeer's abdication of his responsibility in 'apathy and torpor', he now asserts roundly that 'To any considering mind, the two sons had between them slain their father', and he adds even more surprisingly, 'and he who took the sword might be even said to have slain him with his hand' (123–4). Despite the fact that Henry 'found a solid gratification in his accession to the title', his doing so has none of the saving merits of the Freudian displacement of the father, which clears the way for the assertion of a new authority. Denied his father's blessing, he certainly lacks Jacob's determination to secure it by fair means or foul, though it has to be conceded that Jacob's courage might also have failed him had it not been for the resourcefulness of the unscrupulous Rebecca. Perhaps Henry's problems have more to do with the absent mother than the absent father. Far from gaining in authority, he declines further and when his son is born he neglects everything but the boy: 'He lost himself in that continual thought: business, friends and wife being all alike forgotten, or only remembered with a painful effort' (127). What troubles Mackellar is that, in his 'slavery to the child' he will end up repeating his father's mistake and his son will 'prove a second Master'. The succession would seem to be moving through one abdication to another and since we are told at the beginning that neither Alexander nor Katherine marries, the decline is to end in the family's 'deletion'.

While all the family members contend (and fail) to secure authority and legitimacy, the vacuum is filled by the hired steward, the 'stranger' who *also* shows himself to be far from a whole man in that his moral being is predicated on division. His vehement claim that he 'belongs' to Durrisdeer is the expression of a deep desire which translates into a determination to get all of the reins of government into his own hand. In a way, it is *he* who plays Jacob to the Master's Esau. That his success in doing so allows him eventually to supplant the legitimate members of the family is strikingly illustrated in the scene already mentioned when he 'takes it on himself' to supply the Master with an allowance and the latter thanks him, with heavy irony, in the name of his ancestors (153). The Master, however, accepts his authority (or appears to) and together they enjoy the father-and-son parody. When the Master needed money, Mackellar tells us, 'He would approach me then after the manner of a schoolboy and I would carry it on by way of being his father: on both sides with an infinity of mirth' (155).[13]

Mackellar plays the role of host and head of the family not just with obvious relish, but, on his own account, with the distinction and address such a position entailed: 'meal-time at Durrisdeer must have been a delight to anyone by reason of the brilliancy of the discourse. He would often express wonder at his former indifference to my society.' Mackellar's true feelings about his own virtues come out even when he concedes that he was being flattered for a purpose: 'it is a most engaging form of flattery when (after many years) tardy justice is done to a man's character and parts' (156). It is a speech more appropriate to Henry, but it makes us realise how fundamental it is for Mackellar to play the role of 'patron' which alone would allow him access to the right sort of discourse to enable him to display the brilliancy of his 'character and parts' and control the creature which (it could be argued) that same imaginative discourse has sired. But if this Caliban is the product of the discourse he is also its most versatile exponent, which allows him to exceed Mackellar's reach and restore himself to the position of master which he had apparently surrendered.

Mackellar's pride in his gift of expression is obvious throughout: his choice of a word or phrase is often quite studied and his pleasure in the Master's company when they are left alone derives in large measure from the fact that they can converse together with comparable fluency and subtlety. I have suggested that this very dexterity with language, his ear for nuances and undertones, may have been the begetter of the Master (as he is represented to us); it is certainly the source of Mackellar's power and the instrument of his self-aggrandisement. So, too, with the Master who uses his verbal facility to undermine meaning conventionally assumed to be inherent in words: 'There are double words for everything', he tells Mackellar, adding 'you cannot fight me with a word' (175). By contrast, the steward's moral identity absolutely depends on particular words – like good and evil – meaning specific things and his conviction gives the advantage to the Master who would never be able to practise his deceit and dissimulation (or, simply, admit and enjoy his own multi-fariousness) if he were what he accuses Mackellar of priding himself on being – *un homme de parole*. One might indeed say that the Master represents the discrepancy between word and thing which the steward cannot admit, and it is from this that he derives the freedom to outplay Mackellar at virtually every turn. (At the same time the distinction illustrates, on the one hand, Mackellar's belief that evil is both clearly identifiable and excisable and, on the other, the Master's conviction that such notions are purely subjective.)

That discourse itself should become a significant part of the book's focus is one of the things which prompts us to align Stevenson with those late Victorians in whose work one can clearly see the early shoots of Modernism (and even, perhaps, the occasional hint of developments which would contribute to Postmodernism). That a concern with authority and authorship, paternity and inheritance is also prominent serves to confirm the trend.

The fragmentation of authorial responsibility at the very start of the book is of crucial significance: a character then takes over as writer of the book who turns out to be less the creator than the creature of a certain sort of discourse through whose forms alone can the realm of the moral occult be approached. As a result, a rogue, piratical discourse rules the House of Durrisdeer; the Master and a whole order of perception are created by it, the steward, who seeks hegemony through it, is manipulated by it. The rights of primogeniture both in parable and family are rendered meaningless, and hierarchy and legitimate inheritance discounted. And rich though this discourse is, one of its key-words is impotence. The propriety of this is obvious for not only are word and referent often blatantly at odds – Colonel Burke, for example, is forever invoking the name of God while going about his murderous piratical enterprise to his great pecuniary advantage, and Mackellar, though constantly denouncing the sinfulness of the Master, flagrantly breaches the Sixth Commandment in his attempt to kill the Master – but nothing is created, no new moral order is established despite all the lavish expenditure of words. 'Here is too much speech', cries Lord Durrisdeer at one point, and it is hard to disagree. Mackellar does *not* lead the Durrisdeer family into the sunny uplands, its fortunes restored and the succession secured. To the contrary, we have known from the beginning (and so have come stored with scepticism) that for all Mackellar's eloquent moralising and inquisitorial reading-of-the-signs, the family will be ruined, the line extinguished and Mackellar himself divorced from it. The world has *not* been purged of evil as happens in the standard melodrama; instead by the end we are less able to define that word than we were at the beginning or to identify it in practice. There is a fine irony in Secundra Dass coming near to having the final passionate word (until then he has said nothing in English) and that that word should be (pointing to Henry and Mackellar) 'all gallows-murderers' (231). Out of the moral opacity that has been created (not lightened) comes, however briefly, Sir William Johnson 'reason's only speaking trumpet'. To him Secundra Dass appeals: 'You no murderer? You true man? You see me safe?' and on his assurance he singles him out in sharp contrast to Henry, Mackellar and Mountain, 'You good man' (230, 231).

With well-chosen irony, words chiselled in the rock end the story, in the process deconstructing the discourse on which Mackellar's perception of truth depends, smashing the prism through which the sombre colours of the moral occult revealed themselves to Mackellar. Replete with contradictions, the memorial-carving for James ends with the words 'lies here forgotten'; and Henry's tablet is followed by a coda which shows Mackellar still constructing the 'truth': 'The piety of his wife and one old servant raised this stone to both.'

If James is forgotten, whose story have we been following with such a sense of intimacy for the past several hours? And is that story itself now to be forgotten, never read? What is certain is that '[t]he full truth of this matter' which, we are told in the first sentence of

Chapter 1, is what the world 'has long been looking for', has not been told, and the cumulative effect of Stevenson's method of writing is to show that it never can be, and that any attempt to convince oneself otherwise is but a snare and a delusion – of the sort that modern writers do not fall into.

It should now be clearer what was intended by my remark that *The Master of Ballantrae*, while on the surface adopting the mode of melodrama (and doing so with great flair), significantly transcends it, though 'subverts' might be a better word. When the moral axis turns out to be so unstable, when authority and authorship are both dealt with so deprecatingly, when an insistent textual reflexivity exposes nothing but the text's impotence, so that even when it is inscribed on rock its erasure is part of its message, thus infusing unreliability retrospectively into everything we have read – what we are left with is a *palimpsestus* waiting for the next melodrama to be superimposed, which will be no more enduring, no more capable of establishing the truth the world has long been looking for, than its predecessor.

While one would not want to go as far here as Barthes did when he said of Balzac's *Sarrasine* that it 'represents the problem ... of representation' nor to claim that that 'representation is replaced by reflexivity',[14] it would not be improper to claim that this is the direction in which Stevenson can be seen to be moving in *The Master of Ballantrae*. A later writer like Ford Madox Ford, who might be thought to be doing in *The Good Soldier* what Barthes perceives in Balzac, has been to some extent anticipated by Stevenson, even to the expression of doubts about the manageability of the task which the narrator has set himself:

> My pen is clear enough to tell a plain tale; but to render the effect
> of an infinity of small things, not one great enough in itself to be
> narrated; and to translate the tale of looks and the message of
> voices when they are saying no great matter; and to put in half a
> page the essence of near eighteen months – this is what I despair
> to accomplish (21).

This passage could be paralleled many times in *The Good Soldier* (ironically, since Ford refers very slightingly to Stevenson); and Stevenson even gilds the comparativist lily by having Mackellar immediately make one of his most obviously contentious – if not downright outrageous – judgements: 'The fault, to be blunt, lay all in Mrs Henry.'

Whether writing of this kind encourages us to see Stevenson as one of the harbingers of Modernism (and capable of peering beyond even that horizon), the extent and importance of reflexive activity in his work demand acknowledgment. The *mise-en-abyme* effect of reflexive texts embedded in the full text of *The Master of Ballantrae* offers riches beyond the imaginings of the Quaker Oats advertising agency. And within *these* texts the process is continued so that what we seem to be getting is a Barthesian 'perspective of quotations'[15] running well-nigh to infinity. Multiplying texts multiplies voices – orphaned voices with (for Barthes) no other origins but language itself, language 'which ceaselessly calls into question all origins'.[16] This last might seem to be not very like Stevenson, yet we should remember that virtually all of his major works (including this one) have somewhere near the centre a son bewailing a father's absence, real or figurative, and struggling to come to terms with his orphaning. And it *is* orphaning, for in only two of these texts is a mother mentioned, one of whom (Mrs Weir) dies early in the piece and the other (Jim Hawkins' mother) disappears before the adventure truly begins and, surprisingly in such a story, is never heard of again.

The *mise-en-abyme* texts of *The Master of Ballantrae* suffer remarkable vicissitudes and are themselves remarkable for their diversity: some vanish, some never fully materialise, others are dismissed as inauthentic or 'false' in some way. The letter which the Master writes to Alison (who is by then Mrs Henry) is presented to her by Colonel Burke but is directed by her, unopened, to her husband. Unwillingly, he receives it, then passes it to her, unopened, so that she can read it by herself in her room. Next morning she passes it back, still unopened, to her husband. He declines to read it and the letter passes to Mackellar who burns it – unopened and so unread.

The letter, thus circulated, acquires a meaning distinct from its inscribed text. Though never being read, it nevertheless communicates much, albeit nothing which can be verified. Alison is still in love with the Master and *does* want to read it but she knows it will be compromising to do so now that she is Mrs Henry Durie. In assigning it to her husband, however, she also runs the risk of making it look as though she, guiltily, believes him to doubt her commitment to him which, following her reaction to the news that the Master has survived, he can't help doing. Her situation is very similar to that of the Queen in Poe's story 'The Purloined Letter', particularly as Lacan represented it in his now well-known essay: 'the letter is the symbol of a pact and ... even should the recipient [the Queen] not assume the pact, the existence of the letter situates her in a symbolic chain foreign to the one which constitutes her faith [that is, her fealty to the King her husband]'.[17] On his part Henry's refusal to open the letter is a bitter recognition that some sort of bond does still exist between the two that excludes him – or at any rate that James still has a place in her heart. The two lines of dialogue which conclude the scene so loaded with subliminal meaning are, though short, remarkably condensed in meaning. The pride and bitterness on each side are extremely well-expressed:

'Oh, read it and be done!' he had cried.
'Spare me that,' said she. (27)

Another letter which never fully materialises is the one Henry receives from his acquaintance in Government to the effect that the Master is no longer at risk if arrested. Henry reads part of it aloud but the crucial point of the date – about which the letter is silent – he gives the impression of withholding in order to trap the Master. We are left to conclude that the ruse would have been successful had Lord Durrisdeer not intervened 'to save his favourite from exposure'.

The letters which vanish are, of course, those which document the Master's activities as a long-term spy for the Government and as such responsible for the deaths of many. Mackellar sees them as the means of securing complete ascendancy over the Master and shows them to Alison – who burns them. Mackellar's almost diabolic glee on discovering them is now turned to ashes. She burns them, however, because to her, as a member of the Durie family, they have no potency for they cannot be used without permanently damaging the honour of the house. Mackellar – *not* a member of the family – in his single-minded desire to gain the upper hand has overlooked this point or is disqualified from seeing it.

The document – it is a pamphlet not a letter – which is of the greatest importance, however, in that it precipitates the death of both brothers, is brushed aside by Mackellar as palpably false. He stresses the irony that, '[a]fter all the desperate episodes of this contention, the insults, the opposing interests, the fraternal duel', it was a literary act which finally brought doom to Henry and James Durie:

it was reserved for some poor devil in Grub Street, scribbling for his dinner, and not caring what he scribbled, to cast a spell over four thousand miles of the salt sea, and send forth both these brothers into savage and wintery deserts, there to die (190).

Mackellar is curiously insistent that the composition was the 'idle, lying words of a Whig pamphleteer' showing himself, once again, to be credally incapable of accepting the arbitrariness of the word.

The cumulative effect of all this reflexive activity is to suggest that any attempt at a literary representation of moral reality is going to be writ in water; that whatever reality exists is going to be found only in the play of signifiers. But Stevenson is not writing in the age of Roland Barthes. He is a transitional writer and what he gives us is a multi-level, multi-voice text where different narrative forms coexist and where the apparently dominant voice of moral realism is never disowned – even though that other, deconstructive voice, whose locutions tell us that meaning and truth are endlessly deferred, essentially unrealisable, is incompatible with it.

Does this mean then (as my earlier remarks might be taken to imply), that Stevenson, adventuring among a variety of different forms, is equably practising a kind of negative capability? I doubt it. He may not be writing in the age of Barthes but he does show very clearly in, for example, *New Arabian Nights, The Dynamiter*, the ending of *Prince Otto* and *Jekyll and Hyde*, that he deliberately engages in subverting his text's most visible (and, to his contemporary readers, most familiar) narrative mode, its – so to speak – most publicly-registered authority.

So if what we get in *The Master of Ballantrae* appears to be at first reading an elegant and subtle exploration of the 'moral occult' where the story is so 'inward', so focused on the drama of moral consciousness, that George Moore saw no story at all, it is gradually borne in on us that Stevenson, not out of negative capability but with malice aforethought, has planted within his text the seeds of this mode's *bouleversement*. And such a procedure, I would argue, is no aberration. Throughout his entire *oeuvre* Stevenson shows great ambivalence towards fiction's aspirations to trade with confidence in moral realities (an ambivalence which is, among other things, the source of that inconclusiveness in some of his tales which annoyed contemporary reviewers). His evasiveness or lack of commitment on this issue allows for a cancelling-out of (almost) everything, even the durable reality of the text itself. 'The Moving Finger writes; and having writ/Moves on ...'; but there the congruency with Fitzgerald's sentiment has to stop since the text left behind is anything but indelible: no sooner has the moving finger writ than its writing fades. Erasure and deletion seem to be not just the common fate but a mark of the futility of human effort. Like a 'child that breathed on a window', says Dr Gotthold in *Prince Otto*, parading his rather shallow scepticism, 'men write and obliterate, write and obliterate idle words' (44); and this is just what seems to be happening in that text where not only does Prince Otto himself end up writing supremely ephemeral verse (like Somerset at the end of *The Dynamiter*), but the narrator suddenly goes feral and, in the 'Bibliographical Postscript', savages all that has gone before. *Weir of Hermiston* starts with a defaced tombstone; and the epitaph chiselled in the memorial stone at the end of *The Master of Ballantrae* contradicts its function and shares in its subject's oblivion. So in a sense not intended by him, Moore is right. If we listen to the subversive voice in the text, there *is* no story, taking that to mean (in Barthes' words) 'a line of words releasing a "theological" meaning (the "message" of the Author-God)'[18] for the text constantly disavows its own authority, and its discourse is as much a moral freebooter as the amoral smugglers who act as vehicles for shipping the amoral Master in and out of Scotland.

If not a story there *is*, however we read the text, a performance, and every now and then the text is frank about this – sometimes explicitly so as when Mackellar, watching the Master's strategy for tormenting his brother unfold, describes it in a way that links it to the idea of a play-performance: 'and the more the Master enjoyed his spiteful entertainment, the more engagingly, the more smilingly, he went! So that the plot, by its own scope and progress, further confirmed itself' (78). At other times it is the casual analogue which links text to performance as when, towards the end, they come to the Master's last camp on a plateau which is referred to as a stage, and Mackellar is made to remark in the next sentence that it is 'always moving to come upon the theatre of tragic accident' (229); and we think back to the duel, that other theatrical scene on another carefully prepared stage.

Songs and ballads play a significant part in nearly all of Stevenson's books, and while they fit well with the melodrama mode, they also, more importantly, contribute to the reflexive movement of the text, reflexive in that the only reality we are left with is found not in the relation of the word to thing but of word to word or text to text. To Barthes, writing is 'a multi-dimensional space in which a variety of writings, none of them original, blend and clash'.[19] This is well-illustrated in the Stevenson 'story'. The text seems to be ceaselessly engaged in a multi-dimensional, self-referencing activity where its concern with itself as an expressive form reveals it as suspended from, and dependent for its animation on, other such forms, almost (but not quite) exclusively textual.

Thus the Master – who 'took from his father the love of serious reading' (2) – in his first appearance lightly dismisses Alison's protests by quoting (or rather singing) some lines from Herrick, angering his father in the process. His credentials as a serious reader are established later when among 'the beautiful lace and linen' in his portmanteau, Mackellar finds 'Caesar's *Commentaries*, a volume of Mr Hobbes, the *Henriade* of M. de Voltaire, a book upon the Indies, one on the mathematics ... ' (110). Later he discloses his admiration for *Clarissa*, provocatively defending his choice by applying the criteria he derives from it to the Bible.

It is clear, then, that the text talks about itself a great deal of the time, constantly raising questions about its status. So while on one level apparently maintaining the illusions of the romance, it refers to James Durie as 'the discredited hero of romance' (89) which would seem to place this text outside the romance, but exactly where is far from clear. In fact, the text acquires its own character frequently by talking about other texts: thus young Alexander plays Dido to the Master's 'diabolical' Aeneas and a page later is Eve to his Satan. References to *Paradise Lost* are widespread, and the *Aeneid* also plays a role here as it does in other books by Stevenson. Much later the Master compares himself to Aeneas when he escapes from India 'with Secundra Dass upon my back', which casts the Indian as Anchises, Aeneas's father. (This doesn't stop him later claiming that Secundra Dass is like a son to him.)

There are occasions, as I have indicated, when the text-to-text relationship is enhanced by music, and intertextual referencing comes to be seen as embracing complementary forms (or 'texts'). It is of some importance to recall Mackellar's remark that there are times when 'the voice grows to be more important than the words' (89) and though he frames it pejoratively ('It is one of the worst things of sentiment'), given his contempt for the finer feelings, it is inevitable that he should do so. The main point is not weakened: that there is a wordless language in music which will extend the affective powers of the text (as there is in silence and in mute gesture both of which are made much use of in the book). And in this dimension Mackellar concedes that James Durie is indeed a master, calling him just that – 'a master-singer' (159–60) – when he sings 'Wandering Willie' on their departure. There is a further 'play' in the fact that the lines which Mackellar is so moved by are, in fact, from a poem by Stevenson.

At times this musical cross-referencing can go quite a long way to undermining the authority of the text. Thus Mackellar takes Burke's preposterous tale of the Master's piratical doings *au grand serieux* even to the point of adding his own lugubrious footnotes. And this despite Burke's patent unreliability as a narrator, demonstrated not just in getting Alan Breck's name wrong but in liberally sprinkling his tale with literary references and getting some of these wrong too. Stevenson is certainly appealing to the reader over Mackellar's head for he must be well aware that this comic pastiche of piratical life on the high seas brings with it a very audible musical accompaniment. In 1888, when he had just completed The Master of Ballantrae, Stevenson is recorded as having told a journalist that the last time he had been in a theatre was 1880 when he was present at a performance of The Pirates of Penzance. At a time when everyone appeared to know the operetta, Stevenson's interpolation of this lengthy tale into his story could scarcely have had as its function anything other than the subversion of the authority of the text, to repeat Barthes' words, seen as 'a line of words releasing a single "theological" meaning'. This tale-within-a-tale is parodistic in character, and in its reflexive allusions to other literary texts – including Stevenson's own Kidnapped – both comic and merciless in its textual iconoclasm.

Roland Barthes holds that a piece of writing cannot be deciphered, only disentangled. While his interpretative voice should not be specially privileged here, it is worth noting that this article in his creed derives from a central tenet which sheds considerable light on the textual processes of The Master of Ballantrae where Mackellar's moralising insistence that the text must embody 'the truth' and disclose an ultimate meaning is challenged by the subversive energies of the text itself. Barthes, defining how literature 'works', writes:

> literature (it would be better to say writing) by refusing to assign a 'secret', an ultimate meaning to the text (and to the world as text) liberates what may be called an anti-theological activity, an activity that is truly revolutionary since to refuse to fix meaning is, in the end, to refuse God and his hypostases – reason, science, law.[20]

On this reading, poor Mackellar was right to feel impotent: he – along with his Presbyterian creed – was 'deleted' before he had even begun!

## Notes

1. Ihab Hassan, The Dismemberment of Orpheus: Towards a Postmodern Literature (New York, 1978), p. 9.
2. Peter Brooks, The Melodramatic Imagination (New York, 1985), p. 12.
3. Ibid., pp. 12–13.

4. Ibid., p. 14

5. Ibid., p. 15.

6. Peter Brooks, op. cit., p. 6.

7. Peter Blos in *Son and Father* stresses the importance of the 'blessing' conferred on the son by the father: 'At the termination of adolescence a new stage in the life of the growing son appears, when the father's affirmation of the manhood attained by his son, conveyed in what we might call the father's blessings of the youth's impatient appropriation of adult prerogatives and entitlements, reaches a critical urgency.' Blos quotes Stephen Dedalus's invocation at the end of *A Portrait of the Artist as a Young Man* – 'Old Father, old artificer, stand me now and forever in good stead' – as a classic pronouncement of 'this fateful condition'. He also brings in Jacob's cheating Esau of his blessing, an act of dishonesty which haunts Jacob until he secures another blessing from the 'angel' with whom he wrestles, and with it a new identity. (See pp. 11–12.)

8. Luke, 15:20, 15:13, 15:29.

9. ' ... the heir was marked out for a social and religious position as head of the family. The bestowal of a blessing by the father, and the possession of the household goods, probably symbolized this ... Isaac's blessing was irrevocable, as the text emphasizes'. (*The New Bible Dictionary*, ed. J. D. Douglas *et al.*, p. 594.)

10. Genesis, 27:36. Esau is playing on the similarity in Hebrew between *ya'qob* and *ya'gebeni* meaning 'deceived', making 'Jacob', by extension, 'deceiver'. The Jacob–Esau story is very much about the legitimacy of title. Having 'stolen' Esau's legitimising blessing, Jacob shows himself almost obsessive in his desire to be blessed even after his struggle with the Angel which has resulted in the bestowal of the accolade of a new name of his own far removed from 'Jacob' with its association with fraud: 'Thy name shall be called no more Jacob, but Israel' (Genesis 32:28). See J. P. Fokkelman, 'Genesis', in *The Literary Guide to the Bible*, ed. Robert Alter and Frank Kermode (Cambridge, Mass., 1987), pp. 46ff.

11. Genesis, 25: 34.

12. Ibid., 25:27.

13. The Master talks of 'wringing shillings from my daddy' (157).

14. See Ann Jefferson, 'Structuralism and Post Structuralism' in *Modern Literary Theory*, ed. Jefferson and Robey (1983), p. 103.

15. Ann Jefferson, ibid., p. 102.

16. Roland Barthes, 'The Death of the Author' in *Modern Criticism and Theory*, ed. David Lodge (1988), p. 170. I am not, of course, suggesting that Stevenson's work exemplifies this essay's basic thesis, nor trying to identify Stevenson with it. Nonetheless, there is a strain in his own theorising which seems to me to be evolving in this direction.

17. Jacques Lacan, 'Seminar on "The Purloined Letter"' in *Yale French Studies*, 48, (1972), p. 58.

18. Op. cit., p. 170.

19. Op. cit., p. 170.

20. Op. cit., p. 171.

# 8

# *The Ebb-Tide*: A Modernist in the South Seas

Full fathom five thy father lies;
Of his bones are coral made;
Those are pearls that were his eyes: ...

*The Tempest*

The text is a tissue of quotations drawn from the innumerable centres
of culture ... the writer can only imitate a gesture that is always
anterior, never original. His only power is to mix writings, to counter
the ones with the others, in such a way as never to rest on any one
of them.

Roland Barthes

If one wanted to be provocative one might say that *The Ebb-Tide* is
Stevenson's only wholly serious book. One would then pay the price
for being provocative.

To put it more decorously, then, there is an *order* of seriousness
here which is quite different from all the other serious books he
wrote, a good deal of whose seriousness is the seriousness of play.
It is also his most complicated book and it suffers because he is complicating things in a new way. What he also lacks, perhaps, is a Marlow
since *The Ebb-Tide* illustrates well what *Lord Jim* and *Heart of Darkness*
gain by having their action sifted though the consciousness of such
a discriminating narrator. Their ambivalence can then become the
ambivalence of novels whose subject is perception but which can be
found catalogued along with novels about moral consciousness. *The
Ebb-Tide is* a novel about moral consciousness but should be catalogued along with novels about fictional representation. This is not
such a Dewey-eyed view of the fiction of these two writers as it
might seem; not least because one could argue that these classifica-
tions can be seen to converge in Conrad's celebrated statement of his
aim: 'by the power of the written word, to make you hear, to make

317

you feel ... before all to make you *see*:[1] a statement which, in its tene-
briousness, is the *Fiat Lux (sed noli modo)* of Modernist writing. The
fact remains, however, that Conrad, strenuously determined to
make us see, is ultimately and surprisingly more confident than
Stevenson that the resources of fictional representation are equal to
the task.

To quote Bradbury once more:

> The search for a style and a typology becomes a self-conscious
> element in the Modernist's literary production; he is perpetually
> engaged in a profound and ceaseless journey through the means
> and integrity of art. In this sense Modernism is less a style than a
> search for a style in a highly individualistic sense; and indeed the
> style of one work is no guarantee for the next.[2]

Stevenson spent the first half of 1893 working on yet another,
quite different kind of novel. By any standard, *The Ebb-Tide* is a distinctive and innovative work, so clear a precursor of Conrad's fiction
that it is impossible to believe that he did not, in fact, make considerable use of it. Because of the general acceptance of Conrad as a
'modern of moderns', in what follows some use will again be made
of him as a prism through which to refract the Stevensonian ray.

The tale is of three morally bankrupt men stranded 'on the beach'
in Papeete. In Part One (called 'Trio') the men get an unexpected
chance to leave when one of their number, a disgraced sea-captain,
is offered temporary command of a schooner whose white officers
have just died of smallpox. They take it but with the intention of
stealing the ship and selling its cargo of champagne. Shortly after
they set sail they make the ironic discovery that their predecessors
were no less reprobate, being participants in an insurance swindle:
the champagne cargo is mostly water.

In Part Two (called 'Quartette') they chance upon an island the
physical existence of which is disputed in 'Findlay's' authoritative
charts and find it occupied by an European called Attwater who is
engaged in pearl-fishing. He is also a monomaniac evangelist. The
three beach-combers decide to steal his pearls and if necessary murder
him, thus setting in motion a perilous cat-and-mouse game between
themselves and the clever and unsentimental evangelist. The outcome
is that Captain Davis is saved at the point of a gun; Huish 'the clerk'
isn't, and Herrick is left where we found him, on a beach (albeit a
different one), staring out to sea waiting for a ship to carry him away

to an unknown destination. The ending is abrupt, almost perfunctory; and deliberately so.

Reviewers' verdicts were mixed but their remarks are of particular interest in the light of any claim for Stevenson to be regarded as a harbinger of Modernism. 'All through the narrative', says one, 'there is a recurrent suggestion of the undeveloped.... The incidents have not the air of inevitableness. They seem to have been designed independently of the end in view'; and his conclusion echoes, by implication, William Archer's earlier objections: 'the story is by no means a model of design or a good example of the art of cumulative construction'.[3] Richard le Gallienne's review also helps to define something of the nature of Stevenson's aesthetic when he criticises the lack of realism in the second part and the marked self-consciousness of the writing. His concluding sentences give some indication of what Stevenson was up against: 'Mr. Stevenson is a little too consciously the literary artist here and there in this new book. If the book were anything but a book of adventure one would not mind so much.'[4]

It is of course very far from being just this as the most perceptive reviewer, Israel Zangwill, recognised clearly. In 'this little masterpiece', as he called the book, he believes that Stevenson has 'struck the true method and achieved a true unity'. Zangwill is not in the least troubled by the imperceptive conclusions of others, for example that *The Ebb-Tide* is 'badly constructed, a mere random series of adventures, sliced out of a chain of heterogeneous episodes that might have gone on forever'. To the contrary, he sees it as a conception of genius to take what yet another reviewer contemptuously described as 'the fag-ends of certain useless and degraded lives' and expose the inter-relationship of these three characters during their joint criminal enterprise. Of the abrupt ending he says, again perceptively, 'when the adventure is over, when the mutual revelations of the quartette have been exhausted, when the interaction and revelation of character are complete, the book is finished and the author wisely lays aside his pen.' The result of Stevenson's 'new' method, he concludes, is 'not only an enthralling romance, but a subtle study of the psychology of blackguardism in diverse shades and degrees'.[5]

The three characters who so disgusted reviewers must take pride of place in any discussion of the book. What annoyed many of the literary critics of the day was the fact that Stevenson had broken with convention and – startlingly – dispensed with a hero altogether. In fact, these three men (four if Attwater is included) form a collective anti-hero. (There is some justification for regarding them as multiple facets of a single consciousness since two of the three originals have the disconcerting habit of sharing the same alias.) In creating four repellent anti-heroes and no hero, Stevenson has 'struck a blow for the literary artist's independence, for his freedom to choose his own subject irrespective of tradition and conventional expectations'. Zangwill saw this very clearly: critics disliked the book, he said, because it was not constructed on 'the parlour-game formula to which the stock British novel invariably reduces itself'.[6]

Add to this interest in a (mostly) subtle exploration of moral delinquency and self-betrayal, a preoccupation with the fictional nature of fiction (the element which suggested to some critics that Stevenson had lost interest in 'the art of cumulative construction', when in fact he'd never really had it), and the result describes a characteristically Modernist approach to the writing of fiction. In their essay 'The Name and Nature of Modernism', Malcolm Bradbury and James McFarlane have written that if anything distinguishes the intellectual and historical character of the last two decades of the nineteenth century, it is a fascination with evolving consciousness: 'consciousness aesthetic, psychological and historical'.[7] In an earlier essay on Virginia Woolf and Ford Madox Ford, which had enlarged on the consequences of such a preoccupation, he had drawn this conclusion:

> One of the consequences was a psychological realism, an intensified impressionism, a novel of Paterian 'quickened, multiplied consciousness'. Another was a heightened concern with authorial consciousness as such, both as a form of apprehension or an artistic awareness, and as a managing instrument, demanding enormous precision of presentation and point of view, increased formalism. These two kinds of novel – the psychological, and the experimental or fictive – both desubstantiated material reality, and they often tended to merge.[8]

This sums up extremely well – particularly in its last sentence – what Stevenson is about in *The Ebb-Tide*.

The story opens in darkness – a darkness characteristic of Modernist writing which 'begins positively to adopt darkness as a primary organising metaphor, an 'écriture d'ombres'.[9] A ship has brought 'flu to the island and the 'dismal sound of men coughing, and strangling as they coughed' (6) painfully lengthens the night. Alastair Fowler in a perceptive and regrettably short essay ('Parables of Adventure: The Debatable Novels of Robert Louis Stevenson') sees this visitation as having something of the same significance as Camus' *peste*, but a nearer alternative suggests itself in the virus found on Conrad's *Narcissus*, organic to the body of James Wait but potentially endemic in the whole crew. A still better comparison might be with *The Shadow Line* where darkness and disease go together and where the young captain is convinced that 'There is something going on in the sky like a decomposition, like a corruption in the air', making him feel 'as if all [his] sins had found [him] out'. Like Lord Jim and Herrick, he is a young man being tested, and at this low point concludes that his worst fears are going to be confirmed: 'I always suspected that I might be no good. And here is proof positive, I am shirking it, I am no good.'[10] In *The Shadow Line* all is ultimately well: the wind returns, the fever and the darkness abate, the ship makes port and the captain completes his *rite de passage*. With the three adventurers (in Conrad's sense of the term) in Papeete, the case will be very different.

One of Conrad's early reviewers described him as an 'impressionistic realist'[11] and the opening scene of *The Ebb-Tide* might suggest that Stevenson could be similarly classified. (Archer did, in fact, do so.) Yet in this first chapter of the book, Stevenson also shows quite clearly how he differs from Conrad, and he does it by his utilisation of a device which he returns to again and again after first having exploited it in *New Arabian Nights*: that is, the tale-within-a-tale.

Characters in stories who proceed to tell stories disconcert us for a number of reasons. For one thing, from the moment they start, they create a *mise-en-abyme* effect which puts a stop to the notion of an end, a definitive end, that is, which will help us to understand (our experience, ourselves). That's bad enough but it also raises the question: where does *fiction* end? The short answer, of course, is that it doesn't; in the end we are a tale that is told, and, as we know from Scheherazade, a tale is *never* definitively told. Which leaves us feeling rather like Esther Summerson in *Bleak House* who, in her fever, thought of herself as a bead on a flaming necklace from which she could not detach herself. Jorge Luis Borges offers another example of such endless torture from the *Arabian Nights*:

The necessity of completing a thousand and one sections obliged the copyists of the work to make all manner of interpolations. None is more perturbing than that of the six hundred and second night, magical among all the nights. On that night, the king hears from the queen his own story. He hears the beginning of the story, which comprises all the others and also – monstrously – itself. Does the reader clearly grasp the vast possibility of this interpolation, the curious danger? That the queen may persist and the motionless king hear forever the truncated story of the *Thousand and One Nights*, now infinite and circular.... [12]

Like chain-smoking, one tale ignites another and even if one set of lungs gives out there is always another pair of bellows somewhere to blow the embers into life. One thinks of Dunyazade the prompter, Scheherazade's sister, crouching at the end of the bed, hearing and seeing everything. John Barth's Genie in *Chimera* sums up her opportunity – and her and the writer's predicament – eloquently:

All those nights at the foot of the bed, Dunyazade! ... You've had the whole literary tradition transmitted to you – and the whole erotic tradition, too! There's no story you haven't heard; there's no way of making love you haven't seen again and again. I think of you, little sister, a virgin in both respects: All that innocence! All that sophistication! And now it's your turn.... [13]

Talking of Tzvetan Todorov's notion of 'embedded stories', Barth interprets his view of narrative to mean that whatever else it is about, 'it is also always about language, and about telling; about itself': to Todorov, 'narrating almost literally equals living'. Barth continues:

Here he joins Borges but on linguistic rather than metaphysical grounds: we tell stories and listen to them because we live stories and live in them. Narrative equals language equals life: to cease to narrate, as the capital example of Scheherazade reminds us, is to die – literally for her, figuratively for the rest of us. One might add that if this is true, then not only is all fiction fiction about fiction, but all fiction about fiction is in fact fiction about life. [14]

Returning to the three adventurers in their misery on Papeete's beach, we note that Huish (who has caught the virus which rages in the native population and is seriously ill) asks the others for a story: 'I think one of you other parties might wake up. Tell a fellow something.' The captain protests that he has nothing to tell, but Herrick offers to tell them what he has been thinking. '"Tell us anything," said the clerk, "I only want to be reminded that I ain't dead."' (7) His and the narrator's interest would seem to coincide; indeed, he joins in the narration, intervening several times to make his contribution once Herrick begins.

Not only does Herrick's tale-within-a-tale turn out to be a narrator's blueprint of how *not* to tell a tale – there is even a second tale planted *en abyme* inside the first one; this is the plot of *Der Freischütz* which is given in marked detail. Herrick tells his companions that he had been fantasising about how he might liberate himself from his sorry predicament, a state so dire, it would appear, that the help of a supernatural agency will be required: 'I wished I had a ring, or had a fairy godmother, or could raise Beelzebub.' That he decides on Beelzebub is, perhaps, initially surprising but with his well-developed sense of worthlessness, he regards himself as already far gone down the road to damnation. So he gives his attention to the fanciful task of raising the Devil and ponders, a little uncertainly, on the *modus operandi* he is to follow.

The conventional first step, he remembers, is to recite the Lord's Prayer backwards – and to make a ring of skulls. But Herrick doesn't arrive at this conclusion directly: he does so via a recollection of Weber's opera *Der Freischütz*; and not only that but with the additional (and obscure) narrative detail that he will do it just as Formes did it. Now Karl Johan Formes was the German baritone who sang the part of the wicked Kaspar in various London productions of *Der Freischütz* between 1850 and 1868 (though, having married an American, he later established a music school in San Francisco where he died in 1889, the year after Stevenson left that city for the South Pacific).

At this point, quite capriciously, Formes, Kaspar and Beelzebub are all dropped and the figure whom Herrick succeeds in summoning is someone else altogether: a Genie who boldly announces that his provenance is the *Arabian Nights*. So what has started as explicitly a parable (which Herrick expounds 'not like a man who has anything to say, but like one talking against time' (7)) and is sardonically likened by Huish to Robert Meek's uplifting treatise, *Ministering Angels*, proceeds via a fairly recondite reference to a highly innovative romantic opera to an *Arabian Nights* conclusion. Except that it doesn't have one, being, to an even greater extent than its original, *end-less*. Herrick's tale, or parable, simply breaks off and Huish who had asked for a tale to remind him that he was still alive is deeply indignant at, so to speak, this betrayal of the art of Scheherazade: '"Well, I think you are about the poorest 'and at a yarn!" cried the clerk'.

Herrick's breaking-off is not, however, another capricious act. His tale has him deposited before a door – his parents' door – which is where it halts; and the significance of that truncation is that it avoids the meeting between son and father, for the 'frame-tale' here *is* a parable, one which haunts Stevenson's fiction: the parable of the prodigal son. Herrick, so 'conscious of talents and acquirements', cannot bring himself to confess his failure to his father and seek his blessing. So his tale stops *outside* the paternal door and one of his listeners has to prompt him, 'and what did you do next?' His reply could not be more lame: 'Oh, I went in.' The captain persists: '"The old folks?" ... "That's about it," said the other, chewing a grass' (10).

Grounded as it is in parable, Herrick's tale departs from the *Arabian Nights* which gave it its form, and the unprincipled Huish resents it for this reason as well as for its inconclusiveness: 'What is this bloomin' drivel?... It's like the rot there is in tracts.' But Herrick's tale is not as digressive as it seems, for as well as being a (moralising) 'yarn' about their plight, it is also a yarn about yarning, about narrative and representational methods in which various genres are tried and quoted: parable, biblical tract, oriental fantasy, romantic opera and all are found to be partial or wanting in some respect.

The new-found textual self-consciousness which this ranging through the genres liberates cannot but undermine the apparently firm moral realism which the opening paragraphs seemed to be laying down as the dominant representational mode, for it is effectively an assault upon the capacity of any single genre or mode to represent or convey moral truth. In turn, this fracturing or fragmentation will imply fundamental doubts about there being any such truth to be conveyed. Robert Herrick himself seems both a *bricoleur* parading his acceptance of fragmentedness almost in the Postmodernist manner *and* a figure like the speaker in *The Waste Land* shoring fragments against his ruin.

Stevenson reveals his sympathies with Modernist (and even Postmodernist) sentiment by clearly questioning whether there is any such thing as a 'single' (in the sense of a 'pure') genre. But this sympathy has plenty of precedents as we see if we glance at Hawthorne's sub-titles, for example, or read Meredith's *The Amazing Marriage*. Thus when Derrida in his 'The Law of Genre' declares 'what I shall call the law of the law of genre ... is precisely a principle of contamination, a law of impurity, a parasitical economy',[15] he is finding a rather sententious way of formulating a new law for what had, in fact, been an old practice. Stevenson's tongue is clearly in his cheek when he calls *Prince Otto* a historical romance, and Andrew Lang recognised this when he, in turn, called it 'a philosophical-humouristical-psychological fantasy'. In fact, Stevenson constantly and gleefully demonstrates the indefensibility of petrifying generic categories, taking particular pleasure in pointing out their artificiality. Much of the interest and a good deal of the pleasure in reading, for example, *New Arabian Nights*, *The Dynamiter* and *Prince Otto* derive from just this source.[16]

## '... The Whither Whose Echo Is Whence'

Looking again, then, at the opening pages of *The Ebb-Tide*, it is clear that their moral realism, skilfully-enough drawn to bring Conrad to mind, is being challenged by the text's watchful self-consciousness; and we become aware that traditional avenues of fictional representation, together with some newer ones, have barricades across them, those barricades being other texts and other genres. Whatever else the tale is 'about', it is also about the art of fiction and the nature of narrative. The authentic realism of the degraded lives on the beach dissolves into a consideration of literary (and literature-related) forms as Herrick reflects on the best vehicle for his tale. That choice made (actually it is made for him by his charitable act), his tale's essentials would seem to be decided and he is swept to London on a magic carpet fully sponsored by the *Arabian Nights*. Perhaps the most arresting aspect of his chosen vehicle, however, is the fact that it contradicts his tale's moral significance and subverts the parable, for the *Arabian Nights* form is utterly amoral, its sole objective being its own perpetuation. Unable to complete his tale according to the dictates of either formula, Herrick graphically reveals himself to be in limbo.

What is happening in the first three chapters of the book is what Edgar Dryden describes as characteristic of the writings selected by him to illustrate his theories on the American romance. There form 'enters into [the] works as an essential theme';[17] and here in *The Ebb-Tide* it enters it tentatively, questioningly. This has crucially important results, for the text's preoccupation with, and uncertainty about, its own status, disturbs the focus on the moral predicament of the three characters. What this means, in effect, is that the moral realism of their representation is accompanied by a subversive provisionality, which has the beneficial consequence of preventing the moral realist perspective from arrogating to itself the exclusive rights to representation. It shows that, as Stevenson said elsewhere about realism in art, it is simply one among a number of possible methods of representation. By denying hegemony to the moral realist mode, it keeps other possibilities in play – including the radical one which questions whether the text can ever represent anything other than itself.

'Pattern and argument live in each other', Stevenson wrote in his essay 'On Some Technical Elements of Style in Literature'; so the idea of form entering into the work as an essential theme is in no way alien to him. In *The Ebb-Tide* he exploits it to pursue in his own way some of the same problems which Conrad approaches by focusing very sharply on a complex consciousness locked in battle with language in order to clarify its relations with the world. The sizeable difference between them remains the fact that Conrad's characters are still seemingly unable to accept that meaning and understanding, which so teasingly seem always to lie just beyond their reach, might not yet be touched – if only in the hem of their garments or, more tentatively still, in the penumbra which surrounds them. It might be said that while Stevenson addresses representational problems by encouraging the complex play of a plurality of fluid forms, Conrad does so by intricate (and almost infinite) refinements of language and discourse, in which the possibility of defeat is an integral part.

It is, arguably, the subversive provisionality just alluded to which partly accounts for the haunting quality in *The Ebb-Tide* where concrete definitions are so elusive. The tale has, in fact, something of that indeterminable character of Keats's 'Ode on a Grecian Urn' where there is a highly creative tension between the shape of the urn and the narrative content of its frieze, a tension which can be both eloquent and baffling: meaning doesn't inhere in one or other but 'haunts about' both. The urn, though it is a 'silent form' in itself, is still a 'silvan historian' which can 'express' a flowery tale.

When we look again at the trio 'on the beach' in the light of these ruminations, we can see that the moral instability in their characters combines with that sense of provisionality I have been discussing. All three have lost (that is, abandoned) their names. Davis has become Brown, Herrick Hay, while Huish, underlining their common false inheritance and his own particularly lawless nature, also chooses Hay but occasionally calls himself Tomkins – 'and laughed at the discrepancy'. He, by far the most reprobate of the three, revels in the freedom inherent in the moral dissolution signified by his loss of identity. (His is the dark reality that underlies the meretricious appeal of Long John Silver.)[18]

The most prominent of the group, Herrick, is the one who brings the two dimensions of the moral and aesthetic together in way that heightens the provisionality in each order for it is through his tale that the textual indeterminacy shows itself when he toys with various narrative modes and genres. But one might reasonably claim that this has begun the moment his name is inscribed in the text, for while Robert Herrick is a drifter on a beach in Tahiti, he is also the embodiment of lyric poetry (and, as such, a favourite of Stevenson's), which is the polar opposite of the moral realist mode initially embraced by what seems increasingly to be a Jekyll and Hyde text.

When an echo as powerful as this strikes our ears it is difficult to know whether the past or the present is the more significant, which is the 'real' voice and which are the reverberations, so that it becomes that much more difficult to see Robert Herrick, beachcomber, clearly. On the one hand he may be a wretch to be pitied, suffering an existential crisis; on the other, a Marabar Cave of literary echoes. Which is he, a moral consciousness looking for a literary form through which to represent itself – or a literary form looking to realise itself in a moral consciousness? The impossibility of answering the question will destabilise the realism of the tale throughout its length, and ensure that it will never establish a clear formal character. In the sustained play in the borderland of forms and genres the book's chameleon identity is situated; but it is a highly fluid one characterised by indeterminacy, incompleteness and fragmentation which will obviate any chance of our finding a map to guide us, complete with a cross in red ink and a legend in 'a small, neat hand' reading 'Bulk of treasure here'.

The echoes and 'quotations' liberated by the name Herrick and by his tale-within-the-tale continue in full cry in the first three chapters. The principal character's wealth of literary baggage is as remarkable as it is improbable. He is a lover of English, German and Latin literature and is in particular devoted to Virgil. Now, there is little that is unusual about a Victorian ne'er-do-well in the South Seas consoling himself with a tattered Virgil: indeed, a well-worn copy of the *Aeneid* is an essential *vade mecum* for the imperial waster.[19] But the frequency and particular occasion of reference is striking: the uncharted island they stumble on later in the book has its marginal physical reality further aestheticised when, improbably, its name turns out to be Zacynthos, one of the islands chanced upon by Aeneas and his companions; and all sorts of ironies consequently accrue round the 'officers' of the *Farallone* as their shaky moral identity dissolves in another generic form. And there is that other use Herrick puts his Virgil to, when, in his many idle moments, he practises *sortes virgilianae*. This, too, in a book where fate and chance play, in the Modernist manner, very important roles.

Pestilence has, it would appear, to compete with echoes for the air in Tahiti. At times the quotations come so thick and fast that they form a perfect maze of cultural cross-referencing. An episode is inserted when Captain Davis is discovered to have 'a fine sweet baritone' and, absurdly, both sings and dances for his supper, running through a considerable repertoire of popular ballads and folk songs, American and Scottish. Equally arbitrarily, the characters interrupt themselves to become writers. This is Davis's idea so that they can all write home, thus (for him and Herrick at least) keeping in touch with their own consciences. Of course what they are writing is fiction, as Davis frankly admits when he is confronted by Herrick's resistance: 'it may be hard to write, and to write lies at that; and God knows it is; but it's the square thing. It don't cost anything to say you're well and happy, and sorry you can't make a remittance this mail' (18). But *is* it the 'square thing to do'? He sounds more than a little like Marlow justifying his telling a lie to Kurtz's fiancée in *Heart of Darkness*. Huish, who has no conscience, gives his imagination full rein ('I've a good fist with a pen when I choose, and this is a prime lark'), writing to a girl he'd picked up in Northampton ('a spanking fine piece, no end of style'). He tells her how he had got rich, 'married a queen in the Hislands, and lived in a blooming palace'. Having just finished making themselves feel better by telling their own lies, the two moralists round indignantly on the romancer telling his more colourful fables utterly without benefit of conscience – because he doesn't pretend to have one. In the short, sharp tussle between genres, what might be called the moral realism of distressed (and paraded) consciences triumphs, and the romance is torn up by a quite understandably 'sullen' Huish.

In his burst of literary activity Herrick predictably gilds the reflexive lily by recalling in his letter a song – 'the masterpiece of love' – of which he gives us the first three words in German, 'Einst, O wunder!'. The words form the beginning of the fourth stanza of Friederich von Matthisohn's *Adelaide*, set to music by Beethoven. Letter-writing is followed quite literally, by the writing of artistic fragments on walls: to be exact, on the wall of the ruinous old *jail* which has served the men as a shelter. Herrick first of all writes the 'famous phrase' from Beethoven's Fifth Symphony. He cannot resist piling Pelion on Ossa (as he might well have said) by adding a line from the *Aeneid*, extolling the blessedness of dying before one's father's door which, from a failed prodigal son, is another act of self-deception.

All this synaesthetic activity (so characteristic of the Modernists, if not always executed upon jail walls) fails to bring consolation and he falls to musing again. Inevitably, another quotation springs to mind and he repeats to himself the whole poem, 'one of the most perfect of the most perfect poets'. He only gives us the fragments 'Ich trage unterträgliches' and 'Du, stolzes Herz, du hast es ja gewollt' but the poem is Heine's *Der Atlas*, though there is, perhaps surprisingly, no reference to Schubert's setting. At this point the reader has only reached page 23 of a 140-page volume.

By allowing these echoes into what is already highly-reflexive writing, Stevenson has created precisely what Roland Barthes has described as a *'scriptible'* or 'writerly' text where the closure of static forms is avoided and the active reader presented with 'a perspective (of fragments, of voices from other texts, other codes), whose vanishing point is nonetheless carelessly pushed back, mysteriously opened'.[20] Writing of the five major codes by which, according to Barthes, literature is constituted, Ann Jefferson concludes with a remark that is relevant here: 'Reality ... is not defined either concretely or semiotically. Instead reality becomes a kind of text itself, constituted by codes.' In this case then, to write about reality is not to relate word to thing, but text to text. A code is no more than a 'perspective of quotations' and 'its only logic that of the *already-done* or the *already-read*'.[21]

It is remarkable how well this describes so much that is central to the artistic process which forms the text of *The Ebb-Tide*. But though this may deny the text fuel from a 'truth' or moral idea gleaned from some hinterland beyond the text and to which the text can be reduced, it does not mean the comprehensive banishment of, for example, that moral realism which initially makes itself so strongly felt in the opening of *The Ebb-Tide*. It simply ensures that it will establish no hegemony over this text, that it will remain just one of the many fragments of alternative texts which litter the foreshore of Papeete beach.

All this feverish intertextual activity involves an excessive proliferation of echoes and it is worth dwelling for a moment on this aspect of the allusive process since there are times when echo *almost* seems to become the book's organising metaphor. Herrick's 'embedded' tale echoes the *Arabian Nights*, *Der Freischütz*, and the parable of the prodigal son. His letter-writing echoes with Heine, von Matthisohn, Beethoven; while the walls of the old calaboose are made to reverberate with the Fifth Symphony and to proclaim sententious extracts from the *Aeneid*.

Virgil is, in fact, such a persistent echo that he often seems about to become a major structural force in the narrative, not least when the disorientated principal character turns to *sortes virgilianae* for help. In the event, his voice remains one among many, even though it periodically reasserts itself strongly in, for example, the fact that the island is named Zacynthos or (to a lesser degree) in Herrick's preparation to leave the island and resume his search for another landfall.

The effect of all this apparently random echoing combines with the text's formal tentativeness to emphasise contingency and directionlessness. Both textual and personal identity are obfuscated by it for the point of origin is lost. Is Robert Herrick the son of a failed English businessman or is he the seventeenth-century lyric poet (also the son of a businessman, incidentally, who jumped to his death from a window of his home)? Identity can only be established with firm reference to a prior term, a *point de départ*. Herrick cannot know who he is, whether an originating voice or a receding echo. No more can the text. Everything seems to have happened before; nothing has a beginning, nothing an end. Character and text lack authority: they float, detached from a clear, originating source, caught up, instead, in an endless recession. Moreover the confusion over priority obscures the father–son relationship on which is based the familial analogy used to 'explain the genesis of story and to ground the authority of literary representation'.[22]

There is a central moment in Part II when the subject of echo figures explicitly in the drama being played out between Attwater and the three adventurers and in doing so it defines brilliantly the secret of Attwater's authority. When he asks his guests to listen while he strikes the bell and sends the echo soaring away into the night, his 'little experiment' serves him as a parable to represent his belief in the existence of God; for space to him is filled with God, and the echo – like all echoes, in his view – will end in the divine ear. There is, therefore, nothing confusing or contingent about this echo because for Attwater there is total belief in a specific origin and a specific end. In his essay 'Echo and Narcissism', Herbert Marks makes an interesting point which has a bearing on this. Having first alluded to the anxiety-attacks which Thomas Mann used sometimes to experience while walking on the beach when he would be overcome by the vastness and featurelessness of the sea and the dunes and be forced to flee to firmer ground and human company, Marks goes on:

> the unique virtue of the Bible and of the most powerful literature in the biblical tradition is to remain defiantly on the shore ... not blind to the fearsome prospect, but armed against it by some obsessive commitment to an arbitrary beginning, to a personal mark or idiosyncracy, whose intensity overcomes any abstract relativity of origins.[23]

Attwater's is just such 'an obsessive commitment to an arbitrary beginning' and from it he derives his immense authority and his unshakable conviction that truth inheres in the singleness of his vision. Unquestionably, he is, to continue Marks's analogy, firmly planted on the shore, which adds all the more point to our discovery that what we find set over against him is a text of almost oceanic fluidity, a plurality of infinitely resonating narrative forms – and the moral instability of three seafarers adrift among echoes, as uncertain of origins and ends as is the speaker in Meredith's poem ('A Faith on Trial') quoted in the sub-heading.

## To Sea without a Bowditch

Disease comes ominously to the 'rescue' of the three men on the beach. Smallpox has killed the officers of the trading-schooner *Farallone* and port officials offer the command to Captain Davis. Again there is the moral realist feint which invites comparison with Conrad. The ship is, however, a travesty of all that a ship normally symbolises in so much Victorian fiction and which Conrad more or less codifies. Far from representing discipline, duty and human solidarity in a common purpose, the *Farallone* is, as its name might imply (Stevenson insisted it should be pronounced 'Far-alone'), a renegade among ships and has come to stand for greed, selfishness, opportunism – and lost directions. This is not a *Nigger of the 'Narcissus'* case where the crew's solidarity (alias cosmic order) is put at risk by the emergence of weakness and unprincipled opportunism among two of their own number, but which is ultimately restored. The *Farallone* may, like the *Narcissus*, carry 'an anguished remnant of sinful humanity'[24] but that remnant constitutes the whole of its white crew (who are contrasted unflatteringly with the more principled Kanakas). This ship is synonymous with corruption and betrayal and general moral disorder, our attention being drawn to the true state of affairs by the yellow flag at the masthead signalling disease on board – and by another, even more recognisable Conradian symbol.

In the small boat taking Huish and him out to the *Farallone*, Herrick sits with the doctor in the stern 'nursing the while between his feet a chronometer, for which they had exchanged that of the *Farallone* long since run down and the rate lost' (31). On his lap, however, Herrick nurses something else: a pile of novels. The juxtaposition of the chronometer – an essential aid to navigation – with 'a pile of paper novels' indicts these adventurers as untrustworthy navigators – at the same time arraigning the notion of fiction as a midwife to moral responsibility. Reflexive allusions of this sort reassert the text's self-consciousness, raising again all those destabilising uncertainties about whether fiction can ever adequately represent human conduct and experience in such a way as to convey its complex reality (or the complexity of consciousness).

Once Davis boards his new command, he goes down to his stateroom (where his predecessor had died) and begins to 'adjust the chronometer in its place at the bed-head'. Some reference is made to the last words of the previous captain and mate and the exchange is concluded by Davis saying 'There; there's that chronometer fixed' (34). Early in the voyage, with Davis drunk, Herrick tries to persuade him to check their position by dead reckoning, adding 'you told me yourself you weren't sure of the chronometer', to which he gets the ominously careless reply: 'Oh, there ain't no flies in the chronometer' (46).

The density of reference is striking. Indeed, the subject is introduced into the dialogue rather laboriously and at some cost to narrative continuity: we have certainly not heard Davis complain about the instrument. Obviously Stevenson wants his readers to notice that the chronometer is there and that it has a symbolic function. The message is clear: these men have already lost their bearings and are morally adrift. In fact, for Davis, this has already been signalled in his having pointedly divorced himself from another navigational aid. When Huish remarks 'Everybody has a false nyme in the Pacific. Lay you five to three the captain 'as', Davis agrees: 'So I have too, ... and I've never told my own since the day I tore the title-page out of my Bowditch and flung the damned thing into the sea.' A 'Bowditch' was Nathaniel Bowditch's *The American Practical Navigator*, 'the American epitome of navigation', without which, apparently, no self-respecting officer of the American merchant marine would go to sea and which, of course, immediately reminds us of Towson's manual in *Heart of Darkness*. From the wording of the passage, it is not clear whether Davis is throwing away the book or only the title page. Not that it makes a great deal of difference since, either way, he is detaching himself from his Bowditch. (If we were not meant to see him as abandoning his navigator's manual why should this be the chosen title-page? No doubt he has a Bible which could have served a similar turn.)

Once they embark on their voyage the three men revert to their assumed names: Davis becomes Captain Brown and Herrick is once more Mr Hay. Even the ship itself, that emblem of moral integrity, loses its name – or what is worse, half-loses it. The episode provides another example of that casual arbitrariness which characterises the arhythmic movement of this narrative between moral realism and textual deliquescence:

> Once, in the forenoon, he had a bo'sun's chair rigged over the rail, stripped to his trousers, and went overboard with a pot of paint. 'I don't like the way this schooner's painted,' said he, 'and I taken a down upon her name.' But he tired of it in half an hour, and the schooner went on her way with an incongruous patch of colour on the stern, and the word *Farallone* part obliterated and part looking through.

Davis's conduct is, of course, also an indicator of how much has been abandoned when he so clearly neglects to fulfil his role as captain of the ship, preferring to drink – and to read novels: 'he laughed out an empty laugh, drained his glass, sprawled back among the lumber in the boat, and fetched out a crumpled novel' (53).[25] His inability to live up to his captain's role, along with the three's failure to sustain their original identity, interacts with that general sense of instability and indeterminacy which is initially formal, being grounded in the text's own self-consciousness and generic tentativeness. To such an extent do aliases proliferate that naming anything seems, paradoxically, to point to its essential unknowability or at least to its unrepresentability through language. For Attwater to call his island Zacynthos, to take one obvious example, is to make it less, not more 'real' (though, of course, one could argue that it ensures the survival of *some* sense of itself in the endless ricocheting of echo).

When Captain Brown is taking the roll-call of his crew he fails to understand the name the old man gives him, dismissing it as 'not English': 'I'll have none of your highway gibberish in my ship', he says, oblivious to the fact that he has just announced to the others that they are all to resume their false names. So he gives the old man a name culled from a children's rhyme: 'We'll call you old Uncle Ned because you've got no wool on the top of your head' (35). When, however, the sympathetic Herrick also calls the seaman 'Uncle Ned', the latter's expostulation is as sharp as Herrick's when, much later, Attwater calls him 'Hay':

> 'Ah, no call me Uncle Ned no mo'!' cried the old man. 'No my name! My name Taveeta, oll-e-same Taveeta King of Islael. Wat for he call that Hawaii? I think no savvy nothing – all-e-same Wise-a-mana' (49).

The irony in this is obvious: Taveeta can only be a missionary-conferred name; but the Kanaka is proud of it, indignantly asking 'Wat for he call that Hawaii?' Taveeta hasn't understood Davis any more than the latter has him, for Davis had *not* called his name Hawaiian but 'highway gibberish'. So from 'Uncle Ned' and children's stories we get back to Taveeta, hence to King David of Israel and so into the infinitely resonating echo-chamber of biblical nomenclature. Which is not all that different from the way 'Hay' had led back to Herrick hence to be dispersed in the large generic field of lyric poetry. What is paradoxically clear is that in neither case is his name exclusively his 'own': Taveeta never gets (or even asks for) his Hawaiian name and 'Robert Herrick' may or may not be Robert Herrick.

When the *Farallone* runs into the storm which seems mandatory for all such literary vessels, it provides, as usual, an opportunity for moral reappraisal. Davis promises to become a responsible captain again but in so doing has to get something off his chest, and that something is, of course, another name. From the start he has been greatly given to invoking the name of his daughter Ada as evidence of his better instincts. (As Fowler points out, however, 'familial sanctities seem in this story to operate more often as means of justifying crime than as ameliorating influences'.)[26] Now he reveals that she has been dead for years, having died, prosaically, of 'a bowel complaint'. His apologetic explanation – 'I never could act up to the plain-cut truth you see, so I pretend' – is, however, something of an evasion; in fact, he is pretending still. The truth he can't act up to is the plain-cut truth about himself. His revelation that the daughter, whose name has always been introduced at moments when he wants to assure his listeners that he does have *some* values which he will never desert and therefore *some* residual moral integrity, no longer exists, is therefore the revelation of a sentimental fraud. Herrick has always respected Davis for the probity that seemed to be vested in his feeling for his family and particularly for Ada. To have this exposed as yet another lie has a profound effect on him, as it strips away one more of those defences whereby he had attempted vicariously to shore up his own self-respect:

> The Captain's eyes were fixed on the horizon, he talked with an extraordinary softness but a complete composure; and Herrick looked upon him with something that was almost terror (57).

Herrick has now one fewer barrier between himself and his own demoralisation and his 'terror' perhaps helps us to understand better why Marlow in *Heart of Darkness* should say with such vehemence 'I hate, detest and can't bear a lie.... There is a flavour of death, a flavour of mortality in lies.... It makes me miserable and sick, like biting something rotten would do.'[27] Allon White points out that Meredith, Conrad and James were all fascinated by liars, and to this list he could quite properly have added Stevenson:

> They persistently return to explore situations in which people are forced to lie to defend themselves or to defend others. Their lies are rarely malicious or calumniating, they are defensive, often so vague or subtle that their relation to the truth is hopelessly perplexed. Lies are as old as the fictions to which they have been assimilated, but in late nineteenth-century fiction lies and liars focus some complex issues of literary obscurity.[28]

And, he adds: 'In the tensions of early modernism, lying takes on a metaphysical importance, it becomes an index of the ubiquitous untrustworthiness of once familiar and dependable responses.' Put more simply, a Conrad character occasionally has recourse to lying because truth cannot be *told* – which, of course, raises the spectre of there being no truth to tell. Stevenson is venturing into the same moral territory albeit with less confidence and certainty, largely because his concerns are more diverse, and he is less successful partly because his concerns are *too* diverse.

## An Island Not in 'Findlay'

With Part II Trio becomes Quartette. The musical reference suggests a number of things, chief among them, perhaps, the abstract nature of Stevenson's conception. It also might be taken to strengthen the notion that this *ensemble* of voices constitutes a single multi-faceted consciousness, or, alternatively that it is the embodiment of that plurality of consciousness which, it sometimes seemed to Stevenson, constitutes a human being. 'My profound conviction,' Stevenson wrote in 1893 (when revising *The Ebb-Tide*), 'is that there are many consciousnesses in a man ... I can feel them working in many directions.'[29] At the least, in Alastair Fowler's words, the four men 'compose a moral spectrum, or form a psychodynamic series'.[30]

The island which these adventurers have stumbled on is not to be found in 'Findlay's' authoritative charts and though this reference-work does acknowledge that rumours of its existence circulate, it insists that the island 'is totally disbelieved in by South Sea traders' (64). But a M. Delille, who is quoted as believing in the island's existence, accounts for this by claiming that 'private interests' would have it remain unknown for very selfish reasons.

So highly problematic is the island's existence that it seems entirely appropriate for its physical outline to be so indistinct and insubstantial as to deny its right to the name:

> Uncle Ned ... pointed to a part of the horizon where a greenish, filmy iridescence could be discerned floating like smoke on the pale heavens. Davis applied his glass to it .... 'Call that land?' said he. 'Well, it's more than I do' (66–7).

But Uncle Ned is confident in his judgement: what they are seeing is a reflection of the island's lagoon 'all-e-same milla'. Davis doubtingly accepts the possible mirror-effect; but Herrick thinks 'there's something in it'; and he offers further endorsement: 'I'll tell you one thing, too, captain; that's all right about the reflection; I heard it in Papeete.' Indefiniteness could scarcely be pushed farther: Herrick has 'heard' of its 'reflection'; now he has seen it and believes 'there's something in it'. So they pore over the 'bulky volume' of Findlay's charts, the realism of whose 'writings' – its diagrams, statistics, annotations – brings solid reassurance to those who would navigate the South Pacific, and contrasts strikingly with spectral islands which are only discernible as a filmy iridescence in the clouds. One should add that there is nothing fictional about Alexander Findlay whose nautical directories were used world-wide.[31]

So, in addition to the chronometer we have now had two celebrated publications, revered among seamen, drawn conspicuously to our attention. But the indisputable reality of Bowditch and Findlay and their respective aids to navigation is not recruited to inject a note of simple realism into the text. Far from it, in fact, as Conrad presumably realised when, following Stevenson, he planted Towson's *An Inquiry into some Points of Seamanship* in the path of Marlow in *Heart of Darkness*. To him, we are told (somewhat disingenuously) the contents of the book looked very dreary, 'with illustrative diagrams and repulsive tables of figures'. Marlow concludes, however:

> Not a very enthralling book; but at the first glance you could see there a singleness of intention, an honest concern for the right way of going to work, which made these humble pages, thought out so many years ago, luminous with another than a professional light. The simple old sailor, with his talk of chains and purchases made me forget the jungle and the pilgrims in a delicious sensation of having come upon something unmistakably real.[32]

The Bowditch and the Findlay are also luminous with an other than professional light: that is, they symbolise moral order rather than chaos and in doing so demonstrate well what Stevenson himself called 'the dense and luminous flow of highly synthetic narrative'.[33]

In truth, their effect goes further than this. Unlike *Heart of Darkness*, *The Ebb-Tide*, as has been pointed out, navigates its way among texts as well as coral islands, and here we have two texts whose precise factual description and measurements offer a textual reality in the sharpest possible contrast to that which seeks to represent the reality of Zacynthos. Only the maximum of indefiniteness and indeterminacy will do to represent something which is itself a reflection and an echo. Indeed, the question is postulated, is there any textual form capable of doing so? Could a Findlay ever describe such a nebulous entity? Even if it doesn't, though, is that a reason for not pursuing the 'faint iridescence'?

The decision to follow the mirage might seem to suggest that, in terms of fictional genre, the novel has settled for the indeterminate mode – the figurative, the evanescent, the echo, rather than for the moral realism discovered in that other much more solid island of Tahiti. In actual fact, this is not altogether so; we continue to play among forms and are led to perceive through or underneath the mirage that which it reflects: an apparently solid physical reality which the senses lock on to. It is not, note, a competition for ascendancy between these forms; in fact, the one asserts – can only assert – its own claim to recognition in the light of the other, for there is a degree of symbiosis in the relationship.

In his essay 'Reality, Leaven of Myth', Ortega y Gasset also uses the same image of the mirage to define two literary forms: the novel of adventure, the tale, the epic, and what he calls the realistic novel. Though the two writers are not using the mirage to define precisely the same forms, it nonetheless can be seen to function for both in a similar way:

> In summer the sun pours down torrents of fire on La Mancha, and frequently the burning earth produces the effect of a mirage. The water which we see is not real water but there is something real in it: its source. This bitter source, which produces the water of the mirage, is the desperate dryness of the land. We can experience a similar phenomenon in two directions: one simple and straight, seeing the water which the sun depicts as actual; another ironic, oblique, seeing it as a mirage, that is to say, seeing through the coolness of the water the dryness of the earth in disguise. The ingenious manner of experiencing imaginary and significant things is found in the novel of adventure, the tale, the epic; the oblique manner in the realistic novel. The latter needs the mirage to make us see it as such. So it is not only that *Quixote* was written against the books of chivalry, and as a result bears them within it, but that the novel as a literary genre consists essentially of such an absorption.[34]

I said earlier that the text's self-consciousness assists in the prevention of any one form establishing a hegemony over it, which, in turn, casts an air of provisionality upon the representation of character and event. The text's tentative questing among forms contributes to a sense of elusiveness which is echoed in the equally tentative representation of the island's physical reality. Indeed, that reality is hardly distinguishable from the text's own, for it first appears *pencilled* against the morning sky. Moreover, the name conferred on it by Attwater is, as has been said, Zacynthos, so that once again a moral or physical reality dissolves into an echo of another text which is itself a gateway to that other reality of myth. First there is the denial of the island's existence, backed up by an authoritative 'realist' text ('Findlay's') which is shown to be unreliable; then the acceptance of the mirage as an earnest of its reality and finally the ebbing away of that particular reality into classical myth. Both text and island lie very low in the water indeed, thus graphically questioning the nature and reliability of our perceptions and the traditional forms of their representation.

Herrick's conviction that 'never in his dreams had he beheld anything more strange and delicate' ensures that the reader has an impressionistic picture of the island as being of the stuff of dreams; and the fact that he can only render its reality in metaphors further attenuates its physical presence at the same time as it liberates more of those echoes and reverberations which, in the end, desubstantiate everything (and which, in the process if not the prose, recall Forster):

> He tortured himself to find analogies. The isle was like the rim of a great vessel sunken in the waters; it was like the embankment of an annular railway grown upon with wood: so slender it seemed amidst the outrageous breakers, so frail and pretty, he would scarce have wondered to see it sink and disappear without a sound, and the waves close smoothly over its descent (72).

Even the metaphors tend to splinter and disperse themselves in a number of images. Thus the 'vessel' here is primarily a receptacle (later it is referred to as a laver) but it can also be a ship, and a question mark immediately materialises over the nature of its 'crew': was it similar to that of the *Farallone*? Initially, the 'annular railway' seems a particularly harsh intrusion from the industrialised world, violating this fragile beauty in more than one sense; a railway circling the lagoon imprisons it in an incongruously brutal piece of nineteenth-century technology. Fortunately, Herrick's imagination doesn't run to trains (or does it?), but it is still hard to overlook the sexual symbolism which echoes the act of imperial repression and control. The incongruity of the railway may even be taken to echo the inappropriateness of the 'realist' text, in itself, in many ways, a product of the Industrial Revolution. And we should note that the railway fails to enclose the lagoon just as the 'realist' text fails to encompass the reality it claims to define.[35] Ultimately the railway is as out-of-place and redundant as the beached figure head. Both are images of a deracinated will-to-power, both are imbued with ironic, even absurdist, possibilities.

The reaction of the adventurers to the island is of the greatest interest: their snailhorn perception of their surroundings is conveyed with such immediacy that they seem to be inside the mirage itself:

> The airs were very light, their speed was small; the heat intense. The decks were scorching underfoot, the sun flamed overhead brazen, out of a brazen sky; the pitch bubbled in the seams, and the brains in the brain-pan. And all the while the excitement of the

three adventurers glowed about their bones like a fever. They whispered, and nodded, and pointed, and put mouth to ear with a singular instinct of secrecy, approaching that island underhand like eavesdroppers and thieves; and even Davis from the cross-trees gave his orders mostly by gestures. The hands shared in this mute strain, like dogs, without comprehending it; and through the roar of so many miles of breakers, it was a silent ship that approached an empty island (72).

The description of the ship approaching the island with its crew inexplicably awed into silence becomes more fanciful and the image less substantial as it proceeds: it turns first into a bird and then a painted ship upon a very painted ocean:

The hour in which the *Farallone* came there was the hour of flood. The sea turned (as with the instinct of the homing pigeon) for the vast receptacle, swept eddying through the gates, was trans-muted, as it did so, into a wonder of watery and silken hues, and brimmed into the inland sea beyond. The schooner looked up close-hauled, and was caught and carried away by the influx like a toy. She skimmed; she flew; a momentary shadow touched her decks from the shore-side trees; the bottom of the channel showed up for a moment and was in a moment gone; the next, she floated on the bosom of the lagoon, and below, in the transparent chamber of waters, a myriad of many-coloured fishes were sporting, a myriad pale flowers of coral diversified the floor (73).

Our expectations as well as those of the adventurers have been raised to such a pitch that we, too, might be inclined to whisper, but whatever the nature of the surprise we have been anticipating, we are not at all prepared for what we get. Despite the prevailing silence, we have assumed the island to be populated, and 'private interests' in full control and hostile to intruders. What we are not prepared for, after holding our breath so long, is an island which is apparently as deserted as the imaginary town in Keats's 'Ode on a Grecian Urn':

The place had the indescribable but unmistakable appearance of being in commission; yet there breathed from it a sense of deser-tion that was almost poignant, no human figure was to be observed going to and fro about the houses, and there was no sound of human industry or enjoyment (74).

More enigmatic still is the figure that is beckoning the crew of the *Farallone* to come ashore among the empty houses:

> on the top of the beach and hard by the flagstaff, a woman of exorbitant stature and as white as snow was to be seen beckoning with uplifted arm. The second glance identified her as a piece of naval sculpture, the figure-head of a ship that had long hovered and plunged into so many running billows, and was now brought ashore to be the ensign and presiding genius of the empty town (74).

This Melvillean figure with its 'leprous whiteness' is challenging and sinister in its mingled fascination and threat, and the crew of the *Farallone* have 'a sense of being watched and played with, and of a blow impending, that was hardly bearable'. At length they are hailed by a voice and given authoritative directions about berthing:

> Mechanically the orders were obeyed, and the ship berthed; and the three adventurers gathered aft beside the house and waited, with galloping pulses and a perfect vacancy of mind, the coming of the stranger who might mean so much to them (75).

The sentence is brilliant in its suggestiveness: the nervous anxiety with which they await the arrival of the master of the island 'who might mean so much to them' invests Attwater with more than casual significance and adds not to the concreteness of an adventure-story narrative but to that numinousness which seems to haunt Zacynthos. Nonetheless it is quite clear that the narrative tide is again on the turn and is beginning to flow in the Conradian, moral impressionist manner once more: a manner which Stevenson had himself commended in his essay, 'On Some Technical Elements of Style in Literature' when he wrote of the importance of attaining 'the highest degree of elegant and pregnant implication unobtrusively'. With a skill that puts us in mind of the later writer (and of *Nostromo* in particular), the unknown man is given other associations, for, if Findlay was right, as now seems likely, 'he was the representative of private reasons' (the last word surely being a misprint for 'interests').

## A Choice of Nightmares

The first thing that they notice about Attwater is his bulk, and the first that *we* notice is the unreal specificity of his height: 'He was a huge fellow, six feet four in height, and of a build proportionate.' It is as though he, too, were an outsize figurehead planted on the island to compete with the other one. (At the end of the book, when the diminutive Huish sets out to kill Attwater, he describes it as a David and Goliath engagement – and that is the title given to the chapter. Such are the moral and aesthetic ambivalences of the tale, we are less than sure that Huish has got it altogether wrong.)

Attwater is of a complexion 'naturally dark', tanned, we are told, to a hue that is 'hardly distinguishable from that of a Tahitian'. Only 'his manners and movements and the living force that dwelt in him, the fire in flint, betrayed the European'. It is his eyes that show his temper most clearly, however: they are 'of an unusual mingled brilliancy and softness, sombre as coal and with lights that outshone the topaz: an eye of unimpaired health and virility; an eye that bids you beware of the man's devastating anger'. To complete the paradox, he is dressed in a manner reminiscent of the chief accountant in *Heart of Darkness*, in white drill 'exquisitely made', while his scarf and tie are of 'tender-coloured silks'; but 'on the thwart beside him there leaned a Winchester rifle'.

The rifle is of central significance. What these adventurers are going to find on the island is what at least Davis and Herrick have been half-hoping for, half-fearing: law and moral discipline. '[I]t's the law does it, every time', Davis is later to say to Attwater – Davis who has broken one of the most sacred laws of his profession. At least these two characters (unlike Huish/Hyde) recognise their desperate need for the imposition of order which they are too weak to impose themselves.[36]

As for that other dimension, the concern of the text with its own textuality, the arrival of Attwater is significant for it too. As might be construed from Herbert Marks's observation quoted earlier, Attwater implicitly promises an end to the destabilising provisionality which had infused the text in the first half of *The Ebb-Tide*. His word is Law; it is imbued with God's authority and transgression means death. The trouble about accepting these monologic certainties, however, is that we have already formed a perspective on them mediated through echo and quotation, which has made us sceptical about all claims to such authority. Of course his confident self-identification with the symbolic order – the Logos – provides a focus for nostalgic desire, but it collides with the scruples of those who have gone a long way towards accepting conditions of existence predicated on notions of contingency, indeterminacy and 'dialogization'.

A hierarchically structured reality and the assumption of a necessary connection between word and thing come with Attwater's creed and they suggest an analogy with the claims of realism in fiction to represent reality. But the privileging of this particular mode is precisely what the first part of the text of *The Ebb-Tide* vigorously challenges. So we end up with a mixture of what I have been calling, rather loosely, novelistic 'genres'.

That a number of forms compete throughout the text for narrative-rights, so to speak, should now be obvious and there are times when Attwater's monologic influence asserts itself strongly. Thus when Herrick (who is ultimately to reject Attwater's appeal) tries to find analogies for the island's delicate appearance, his attempt – surprisingly – results in the extremely physical image of male dominance suggested by the railway superimposed upon the tree-clad embankment which encircles the passive waters of the lagoon. Now the massive figure of the entrepreneur, who has also built the jetty (and whose name thus takes on a sexual as well as a baptismal significance), combines with it as lord of this coral-fringed lagoon. With the emphasis given to his bulk, he seems to be linked to that other symbol of authority, the figurehead: 'a woman of exorbitant stature and as white as snow' (74). Though larger, the figurehead is less potent: she is beached, immobilised, captive, becoming at once a figure for the island under Attwater's ruthless domination and a reflection of the supremacy of male law. She is a figure, therefore, both of imperial domination – she is a helmeted piece of *naval* sculpture, and she is located 'hard by the flagstaff' – and of female subjugation to the male. The sexual symbolism is further strengthened by the fact that this, too, is a treasure-island (with all that that implies in Jungian terms) whose treasure the adventurers are determined to get their hands on.

Once on board the schooner it takes Attwater only a very few minutes to size up the situation and almost immediately he throws what could be either a life-line or a grappling-hook to Herrick:

Attwater leaned to him swiftly. 'University man?' said he.

'Yes, Merton,' said Herrick, and the next moment blushed scarlet at his indiscretion.

'I am of the other lot,' said Attwater: 'Trinity Hall, Cambridge, I called my schooner after the old shop' (77).

The hierarchies and complicities of class have been invoked as a divide-and-rule tactic which has the effect of asserting a kind of family bond between Attwater and Herrick – who later admits to Davis that he had been both 'attracted and repelled'. That he should be so is easily explained. Attwater once again embodies that father-figure whose blessing the alienated, unworthy son so desperately seeks, yet the judgemental authority that he wields – in this case with 'silken brutality' – is anathema to the young man, reminding him as it does, of his emasculation or, at any rate, his disempowerment.

To explain to himself – even to justify – that disempowerment the young man exaggerates the father-figure's potency and virility – something much in evidence in the depiction of Attwater. In the conclave which follows Attwater's departure, Herrick is given the – to him – monstrous task of delivering Attwater into the hands of the other two precisely because of what might be called their consanguinity: 'He's your kind, he's not ours', says Davis. Even before the captain spells out what is expected of him, Herrick knows what's coming and the brief passage where this is made clear is masterly:

> The captain drummed with his thick hands on the board in front of him; he looked steadily in Herrick's face, and Herrick as steadily looked upon the table and the pattering fingers; there was a gentle oscillation of the anchored ship, and a big patch of sunlight travelled to and fro between the one and the other.

Davis's instructions are delivered in an odd command around which other meanings cohere:

> 'Save him if you can!'
>     'Save him?' repeated Herrick.
>     'Save him, if you're able!' reiterated Davis with a blow of his clenched fist (83).

What Davis means is that if Herrick can inveigle Attwater on board, together with his pearls, his life will be spared. Otherwise he will be robbed of his treasure and killed.

For Herrick, so conscious of his own need for salvation, to be given a commission to 'save' Attwater is to heap coals of fire on his head and to force him to confront his own weakness:

> 'Well, and if I can't?' cried Herrick, while the sweat streamed upon his face. 'You talk to me as if I was God Almighty, to do this and that! But if I can't?'
>     'My son,' said the captain, 'you better do your level best, or you'll see sights!' (83)

Once on the island to meet Attwater, Herrick discovers a shed full of the detritus of two wrecks: a binnacle with its compass 'idly pointing', a steering wheel, windlasses, anchors and so on – all of which seem to him to be 'romantic things' and it seems to him as if he 'heard the tread of feet and whisperings and saw with the tail of his eye the commonplace ghosts of sailormen' (86). To the uncompassionate Attwater whose voice cuts in on Herrick's Conradian reverie, it is all simply 'Junk ... only old junk.'

The monomaniac evangelist seems to prefer to think of human beings as abstractions or, when dead, as dehumanised artefacts, referring to the population as 'souls' not people and to the dead bodies of the smallpox victims as empty bottles. When Herrick, misunderstanding him, queries 'You loved these people?' he replies 'I ... Dear no! Don't think me a philanthropist. I dislike men and hate women' (90). One islander only does he admit to liking as he stands by his grave and this, one suspects, is because he offered the evangelist a challenge: 'He was a fine savage fellow; he had a dark soul; yes, I liked this one. I am fanciful,' he added, looking hard at Herrick, 'and I take fads. I like you.' Herrick's self-loathing ensures his response 'No-one can like me', to which Attwater replies 'You are wrong there.... You are attractive, very attractive.' Though there is always a certain degree of sexual ambiguity in these father–son tensions in Stevenson, Attwater is surely speaking here as the evangelist to whom Herrick appeals because of his moral degradation. It had been the islander's 'dark soul' which had interested Attwater and what he perceives in Herrick, with his usual penetration, is another deeply troubled soul.

In a way it is Herrick's vulnerability that attracts the pearl-fisher who would be a fisher of souls. So powerfully is he attracted that it is fitting that the expression of his attraction should seem to have something in common with a sexual response. He *is* trying to seduce him; the sight of a conscience in dire distress acts like a spiritual aphrodisiac on the predatory evangelist. Moreover, his physical presence is asserted with an almost sexual aggressiveness:

> Attwater stood in the doorway, which he almost wholly filled; his hands stretched above his head and grasping the architrave. He smiled when their eyes met, but the expression was inscrutable (87).

Later, when he has rebuked Herrick for what he regards as the cynicism of the latter's reading of the parable he has propounded, he becomes menacing in his fervour: 'The huge dark man stood over against Herrick by the line of the divers' helmets, and seemed to swell and glow' (88).

Herrick's vulnerability is completely exposed in the exchange between the two over the allegory suggested by the diving suits. Herrick would like to think that a well-founded self-respect could act as that diving-suit and protect its wearer from whatever danger threatened him; but after his discovery of his own moral insufficiency he is inclined to think that what he has donned is, rather, self-conceit – which is going to offer very little protection.

The crucial importance of what might, a little loosely, be called 'self-respect' in a world imbued with sceptics and devoid of religious belief is a preoccupation of a great many of Conrad's characters, including Marlow. To these men, moral integrity and the discipline it demands – fidelity to 'the sovereign power enthroned in a fixed standard of conduct' – is all-important. It is this code which Lord Jim would seem to have betrayed though he himself never accepts such a reading of his conduct and insists that, when circumstances are not against him, he will prove how stalwart he is in defence of that 'standard' on which self-respect depends. At Patusan he finally gets his opportunity – and apparently triumphantly meets the challenge: 'Not in the wildest days of his boyish visions could he have seen the alluring shape of such an extraordinary success!', writes Marlow who, nonetheless, casts a somewhat equivocal light on that 'success'.

Herrick has also betrayed his own ideals but, unlike Jim, 'he had struck his flag' and 'entertained no hope to reinstate himself' (4). So he has sought refuge in the islands but not in the same way as Jim, who repeatedly moved on when his act of self-betrayal caught up with him (at least Jim would not have seen any similarity). Herrick arrives 'a skulker from life's battles and his own immediate duty'. He is a Jim, then, who would never earn the honorific 'Lord': a Jim gone determinedly to the bad but with a Calvinist conscience which won't lie down, or let him lie down either. And in this (leaving aside the Calvinism, though Jim's father *is* an Anglican priest) there may be a glimmer of resemblance to 'Lord' Jim. For however much Herrick may be revolted by his own debasement, he is still unwilling to surrender himself to the absolutist authority of the master of the island, the 'dark apostle' Attwater; and at the end he is to be found waiting on the beach for a ship which will carry him away possibly – *just* possibly – to discover his own Patusan.

That what Attwater wants of him is total submission, Herrick is well aware; for he knows that the evangelist's religion is altogether uncompromising. The latter has told him that he gave up his interest in missions because they were too 'parsonish'. For him 'religion is a savage thing, like the universe it illuminates; savage, cold and bare but infinitely strong' (89). So he set up his own colony, mission and business and now applies the same authoritarian principles to all three:

> 'I was a man of the world before I was a Christian; I'm a man of the world still and I made my mission pay…. I gave these beggars what they wanted: a judge in Israel, the bearer of the sword and scourge …' (89).

Sounding like a contemporary university Vice-Chancellor, Attwater's creed is all about power, and his brutal exercise of it upon the weak and self-despising Herrick comes near to intellectual rape.

Initially, the discovery of Attwater's religious zeal greatly disconcerts Herrick and he finds it hard to fit his perceptions of this man into a coherent whole. The incompleteness of his comprehension – a little later he is to admit 'I do not understand what manner of man you are' (96) – revives in him the feeling that he is still in a dream, and suggests to us some affinity between Herrick's difficulty in establishing a clear focus and the text's:

> Herrick was like one in a dream. He had come there with a mind divided; come prepared to study that ambiguous and sneering mask, drag out the essential man from underneath, and act accordingly; decision being till then postponed. Iron cruelty, an iron insensibility to the suffering of others, the uncompromising pursuit of his own interests, cold culture, manners without humanity; these he had looked for, these he still thought he saw. But to find the whole machine thus glow with the reverberation of religious zeal, surprised him beyond words; and he laboured in vain, as he walked, to piece together into any kind of whole his odds and ends of knowledge – to adjust again into any kind of focus with itself, his picture of the man beside him (88–9).

The island itself had at first seemed like something in a dream in its fanciful beauty; now another dream verging on nightmare is displacing the first one: in it things appear to be fragmented, out of focus, beyond his comprehension. And it has a monster, too, in the overbearing, evangelising, bullying father-figure. Nonetheless the importance of Herrick's refusal to make submission to Attwater must not be underestimated. Earlier we had heard that 'something that was scarcely pride or strength, that was perhaps only refinement withheld him from capitulation; but he looked upon his own misfortune with a growing rage ...' (5). There *is* something more than a trace of a saving egotism in Herrick's refusal to offer Attwater the complete self-abnegation he wants; not as much as there is in Lord Jim and certainly not of such an exalted order, but undoubtedly it is there in his 'growing rage' and in his response here to his tormentor: '"Attwater," he said, "you push me beyond bearing. What am I to do? I do not believe. It is living truth to you; to me, upon my conscience, only folk-lore"' (42). When Herrick rejects his appeal he has nothing but contempt for him: 'The rapture was all gone from Attwater's countenance; the dark apostle had disappeared; and in his place there stood an easy, smiling gentleman who took off his hat and bowed' (92).

Herrick's struggle with the 'dark apostle' is almost as fierce as Jacob's with the angel, but here the ability to resist is a sign of his *refusal* to seek reconciliation with the law; as is his inability or unwillingness to dissociate himself from his two fellow-criminals. When Attwater asks what 'a poor lost puppy' is doing with two wolves, he is driven to defend his companions in iniquity and he does so in a manner we now think of as Conradian:

> 'There is nothing wrong; all is above-board; Captain Brown is a good soul; he is a ... he is ....' The phantom voice of Davis called in his ear: 'There's going to be a funeral'; and the sweat burst forth and streamed on his brow. 'He is a family man,' he resumed again, swallowing; 'he has children at home – and a wife.'
>
> 'And a very nice man?' said Attwater. 'And so is Mr Whish, no doubt?'
>
> 'I won't go so far as that,' said Herrick. 'I do not like Huish. And yet ... he has his merits too' (91).

Herrick's difficulty is extremely well done. What he has been asked to define is his own moral degradation and language fails him, not being equal to the task any more than it was for Kurtz. (Later he is to say that the only thing he believes in is the 'living horror' of himself, which is one possible reading of Kurtz's famous broken statement at the end of *Heart of Darkness* and for whom, as Marlow says, it is some sort of achievement – after all it is something for

Kurtz to get back to a position where he has, in Marlow's phrase, 'a choice of nightmares'.) Herrick's dilemma *vis-à-vis* his companions also recalls Jim's when confronted by another seaman who had betrayed their code, who is also called Captain Brown, and who appeals to Jim for help in the name of their common weakness.

> He asked Jim whether he had nothing fishy in his life to remember that he was so damnedly hard upon a man trying to get out of a deadly hole by the first means that came to hand – and so on, and so on. And there ran through the rough talk a vein of subtle reference to their common blood, an assumption of common experience; a sickening suggestion of common guilt, of secret knowledge that was like a bond of their minds and of their hearts.[37]

What Herrick does is to seek to conceal the truth about the captain by invoking the one moral commitment Davis has remained true to (or at least has continued to pay lip-service to), that is, his family. By making it part of a lie, Herrick corrupts and desecrates it – in much the same way that Marlow corrupts Kurtz's fiancée by persuading her to believe (and so to live) a lie. So his defence of his companions turns into a self-indictment.

At the same time, Herrick also feels some sort of duty towards Attwater and experiences an 'immense temptation' to go up to him and 'breath a word in his ear: "Beware, they are going to murder you"'. To do so, however would be to betray Davis and Huish and what follows is another bout of agonised soul-searching, confronting the fact that he of the 'bedevilled and dishonoured soul' must now choose between the lives of Attwater and Davis. Like Marlow, Herrick's preoccupation is very much with his own consciousness; with, in this case, how he perceives and values Attwater. To understand the evangelist would be successfully to orientate himself, and the frustration of the attempt does nothing to diminish his sense of being caught in the toils of an existential imbroglio he has no hope of resolving.

The Conradian struggle is, however, complicated by the overt presence of a Freudian aspect to Herrick's predicament. Attwater, as superego, is an altogether overpowering father-figure who can, in every sense, lay down the law. While this is part of his appeal, it is also a challenge and, weak as he is, Herrick is sufficiently a Stevenson character to harbour deep resistance, even animosity, towards any demand that he should subordinate himself completely to the authority of such a figure. That he should kill, or help to kill, this man is, however, altogether a different matter and the prospect appals him. The image in which he envisages that death recreates the primal murder: the brothers banding together to slay the tribal father whom they both love and envy and who stands in their way. At this moment, let us recall, Attwater appears even larger than life; he is totemic:

> He considered the men. Attwater intrigued, puzzled, dazzled, enchanted and revolted him; alive, he seemed but a doubtful good; and the thought of him lying dead was so unwelcome that it pursued him like a vision, with every circumstance of colour and sound. Incessantly, he had before him the image of that great mass of man stricken down in varying attitudes and with varying words; fallen prone, fallen supine, fallen on his side; or clinging to a doorpost with the changing face and the relaxing fingers of the death-agony. He heard the click of the trigger, the thud of the ball, the cry of the victim; he saw the blood flow. And this building up of circumstance was like a consecration of the man, till he seemed to walk in sacrificial fillets (93).

From the start, Herrick's problem has been rooted in the knowledge that he has failed his 'intelligent, active and ambitious' father. Even while at Oxford he had shown himself deficient in 'intellectual manhood' and when the family fortunes collapse, he is obliged to follow the career of merchant's clerk which he 'detested and despised'. Having taken up the job to help his family, he does so 'with a mind divided' and proceeds to go steadily downhill. His voyage to the South Seas was a half-hearted attempt to redeem his fortunes but, the narrator tells us pointedly, had he gone there 'with any manful purpose he would have kept his father's name: the *alias* betrayed his moral bankruptcy ...' (4).

In that curious letter-writing episode on the beach, it is noteworthy that though Herrick addresses his letter to the woman he had loved, he first attempts to address his father and then, having been unable to do so, falls back on using the girl as a messenger. He asks her to break the news of his failure to his father and also to disclose the fact that he now passes under a false name – a classic avoidance of that confrontation with the father which would allow him to assert his manhood. Appropriately enough, he abjectly confesses to the girl that he 'had not the manhood of a common clerk' and encourages her to 'turn the key in the door ... [and] be done with the poor ghost that pretended he was a man' (19–20).

Herrick's failure to make good is thus a reflection of his failure in manhood – his unwillingness (as we saw from his parable) even to confess himself to his father as a prodigal son. As so often in Stevenson's own case and in the case of so many of his weak young male characters, one is reminded of Franz Kafka's reaction to his perceived problems with *his* father. True, Kafka could neither revolt nor simply leave the family-circle but then, in a sense, neither did Herrick. He was abroad (at his father's expense) when disaster struck the family, and he simply never returned. In 'the sense of utter helplessness mingled with rage and hatred'[38] which assailed Kafka from time to time, there is a parallel for Herrick's own bouts of helplessness, despair and rage which occasionally 'rose and flooded him', as well as that hatred which he pours out hysterically on Attwater during the dinner party.

Frederick J. Hoffman has written of Kafka that:

> His struggle for peace is characterised by an ambivalence of protest and submission – a protest against the unreasonableness, often absurdity of authority, and a submission to its inevitablity and its power.[39]

This seems to me to describe Herrick's case (and quite a number of other Stevensonian cases, too) very well: what fuels (and explains) so much of his inner turmoil is the absent father whom he cannot or will not confront psychologically or physically. And if his struggle with the 'dark apostle' may suggest that phantasmagoric wrestling-match between Jacob and the mysterious stranger – a recurring biblical episode which seems to occupy as large a place in Stevenson's imagination as the parable of the prodigal son – that, too, fits for surely it is a surrogate conflict for the son–father confrontation which never took place.[40]

After vividly rehearsing in his mind's eye the death of Attwater, Herrick goes on to consider the fate of another man whose life now lies in his hands. Davis has also been something of a father-substitute to the distressed 'puppy in pyjamas' (as Attwater calls him), greatly given to addressing him as 'my son' and even occasionally saying 'I love you'. In fact, Davis exemplifies the 'bad father' in that he explicitly tempts his son to moral destruction. After Herrick's clumsy move to 'tempt' Davis into joining him in a suicide pact – 'both of us together ... a few strokes in the lagoon – and rest!' – Davis turns the tables on him and mounts his own far more successful enticement:

'I tell you, Herrick, I'm 'most tempted to answer you the way the man does in the Bible, and say, *"Get thee behind me, Satan!"'* said the captain. 'What! you think I would go drown myself, and I got children starving? Enjoy it? No, by God, I do not enjoy it! but it's the row I've got to hoe, and I'll hoe it till I drop right here. I have three of them, you see, two boys and the one girl, Ada. The trouble is that you are not a parent yourself. I tell you, Herrick, I love you,' the man broke out; 'I didn't take to you at first you were so angli-fied and tony, but I love you now; it's a man that loves you stands here and wrestles with you.... Ah, you've no family, and that's where the trouble is!' (28)

So we have yet another wrestling-match between a surrogate father and his son. The inversions in the passage are quite extraor-dinary. 'The man in the Bible' is, of course, Christ; so Stevenson has Davis, the miscreant father, invoke Christ's name to reject Herrick's 'temptation' to end his wrong-doing, and to tempt the son into further crimes.[41] There could surely be no more graphic example of how profoundly these men have lost their moral bearings as the text itself stumbles among corrupted texts. The 'bad father' seeks the corruption of the son by recruiting to his corrupt cause the Son himself. In this chaotic universe Christ becomes a confidence trick practised by the father whose law is reinforced by being seen to be absolute, capricious and destructive. It is utterly preposterous for this humbug who has deserted his wife and children to say to Herrick 'Ah, you've no family, and that's where the trouble is', adding 'And if you thought a cent about this father that I hear you talk of ... you would feel like me. You would say, What matter laws, and God, and that?' (28–9) This from the man who has just invoked the name of Christ to assert the law of the 'bad' father!

As usual, however, Herrick is cowed by the (always outsize) figure of the bullying father. When the captain finishes prophesying Herrick's doom if he sticks to what few principles he has left ('Don't think, if you refuse this chance, that you'll go on doing the evangel-ical; you're about through with your stock ...' [29]), Herrick submits:

as the man stood and shook through his great stature, he seemed indeed like one in whom the spirit of divination worked and might utter oracles. Herrick looked at him, and looked away; it seemed not decent to spy on such agitation; and the young man's courage sank (30).

Thus, in being driven to choose between 'saving' Davis or Attwater, Herrick is, like Marlow, confronted by a choice of nightmares – which in his case take the shape of *two* 'bad' fathers.

> Next he considered Davis, with his thick-fingered, coarse-grained, oat-bread commonness of nature, his indomitable valour and mirth in the old days of their starvation, the endearing blend of his faults and virtues, the sudden shining forth of a tenderness that lay too deep for tears; his children, Ada and her bowel complaint, and Ada's doll. No, death could not be suffered to approach that head even in fancy; with a general heat and a bracing of his muscles, it was borne in on Herrick that Ada's father would find in him a son to the death (93–4).

So the weaker but (by his own lights) the more loving father wins: 'it must be Attwater'. Amazingly, after all we've heard, the familial bond surfaces again as a moral standard – and even more amazingly is extended to include the disreputable Huish: 'even Huish showed [shared?] a little in that sacredness; by the tacit adoption of daily life they were to become brothers' (94). It is through an appeal to precisely this sort of bond, the bond of delinquent weakness, that 'Gentleman' Brown brings about Lord Jim's destruction: 'there ran through the rough talk a vein of subtle reference to their common blood, an assumption of common experience; a sickening suggestion of common guilt, of secret knowledge that was like a bond of their minds and of their hearts'.[42]

Of course, as soon as the hopelessly irresolute Herrick decides that 'it must be Attwater', panic sets in and he swings the other way: 'when he looked within himself he was aware only of turbulence and inarticulate outcry'. Yet in an almost Bunyanesque way (there are as many covert allusions to *The Pilgrim's Progress* in this text as there are in *Heart of Darkness*) Herrick emerges from his struggle with the false fathers sufficiently intact to leave alive the faint possibility of faring better at another time and place. The question is: can he reach his Patusan without ever having confronted his father at a crossroads or the 'Angel' at the brook Jabok? Come to that, did Jim?

That hope is, however, diminished by the fact that it is at this precise point the text's own 'figurehead', its title, is found to be planted. In a highly ambivalent paragraph we learn that in all his inner debate over the fate of Attwater and Davis 'there was no thought of Robert Herrick'. This is palpably untrue: the entire argument about these men's fate has been filtered through a moral consciousness preoccupied with its own health. The paragraph intrudes a note of passivity which Herrick's stream-of-consciousness analysis has not reflected, and may be an authorial attempt to rein in a moral discrimination which was becoming too active. At any rate, this is by no means the moment when Herrick seems most to have complied with 'the ebb-tide in men's affairs' and to make it so here, with all that it implies for the shaping imagination, is to upset the equilibrium of the text.

In fact, the paragraph is both damaging and unnecessary; for what follows says virtually all that needs to be said while remaining not just relevant to the preceding debate but concluding it in a telling way:

> For how long he walked silent by his companion Herrick had no guess. The clouds rolled suddenly away; the orgasm was over; he found himself placid with the placidity of despair; there returned to him the power of common-place speech; and he heard with surprise his own voice say: 'What a lovely evening!' (94)

Despite its obliqueness, this is so much more satisfactory as a representation of Herrick's turmoil and its aftermath that it adds to our deprecation of the previous paragraph. That the wrestling-match *has* been about a young man's struggle to wean himself from dependence on the authority of the father is surely clear, as has been the fact that his problem has been compounded by his deep desire *for* that dependent status – and the love that is felt should come with it. The complex, intense nature of the struggle is much more effectively conveyed in 'the orgasm was over; he found himself placid with the placidity of despair', than in exalted talk about his 'bedevilled and dishonoured soul'.

The timid emergence of a judging centre has collapsed, a waste of spirit in an expense of shame. By contrast, Attwater's potency is reasserted with considerable force in the dialogue which ensues:

> 'Yes, the evenings here would be very pleasant if one had anything to do. By day, of course one can shoot.'
>
> 'You shoot?' asked Herrick.
>
> 'Yes, I am what you would call a fine shot,' said Attwater. 'It is faith; I believe my balls will go true; if I were to miss once, it would spoil me for nine months.'
>
> 'You never miss, then?' said Herrick.
>
> 'Not unless I mean to,' said Attwater. 'But to miss nicely is the art. There was an old king one knew in the western islands who

used to empty a Winchester all round a man, and stir his hair or nick a rag out of his clothes with every ball except the last; and that went plump between the eyes. It was pretty practice.'

'You could do that?' asked Herrick, with a sudden chill.

'Oh, I can do anything,' returned the other. 'You do not understand: what must be, must' (94–5).

The evangelist, with his lust for justice at the point of a Winchester, is, as Herrick later describes him, 'a sinister man'. Indeed, having been alerted earlier by the allusion to *Der Freischütz*, we might be inclined to interpret his confidence in the trajectory of his bullets as a sign of his complicity with some very dark powers indeed. What is signified in all this, however, is the characteristic Stevensonian refusal to represent good and evil as a clear-cut polarity. The angel of the Lord's wrath is quite as terrifying as Kaspar:

> till then he had seen Attwater trussed and gagged, a helpless victim, and had longed to run in and save him; he saw him now tower up mysterious and menacing, the angel of the Lord's wrath, armed with knowledge and threatening judgment (97).

## Emissaries of Light

When the two men reach Attwater's house, incongruity and paradox force themselves on the reader's attention. Among the trees of this coral atoll the hanging lamps on the verandah illuminate a scene altogether artificial and out-of-place. The house becomes an island-within-an-island: an island of glimmering light amid surrounding darkness. Under the lamps 'the table shone with napery and crystal' and the house itself, as though under a spot-light, 'shone abroad in the dusk of the trees with many complicated shadows' (95). Mellow though the light is, it signifies an aggressive alien presence, forcing the soft and yielding darkness back upon itself, splitting it with 'complicated shadows'. The formal dinner table, the ritual sampling of vintage wine, the hovering, well-trained native servants – all bespeak a dominating foreign culture which carries with it, and imposes on others, its own overbearing self-sufficiency and its own discipline.

In *Heart of Darkness*, Marlow sees himself, with self-deprecating irony, being cast in the role of 'an emissary of light, something like a lower sort of apostle'.[43] The same irony is at work here, though unspoken: into this pool of light come the trio of dilapidated adventurers, representative of those European races we heard about in the book's first sentence who 'throughout the island world of the Pacific … carry activity and disseminate disease'. They are, of course, the guests of the ruthless trader-evangelist whose acquisition of wealth has been as rapacious and unscrupulous as Kurtz's, though he deals in pearls rather than ivory: 'Here are ten years' accumulation from the lagoon, where I have had as many as ten divers going all day long; and I went further than people usually do in these waters, for I rotted a bit of shell, and did splendidly' (96). Unlike Kurtz, however, he has not sold out to the 'wilderness'. In some ways – and most of all, perhaps, in his fastidiousness and exquisitely tailored appearance – he resembles more (as has been said) the Company's chief accountant in *Heart of Darkness* who, despite living in the depths of the jungle, manages to maintain 'such an unexpected elegance of get up that in the first moment [Marlow] took him for a vision':

> I saw a high starched collar, white cuffs, a light alpaca jacket, snowy trousers, a clear necktie, and varnished boots. No hat. Hair parted, brushed, oiled, under a green-lined parasol held in a big white hand.[44]

Attwater, we recall, when first seen by the men on the *Farallone*, 'was dressed in white drill, exquisitely made, his scarf and tie … of tender-coloured silks'. And just as the accountant's 'faultless appearance' (ironically described by Marlow as, 'in the great demoralization of the land', an achievement of character) is contrasted with his inhumanity towards the sick person whose groans distract him from his calculations, so Attwater's fastidiousness is set against his heartlessness towards the islanders.

Another similarity is their attitude to women. When Marlow asks the chief accountant 'how he managed to sport such linen' he replies: 'I've been teaching one of the native women about the station. It was difficult. She had a distaste for the work.' Similarly, when Herrick remarks on the beauty of one of Attwater's servants, Attwater responds:'Too pretty.... That was why I had her married … I had the pair of them to the chapel and performed the ceremony. She made a lot of fuss. I do not take at all the romantic view of marriage.'

The dinner party is something of a master-stroke in the structure of the book. For characters in a novel to arrange themselves round a dinner-table like characters on a stage (Attwater actually talks of their sitting 'on a lighted stage') again underlies the text's self-consciousness. But they do more: they provide a graphic tableau of the incongruous, even absurdist, intrusion of Europeans on the South Pacific scene, exposing their pretentiousness and the essential falseness of their position. Dragging their metropolitan baggage with them, these four adventurers stand for imperial entrepreneurship at its sordid and disreputable worst, constituting them fit companions for the squalid 'pilgrims' in *Heart of Darkness*. Their alien imaginations contaminate everything they come in contact with:

> The isle, at this hour, with its smooth floor of sand, the pillared roof overhead, and the prevalent illumination of the lamps, wore an air of unreality like a deserted theatre or a public garden at midnight. A man looked about him for the statues and tables. Not the least air of wind was stirring among the palms, and the silence was emphasised by the continuous clamour of the surf from the seashore as it might be of traffic in the next street (107).

The scene around the table is, at the same time, full of suspense so that it becomes a very modern sort of theatre where disjunction, incongruity and a pervading sense of incoherence dominate the action. There is an overwhelming feeling of things only part-understood, of watchful uncertainty, of action only partly complete. How much has Attwater guessed? What is he going to do – and when? Attwater dexterously manipulates the others' ignorance and uncertainty. At the end of a series of highly ambiguous remarks from him, Davis finds himself '[reaching] out far and wide to find any coherency in these remarks', and his difficulty expresses well the deliberate indefiniteness of so much that refuses to come intelligibly together.

That indefiniteness is given further impetus by Attwater very deliberately setting up yet another in the long sequence of echoes. When Huish declares his dislike of solitude and his preference for the sound of Bow Bells, his remark not only heightens the alien character of these men to their surroundings (given their position in the middle of the South Pacific, surely *nothing* could be more inapposite than an echo of Bow Bells), it gives Attwater his opportunity to claim that there can be no such thing as solitude since space is filled by God:

> 'And talking of the sound of bells, kindly follow a little experiment of mine in silence.' There was a silver bell at his right hand to call the servants; he made them a sign to stand still, struck the

bell with force, and leaned eagerly forward. The note rose clear
and strong; it rang out clear and far into the night and over the
deserted island; it died into the distance until there only lingered
in the porches of the ear a vibration that was sound no longer.
'Empty houses, empty sea, solitary beaches!' said Attwater. 'And
yet God hears the bell! And yet we sit in this verandah on a lighted
stage with all heaven for spectators!' (100–1)

For Attwater there can be no such thing as an *ending*: the note he
liberates goes on forever yet is not lost because space is not just infinite, it is the Infinite. Every pulse of sound or being is repeated *ad
infinitum* but in no empty, mocking sense:

'Why ring a bell, when there flows, out from oneself and everything about one a far more momentous silence? the least beat of
my heart and the least thought in my mind echoing into eternity
for ever and for ever and for ever' (101).

Though Davis, the sea captain, is mesmerised by this idea, Huish
refuses to be impressed, seeing it as familiar evangelical mumbo-
jumbo – 'turn down the lights at once, and the Band of 'Ope will
oblige!'

The persistent return to the echo motif is, however, of real significance in the questions being posed by the text. In fact, Attwater's
contribution focuses the issues sharply. Does echo signify anything
other than endless repetition devoid of meaning, like the 'ou-boum'
in Forster's Marabar caves? Are all the literary or musical echoes we
have been bombarded with simply lost in space – or do they survive
by being absorbed or reabsorbed in religion or myth? Has Herrick
no hope but simply to plod on, from one defeat to another, caught
in an endless chain of repetition? To him the religious solution is
simply folklore; but to the 'dark apostle' it is salvation – and power.
To emphasise the iron fist in the evangelical glove, when Attwater
next strikes the bell it is to discipline the native servants – who 'stood
mute and trembling' – after one of them has dropped and broken a
bottle of wine while serving.

Central to Attwater's belief in God is his belief in Law while he
himself becomes an image of 'the stern, judgmental, prohibiting father
Freud evokes in *Totem and Taboo* – the God of Protestantism … the
symbolic representative of law'.[45] It is this law of the Father which
both attracts and repels Herrick. But it is law, too, which impresses
Davis (delinquent though he now is) and Attwater's achievement in
drilling his forced labour without the assistance of legal sanctions

earns him the captain's unqualified respect. "'By God, but you must be a holy terror!" cried the captain in a glow of admiration'; to which their host modestly replies 'One does one's best' (102). Davis is not to be denied his eulogy, however:

> 'In a ship, why, there ain't nothing to it! You've got the law with you, that's what does it. But put me down on this blame' beach alone with nothing but a whip and a mouthful of bad words, and ask me to ... no, *sir!* it's not good enough! I haven't got the sand for that!' cried Davis. 'It's the law behind,' he added; 'it's the law does it, every time!' (102)

To which the 'holy terror' replies dryly: 'Well, one got the law after a fashion ...'; by which, he means, of course *his* law.

Herrick, so conscious of his own wrong-doing, is both fascinated and fearful and asks: 'Did you – did you ever have crime here?' In reply Attwater offers him a vivid tale of crime and punishment which shocks Herrick by the way it exposes the inhuman savagery at the heart of his grim version of Christianity.[46] *Caritas*, forgiveness, have no place in it: prodigal sons need not apply. Hence his extreme reaction when Attwater describes the punishment he meted out to a native who had, he decides, made a fool of his justice by shifting the blame for an offence from himself to another who had then committed suicide. To Herrick, profoundly aware of his need for a forgiving father, the execution of the islander is a travesty of justice, having been turned into a grisly game:

> 'It was a murder,' he screamed. 'a cold-hearted, bloody-minded murder! You monstrous being! Murderer and hypocrite – murderer and hypocrite – murderer and hypocrite –' he repeated, and his tongue stumbled among the words (105).

Davis recognises the threat to their plans in Herrick's hysterical outburst and hastens to calm him down, restraining him by putting his arms round him. The description is significant:

> Herrick struggled in his embrace like a frantic child, and suddenly bowing his face in his hands, choked into a sob, the first of many, which now convulsed his body silently, and now jerked from him indescribable and meaningless sounds (106).

It is impossible not to recognise in this scene the portrayal of a crisis very close to the one which Archie Weir experiences early in *Weir of Hermiston*. Archie having just witnessed the hanging of the miserable

Duncan Jopp, condemned to death by Lord Hermiston, 'stood a moment silent, and then – "I denounce this God-defying murder," he shouted; and his father if he must have disclaimed the sentiment, might have owned the stentorian voice with which it was uttered' (26). Herrick's horror of Attwater's relish for the role of the punitive judge ('a judge in Israel, the bearer of the sword and scourge') is a forerunner of Archie's and helps to make his relationship to Attwater clearer. What most appalled Archie, watching the trial of Jopp, was the 'gusto' with which his father applied himself to the task and he uses one of Herrick's words of denunciation to describe the effect: 'And the judge had pursued him with a monstrous, relishing gaiety, horrible to be conceived, a trait for nightmares' (25). Perhaps because of his nurse 'Cummy's' indoctrination, Stevenson had from an extremely tender age a rooted sense of personal guilt so that fear of an all-judging Father seems to have been translated into an abiding terror of the father, whom he loved, cast in the antagonistic role of the 'hanging judge'.

In the end, Herrick returns to Attwater but only after his last shred of belief in his capacity to transcend circumstances has been exposed as self-delusion. In the paradoxically-named chapter 'The Open Door', he discovers that he cannot pass through this door to his death as he had always told himself he could. When Herrick slips into the water with the intention of drowning himself, he thanks 'whatever Gods there be' for that open door of suicide: 'In such a little time he would be done with it, the random business at an end, the prodigal son come home' (115). But what he is about is a travesty of the parable, for suicide is a means for the prodigal son *avoiding* 'coming home'. Predictably, he cannot go through with it and he finds himself clinging to life, utterly devoid of that 'single manly thought' which would strengthen his resolve to die:

> The open door was closed in his recreant face. He must go back into the world and amongst men without illusion. He must stagger on to the end with the pack of his responsibility and his disgrace ... (116).

So he delivers himself up to Attwater to be repaired – if that is possible. 'Can you do anything with me?' he asks the evangelist and goes on abjectly: 'I am broken crockery, I am a burst drum ...'. Again the emphasis is on fragmentation and his surrendering to Attwater comes about explicitly because Attwater sees through deceit and masquerade – and is an upholder of forms:

Why do I come to you? I don't know; you are cold, cruel, hateful; and I hate you, or I think I hate you. But you are an honest man, an honest gentleman. I put myself, helpless, in your hands. What must I do? If I can't do anything, be merciful and put a bullet through me; ... (118).

There is, as Attwater admits, not much he *can* do and it would be hard to criticise him if he took up Herrick's suggestion to put a bullet through him then and there. The prospect of having this whingeing Oxford drop-out as a house-guest on a coral atoll would try the patience of a far more benign religionist than the lord of Zacynthos. When, however, Herrick attributes his decision to come over to Attwater's side – despite hating him – to the fact that he's not just a honest man but an honest *gentleman*, he voices again that link between them which had first been established when Herrick blurted out the name of his Oxford college. As Davis and Huish had immediately realised, what links the two is class consciousness. In fact we have had a sample of Herrick's snobbery in the early pages of the book when he complained of starving on Tahiti 'with worse than banditti'. When he writes the phrase from the Fifth Symphony and the lines from the *Aeneid* on the wall, he thinks 'So ... they will know that I loved music and had classical tastes' (23).

For the last chapter to be called 'David and Goliath' is to re-assert at the book's end that moral opacity in which the characters have been seen to lose their way from the very beginning. Huish is by far the most evil of the trio, not just devoid of principle but actively relishing his freedom from all restraining scruples. His is the sort of freedom Milton's Satan revels in and the two have much in common as 'Mr Whish' – the 'clerk' who laughs at his own namelessness – materialises under the awed scrutiny of Davis after he has disclosed his plan to destroy Attwater:

The Captain looked at him. Huish sat there, preening his sinister vanity, glorying in his precedency in evil; and the villainous courage and readiness of the creature shone out of him like a candle from a lantern. Dismay and a kind of respect seized hold on Davis in his own despite .... He had raised the devil, he thought; and asked who was to control him? and his spirits quailed (126).

The echoes released by the two names David and Goliath are of course, entirely misleading and mocking (greatly complicating Attwater's parable of the bell). The evangelist may be an unattractive even sinister figure but, except in stature, he is no Goliath who would defy the

God of the armies of Israel. Neither is Huish's intention to destroy Attwater designed to ensure that 'all the earth may know that there is a God in Israel'. He is no David: he is not 'of a fair countenance', and he is certainly not 'a cunning player on a harp'.[47]

When Attwater appears, ready to confront Huish and Davis as they make for the shore, he is accompanied by Herrick and by two natives clad in the huge diving helmets, the point of which seems to be to replicate Goliath's armour (particularly his brass headgear) and – possibly – the 'one bearing a shield [who] went before him',[48] to frighten Davis (which it does, for the heads are faceless), and to give Huish the chance to say 'Wot did I tell you ... Dyvid and Goliar all the w'y and back' (132). Whatever comfort he may have got from the analogy is short-lived, for he pays the price for misapplying a text which in this case means inverting biblical morality. Goliath wins.

Biblical allusions gone wrong are of great significance (again they are a means of casting doubt upon the text's authority) but such echoes in this chapter are almost dwarfed by those emanating from the ship's figurehead. Earlier, we may recall, when Herrick first went ashore the figurehead confronted him 'with what seemed irony'. She was like a 'defiant deity from the island' rushing forth to wreak vengeance on the intruders 'her helmeted head tossed back, her formidable arm apparently hurling something, whether shell or missile in the direction of the anchored schooner'. Herrick saw her as having for long been 'the blind conductress of a ship among the waves' and wonders whether her adventures now are really ended. He obviously hoped not, thinking that she might become *his* 'conductress': 'he could have found it in his heart to regret that she was not a goddess, nor yet he a pagan, that he might have bowed down before her in that hour of difficulty' (85).

As we see from the last chapter her adventures do continue and in a quite striking way. When Huish steps ashore on his dastardly mission, he is met by Herrick with a rifle in his hands ordering him to put his hands above his head:

> The clerk turned away from him and towards the figure-head, as though he were about to address to it his devotions; he was seen to heave a deep breath; and raised his arms (133).

He appears to be doing what Herrick had earlier said he felt like doing – offering the figurehead his obeisance. She, we have to remember, has *her* arm upraised but whether in a blessing or a threat is deliberately left vague. There is a large irony in these two faith-less, corrupt men who have so badly lost their way *seeming* to treat the figurehead with reverence and investing her with something of the aura of a divinity. For the evil Huish to be seen to be offering his devotion to the quasi-sacred symbol of seafarers is another of those moral inversions which spell out their bankruptcy.

Davis, who had started to follow Huish 'as the mesmerised follow the mesmeriser; all human considerations ... swallowed up in one abominable and burning curiosity', is summarily ordered by Herrick to halt: 'Put your back to that figure-head, do you hear me, and stand fast!' When Huish is killed, Davis watches the action, transfixed:

> Davis had not yet moved; he stood astonished, with his back to the figure-head, his hands clutching it behind him, his body inclined forward from the waist (136).

The description is a careful one: Davis's body seems to parallel the outline of the figurehead as it leans outward from the ship's bow; and we realise that what we are presented with is another example of that reflexive doubling or echoing which has characterised so much of the text's movement. The *captain* is thus 'worn' as a replica ship's figure-head on the towering body of the helmeted goddess. He becomes the talisman of the ship's talisman – an inversion which is doubly grotesque because they are both 'beached' and bereft of command. It is difficult to conceive of a more fitting symbol of absurdist alienation: the ship itself has disappeared (though it may have left an echo in the shape of the coral atoll which reminded Herrick of the 'rim of a sunken vessel'), its figurehead is firmly planted on land, and the captain, whose role it is to preside as law-giver in both a practical and moral sense to the ship's community, is now reduced to a startlingly literal example of the *mise-en-abyme* by travestying himself as a badge on the front of the figurehead.

There is irony in Davis standing with his back to this desacralised totem, facing Attwater who 'along the levelled rifle ... smiled like a red Indian'. Nothing could make clearer the hollowness of the once-protective symbol as Attwater tortures his victim by firing his bullets into the totem so that they will just graze his victim's head:

> The cruel game of which he was the puppet was now clear to Davis; three times he had drunk of death, and he must look to drink of it seven times more before he was despatched. He held up his hand.

'Steady!' he cried; 'I'll take your sixty seconds.'

'Good!' said Attwater.

The captain shut his eyes tight like a child: he held his hands up at last with a tragic and ridiculous gesture.

'My God, for Christ's sake, look after my two kids,' he said; and then, after a pause and a falter, 'for Christ's sake, Amen' (136).

Why is Davis's holding his hands up a 'tragic and ridiculous gesture'? Part of the explanation is that this traditional sign for surrender comes too late: Attwater has him at his mercy and is going to shoot him. Too late, too, one might think, for him to surrender to God after all he has done and been a party to. But part of the ridiculousness (and even some of the tragic element) can be attributed to the spectacle he presents, with his upraised arms and his back to the figurehead whose hand is outstretched above him, as though he were a priestly celebrant of his divinity's (demystified) mysteries. He provides the ironic culmination to that sequence which begins with Herrick's instinct to bow down before the figurehead as to a pagan goddess, and which was, in visual terms, replicated in Huish appearing to offer obeisance to her.

These gestures are echoed – consciously or unconsciously – some six years later in the ending of another novel, *Heart of Darkness*, where false gods are again worshipped. After hearing Marlow's account of Kurtz's death, the latter's fiancée puts out her arms, 'stretching them back' as if she, too, were about to worship the corrupt Kurtz; much as the native woman 'bedecked with powerless charms' had thrown up her arms 'rigid above her head, as though in an uncontrollable urge to touch the sky', as Kurtz is about to be carried away from her in the steamer.[49]

Davis's prayer for his children earns him his reprieve but the rebuke which accompanies it signals his deposition from authority. 'Go, and sin no more, sinful father', the 'bad' super-father commands the other. With his voice breaking 'like that of a child among the nightmares of fever', Davis delivers himself up to Attwater crying 'O! what must I do to be saved?'; and the highly-gratified pearl-fisher congratulates himself on having at last found 'the true penitent'.

Irony gets in the way here, too, however, as our suspicion that Davis is a broken reed rather than a prodigal father is confirmed in the last chapter, 'A Tail-Piece'.[50] When Herrick comes across Davis gabbling his prayers on the beach his reaction is significant – and is given twice. An exclamation 'Part of annoyance, part of amusement' breaks from him when he first catches sight of Davis on his knees 'immersed in his devotion'. When he gets near enough to overhear, he listens 'in a very mingled mood of humour and pity' (139). What does the unexpected sequence of 'annoyance', 'amusement', 'humour' and 'pity' signify? Amusement at Davis's fervour, if his conversion is real, is as out-of-place as 'annoyance', and all the more so if, as 'pity' suggests, Davis is now slightly crazed. Herrick has not shown himself to be cynical (except about his own moral capacity), so one is left with the possibility that Davis is putting on an act which serves his turn well, though Herrick's 'pity' would imply that he, at least recognises it as an opting-out, a final capitulation. The ambiguity is sustained when Davis, interrupted in the middle of his prayers by Herrick, scrambles to his feet protesting '"Mr. Herrick, don't startle a man like that! ... I don't seem some ways rightly myself since ..." he broke off' (139). In one sense Davis *should* feel alienated from his old reprobate self (assuming he had a 'self' in the first place) but the incomplete statement would suggest that his conversion hasn't supplied him with a self either. What lies beyond that 'since'? Does he mean since witnessing the death of Huish (who was very much a part of himself) and coming very near to his own? In which case he certainly seems to have derived little benefit from his conversion. Yet it is hard to believe in his derangement when he instantly grasps the significance of the *Farallone* having been set on fire. '"...you may guess from that what the news is". "The *Trinity Hall*, I guess," said the captain.'

The book ends on a note of appeal: 'why not be one of us?' – but to Herrick this is the voice of the 'dark apostle'. The 'us' he would like to be part of is not that of the Band of 'Ope as Huish derisorily put it but that Marlovian brotherhood which is founded on a clear-cut ideal of conduct and mutual self-respect. So Herrick rejects Davis's appeal and, alone once more, waits to resume his wanderings on the *Trinity Hall*; and though that is, in one sense, a ghost-ship, reminding a 'University-man' of a past existence and complacent assumptions about his place in the world, it also carries with it a reminder of aspirations which have not yet been completely extinguished. In Herrick's decision to continue his voyaging there is something, however vestigial, of that questing, Marlovian restlessness which comes from an inability to give up altogether on the notion that some moral basis *can* be discovered on which to construct a coherent and sustainable identity.

Of such a reality we shall, however, always be sceptical: as sceptical as Findlay is about the existence of Zacynthos. It will, *The

*Ebb-Tide* tells us, always remain intangible, merely rumoured, because art – which offers the only hope of representing it – cannot find any way of doing so which does not involve our getting lost in a quest among forms and endlessly receding echoes which do not necessarily reach the ear of God.

## Notes

1. Joseph Conrad, Preface to *The Nigger of the 'Narcissus'* (1955), p. 23.
2. Malcolm Bradbury and James McFarlane (eds), op. cit., p. 29.
3. Paul Maixner (ed.), op. cit., 1981, pp. 454, 455.
4. Ibid., pp. 456, 457.
5. Ibid., pp. 460, 461.
6. Ibid., p. 460.
7. Op. cit., p. 47.
8. *Possibilities*, p. 123.
9. Allon White, *The Uses of Obscurity: The Fiction of Early Modernism* (1981), p. 17.
10. Joseph Conrad, *The Shadow Line*, World's Classics (1985) pp. 106, 107.
11. Quoted in Ian Watt, *Conrad in the Nineteenth Century* (1980), p. 172.
12. 'Partial Magic in the *Quixote*', in *Labyrinths* (Norfolk, Conn., 1962), p. 189. Frustratingly, this does *not* happen in the six hundred-and-second tale in any edition I have seen. However, something *like* it happens in the tale of the five-hundred-and-seventy-sixth night ('The Adventures of Hasan of Basrah') in the Powys Mathers edition.
13. John Barth, *Chimera* (Greenwich, Conn., 1972), p. 40.
14. John Barth, 'Tales Within Tales', in *The Friday Book: Essays and Other Non-Fiction* (New York, 1984), p. 236.
15. Jacques Derrida, 'The Law of Genre' in *On Narrative*, ed. W.J.T. Mitchell (Chicago, 1981), p. 61.
16. As will have been obvious, I am applying the word *genre* here to different forms and concepts of the novel.
17. Edgar A. Dryden, *The Form of American Romance* (Baltimore, 1988), p. x.
18. It is, as has been suggested, possible to see these three beachcombers as constituting three sides of collective personality, and a number of critics have done so, including Alastair Fowler: 'The four characters make up a quartette indeed, of psychological forces contending for a single mind.' ('Parables of Adventure: The Debatable Novels of Robert Louis Stevenson', in *Nineteenth Century Scottish Fiction*, ed. Ian Campbell, p. 118.)
19. Perhaps for the same reason as that attributed to Austin Roxburgh in Patrick White's *A Fringe of Leaves* after he has rescued his copy of Virgil from the bilge-water of the *Bristol Maid*: 'This sodden, and to any other eyes, repulsive trophy had the feel of a familiar and beloved object which assured him of his own reality' (p. 161).
20. Roland Barthes, *S/Z*, p. 12, quoted in *Modern Literary Theory: A Comparative Introduction* (1983), ed. Jefferson and Robey, p. 101. Ann Jefferson defines

the 'writerly' text (as opposed to the *lisible* or 'readerly') as the text
which 'demands the reader's active co-operation, and requires him to
contribute in the production and writing of the text' (p. 100).
21. Ibid., p. 102.
22. Edgar A. Dryden, op. cit., p. 213.
23. Herbert Marks, 'Echo and Narcissism', *University of Toronto Quarterly*,
   61:3 (Spring) 1992.
24. Joseph Conrad, *The Nigger of the 'Narcissus'*, p. 57.
25. Cf. p. 45 where the drunken captain is described as a 'drooping, unbut-
   toned figure that sprawled all day upon the lockers, tippling and reading
   novels'. Perhaps a little oddly, neither before nor after the voyage is
   there any other indication of Davis having such a passion for reading.
26. Op. cit., p. 124.
27. Joseph Conrad, *Heart of Darkness* (1975), p. 38–9.
28. Allon White, op. cit., p. 62.
29. Quoted by Fowler, op. cit., p. 123.
30. Fowler, op. cit., p. 123.
31. Alexander John Findlay (1812–75) published six large nautical directories, including one on the South Pacific Ocean. He is linked indirectly
   with the Stevenson family and he wrote a dissertation on *The English
   Lighthouse System* (for which he won the Society of Arts medal), later
   published as *Lighthouses and Coast Fog Signals of the World*.
32. *Heart of Darkness*, p. 54.
33. 'On Some Technical Elements of Style in Literature', p. 37.
34. José Ortega y Gasset, 'Reality, Leaven of Myth', in *Meditations on Quixote*
   (New York, 1961), p. 139. I was reminded of this passage by coming
   across it in Edgar Dryden's *The Form of American Romance*.
35. I am indebted to Dr. Robert Dingley for this suggestion.
36. Huish is the one who glories 'in his precedency in evil' (126) and is
   completely without conscience. The name is unusual enough to call attention to itself. In Cottle's *Dictionary of Surnames* it is given as an alternative
   spelling of Hewish. Originally the word signified a measure or hide of
   land and the name is thus, according to Cottle, the equivalent of Hyde.
   Huish also calls himself 'Hay' and in his much-insisted-on cockney dialect
   this is also going to sound something like Hyde.
37. Joseph Conrad, *Lord Jim* (1966), p. 291.
38. Frederick J. Hoffman, *Freudianism and the Literary Mind* (Baton Rouge,
   1957), p. 186.
39. Ibid., p. 186.
40. What happens at the brook Jabok is surely one of the most powerful of
   all representations of the impact on the erring son of the conflict between
   filial ambitions and paternal authority. At the core of the story is the fact
   that Jacob cheats his father into conferring on him his authority (the
   blessing) by assuming the identity of another, so acquiring that authority
   by the avoidance of confrontation. The fact that he has gained the
   blessing by a stratagem which involves denying his own identity haunts
   Jacob. In the struggle with the stranger he refuses to let him go until he
   gets the absolving blessing *and with it acquires a new name* (Genesis
   32:28).

41. In Luke 4:8 Christ addresses these words to the devil but in Matthew 16:23 he uses them to rebuke Peter, adding 'thou art an offence unto me for thou savourest not the things that be of God but those that be of men.'

42. *Lord Jim*, p. 291.

43. *Heart of Darkness*, p. 18.

44. Ibid., p. 25.

45. The words are those of Elizabeth Grosz, distinguishing between Freud's postulate and Kristeva's notion of the 'imaginary' father in *Sexual Subversions*, p. 88.

46. His is the philosophy of the administrator at the Central Station in *Heart of Darkness*: 'Serve him right. Transgression – punishment – bang! Pitiless, pitiless. That's the only way' (p. 37).

47. 1 Samuel 17:45; 17:42; 16:16.

48. Ibid., 17:7.

49. *Heart of Darkness*, p. 88.

50. Interestingly, in 'The Story of a Lie' (which is bound in with *The Ebb-Tide* in the Tusitala edition), the short title of Chaper IV is 'The Filial Relation', of Chaper V it is 'The Prodigal Father at Home' and of Chapter VI it is 'The Prodigal Father Goes On'.

# 9

# *Weir of Hermiston:*
# The Horizon of Silence

What is there to say at this late date? Let me think; I'm trying to
think. Same old story. Or. Or? Silence.

> John Barth, *Lost in the Funhouse*

' ... the lighted strip of history is past and all our Kings and
Queens; we are gone; our civilization; the Nile; and all life. Our
separate drops are dissolved; we are extinct, lost in the abysses of
time, in the darkness.'

> Louis, in Virginia Woolf's *The Waves*

'Son and father?' he cried. 'Father and son? What d - d unnatural
comedy is all this?'

> 'The Rajah's Diamond'

Reading through *The Ebb-Tide* when he received his copy, Stevenson
confessed to being delighted with it: 'I did not dream it was near as
good.' What he takes particular pride in is having surmounted the
formal challenge he had quite consciously set himself: 'It gives me
great hope, as I see I *can* work in that constipated mosaic manner,
which is what I have to do just now with "Weir of Hermiston".'[1]
There are surely few readers of Stevenson who would not be surprised
at the application of what seems to be a quite reasonable summary
of *The Ebb-Tide*'s narrative form to *Weir of Hermiston*. Several readings later, however, the analysis will seem more just, though it has
to be said that there is nothing at all costive about the style of the
book which is, on the contrary, quite exceptionally well-regulated.

In truth, what is perhaps the most striking stylistic feature of the
work is its poise, for this is a text finely balanced on the brink of
dissolution. While the brilliant 'Introductory' is, without doubt, the
most succinctly powerful of all Stevenson's openings, its sombre

message forecasts silence, disappearance and death. Initially it might seem as though the author were simply giving his own tale a firm place in Scottish cultural history, but almost the contrary is true for, underneath it, there is no solid ground. Instead, there is a haunting sense of instability and evanescence in all things (even the art of narrative) which dissolves into an endlessly receding echo.

## Of First and Last Things

The first image our eye is drawn to is the embodiment of isolation and eschatological loneliness: a tombstone set 'in the wild end of a moorland parish'. Upon this monument there is further discouragement, not least for the writer and reader of novels: an inscription which has not stood up well to the passage of time, for its 'verses' are 'half-defaced'. Nor is the name of the man commemorated by the stone revealed to us which suggests that it has been part of the defacement: that it, too, has been rendered illegible or, to use a word which recurs throughout most of Stevenson's novels (including this one), obliterated. But, nameless though the dead man may be, through having carved for himself a place in the mind and the lore of the *volk* as representative of that constituency which has suffered death for its beliefs, he has had conferred upon him the generic identity of the Praying Weaver of Balweary.

A disjunction has none the less occurred between the historical and the mythic; in fact, it is a double disjunction. Claverhouse, who is alleged to have killed the weaver, we know to have existed historically. That the weaver himself did, we have only the word of the author whose proof is the tombstone. Except, of course, that it isn't, for no (legible) name appears upon it. For the weaver to be detached from his tombstone and his name is to cast doubts not just on his historical reality but on his fictional reality as well. The author tells us he existed and then conspicuously fails to supply the written evidence.

Empty tombs make good absent centres, it would seem. It is around the alleged weaver under his alleged tombstone that a significant amount of the action revolves. Both Archie and Kirstie, having kept their respective trysts by the Weaver's Stone, testify to their awareness of the weaver's presence, Kirstie providing the best *reprise*, '"God but yon puir, thrawn, auld Covenanter's seen a heap o' human natur since he lookit his last on the musket-barrels, if he

never saw nane afore", she added, with a kind of wonder in her eyes'
(116). But proof of that presence is nowhere to be found – certainly
not in the written text of the tomb which is illegible – and so all we
are left to fall back on is the legend which haunts about the tombstone and which comes to us readers through the prism of another
legend. The Praying Weaver, then, exists only in folk-memory, that
same folk-memory which we see a few sentences later busily – but
by no means reliably so – amending and correcting itself as it fash-
ions yet another legend out of the events surrounding yet another
tragedy in the Deil's Hags whereby one man died and another – the
principal character in *this* story – 'vanished from men's knowledge'.

At some point in the past, John Graham of Claverhouse, Viscount
Dundee, killed a large number of Covenanters (a fundamentalist
Presbyterian sect which had challenged the authority of Anglicanism)
and was himself killed defending the Stewarts and Catholicism in
1689. This first event sets in train a series of echoes which, many generations later, reaches the ear of the narrator of Archie's story. But there's
nothing romantic about this continuum with the past – in fact,
there's not really a continuum. After Claverhouse all historical fact
dissolves in folk-lore whereby the 'folk' *constructs* its past to maintain its coherence and give itself the illusion of participating in a
continuum and a shared destiny. This is the shadowy *provenance* of
the Praying Weaver who, in investing the tale with his presence,
invests the past with doubt and uncertainty. As such he is more the
expression of a *desire* for that continuum with the past than its proof.

To pursue this argument further might seem to be flogging a dead
echo. It is a risk that has to be run, however, for into his very first
paragraph Stevenson has unobtrusively introduced another tale of
another dedicated Covenanter; one whose verifiable historical reality
is distilled in yet another text, that of Sir Walter Scott's *Old Mortality*,
the true author of which, we are invited to believe, is the itinerant
Covenanter himself.

The one-time existence of 'Old Mortality' is, like that of Claverhouse,
beyond doubt. Scott gives a deliberately precise and detailed account
of his life in *his* 'Author's Introduction' printed along with the 1830
edition of his novel. There we learn that Robert Paterson *alias* 'Old
Mortality', was born in 1715, became an ardent Cameronian and
from about 1758 deserted his sizeable family in favour of his calling.
His interpretation of the latter led to a passionate commitment to
keeping alive the memory of fallen Covenanters. Accordingly, he
travelled the southern moorlands erecting monuments – he was

fortunately the leaseholder of a quarry – and cleaning and repairing those which had suffered the ravages of time. He died, the 'Author's Introduction' tells us with precision, on 14 February 1801, having sired two daughters and three sons, one of whom set a precedent for Archie Weir by emigrating to America.

All of these details are vouched for by a respected antiquarian friend (John Train) of Scott's whose testimony in the form of a letter forms a substantial part of the Introduction. So, far from there being a paucity of evidence about *this* Covenanter, we are almost smothered by a wealth of scrupulously recorded detail (for a further example, both living and funeral expenses are considerately provided). No obliterated tombstone here, we might conclude; and we would be wrong. The most interesting of all the details supplied is the one the antiquarian is unable to verify: the whereabouts of 'Old Mortality's' own grave. Despite the strenuous efforts by Scott's correspondent ('for the purpose of erecting a small monument to his memory') no trace of his resting-place has been found since 'his death is not registered in the session book of any of the neighbouring parishes'. Lest we have missed the poignancy of this monumental lapse, Mr Train dilates upon it:

> I am sorry to think, that in all probability, this singular person, who spent so many years of his lengthened existence in striving with his chisel and mallet to perpetuate the memory of many less deserving than himself, must remain even without a single stone to mark out the resting-place of his mortal remains.[2]

Thus if, initially, Stevenson's nameless Covenanter seems to contrast sharply with the almost over-documented life of Robert Paterson, the two novels do meet at the vanishing-point of a nameless grave. But thereafter they take very different directions.

Scott, having apparently casually taken the edge off the clarity of his own historical documentation by, so to speak, planting an absent headstone, goes on to provide a *second* frame-tale for his narrative in which a *second* headstone is foregrounded. 'Old Mortality' has told the bits and pieces of the story we are about to hear to Peter Pattieson, a schoolmaster, who has, in his own words embodied them '[in] one compressed narrative'. But Pattieson – as well as 'Old Mortality' – has vanished before his narrative appears in print, and so the text becomes a monument to both. However, in contrast to the small but troubling detail which leaves the old Covenanter's history incomplete, Pattieson (that faint echo of Paterson) is provided with an amply-inscribed, 'handsome' headstone by his 'superior and patron', Jedediah Cleishbotham. The latter is a figure (or a device) of some importance whose intrusive annotations help to frame Pattieson's tale and in doing so gives a garrulous voice to the 'present'. That framing is, of course, extended in his Introduction to *Tales of My Landlord* where he sets himself up as a competitor (just as he has done with 'Old Mortality' on the matter of tombstones), taking issue with Pattieson's method and casting aspersions on his judgement.[3]

No such figure as Jedediah Cleishbotham occurs in *Weir of Hermiston*. The tale told by the narrator-author here takes as its *point de départ* a tombstone with no legible inscription, and the vista he opens up discloses not the colour and vitality of Scott's historical realism but a grey desolation peopled by ghosts and ending, full circle, in silence and death. Interestingly, the reminder of 'Old Mortality', whose chisel had 'clinked on that lonely gravestone', leads us back not to Peter Pattieson's 'compressed narrative' of stirring deeds, but through Pattieson, who had *heard* '[t]he clink of a hammer' and seen the old man busy with his chisel, to 'Old Mortality' himself – of whom no physical trace remained by the time his tale was told. Introduction is speaking to Introduction, it would seem; frame-tale to frame-tale.[4]

Time may have obscured the details of that earlier death on the moor, but, since then, 'the silence of the moss has been broken once again by the cry of the dying'. Already time has been at work on this more recent tragedy and the facts of the story have to be disinterred from the buried past and guessingly reassembled like the bones of an incomplete skeleton. It is a telling metaphor in this tale where *everything* stands on the edge of oblivion: 'the facts of the story itself, like the bones of a giant buried there and half dug up, survived, naked and imperfect, in the memory of the scattered neighbours'. Fragmentation and indeterminacy will therefore once again characterise the story though much more subtly than in *The Ebb-Tide*; and permeating everything is a sense of loss, loss realised or impending, and an unassuaged hunger for fulfilment. The past can, of course, never be retrieved, however much Kirstie may ache for her lost motherhood or Archie for the dyadic relationship with his father – or the tale for the lost bones of its own incomplete skeleton. That last consideration alone will infuse into the text a provisionality as the tale seeks to reconstruct itself 'amid the silence of the young and the additions and corrections of the old'. The silence is surely ominous, suggesting that it is to this it will return – a reading which can only be reinforced by the ambiguous closing words of the 'Introductory' which refer to the resurrected story as 'the tale of the Justice-Clerk and of his son, young Hermiston, that vanished from men's knowledge'.

In a text which is itself so assured and so eloquent, it is remarkable that at every turn it is threatened by silence. Retrospectively, we can see that every one of the constituent dramas has death at its centre. From the Praying Weaver who fell victim to Claverhouse we pass first to a catalogue of fatalities which, hardly surprisingly, led to the extinction of the male Rutherfords:

> One bit the dust at Flodden; one was hanged at his peel door by James the Fifth; another fell dead in a carouse with Tom Dalyell; while a fourth (and that was Jean's own father) died presiding at a Hell-Fire Club, of which he was the founder (3).

Then Mrs Weir, after her brief but not unproductive sojourn in what to her was unquestionably a vale of tears, succumbs early in the piece, thus eliciting her husband's only known compassionate remark addressed to her in public: 'puir bitch'. This is followed by the *casus belli* between Archie and his father, the graphically described execution of Duncan Jopp, Archie's vocal objection to which leads to his exile at Hermiston. This will, of course, culminate in the central episode of the death of Frank Innes, but before then Archie will have been fully briefed by Kirstie on the remarkably uniform end of her ancestors of whom 'one after another closed his obscure adventures in mid-air, triced up to the arm of the royal gibbet or the Baron's dule-tree' (54). Kirstie's own father had come to a bloody but respectable end, having been set upon by no fewer than six thieves at a ford where he acquitted himself so well that he was able to '[ride] for home with a pistol-ball in him, three knife-wounds, the loss of his front teeth, a broken rib and bridle, and a dying horse'. Once over his threshold he finally allows himself to expire of his 'honourable injuries and in the savour of fame' (59). Lastly, death takes Kirstie's only lover, Tam, so blighting her life forever.

But silence threatens in other ways. All significant incidents and action seem to stand at a vanishing-point and the characters themselves are either, like Mrs Weir, the last of a line, like Frank Innes, doomed to an early death, or, like Weir, so lapped in isolation that silence becomes the not unwelcome condition of his paraded self-sufficiency (which so effectively repels his son). The loneliness which Kirstie feels, and the silence she sees being imposed upon her, affect the text itself, for she is the teller of tales and without her voice (and the voices of others like her) there will be no text.

The sense of isolation which pervades the text is underscored – indeed it is partly occasioned – by the discontinuity with the past and by the fact that the past itself is not a comforting and coherent reference-point but something disconcertingly elusive and indeterminate. When Archie says

'On days like this ... everything appears so brief, and fragile, and exquisite, that I am afraid to touch life. We are here for so short a time; and all the old people before us – that were here but a while since, riding about and keeping up a great noise in this quiet corner – making love too, and marrying – why, where are they now?' (89)

– when he says this, he is counterpointing the 'great noise' they kept up against silence. These ancestors are lost to them, and what colours this thinking is the fragility of the moment on the brink of an eternal eclipse rather than the comfort of family history, family succession and the transcendence of time.

If this argument is justified, the opening paragraph of Chapter 1 ('The Life and Death of Mrs Weir') takes from Adam Weir a good deal more than it gives: 'The Lord Justice-Clerk was a stranger in that part of the country; but his wife was known there from a child, as her race had been before her.' The title is a sounding one, redolent of power and Scottish history. To be described as a 'stranger in that part of the country' means, however, that there will also attach to him the notion of isolation. It is an association which will be strengthened as the paragraph goes on to detail something of the colourful and lengthy history of his wife's family, the Rutherfords of Hermiston – the first, rather casual, reference to Flodden taking them back to somewhere beyond 1513.

Weir, then, is emphatically *not* of the *volk*, and his conspicuous lack of a *provenance* draws attention to a loss of contact with the past rather than any sort of continuity. When Frank Innes tries his hand at a piece of spiteful (and patently false) etymology suggesting that 'Weir' is derived from 'weaver' (101), he merely emphasises the lack of any connection between the Lord Justice-Clerk and all that accrues round the Weaver's Stone.

Thus though it would appear that the tale we are listening to (before it vanishes from men's knowledge) deals very much with the past, it is a lost and misread past, which is one reason why the voice of the narrator, piecing together the tale, often sounds hesitant and lonely. More surprisingly, Weir's voice also imparts something of that loneliness as it clings tenaciously to a dialect from whose ethnic background its owner has become estranged (while at the same time ostentatiously distancing himself from his son's English).

If Weir appears not to be rooted anywhere in particular, to have no discernible past (one of Jean Rutherford's attractions in his eyes is that *her* estate will supply him with a title when he gets to the Bench), it would seem that his wife is anchored very securely in a line reaching back many centuries. Yet she, too, is an isolated figure, alienated from her turbulent ancestors by being so utterly unlike them that she seems to have contrived a separate line of uncontaminated descent. And she is the last of the race; after her the voice of these Rutherfords falls silent.

In an early review (1896) Quiller-Couch noted that, in his new style of narrative, Stevenson gives his characters 'a formal and sometimes ... very lengthy introduction' when even 'the unfortunate Mrs Weir is prefaced with a list of ancestors whom she did not resemble'. And he adds that Weir, Kirstie and her four brothers all 'sit for their portraits (like the Australian cricketers) before they begin to play'.[5] Quiller-Couch is quite right in his observation but he misses Stevenson's point: they are deliberately introduced formally and placed like figures sitting for a portrait – against a past from which they have become, or are in process of becoming, alienated. All are, in the words of a critic of our own day, heading towards 'the horizon of silence'.

The wraith-like Jean Rutherford is represented almost as the ghost of the past, seemingly more a biological sport than a true descendant of her line, embodying nothing of the vigour which had sustained it for so long. A withered, *defaced* figure, she provides rapidly-fading testimony to the obliteration of her 'race':

> At the first she was not wholly without charm. Neighbours recalled in her, as a child, a strain of elfin wilfulness, gentle little mutinies, sad little gaieties, even a morning gleam of beauty that was not to be fulfilled. She withered in the growing, and (whether it was the sins of her sires or the sorrows of her mothers) came to her maturity depressed, and, as it were, defaced; no blood of life in her, no grasp or gaiety; pious, anxious, tender, tearful, and incompetent (4).

Yet though the last of the Rutherfords may have inherited nothing of the red-blooded, brawling temper of the tribal fathers, she is still the expression of one aspect of their turbulent history, at the centre of which there had been an almost institutionalised injustice. The successful perpetuation of the line over so many generations, which has been a matter of such pride in the Rutherford men, has been achieved at great costs to wives and mothers. Thus in a text resonant with voices, we hear not only the loud, potent and unruly voice of the Rutherford males, but, through (if not in) Jean, the long-suppressed voice of their women. Like a Greek chorus, they *condemn* that 'heroic' past which has ensured their subjugation and, through the last descendant, seek an end to its tyranny:

> In all these generations, while a male Rutherford was in the saddle with his lads, or brawling in a change-house, there would be always a white-faced wife immured at home in the old peel or the later mansion-house. It seemed this succession of martyrs bided long, but took their vengeance in the end, and that was in the person of the last descendant, Jean. She bore the name of the Rutherfords, but she was the daughter of their trembling wives (3–4).

What the voice of these 'martyrs' (a strong word, perhaps not untouched with irony, which postulates a link with the Praying Weaver) bears witness to is that no uniform view of the past is possible; that the past itself is not so much all of a piece as all in pieces. Systematically and even ruthlessly, Stevenson has deconstructed it as a point of reference, and there are times when he invests the process with a sort of cosmic irony.

Thus when 'chance cast [Jean Rutherford] in the path of Adam Weir' the resulting marriage might, regarded theoretically and historically, appear eminently sensible: the last of an old Border family making an alliance with the then new Lord Advocate, a 'risen' man destined to become a power in the land. It is the sort of arrangement which has traditionally been regarded as conferring benefit all round by ensuring the old family's future health and welfare, enabling the newcomer to assimilate himself, and greatly strengthening society.

But the character of the participants here suggests an almost Hogarthian parody of such a process. Of course mismatches were not uncommon when a union was brought about primarily for dynastic reasons but the sheer incongruity of this one baffles even the narrator who searches in vain for an explanation: 'perhaps [Weir] belonged to that class of men who think a weak head the ornament of women – an opinion invariably punished in this life' (5). Perhaps the attraction was something more material: 'There was ready money and there were broad acres, ready to fall wholly to the husband, to lend dignity to his descendants, and to himself a title, when he should be called upon the Bench.' Perhaps there was even a hint of a deeply buried personal feeling – but one which, unflatteringly, turns the already wraith-like Jean into even more of a ghost:

> it would seem he was struck with her at the first look. 'Wha's she?' he said, turning to his host; and, when he had been told, 'Ay,' says he, 'she looks menseful. She minds me –'; and then after a pause (which some have been daring enough to set down to sentimental recollections), 'Is she releegious?' (4)

If part of poor Jean's attractions was her capacity to remind Weir of someone else, his attraction to her (if it existed at all) was that of the utterly unknown. The narrator can do no more than speculate:

> On the side of Jean, there was perhaps some fascination of curiosity as to this unknown male animal that approached her with the roughness of a ploughman and the aplomb of an advocate. Being so trenchantly opposed to all she knew, loved, or understood, he may well have seemed to her the extreme, if scarcely the ideal, of his sex (5).

Reinvigorating a dynasty asserts a continuum with the past and a hopeful confidence in the future; but the characterisation of Adam Weir and Jean Rutherford argues for neither of these necessary conditions. Isolation and self-sufficiency distinguish the former and dynastic exhaustion and domestic incompetence the latter. Weir may be a 'risen' man but he is not a 'new' man bringing a dynamic, innovative spirit to re-animate an all-but-defunct line. He cannot be compared with, for example, Donald Farfrae arriving in Casterbridge. It is acknowledgedly 'late in the day' that he begins 'to think upon a wife', for he is by then over forty. Moreover he is deeply conservative, a fervent upholder of the *status quo* – it is his profession – and hostile to new ideas. He is even something of an anachronism with his defiant adherence to the dialect (despite his deracination) and his parading of a plebeian coarseness on (and off) the Bench.

As for Jean Rutherford, she is so much a ghost that when she dies there is not much change to be noticed:

> She was never interesting in life; in death she was not impressive; and as her husband stood before her, with his hands crossed

behind his powerful back, that which he looked upon was the very image of insignificance.

Like virtually everyone else in *Weir of Hermiston* (the exception is Weir himself) her vocation has not been fulfilled, but it is one which would have done nothing for the House of Rutherford and would have been derided by her philoprogenitive forbears:

> It seems strange to say of this colourless and ineffectual woman, but she was a true enthusiast, and might have made the sunshine and the glory of a cloister. Perhaps none but Archie knew that she could be eloquent; perhaps none but he had seen her – her colour raised, her hands clasped or quivering – glow with gentle ardour (10).

As Mrs Weir, however, she has virtually no voice of her own. Utterly inept at housekeeping, she cowers under her lord's wrathful expostulations, 'speechless and fluttering'. At other times she seems to converse almost entirely in biblical texts which constitute her 'body of divinity'. They very nearly constitute her own body as well, for 'she put them on in the morning with her clothes and lay down to sleep with them at night' (9). Nonetheless it is through these texts that she comes to assert herself against her husband.

To the surprise of all, it would seem, this 'scarce natural union' produces a son. Not the least astonished is Mrs Weir herself who, though she finds great difficulty in comprehending 'the miracle of her motherhood', nonetheless seems to take on a new lease of life when she is with the boy: 'her frosted sentiment bloomed again, she breathed deep of life, she let loose her heart in that society' (8). She does quite a bit more, in fact, for she exerts herself strenuously to indoctrinate the child with her own religious precepts and to infuse into him her altogether excessive piety. In this one connection alone, we are told, she had 'conceived and managed to pursue a scheme of conduct'. It was a predictable one: 'Archie was to be a great man and a good; a minister if possible, a saint for certain' (8). His feet must, therefore, be placed firmly on the paths of righteousness and the right models put before him; so he is subjected to a course of reading in Rutherford's *Letters* and Scougal's *Grace Abounding*. To bring home to him her message, she would take the child to the Deil's Hags and sit with him on the Weaver's Stone recounting the persecutions of the past 'till their tears ran down'.

Thus from an early stage, young Archie has been made to confront death in the putative company of the martyred weaver. For the reader, however, who has been already conditioned to regard the past with a certain mistrust, Mrs Weir's hopes that by 'blooding' Archie at the Weaver's Stone she will recruit her son to the cause, do not strike him as very promising. That feeling is greatly reinforced by the fact that the past she, Jean Rutherford, weeps for – the past which witnessed the persecution of the Covenanters – is for her as much as for anyone else a great muddle. For a member of her own house had taken part in the persecution which was so hateful to her spiritual sympathies: 'Her great-great-grandfather had drawn the sword against the Lord's anointed on the field of Rullion Green and breathed his last (tradition said) in the arms of the detestable Dalyell' (8). It is clear from the parenthesis that some of these matters are not beyond dispute, that 'tradition' may be refining and intensifying the lady's suffering by virtue of the credence allowed to it; and the sense of confusion about the 'reality' of the past grows along with signs of its capricious reconstruction in the folk-memory.

As if the past were not confused and confusing enough for Mrs Weir, she tortures herself further by transplanting her husband into it (a worrying enough initiative in itself) and reaches an alarming conclusion:

> Nor could she blind herself to this, that had they lived in those old days, Hermiston himself would have been numbered alongside of Bloody Mackenzie and the politic Lauderdale and Rothes, in the band of God's immediate enemies (8).

In a sense she *succeeds* in translating him into the past. '*Persecutor*', we are told 'was a word that knocked upon the woman's heart; it was her highest thought of wickedness … '. What is more, she 'had a voice for that name of *persecutor* that thrilled in the child's marrow', so that when the three of them are travelling in Hermiston's carriage and the crowd cries 'Down with the persecutor! down with Hanging Hermiston!' young Archie immediately confronts his mother with the implications of her teachings, *vis-à-vis* the conduct of his father. Mrs Weir can only label such questions 'undutiful' and pass on to safer subjects, leaving on the child's mind 'an obscure but ineradicable sense of something wrong' (9).

Not unlike Stevenson's nurse, 'Cummy', Mrs Weir's view of the universe was 'all lighted up with a glow out of the doors of hell'. So, determined above all things on her son's salvation, she has from earliest days swaddled him in an asbestos-blanket of biblical texts.

What she has been unwilling to recognise, however, is that her heroic fire-fighting also involves her in a secret war against her husband:

> The mother's honesty was scarce complete. There was one influence she feared for the child and still secretly combated; that was my lord's; and half unconsciously, half in a wilful blindness, she continued to undermine her husband with his son. As long as Archie remained silent, she did so ruthlessly, with a single eye to heaven and the child's salvation; but the day came when Archie spoke (11).

Archie has become increasingly aware of the discrepancies between his father's conduct and his mother's precepts. It didn't really need the abuse from the populace and his father's investiture with the word 'persecutor', abhorred above all other words, to convince the child that there was 'something wrong'. There were other, perhaps less significant, indications such as Weir's language 'that the child had been schooled to think coarse', and which included words 'that Archie knew to be sins in themselves'. But the tally didn't end there:

> Tenderness was the first duty, and my lord was invariably harsh. God was love; the name of my lord (to all who knew him) was fear. In the world, as schematised for Archie by his mother, the place was marked for such a creature. There were some whom it was good to pity and well (though very likely useless) to pray for; they were named reprobates, goats, God's enemies, brands for the burning; and Archie tallied every mark of identification, and drew the inevitable private inference that the Lord Justice-Clerk was the chief of sinners (11).

The vengeance of the downtrodden Rutherford women is, it seems, taking its toll.

What brings matters to a head between mother and son and causes the latter to speak out is the impact which one text in particular has had on the child. As it happens, it is the same text from Matthew (7:1) which so troubled Stevenson, young and old: 'Judge not, that ye be not judged'.[6] Archie's emerging oedipal instinct is a sure one as he turns his mother's text against the seat of his father's power: 'If judging were sinful and forbidden, how came papa to be a judge? to have that sin for a trade? to bear the name of it for a distinction?' So the narrator renders Archie's question.

Being precociously logical, Archie concludes that, given the obviously deplorable state of the paternal soul, the continued cohabitation
of himself and his mother with such a reprobate cannot be justified.
His mother is appalled at the comprehensive success of her instruction:

> The woman awoke to remorse; she saw herself disloyal to her
> man, her sovereign and bread-winner, in whom (with what she
> had of worldliness) she took a certain subdued pride. She expati-
> ated in reply on my lord's honour and greatness; his useful services
> in this world of sorrow and wrong, and the place in which he
> stood, far above where babes and innocents could hope to see or
> criticise. But she had builded too well (12).

The texts have triumphed. Archie is relentless, showing himself a
true son of Stevenson as well as his mother by taking particular
exception to his father's sobriquet of 'the Hanging Judge' ('it seems
he's crooool!'). To his mother's consternation he caps his exegesis
with another of her texts (interestingly misapplied): 'It were better
for that man if a mile-stone [sic] were bound upon his back and him
flung into the deepestmost pairts of the sea' (12). Mrs Weir is duly
horrified and rather lamely tries to undo the damage by reminding
her son that 'Ye're to honour faither and mother, dear, that your
days may be long in the land.' More usefully, she attempts to turn
the tables on him by asking 'arena *you* setting up to *judge*?' But her
success is distinctly limited:

> no doubt it is easy thus to circumvent a child with catchwords, but
> it may be questioned how far it is effectual. An instinct in his
> breast detects the quibble, and a voice condemns it. He will instantly
> submit, privately hold the same opinion. For even in this simple
> and antique relation of the mother and the child, hypocrisies are
> multiplied (12–13).

Inherent in that last sentence there is a sad inevitability and again
a sense of loss. Alienation of son from father is clearly in prospect,
but the rupturing of the umbilical line of communication between
mother and child seems particularly definitive, as though moral
isolation were a condition of existence; and it brings with it its own
corrupting form of silence implicit in those multiplying hypocrisies.
Clearly this is not a simple description of the process of growing up:
the child is *not* finding his own voice, he is repressing it and finding
an aggrieved silence instead.

To review what has been argued, explicitly and implicitly, so far. *Weir of Hermiston*, even in its very title, might seem to be postulating a healthy continuum with the past which will link Scottish society of the early nineteenth century with its political and cultural antecedents in the later seventeenth century, all interpreted by a narrator from his vantage point in the present day of the eighteen-nineties. But to construe the text thus is, in fact, to show how hard the reader strives to become author, to 'write' a certain comforting sort of historical romance more or less in the manner of Sir Walter Scott. In fact, no continuum with the past is asserted in *Weir of Hermiston*, no Scott-like assumption put forward that there is a past there to be read (if only it can be approached with appropriate qualifications). True, the author would seem almost to encourage such expectations testifying to his awareness of his reader's needs, or, at least, demands; but his constant thwarting of such an expectation is proof of his own greater need to deny it. At times the whole of *Weir of Hermiston* seems to be predicated on a dialectic of disappointed hopes and it is one which informs its structure as well as its individual dramas.

Thus the Scott-like possibilities inherent in the Weaver's Stone are converted into disappointment – with the conspicuous assistance of Scott himself. First, hopes are raised by the invocation of the name of 'Old Mortality'; then they are dashed when it is revealed that, despite the efforts of 'Old Mortality' himself (and despite the legend recounted in the Introduction to Scott's novel that such chiselled incisions remain in their pristine condition forever), the tombstone's inscription is illegible.

Readers who expect a historical romance may again feel their hearts rise and again reach for their quills when they come across the Lord Justice Clerk's name flourishing in the first few words at the beginning of Chapter 1, for the title itself is the embodiment of so much Scottish political and legal history. But even before the end of the sentence the hopeful prospect has been extinguished. Far from being a figure of authority with his roots deep in the nation's culture, he is 'a stranger in this country', and as the tale progresses he is more and more seen to be an exceptionally isolated and self-sufficient figure who has come from nowhere and who is going to disappear leaving nothing behind but his legal judgements.

If the Weirs of Hermiston are doomed to vanish, the old warring race of the Rutherfords, with the death of Jean, have done so. Again, the opening roll-call of their colourful exploits promises a stirring foray into Scottish history only for the reader's attention to be re-directed to the last of the family so that he can appreciate how little she resembles them. When she dies, so does the name of these Rutherfords. Ironically, this meekest of women is partly responsible for blocking off the one remaining hope that survives in her son, for she has helped to instil into Archie a deep antagonism towards his father, further ensuring the isolation of both. Weir's responsibility for this situation is, of course, also considerable, priding himself as he does on his self-sufficiency and his domestic unsociability. Rarely speaking himself, when he does so it often results in others being left speechless: we hear of a family home which 'at the least ruffle in the master's voice ... shuddered into silence' (29), or, at another time, that ' [t]he man was mostly silent; when he spoke at all, it was to speak of the things of the world, always in a worldly spirit' (11), and Archie is duly repelled.

As the generations within the tale are alienated from each other, so are they all from their cultural and political history. Defaced tombstones, silently eloquent of an obliterated or at least an inaccessible and uncertain past, constitute their inheritance, and they are replicated in dying dynasties whose names are disappearing and (as we shall see) in the dying art of narrative itself.

In Randolph Stow's remarkable book *Tourmaline*, the Law, who is the principal character and narrator, pays a daily visit to the War Memorial, his 'rendez-vous with the world', by means of which he can bolster the sense of his own reality ('Those names give me a name'). The characters in *Weir of Hermiston* are constantly keeping a rendez-vous at *their* war memorial – but with what? With, I would argue, a simulacrum of the past which is hollow: theirs is a rendezvous with emptiness. The result is that all of them – including the markedly tentative narrator from a still later generation – suffer a diminution of their reality. All of them seem to be about to move out of focus, to fade from the scene just as Jean Weir has done. For this we have been prepared by the Introductory which, unusually, alerts us to the emptiness at the end of the tale before we have even heard the beginning.

'If you are going to make a book end badly, it must end badly from the beginning', Stevenson wrote to J. M. Barrie in November 1892 when he was working on *Weir of Hermiston*. In this case, however, the story doesn't so much end badly as disappear; nonetheless its disappearance has been predicated from the very beginning when, in the Introductory, our attention is firmly drawn to that horizon of silence.

## A Moorland Helen

When re-telling Kirstie's violent tale of the vengeance exacted by her nephews for the death of their father, the narrator notes:

> Some century earlier the last of the minstrels might have fashioned the last of the ballads out of the Homeric fight and chase; but the spirit was dead, or had been reincarnated already in Mr Sheriff Scott, and the degenerate moorsmen must be content to tell the tale in prose and to make of the 'Four Black Brothers' a unit after the fashion of the 'Twelve Apostles' or the 'Three Musketeers' (59).

Once again the past is made to seem particularly remote and inaccessible: a series of arches through which the reality of these colourful events recedes to distant and obscure horizons of myth and epic. The exploits of the Elliotts come a hundred years too late for even the last of the true minstrels and the last of the genuine ballads, later even than that, then, for the heyday of minstrel and ballad, and centuries behind the great Homeric epics which are posited as their far-off progenitors. They are even too late, the narrator points out with a hint of irony, for inclusion in *The Minstrelsy of the Scottish Border*. Scott's 'reincarnation' of the Homeric spirit is in itself sufficient to confirm that, in Keats's words, it is 'too late for the fond believing lyre'; that the spirit in its original vitality and spontaneity can not *be* resurrected any more than can the complete skeleton of the tale we are reading. What Sheriff Scott has done is to arrest its ghost and imprison it in the pages of a pseudo-minstrelsy so that it might be abused by pseudo-antiquarians. 'Degenerate moorsmen' – and latter-day narrators, presumably – are deprived of access to the passion which inspired 'these ballad heroes', the Elliotts and others like them, to their individual feats of courage and devotion, and are reduced to portraying them from the outside, as it were, *en bloc* and in prose.

The narrator – degenerate or otherwise – voices a paradox. On the one hand, in his capacity as cultural guide, he assures us that the Scot 'stands in an attitude to the past unthinkable to Englishmen, and remembers and cherishes the memory of his forbears, good or bad; and there burns alive in him a sense of identity with the dead even to the twentieth generation' (54). On the other hand the whole of *Weir of Hermiston* is suffused with a modern consciousness expressive of dislocation, isolation and loneliness and an inability to

communicate with the past, the key to which seems, at times, to have
been lost. Increasingly, the tenor of the discourse on the past seems
to be gravitating towards the view expressed by Louis in the extract
from *The Waves* at the beginning of the chapter.

The paradox is exemplified in Kirstie Elliott and her family:

> No more characteristic instance could be found than in the family
> of Kirstie Elliott. They were all, and Kirstie the first of all, ready
> and eager to pour forth the particulars of their genealogy, embell-
> ished with every detail that memory had handed down or fancy
> fabricated; and, behold! from every ramification of that tree there
> dangled a halter (54).

Perhaps that last sentence offers a way of resolving the paradox:
the vitality (which Kirstie records so well) always ends in death; and
we recall the narrator's expression when he informed us that 'there
*burns alive*' in the Scot 'a sense of *identity with the dead*'. His kind of
ancestor-worship would appear to incline towards the Egyptian rather
than the Oriental. Filtered through the narrator's gloomy, sceptical
1890s' consciousness, the living past succumbs to those long perspectives which Philip Larkin talks about, and becomes imbued with a
sense of loss:

> Truly, though our element is time,
> We are not suited to the long perspectives
> Open at each instant of our lives.
> They link us to our losses ....[7]

If the past is dead and lost, what about Kirstie and her animated and
animating account of it? The answer is that Kirstie, once regarded as
a 'moorland Helen'(7) (an allusion which, in itself, presents her as a
receding figure) marks yet another ending, and it is in his portrayal
of this fact that Stevenson produces some of his finest and most memorable writing. Essentially it is a poignant representation of a woman
cheated of her destiny and all too aware of the fact.

In the Elliott family, though the men might resemble the Rutherfords
in being 'proud, lawless, violent as of right, cherishing and prolonging
a tradition' (55), in one respect there was a notable difference: the
women were their equals, and Kirstie represents them well. Though
'essentially passionate and reckless', Kirstie has 'cherished through
life a wild integrity of virtue' (55). We are introduced to her soon
after she has reached a turning-point in her life:

Kirstie was now over fifty, and might have sat to a sculptor. Long of limb, and still light of foot, deep-breasted, robust-loined, her golden hair not yet mingled with any trace of silver, the years had but caressed and embellished her. By the lines of a rich and vigorous maternity, she seemed destined to be the bride of heroes and the mother of their children; and behold, by the iniquity of fate, she had passed through her youth alone, and drew near to the confines of age, a childless woman (50).

She who had so much to contribute to the future of her 'race' will now never do so. Humiliatingly, her potent energy which should have resulted in the renewal of her line of heroes, has now to be sublimated in the drudgery of housework:

> The tender ambitions that she had received at birth had been, by time and disappointment, diverted into a certain barren zeal of industry and fury of interference. She carried her thwarted ardours into housework, she washed floors with an empty heart (51).

It has already been said that the whole of *Weir of Hermiston* seems delicately balanced on the edge of oblivion. Everything stands at a vanishing-point and the embodiment of this impending change is Kirstie herself. For this to endow her with a special poignancy depended on Stevenson being able to portray the reality of her physical appeal and her maternal needs at the same time as he revealed her own recognition that it was now too late for her ever to achieve the ambition she had long held dearest: to bear her own children. In the event, no other writer in the language (it seems to me) has bettered Stevenson's representation of such a situation in all its vibrant need, its pride and its anguish; all touched with, but not overwhelmed by, the bitterness of acknowledged defeat.

What crystallises her predicament is the arrival of Archie, banished by his father to Hermiston. 'To Kirstie, thus situate and in the Indian summer of her heart, which was slow to submit to age, the gods sent this equivocal good thing of Archie's presence' (51). She had last seen him when he was eleven; now he is a 'tall, slender, refined, and rather melancholy young gentleman of twenty', and Kirstie is deeply and complicatedly attracted to him. The list of things which impress her about him concludes thus: 'And lastly he was dark and she fair, and he was male and she was female, the everlasting fountains of interest' (52).

Of course she – already over fifty – entertains no notion of a relationship other than that of being his utterly devoted servant:

No matter what he had asked of her, ridiculous or tragic, she would have done it and joyed to do it. Her passion, for it was nothing less, entirely filled her. It was a rich physical pleasure to make his bed or light his lamp for him when he was absent, to pull off his wet boots or wait on him at dinner when he returned (52).

The narrator acknowledges that had a young man behaved towards a woman as she did towards him, it would be fair to talk of him as being in love. But Kirstie 'had not a hope or thought beyond the present moment and its perpetuation to the end of time. Till the end of time she would have had nothing altered, but still continued delight-edly to serve her idol, and be repaid (say twice in the month) with a clap on the shoulder' (52).

Her greatest pleasure is her occasional long conversation with him when she takes his late supper to his room and brings to bear all her power as an accomplished raconteur to prolong her visit. Clearly the rendering of her feelings had to be done with enormous sensitivity and tact, for the least misjudgement could have upset the balance between sentiments which 'partook of the loyalty of a clanswoman, the hero-worship of a maiden aunt, and the idolatry due to a god' – between all that and something else summed up by its *absence* in her having 'not a hope or a thought beyond the present moment and its perpetuation to the end of time'.

When Frank Innes imposes himself on Archie, Kirstie finds access to her idol less easy and that obstruction increases when Archie falls under the spell of Christina, the younger Kirstie. This last is the hardest blow to bear, for Kirstie has comforted herself with the hope that when she does lose Archie it will be to someone very much like herself: 'She had seen, in imagination, Archie wedded to some tall, powerful, and rosy heroine of the golden locks, made in her own image, for whom she would have strewed the bride-bed with delight' (112). Even such a vicarious triumph as this is to be denied her, however:

> With a sense of justice that Lord Hermiston might have envied, she had that day in church considered and admitted the attrac-tions of the younger Kirstie; and with the profound humanity and sentimentality of her nature, she had recognised the coming of fate (112).

Too clearly Kirstie sees what this means for her and for the cherished intimacy with her idol:

And again she had a vision of herself, the day over for her old-world tales and local gossip, bidding farewell to her last link with life and brightness and love; and behind and beyond, she saw but the blank butt-end where she must crawl to die. Had she then come to the lees? she, so great, so beautiful, with a heart as fresh as a girl's and strong as womanhood? It could not be, and yet it was so; and for a moment her bed was horrible to her as the sides of the grave (112–13).

In its lacerating honesty, her recognition of her fate is poignant in itself as well as being a masterpiece of authorial tact.

It is then that she hears Archie going upstairs to his room after his disagreeable conversation with Frank Innes, and, seeing the opportunity for one more of her 'night cracks', she gets up:

She rose, all woman, and all the best of woman, tender, pitiful, hating the wrong, loyal to her own sex – and all the weakest of that dear miscellany, nourishing, cherishing next her soft heart, voicelessly flattering, hopes that she would have died sooner than have acknowledged. She tore off her night-cap, and her hair fell about her shoulders in profusion. Undying coquetry awoke. By the faint light of her nocturnal rush, she stood before the looking-glass, carried her shapely arms above her head, and gathered up the treasures of her tresses. She was never backward to admire herself; that kind of modesty was a stranger to her nature; and she paused, struck with a pleased wonder at the sight. 'Ye daft auld wife!' she said, answering a thought that was not; and she blushed with the innocent consciousness of a child. Hastily she did up the massive and shining coils, hastily donned a wrapper, and with the rush-light in her hand, stole into the hall (13).

Twice in this intense and marvellously controlled passage, subliminal, voiceless thoughts animate Kirstie with a sensuous energy which, for the moment at least, banishes her earlier despondency. Nothing has changed fundamentally; this is still the woman who had clear-sightedly 'recognised the coming of fate' conveying the unwelcome, almost inconceivable, message of her own decline. Yet when she appears before Archie with her rush-light in her hand, time seems to have been vanquished:

Something – it might be in the comparative disorder of her dress, it might be the emotion that now welled in her bosom – had touched her with a wand of transformation, and she seemed young with the youth of goddesses (114).

The scene is charged with sexual significance since Kirstie's objective is the complex one of letting Archie know that she has divined his secret, defending her niece's honour which she fears is at risk, and warning Archie of the danger to himself in such an entanglement. Anxious to make clear that she is speaking in no censorious or unsympathetic spirit, she tells of her own lover and of their trysting in the same spot of the Deil's Hag and of her loss of Tam (the last with the economy of the ballad – 'he dee'd, and I wasna at the buryin'):

> Kirstie, her eyes shining with unshed tears, stretched out her hand towards him appealingly; the bright and the dull gold of her hair flashed and smouldered in the coils behind her comely head, like the rays of an eternal youth; the pure colour had risen in her face; and Archie was abashed alike by her beauty and her story. He came towards her slowly from the window, took up her hand in his and kissed it (116).

Within the structure of the text as we have it Kirstie is the fulcrum on which balances past and present; burgeoning promise, the *embonpoint* of a rich tradition, and cruel disappointment; replenishment and sterility; love and creativity and barren emptiness. What Stevenson has achieved in his fine description of her is to make her a glorious embodiment of her own descending sun: 'the bright and the dull gold of her hair flashed and smouldered in the coils behind her comely head, like the rays of an eternal youth ...'. With the light behind her, the illusion of youth can be sustained for a moment longer but what is affecting in the portrayal is the acknowledgement that it *is* an illusion. Like Cleopatra, Kirstie is well aware of her 'becomings' and like her she is well aware that they are not proof against the encroachment of time.

## The Unnatural Comedy

Into his fine representation of mature womanliness and generosity of love, Stevenson has deliberately introduced a massively discordant note: the hostile image of the Hanging Judge. That it should be made to intrude here is, however, altogether apt.

Throughout all of Stevenson's work, the youthful protagonist finds himself embroiled in conflict with the father or father-substitute. Here in the last novel of all, that conflict finds its most powerful and bitter expression. It would be that even if we did not know that Stevenson intended the judge to condemn his son to death (or, somehow, to be party to that verdict) and then to die as a direct or indirect consequence of the decision. That the long-running conflict which has smouldered on through all the novels should burst into such violent flames *à la fin des fins* is an almost shocking proof of how fiercely it had consumed Stevenson despite that large part of him which deeply loved his difficult parent.

The death of Weir, had it occurred as it was seemingly planned to do, would not have been the final oedipal resolution we might take it to be. For that to happen the son would have had to come fully into his own as a paterfamilias and survive. In breaking out of jail, thus defying paternal law, and in marrying young Kirstie and carrying her off to America (all of which seems to have been intended), Archie apparently completes the necessary rites of passage. But does *he* survive the effort? Is the victory over the father a pyrrhic one? The 'Introductory' is surely ominous when it tells us that 'young Hermiston vanished from men's knowledge'.

At any rate, the moment of his re-introduction in the middle of Kirstie's warning about sexual indulgence suggests once again the figure of a jealous father prohibiting the son's accession to manhood. And the image loses nothing of its judgemental severity in Kirstie's representation:

'I'm feared for ye, my dear. Remember, your father is a hard man, reapin' where he hasna sowed and gatherin' where he hasna strawed. It's easy speakin' but mind! Ye'll have to look in the gurly face o'm, where it's ill to look, and vain to look for mercy' (114–15).

Having delivered her sermon and won from Archie the promise that he would 'spare the girl' Kirstie suddenly 'saw in a flash how barren had been her triumph' for 'who had promised to spare Archie?' (117). What, she asks herself, was to be the end of it? Archie will 'spare' young Kirstie, but if she doesn't spare him what will *his* future be? Kirstie has little doubt: 'Over a maze of difficulties she glanced, and saw at the end of every passage, the flinty countenance of Hermiston' (117). The multiple image of Hermiston blocking off every route along which his son might navigate *his* passage to independence and maturity, imprisoning him instead in a labyrinth, is one of the most dramatic and powerful of all Stevenson's illustrations of the son's disempowerment at the hands of the father, though, significantly perhaps, the image of the labyrinth recurs with great frequency throughout his work.

Kirstie's vision of the implacable father thwarting his son's passion is replicated in the meeting between the two lovers which constitutes the next and last chapter. Ominous shadows are lengthening as the chapter opens and once more everything which gives particularity and significance to the world seems on the point of vanishing:

> It was late in the afternoon when Archie drew near by the hill path to the Praying Weaver's Stone. The Hags were in shadow. But still, through the gate of the Slap, the sun shot a last arrow, which sped far and straight across the surface of the moss, here and there touching and shining on a tussock, and lighted at length on the gravestone and the small figure awaiting him there.... His first sight of her was thus excruciatingly sad, like a glimpse of a world from which all light, comfort and society were on the point of vanishing (119).

The meeting is doomed from the start and it is so by the shadow of Lord Hermiston which Archie has brought with him from his conversation with the elder Kirstie. The disappointment of expectations for the younger woman is thus intense when she is confronted by a 'grey-faced, harsh schoolmaster' in place of her lover. Young Kirstie had been ready not just to tempt but to fall: 'to have been ready there, breathless, wholly passive, his to do what he would with', and now to be denied him is 'too rude a shock'. Archie's remonstrations about the need to be wise are therefore unlikely to be taken kindly and when he incautiously adds, '[t]he first thing that we must see to, is that there shall be no scandal about, for my father's sake. That would ruin all', he makes a fatal mistake, for 'there had come out the word she had always feared to hear from his lips, the name of his father'.

Kirstie well knows that Lord Hermiston has always been the enemy. When they talked of their future the forbidding presence of Archie's father was in both their minds – except that she 'wilfully closed the eye of thought'. For Archie, however, he was an insurmountable obstacle: 'Again and again he had touched on marriage, again and again been driven back into indistinctness by a memory of Lord Hermiston.' Kirstie has understood the source of his 'stumbling or throttled utterance' on the subject of their marriage and has suffered intensely at watching her fondest hopes thus blighted: 'these unfinished references, these blinks in which his heart spoke, and his memory and reason rose up to silence it before the words were well uttered, gave her unqualifiable agony' (122). Repeatedly this threat has supervened to disappoint her growing hopes and now it seems to her that this terrible father had 'accompanied them in their whole moorland courtship, an awful figure in a wig with an ironical and bitter smile'. Archie does not realise how deeply he has hurt Kirstie, his intentions having been of the best:

> He had come, braced and resolute; he was to trace out a line of conduct for the pair of them in a few cold, convincing sentences; he had now been there some time, and he was still staggering round the outworks and undergoing what he felt to be a savage cross-examination (123).

All he succeeds in doing in his response is to exacerbate the situation to a point were he drives her away 'shaking ... from head to foot with the barren ecstasy of temper'. Assuredly this was not the sort of ecstasy she had been anticipating and that one word 'barren' which we have heard before (once in connection with the elder Kirstie) resonates with significance: it echoes much of the contextual sterility which so blights hopes for the future, it signals the apparent failure of her relationship with Archie and her repudiation by him, and it exposes her vulnerability to Frank Innes.

Archie reacts to her outburst with bewilderment and dismay. In his inability to 'read' her or to grasp the complexity of her feelings he is his father's son, yet she is partly to blame for she *had* 'wilfully closed the eye of thought', and her ambitions to be Mrs Weir of Hermiston seem to matter as much to her as to be Archie's wife. What status, we wonder, was Frank Innes to promise to confer on her? The question reflects no unworthy suspicions: the narrator has been studiedly benign in his presentation of her but latitude has been left us in which to see her as both coquette and schemer who calculates all her effects to a nicety whether it be in the careful colour coordination of her dress or the pose she adopts on the tombstone. A great deal is said about the lengths she is prepared to go to in her brief exchange with her brother Dand, the libertine, as she leaves to go on her Sunday afternoon walk. The words are few but she and Dand understand each other very well.

It is fitting that the novel, as we have it, ends on a note of bewilderment, of hope disappointed and fulfilment indefinitely postponed. Had it been twice as long there is every indication that the ending would not have been very different. It is fitting, too, that the figure who is central to the frustration of these aspirations is that of the father. From the start Adam Weir has been perceived by his son to be the authoritarian embodiment of everything which denies dignity, grace and refinement to human society. Spurning the whole company of those who, recognising their own incompleteness, their hunger for a fuller quality of being, he derides all liberal and humane sentiment, all dissenting opinion. Inherently, life may be, as the book's author elsewhere claimed, 'monstrous, infinite, illogical, abrupt, and poignant' but Weir is single-mindedly determined that it will be regulated within the clear constraints of the law whose rigorous implementation he sees to with a relish and a punctiliousness which far exceeds even that of Attwater, his prototype in *The Ebb-Tide*.

That Weir is not without feelings one or two incidents attest, but he places no value on these and has no wish to cultivate their expression. The result is a splendid (moral) isolation, both from that putative inner self and from his fellow-men: 'My Lord Justice-Clerk was known to many; the man Adam Weir perhaps to none. He had nothing to explain or to conceal; he sufficed wholly and silently to himself' (17). He prides himself on having no need 'either of love or of popularity', with predictable consequences when, in the fullness of time, 'the tough and rough old sinner felt himself drawn to the son of his loins and sole continuator of his new family, with softnesses of sentiment that he could hardly credit and was wholly impotent to express' (21). His attempts at propitiating Archie ('so inconspicuously made') are a complete failure but the outcome is accepted with stoical equanimity. So much so that we are warned against wasting our compassion:

> Sympathy is not due these steadfast iron natures. If he failed to get his son's friendship, or even his son's toleration, on he went up the great bare staircase of his duty, uncheered and undepressed (21).

The re-appearance of the image of the staircase here is striking, and though it may seem to take its character from the endlessly repetitive treadmill in 'A Chapter on Dreams', it is actually more like its counterpart in *Kidnapped* which *does* end – in a void. In both cases, too, the isolation which surrounds the climber of the stairs is the product of the father–son conflict (Uncle Ebenezer being very much the surrogate obstructing father).

Isolation and loneliness are hallmarks of the relationship between Archie and his father – 'there were not, perhaps, in Christendom two men more radically strangers' (22) – but, as has been noted, Weir is no more intimate with his colleagues and peers. In this account of the conflict, however, Stevenson is at much greater pains than elsewhere to stress the similarities between father and son. Thus if many know the Lord Justice-Clerk but few Adam Weir, so when Frank Innes is asked if he is a friend of Archie Weir, he replies 'with his usual flippancy and more than his usual insight: "I know Weir, but I never met Archie"' and the narrator endorses this with a feeling which reflects his author's on the subject: 'No one knew Archie, a malady most incident to only sons. He flew his private signal, and none heeded it; it seemed he was abroad in a world from which the very hope of intimacy was banished' (21). To his contemporaries this simply means that he was 'thought to be a chip of the old block' (21).

The narrator also makes clear something else which scarcely figures in earlier examples of the conflict: the degree of responsibility which the son bears for the bad relations between them. True, the implicit criticism is moderated by the explanation that he has been already so wounded that he fears the pain of the likely rebuff; but, then, perhaps the charge against him becomes one of a lack of moral courage:

He made no attempt whatsoever to understand the man with whom he dined and breakfasted. Parsimony of pain, glut of pleasure, these are the two alternating ends of youth; and Archie was of the parsimonious. The wind blew cold out of a certain quarter – he turned his back upon it; stayed as little as was possible in his father's presence; and when there, averted his eyes as much as was decent from his father's face (22).

Their similarities and their shared responsibility for the bad relationship are brought out in the way the figure of silence is symmetrically deployed. Weir, we are told, 'sufficed wholly and silently to himself' (17); Archie, confronted at the dinner-table when guests are present by his father's inebriated coarseness, 'turned pale and sickened in silence' (19). When they dined alone together the father 'either spoke of what interested himself, or maintained an unaffected silence', while the son would search with exaggerated sensitivity ('like a lady's gathering up her skirts in a by-path') for a subject that would 'spare him fresh evidence either of my lord's inherent grossness or of the innocence of his inhumanity'. If he touched the wrong chord and his father 'began to abound in matter of offence', Archie would allow his share of the talk to expire, while 'my lord would faithfully and cheerfully continue to pour out the worst of himself before his silent and offended son' (22). When on such occasions his father departs for his study, Archie goes forth 'into the night and the city, quivering with animosity and scorn' (22). Clearly we are not being asked to be uncritical partisans in Archie's cause.

The self-indulgence in his animus towards his father is brought out well in his setting up a surrogate parent in Lord Glenalmond. Archie reflects the insatiable hunger for love that the Stevensonian son always reveals at some point in the conflict with the father. Here he does so (not for the first time) by precipitating a situation in which that love is charged, however lightly, with a sexual appeal. Lord Glenalmond first 'riveted' the boy's attention because of his 'exquisite disparity' with his fellow-guests at dinner, and 'as curiosity and interest are the things in the world that are the most immediately and certainly rewarded, Lord Glenalmond was attracted to the boy'. Baldly as he puts the word before us, it would be disingenuous of Stevenson if he were to pretend that 'attracted' did not have *some* libidinal suggestiveness about it.

Glenalmond disregards Weir's contemptuous dismissal of his son ('just his mother over again – daurna say boo to a goose!'), finding in Archie 'a taste for letters and a fine, ardent, modest youthful soul' and he encourages him 'to be a visitor on Sunday evenings in his bare, cold, lonely dining-room, where he sat and read in the isolation of a bachelor grown old in refinement' (19). Once again those themes of loneliness and barren emptiness recur in the context of unfulfilled parental relationship and filial longing. It is doubtful whether our hearts should be going out to Archie at this moment, however, for, in reality, he is in predatory mode and the old judge might seem to be his ideal prey:

> The beautiful gentleness and grace of the old Judge, and the delicacy of his person, thoughts, and language, spoke to Archie's heart in its own tongue. He conceived the ambition to be such another; and, when the day came for him to choose a profession, it was in emulation of Lord Glenalmond, not of Lord Hermiston, that he chose the Bar (19).

Baulked by a father who refuses to concede to the son even that much of the father's territorial dominion necessary for them to meet on, the son retaliates by creating – or seeking to create – a father in his own image which he can then fall in love with assured of a full narcissistic reciprocity.[8] Loneliness and paternal conflict will be forever abrogated for someone who can father himself and in that image also find a lover.

But Archie's stratagem doesn't really work though his appeal is eloquent:

> 'You and my father are great friends, are you not?' asked Archie once.
> 'There is no man that I more respect, Archie', replied Lord Glenalmond....
> 'You and he are so different,' said the boy, his eyes dwelling on those of his old friend, like a lover's on his mistress's (20).

But when Archie vehemently refuses to admit any pride in his father, Glenalmond dismisses his colourful expressions as 'merely literary and decorative' and Archie, reading in the 'slight tartness of the words' a prohibition, henceforth avoids the subject.

The crisis in the relationship between father and son comes to a head over the trial of Duncan Jopp. In George Orwell's celebrated essay 'A Hanging' there is a moving account of a man who, on the way to the gallows, delicately side-steps a puddle. Once accepted as factual, there is some doubt now as to whether Orwell might not have invented the incident. If so, the imaginative achievement is eclipsed by Stevenson's. Looking at the 'whey-faced, misbegotten caitiff' in the dock, Archie's attention focuses on a seemingly nonde-script detail of his dress:

> There was pinned about his throat a piece of dingy flannel; and this it was perhaps that turned the scale in Archie's mind between disgust and pity. The creature stood in a vanishing point; yet a little while, and he was still a man, and had eyes and apprehen-sion; yet a little longer, and with a last sordid piece of pageantry, he would cease to be. And here, in the meantime, with a trait of human nature that caught at the beholder's breath, he was tending a sore throat (23).

Against this insignificant creature there is ranged the full panoply of the court of justice dominated by Archie's father.

Over against him, my Lord Hermiston occupied the bench in the red robes of criminal jurisdiction, his face framed in the white wig.

Honest all through, he did not affect the virtue of impartiality; this was no case for refinement; there was a man to be hanged, he would have said, and he was hanging him. Nor was it possible to see his lordship, and acquit him of gusto in the task. It was plain he gloried in the exercise of his trained faculties, in the clear sight which pierced at once into the joint of fact, in the rude, unvarnished gibes with which he demolished every figment of defence. He took his ease and jested, unbending in that solemn place with some of the freedom of the tavern; and the rag of man with the flannel round his neck was hunted gallowsward with jeers (23–4).

The effect on Archie of the judge's treatment of the defendant (not least in his summing-up where 'the savage pleasure of the speaker in his task' reverberates through the court) is nothing less than traumatic:

> When all was over, Archie came forth again into a changed world. Had there been the least redeeming greatness in the crime, any obscurity, any dubiety, perhaps he might have understood. But the culprit stood, with his sore throat, in the sweat of his mortal agony, without defence or excuse; a thing to cover up with blushes; a being so much sunk beneath the zones of sympathy that pity might seem harmless. And the judge had pursued him with a monstrous, relishing gaiety, horrible to be conceived, a trait for nightmares. It is one thing to spear a tiger, another to crush a toad; there are æsthetics even of the slaughter-house; and the loathsomeness of Duncan Jopp enveloped and infected the image of his judge (25).

Archie's revulsion against his father (who seems less than human) is now complete; he thinks of fleeing, of some other life, but neither of these solutions will ensure his escape from 'this den of savage and jeering animals'. When he meets his father he '[will] not look at him … [can] not speak to him' and Weir himself is 'in one of his humours of sour silence'.

Archie is further appalled when he witnesses the execution of the worthless and insignificant Jopp – 'He had been prepared for something terrible not this tragic meanness' – and denounces it then and there as a 'God-defying murder'. Hurried from the scene by Frank Innes, he later makes his appearance at the Speculative Society of which he was to be the evening's president. Of course he uses the occasion to pursue his vendetta against his father but of equal importance is the common perception by his fellow members that in the conduct of the evening's business, he greatly resembles Lord Hermiston.

It is curious that in only two of Stevenson's works where the youth or young man is pitted against the power of the father does the former seriously challenge the paternal power, and these two are his first major work and his last, *Treasure Island* and *Weir of Hermiston*. And in the last-mentioned the challenge is a powerful one precisely because the son has already acquired something of the authority of the father and is willing to confront him, effectively to challenge him for more:

> under the very guns of [the Lord Justice-Clerk's] broadside Archie nursed the enthusiasm of rebellion. It seemed to him, from the top of his nineteen years' experience, as if he were marked at birth to be the perpetrator of some signal action, to set back fallen Mercy, to overthrow the usurping devil that sat, horned and hoofed, on her throne. Seductive Jacobin figments, which he had often refuted at the Speculative, swam up in his mind and startled him as with voices and he seemed to himself to walk accompanied by an almost tangible presence of new beliefs and duties (25–6).

It would, however, be too much to expect that a young man descended of such as David Balfour and Robert Herrick would not suffer a signal loss of self-confidence when he has time to size up the extent of his temerity in throwing down such a challenge to such an archetypally formidable parent. After the meeting of the 'Spec.', Archie's isolation weighs heavily on him and he sees himself 'on the brink of the red valley of war, and measured the danger and length of it with awe' (29). It is at this juncture that he learns for the first time (from Dr Gregory) that his father *does* have some feeling for him. When Weir heard from Gregory of a change in his son's condition when Archie was critically ill, he interpreted it as a change for the worse: 'He never said a word, just glowered at me (if ye'll pardon the phrase) like a wild beast.' When Gregory tells him it is a change for the better he 'distinctly heard him catch his breath'.

Though, as Archie says, the anecdote 'might be called infinitely little' it is enough to open his eyes, and enough, too, to indicate how wilful had been their closure: 'He had never dreamed this sire of his, this aboriginal antique, this adamantine Adam, had even so much heart as to be moved in the least degree for another ...' (31). With this new awareness Archie is disarmed before the combat begins. Characteristically, he now invests his father with superhuman and

irresistible powers to sift his soul, leaving himself the abject role of
the sinner waiting his proper judgement (evoking again one of
Stevenson's own most persistent nightmares): 'Words were needless, [Weir] knew all – perhaps more than all – and the hour of
judgement was at hand' (32). Words may be needless so far as Archie's
intended explanation goes, but their absence deepens and perpetu-
ates the growing rift. The father summons the son into his presence
by making him 'an imperative and silent gesture with his thumb'
and though they proceed to dine together 'there reigned over the
Judge's table a palpable silence' (32).

What follows is a sort of mini-trial: Archie remains standing before
his father, who 'took his usual seat', and is subjected to the same harsh
and jeering cross-examination which he had seen visited upon the
hapless Duncan Jopp. (Later he is to refer to himself as 'the offender'.)
As the exchange continues it takes on something of the character of
the scene in *Paradise Lost* where Christ pleads with his Father to show
more mercy to humanity's weakness.[9] Archie finds the strength to stand
by his denunciation of the treatment meted out to Jopp:

> 'It was a hideous business, Father, it was a hideous thing! Grant
> he was vile, why should you hunt him with a vileness equal to his
> own? It was done with glee – that is the word – you did it with
> glee, and I looked on, God help me! with horror' (33–4).

Hermiston is unmoved and his reply has a succinctness Attwater
might have envied:

> 'You're a young gentleman that doesna approve of Caapital
> Punishment,' said Hermiston. 'Weel, I'm an auld man that does. I
> was glad to get Jopp haangit, and what for would I pretend I wasna?
> You're all for honesty, it seems; you couldna even steik your
> mouth on the public street. What for should I steik mines upon
> the bench, the King's officer, bearing the sword, a dreid to evil-
> doers, as I was from the beginning, and as I will be to the end!
> Mair than enough of it! Heedious! I never gave twa thoughts to
> heediousness, I have no call to be bonny. I'm a man that gets through
> with my day's business, and let that suffice.' (34)

Archie *is* being judged – and against an alien, impersonal creed which,
however, is more justly perceived to have its own formidable integrity.
More than ever Hermiston sounds like Milton's God: 'The ring of
sarcasm had died out of his voice as he went on; the plain words
became invested with some of the dignity of the Justice-seat.' As

usual in such interviews in Stevenson, precisely which bar the young man is being obliged to plead at is made deliberately ambiguous. Contemptuously, Hermiston considers the young man's future – 'what am I to do with ye next?' – dismissing the idea of the church on the grounds that 'Him that the law of man whammels is no likely to do muckle better by the law of God ... there's no room for splairgers under the fower quarters of John Calvin' (34–5).

In the first full confrontation between father and son in Stevenson's work there is clearly *some* therapeutic benefit: though Archie is aware that his father had been 'coarse and cruel', he is also able to recognise the presence of 'a bloomless nobility, an ungracious abnegation of the man's self in the man's office'. Nonetheless, the fact remains that the son is once again crushed – 'Archie was now dominated' – and even as he concedes the greatness of Lord Hermiston's spirit, he is aware of his own disempowerment represented once again in the word which haunts nearly all of Stevenson's youths in conflict with their father. Along with his awareness of Hermiston's greatness comes 'that of his own impotence, who had struck ... at his own father, and not reached so far as to have even nettled him' (36). The failed patricide capitulates: 'I place myself in your hands without reserve,'; and the father is not magnanimous in victory:

> 'That's the first sensible word I've had of ye the night,' said Hermiston. 'I can tell ye that would have been the end of it, the one way or the other; but it's better you should come there yourself, than what I would have to hirstle ye. Weel, by my way of it – and my way is the best – there's just one thing it's possible that ye might be with decency, and that's a laird' (36).

But being a laird is not to have independent authority. Archie is to be despatched to Hermiston as estate manager: 'ye must be my grieve there, and I'll see that I gain by you. Is that understood?' (37) And Weir concludes the hearing 'with a freezing smile'.

Archie goes straight from his 'trial' to his surrogate father Glenalmond. Having all but lost confidence in the merits of his own case – 'I have made a fool of myself, if I have not made something else' – he tries, this time, to create a judge in something like his own image. (Fathers and judges, of course, amount to much the same thing in Stevenson's generational wars.) In the most naked exposure of one of his principal objectives in all these battles, Stevenson has Archie demand that the sympathetic Glenalmond sit in judgement on father and son.

'Do you judge between us – judge between a father and a son. I
can speak to you; it's not like.... I will tell you what I feel and what
I mean to do and you shall be the judge,' he repeated (46).

Of course what this amounts to is a strategy for paternal disempowerment. Glenalmond knows very well the full extent of what
he's being asked to do, of the role he is being forced into, and he
resists the attempt to compromise him (much as Marlow resists Jim's
appeal to do something of the same sort in *Lord Jim*): '"I decline jurisdiction," said Glenalmond, with extreme seriousness.'

Nonetheless Glenalmond goes some way to meeting Archie's filial
needs in encouraging him to talk and at the same time surrendering
some of the authority Archie has conferred on him: 'my dear boy, if
it will do you any good to talk, and if it will interest you at all to hear
what I may choose to say when I have heard you, I am quite at your
command'. He follows this graceful concession with an expression
of affection so much in tune with Archie's needs that it is clear that
though he declined to judge between father and son he has not
declined Archie's tempting offer of surrogate fatherhood: 'Let an old
man say it, for once, and not need to blush: I love you like a son'
(40).

This is, of course, the word Archie promiscuously hungers for:
'"Ay," he cried, "and there it is! Love! Like a son! And how do you
think I love my father?"' Glenalmond tries to soothe him and Archie
responds:

'I will be very quiet,' replied Archie. 'And I will be baldly frank. I
do not love my father; I wonder sometimes if I do not hate him.
There's my shame; perhaps my sin; at least, and in the sight of
God, not my fault. How was I to love him? He has never spoken
to me, never smiled upon me; I do not think he ever touched me.
You know the way he talks? You do not talk so, yet you can sit
and hear him without shuddering, and I cannot. My soul is sick
when he begins with it; I could smite him in the mouth. And all
that's nothing. I was at the trial of this Jopp. You were not there,
but you must have heard him often; the man's notorious for it, for
being – look at my position! he's my father and this is how I have
to speak of him – notorious for being a brute and cruel and a coward'
(40).

Then the self-doubt reappears and with it the ever-present tendency
in a Stevensonian youth to minimise his readiness for manhood. The

nineteen-year-old confronts Glenalmond with what is, in effect, another appeal:

'Well, who am I? A boy, who have never been tried, have never done anything except this twopenny impotent folly with my father. But I tell you, my lord, and I know myself, I am at least that kind of a man – or that kind of a boy, if you prefer it – that I could die in torments rather than that any one should suffer as that scoundrel suffered. Well, and what have I done? I see it now. I have made a fool of myself, as I said in the beginning; and I have gone back, and asked my father's pardon, and placed myself wholly in his hands – and he has sent me to Hermiston,' with a wretched smile, 'for life, I suppose – and what can I say? he strikes me as having done quite right, and let me off better than I had deserved' (41).

Glenalmond's response is wryly perceptive, acknowledging that for someone like Archie relationship will always be problematic: 'My poor dear boy! ... You are only discovering where you are; to one of your temperament, or of mine, a painful discovery. The world was not made for us; it was made for ten hundred millions of men, all different from each other and from us ...' (41).

Having found himself a surrogate father more to his taste, Archie is then led by the latter's sympathetic review of Hermiston's qualities to come to a greater understanding of his parent. The device is a deeply interesting one. It is the accommodating father – the son's bit of father-fathering, which really means father disempowerment – which eventually assists the son to a more tolerant attitude towards the all-judging, all-prohibiting Law-giver who is his natural father. He wants now to 'make it up to him', he says, but the paternal mass so dwarfs him that he finds it difficult to know how to go about it: 'How do you pay attentions to a – an Alp like that?' (44). Again Glenalmond offers him advice that Archie could only readily accept when mediated through *this* kind of father-figure: 'Only by obedience, punctual, prompt, and scrupulous.' Archie promises that he shall have it and he says *to Glenalmond*: 'I offer you my hand in pledge of it.' The old judge accepts, like the true surrogate he is, and adds the paternal blessing which Stevenson's aspiring young men seek with the obsessiveness of Jacob himself: 'God bless you, my dear, and enable you to keep your promise. God guide you in the true way, and spare your days, and preserve to you your honest heart.' At that, he kissed the young man upon the forehead in a gracious, distant, antiquated way ...' (44).

For all his success in broadening Archie's view of his father, Glenalmond's mediation may mitigate his anguish but it cannot extirpate its source: in this sort of conflict, a pseudo-father can only provide a pseudo-solution. To a considerable extent Glenalmond is a fantasy father – and so an evasion of the realities and the inescapable conflicts inherent in the father–son relationship. Obviously there is going to be no serious conflict with *this* surrogate since Archie has *chosen* him. Like a well-modulated Miltonic voice, Glenalmond has been interposed between Archie and the 'terrible father' with a task roughly comparable to justifying the ways of God to man. His function (again like that of the Miltonic voice) is to enable Archie to express his love and his willingness to accept his father's law while taking responsibility for the growth of an independent selfhood and seeing it through to man's estate. But is this last possible without bringing father and son, later if not now, into renewed conflict? Should this happen it is improbable that Lord Glenalmond would be able to mediate again; he has given his discreet judgement and his blessing which is the most a surrogate father can do, and, moreover, there are various pointers to an early demise. So what will happen when Archie next confronts the father? Will the young man whose wooing of Christina Elliott is blighted by the presence of a figure 'with an ironical and bitter smile' submit to being 'dominated' all over again? The question remains unanswered, which is as fitting a conclusion as any to a conflict which is renewed in every generation.

### Straining towards Silence

In trying to delineate something of this drama of unfulfilment, I have touched on the counterpointing of speech and silence and of the deployment of silence as a rhetorical device throughout the text. The device is not just central to that drama, it is also an integral part of the text's structure. The narrative begins with an illegible inscription on a gravestone and ends in the paradox of the curtain going up on … the end, on silence. But, as Susan Sontag puts it, 'if a work exists at all, its silence is only one element in it'. What this means in literary practice is that: 'Instead of raw or achieved silence, one finds various moves towards an ever-receding horizon of silence – moves which, by definition, can never be fully consummated.'[10] The 'end' that the curtain goes up on here is, in fact, resonant with future possibilities for what it describes is the point at which maladroit youth is about to give way to the (bewildered) man. Archie has, without knowing how, bitterly offended Christina and now tries to comfort her as she sobs in his arms:

> He felt her whole body shaken by the throes of distress, and had pity upon her beyond speech. Pity, and at the same time a bewildered fear of this explosive engine in his arms, whose works he did not understand, and yet had been tampering with. There arose from before him the curtains of boyhood, and he saw for the first time the ambiguous face of woman as she is. In vain he looked back over the interview; he saw not where he had offended. It seemed unprovoked, a wilful convulsion of brute nature ... (124).

This last meeting which ends (perfectly, one might say) in puzzled silence takes place at the Deil's Hags, which is where the story had opened. It was there that we heard for the first time of the silence of the moss and of the fact that the silence was to be *once again* broken 'by the report of firearms and the cry of the dying'. So, though silence descends, perhaps prematurely, with the word 'nature', a ghostly echo of the first report of firearms and of the cry of the dying survives the cessation of the narrating voice, continuing to pursue an event that is *not* narrated. Thus not only is *Weir of Hermiston* surprisingly symmetrical for a fragment, the text itself displays a remarkable durability, projecting the echoes which had been set going at its very beginning beyond the life of the narrative and the (literal) death of the author. But such an ending has been in a sense prepared for in the emphasis from the start on silence, disappearance and death.

The voice of the narrator has had an interesting role to play in this context not least because at various times it lays explicit claim to being the voice of the author. It is also a musing voice which is not slow to bring the perspective of its owner's experience to bear upon the text: 'perhaps [Mr Weir] belonged to that class of men who think a weak head the ornament of women – an opinion invariably punished in his life'; and *his* opinion is reiterated in the next paragraph: 'The heresy about foolish women is always punished, I have said, and Lord Hermiston began to pay the penalty at once' (5). This voice continues to examine, interrogate and speculate about the material of the tale with a proprietorial freedom which gives it a degree of apparent autonomy – as though the owner of the voice were indeed piecing together the bones of its skeleton, providing a running commentary the while. Thus: 'I doubt if Frank Innes had the least belief in his predictions: I think it flowed from a wish to make the story as good and the scandal as great as possible' (27). At the same time the voice identifies its owner as being in a dynastic line with Archie Weir. Recounting the latter's presidency of the 'Spec.', there seems to be a considerable identification: 'He sat in the same room where the Society still meets.... The same lustre of many tapers shed its light over the meeting; the same chair, perhaps, supported him that so many of us have sat in since' (27). Tempting as it is to see this as a piece of Samoan nostalgia since it is the only time that sympathy has been shown for a continuum of any sort, it is more profitable to view it as a tactful way for the narrator to express his affinity with Archie in his family difficulties. Given Stevenson's own occupancy of the same chair (with consequences occasionally mortifying to the patriarch in Heriot Row), the narrating voice is also linked to his. Thus when that voice lays claim to being the author of the text before us, we are encouraged to complete the identification with Stevenson even though we are under no necessity of doing so.

The voice's claim to authorship is established with fluency and discretion: 'He ... rode to hounds with my Lord Muirfell, upon whose name, as that of a legitimate Lord of Parliament, in a work so full of Lords of Session, my pen should pause reverently' (49). This pen is busily inditing a work which attempts with a good deal of tentativeness ('I doubt', 'I think', 'perhaps') to set down 'the tale of the Justice-Clerk and of his son, young Hermiston, that vanished'. It is a tale, now lost, which can never be fully verified, which is still the subject of 'additions and corrections by the old' when retold amidst the enigmatic but unpromising 'silence of the young' – a disconcerting reception which adds to the dying fall.

Just how much this authorial voice wishes to be regarded as contemporary and literary can be judged from its allusions when seeking to describe Innes's exaggerated belief in his 'unusual quickness and penetration'. The obvious comparison, it says, would be with Sherlock Holmes but 'They knew nothing of Sherlock Holmes in these days', and it has to settle for Talleyrand instead (103). To contrive such a dissonant mention of Sherlock Holmes here is to register strongly the modernity of the authorial voice and at the same time to effect an extreme disjunction between the period of the tale (and its literary and historical antecedents) and the modern age represented by the figure of the urban detective. (*The Adventures of Sherlock Holmes* and *The Memoirs of Sherlock Holmes* both came out while Stevenson was working on *Weir of Hermiston*.) The polar separation of the two periods could hardly be more dramatically represented than by having *Old Mortality* at one end and Sherlock Holmes at the other.

Sherlock Holmes's name is invoked only to be discarded as an anachronism; but Talleyrand's is also discarded, if for different reasons. Sifting through the skeletal evidence, the voice establishes its editorial function by returning to debate inferences which it has itself supplied. Thus having been the source of the suggestion that Innes might think of himself as a Talleyrand when it came to the quickness of his perceptions, the voice then demurs: 'Frank's resemblance to Talleyrand strikes me as imaginary ...' (105). The same voice enters into gentle adjudications: 'In the early stages I am persuaded there was no malice' (102); and words of caution are addressed to the reader's interests: 'I must guard the reader against accepting Kirstie's epithets as evidence' (97). Occasionally, in mild self-reproof, the self-proclaimed authorial voice notes that it has lapsed into the clichéd conventions of narrative and paid the price in inexactness: 'I have said her heart leaped – it is the accepted phrase. But rather, when she was alone in any chamber of the house, and heard his foot passing on the corridors, something in her bosom rose slowly until her breath was suspended, and as slowly fell again with a deep sigh, when the steps had passed and she was disappointed of her eyes' desire' (52).

At other times the voice expresses more serious doubts – the doubts of a writer struggling with the essential intractability of language, in particular with its questionable capacity to render the moral and psychological complexity of human behaviour:

> Had it been a doctor of psychology, he might have been pardoned for divining in the girl a passion of childish vanity, self-love *in excelsis*, and no more. It is to be understood that I have been painting chaos and describing the inarticulate. Every lineament that appears is too precise, almost every word used too strong. Take a fingerpost in the mountains on a day of rolling mists; I have but copied the names that appear upon the pointers, the names of definite and famous cities far distant, and now perhaps basking in sunshine; but Christina remained all these hours, as it were, at the foot of the post itself, not moving, and enveloped in mutable and blinding wreaths of haze (82–3).

If doctors of medicine and psychology – references which again 'place' the narrator – cannot diagnose Christina's condition, neither can the writer adequately cut through the 'mutable wreaths of haze' which envelop her and identify the moral truth of her condition. The problem which the *soi-disant* author discovers here is the one which

Conrad, for example, made the subject of much of his writing, but it is one which, carried to the extreme, defines Modernist and even some aspects of Postmodernist literary development. 'There are no words for the deepest experience' wrote Ionesco. 'The more I try to explain myself, the less I understand myself. Of course not everything is unsayable in words, only the living truth.' In quoting these words from Ionesco's *Journal*, George Steiner notes that the conclusion that the living truth is no longer sayable has been reached by many others. He goes on: 'The theatre of Beckett is haunted by this insight. Developing Chekhov's notion of the near-impossibility of effective verbal interchange, it strains towards silence, towards an *Act Without Words*.'"[11]

What all this means is that very different things are being asked of language by the Modernists but, as Susan Sontag has pointed out, the radical critique of consciousness which is taking place 'always lays the blame on language'.[12] There is a necessary corrective in Norman Brown's pungent assertion that 'The problem is not the disease called language, but the disease called man.'[13] What Stevenson's narrator reveals in his moment of authorial frustration is his preoccupation with his *own* consciousness and perceptions: with how he can justly render *their* complexity. Finding words adequate to represent this reality would seem to be a near impossibility – indeed something like the recognition of this prompted Roland Barthes to say that Modernism begins with the search for 'a literature no longer possible'.[14] Language, it seems, now 'calls our attention to silence, and literary forms take shape in the perpetual presence of consciousness'.[15]

The problematics of language would seem to do little to inhibit another narratorial voice in *Weir of Hermiston* which, in its fluency and confidence, the narrator-author's own voice seems at times almost to envy. Yet the crucially important voice of the elder Kirstie obsessively narrating her family-history, hungrily raiding the cupboard of folk-memory in the process, is doing so against time. Increasingly she comes to sound like a Beckett character talking compulsively against the encroachment of silence.

We have already heard of Kirstie having been in her youth 'a moorland Helen'. But her skill as a storyteller is at least a match for her beauty and it might be equally apposite to think of her as a moorland Scheherazade. Her narrative resources and her skills are almost as great, and her threatened nemesis, too, comes with silence. If occasionally she seems to have some of Scheherazade's sexual energy – 'the woman, essentially passionate and reckless, who crouched on the rug, in the shine of the peat fire, telling these tales, had cherished through life a wild integrity of virtue' – the erotic is thoroughly subordinated to the storytelling and that dangerous locale, the hearthrug, becomes a stage for the raconteur telling an endless tale:

> Like so many people of her class, she was a brave narrator; her place was on the hearthrug and she made it a rostrum, miming her stories as she told them, fitting them with vital details, spinning them out with endless 'quo' he's' and 'quo' she's', her voice sinking into a whisper over the supernatural or the horrific; until she would suddenly spring up in affected surprise, and pointing to the clock, 'Mercy, Mr Archie!' she would say, 'whatten a time o'night is this of it! God forgive me for a daft wife!' So it befell, by good management, that she was not only the first to begin these nocturnal conversations, but invariably the first to break them off; so she managed to retire and not to be dismissed (53).

The tale she tells of her own family records their doings over many generations but their reality is fitful rather than substantial. Their moment seems supremely fleeting, all too often confirmed by an untimely and violent death.

> One ancestor after another might be seen appearing a moment out of the rain and the hill mist upon his furtive business, speeding home, perhaps, with a paltry booty of lame horses and lean kine, or squealing and dealing death in some moorland feud of the ferrets and the wild cats. One after another closed his obscure adventures in mid-air, triced up to the arm of the royal gibbet or the Baron's dule-tree (54).

The increasing shadowiness of these heroic exploits signals not just the passage of time but the decline of the oral tradition, the spirit of which, if it survives at all, does so in the printed pages of Mr Sheriff Scott. In this context, it is worth noting that Christina's brother, Dand, functions within the old bardic tradition: 'Either I'm a poet or else I'm nothing', he tells his elder brother, and when it is quietly revealed that he has not been printed himself, he is made to seem more genuinely (if belatedly) part of that tradition:

> No question but he had a certain accomplishment in minor verse. His 'Hermiston Burn,' with its pretty refrain –
>
> > 'I love to gang thinking whaur ye gang linking
> > Hermiston burn, in the howe;'

his 'Auld, auld Elliotts, clay-cauld Elliotts, dour, bauld Elliotts of auld,' and his really fascinating piece about the Praying Weaver's Stone, had gained him in the neighbourhood the reputation, still possible in Scotland, of a local bard; and, though not printed himself, he was recognised by others who were and who had become famous. Walter Scott owed to Dandie the text of the 'Raid of Wearie' in the *Minstrelsy* and made him welcome at his house, and appreciated his talents, such as they were, with all his usual generosity. The Ettrick Shepherd was his sworn crony; they would meet, drink to excess, roar out their lyrics in each other's faces, and quarrel and make it up again till bedtime (64).

Not being printed, however, means that his voice, too, is under threat from that silence which seems to be the destiny of the oral tradition; for it is another of those things on the point of vanishing.

When we hear for a second time of his 'failure' to get printed, it is in a manner which both compliments him and casts a shadow over the future. Young Kirstie draws his ballad on the Elliotts to Archie's attention and he asks her to sing it to him. She is reluctant to do so because it is the Lord's Day, though she adds that she doesn't really see anything inherently sacrilegious in reciting it: 'By my way of thinking it's just as serious as a psalm.' She compromises by 'soothing' it to him ('I wouldna like to sing out loud on the Sabbath'), and she does so seated on the Weaver's Stone – about which her brother has also written. Finally, she prefaces her rendering of the ballad with the remark that 'there's few bonnier bits in the book-poets, though Dand has never got printed yet' (90). The effect of the careful preparation and presentation of her recital is, however, *not* to demonstrate a secure and reassuring lodgement of the past in the present and *vice versa*, so strengthening the picture of a rural community strong in its inherited cultural values, but almost its opposite: a sense of the instability and evanescence of things, an allusion to something that is about to be lost.

I have said that the narrator-author seems at times to envy Kirstie's narratorial voice but there is nothing ungenerous about his reaction. At one point he gracefully concedes precedence as Kirstie's dramatic account reaches a peak:

At that sight, at that word, gasped out at them from a toothless and bleeding mouth, the old Elliott spirit awoke with a shout in her four sons. 'Wanting the hat,' continues my author, Kirstie, whom I but haltingly follow, for she told this tale like one inspired, 'wanting guns, for there wasna twa grains o' pouder in the house, wi' nae mair weepons than their sticks into their hands, the fower o' them took the road' (57).

'My author' is nicely ambiguous. The voice we have grown accustomed to as the authorial voice (because it has insisted on being seen, or heard, as such) now concedes the authority of origination to another – who seems to beget *him*. Appropriately enough he then follows after – 'haltingly' – in her voice-print.

What is dangerous about this for the voice of the narrator-author is that that voice-print is carried to the edge of extinction with every possibility that it will soon disappear. Not that this is a prospect at all new to this voice which from the start has been concerned with – almost preoccupied with – that which vanishes. Sometimes such presentiments are communicated in the construed voice of the characters: Archie Weir, for example, at the outset of his wooing tests Christina to see if she is sensitive to the tragic possibilities in 'the long perspectives'; and young Kirstie rises to the occasion and sings (sitting on the tombstone) one of her brother Dand's songs:

'O they rade in the rain, in the days that are gane,
   In the rain and the wind and the lave,
They shoutit in the ha' and they routit on the hill,
   But they're a' quaitit noo in the grave.
Auld, auld Elliotts, clay-cauld Elliotts, dour, bauld Elliotts of auld!'

Archie thinks his soundings have returned the answer he was hoping for: 'She was a human being tuned to a sense of the tragedy of life, there were pathos and music and a great heart in the girl' (91).

Kirstie's young voice singing of the 'Auld, auld Elliotts' blends with that of her aunt, thus participating in, yet at the same time extending, the perspective of the latter's tales. After the two have parted, however, Kirstie seems already to be receding into one of those long perspectives which link us to our losses: 'In the falling greyness of the evening he watched her figure winding through the morass, saw it turn a last time and wave a hand, and then pass through the Slap.' The process is accentuated by her being associated with the Praying Weaver and with Archie's dead mother.

He had retained from childhood a picture, now half-obliterated by the passage of time and the multitude of fresh impressions, of his mother telling him, with the fluttered earnestness of her voice, and often with dropping tears, the tale of the 'Praying Weaver,' on the very scene of his brief tragedy and long repose. And now there was a companion piece; and he beheld, and he should behold for ever, Christina perched on the same tomb, in the grey colours of the evening, gracious, dainty, perfect as a flower, and she also singing –

> 'Of old, unhappy far-off things,
> And battles long ago,'

– of their common ancestors now dead, of their rude wars composed, their weapons buried with them and of these strange changelings, their descendants, who lingered a little in their places, and would soon be gone also, and perhaps sung of by others at the gloaming hour (91).

As if she were already dead, Kirstie is given a place in the perspective of Archie's memory close to that of the long-dead weaver and his dead mother, a remarkable foreclosure on the future given that his lover has not yet become his bride:

> By one of the unconscious arts of tenderness the two women were enshrined together in his memory. Tears, in that hour of sensibility, came into his eyes indifferently at the thought of either, and the girl, from being something merely bright and shapely, was caught up into the zone of things serious as life and death and his dead mother (92).

It is extraordinary that, once again in a Stevenson text, we get the elision of the figures of mother and lover, brought about, in this case, with a conspicuousness that ensures our attention.

When the elder Kirstie had examined the 'maze of difficulties' she saw obstructing Archie's future, she had found 'at the end of every passage, the flinty countenance of Hermiston'. Here at the end of every passage or every perspective, there seems to be death; and nothing evokes this better than Kirstie's own story which is the story of the storyteller for whom silence is death. In an earlier chapter, I quoted John Barth quoting Todorov to the effect that all narrative is always about language and about telling; about itself, in other words. Barth had continued his paraphrase by reference to *The Thousand and One Nights*: 'Narrative equals language equals life. To cease to narrate, as the capital example of Scheherazade reminds us, is to die – literally for her, figuratively for the rest of us.'[16] In the penultimate chapter of *Weir of Hermiston*, the storytelling voice also speaks – and with great compassion – of the fear which besets all narrators, indeed, all talkers. It is a remarkable passage and merits extensive quotation:

Kirstie had many causes of distress. More and more as we grow old – and yet more and more as we grow old and are women, frozen by the fear of age – we come to rely on the voice as the single outlet of the soul. Only thus, in the curtailment of our means, can we relieve the straitened cry of the passion within us; only thus, in the bitter and sensitive shyness of advancing years, can we maintain relations with those vivacious figures of the young that still show before us and tend daily to become no more than the moving wall-paper of life. Talk is the last link, the last relation. But with the end of the conversation, when the voice stops and the bright face of the listener is turned away, solitude falls again on the bruised heart. Kirstie had lost her 'cannie hour at e'en'; she could no more wander with Archie, a ghost, if you will, but a happy ghost, in fields Elysian. And to her it was as if the whole world had fallen silent (111).

Could anyone argue after such a passage that Stevenson's writing did *not* embody 'a future feeling'?

Earlier, the narrator-author had acknowledged in Kirstie a supe-rior teller of tales; but his defence is that of one storyteller to another: they are, so to speak, both of the same guild. When we come across the conspicuously-placed, oft-repeated plural pronoun in the passage just quoted, we are reminded of this mutuality, and of other things as well. For example, it prompts us to recall the narrator's compas-sionate regard for the plight of women and his repeated attempts to see things through their eyes. Above all, however, the pronoun ensures that the threat of silence and death will be seen not only to pervade all levels of the narration, so strengthening the impression of a text balanced at vanishing-point, but also to touch us personally. Like the sound of Attwater's bell, its message echoes far beyond Hermiston and Scotland, beyond, even, the islands of the South Pacific where, for Robert Louis Stevenson, as he concluded the day's drafting of *Weir of Hermiston*, the horizon of silence finally stopped receding.

### Notes

1. Letter to Colvin, February, 1894; quoted in Maixner, op. cit., p. 453.
2. Sir Walter Scott, *Old Mortality* (1954), p. 23.
3. 'Note, by Mr Jedediah Cleishbotham – That I kept my plight in this melan-choly matter with my deceased and lamented friend, appeareth from a handsome headstone, erected at my proper charges in this spot, bearing the name and calling of Peter Pattieson, with the date of his nativity and sepulture; together also with a testimony of his merits, attested by

myself, as his superior and patron – J. C.'(*Old Mortality*, p. 26) The extraordinary involutions of the frame-tales in this novel may be an example of the influence of the *Arabian Nights*. Henry Weber, who had published them in his *Tales of the East* (1812), had acted, as has been mentioned earlier, as Scott's amanuensis from 1804 to 1813. *Old Mortality* was published in 1816.

4. Through the use of multiple frames, Scott has deliberately distanced 'Old Mortality', 'the author', from his own tale. For a brief discussion of some other effects of Scott's layered narrative structure, see James Kerr's *Fiction Against History: Scott as Storyteller* (Cambridge, 1984), pp. 40ff.

5. Quoted by Maixner, op. cit., p. 470.

6  It is tempting to again see the admonitions of 'Cummy' in this, her relish for judgement-and-damnation being every bit as capable of thrilling young Stevenson to the marrow as Mrs Weir's account of the persecutions was Archie.

7. Philip Larkin, 'Reference Back', *Collected Poems*, ed. Anthony Thwaite (1988), p. 106.

8. The filial hunger evident in all the father–son conflicts in Stevenson's work is, it can be argued, narcissistic in nature. By creating a father in his own image which he can then fall in love with, the son secures an ideal self-completion. A hostile father is a useful element in this play since he supplies a negative definition of the ideal.

9. For should man finally be lost, should man
Thy creature late so loved, thy youngest son
Fall circumvented thus by fraud, though joined
With his own folly? That be from thee far,
That far be from thee, Father, who art judge
Of all things made, and judgest only right.
                              Book III, 150–5.

10. Susan Sontag, 'The Aesthetics of Silence' in *A Susan Sontag Reader* (1982), p. 186.

11. George Steiner, 'Silence and the Poet', in *Language and Silence: Essays 1958–66* (1967), p. 72.

12. Susan Sontag, op. cit., p. 196.

13. Quoted in Ihab Hassan, *The Dismemberment of Orpheus*, p. 16.

14. Ibid., p. 20.

15. Ibid., p. 22.

16. John Barth, 'Tales within Tales', *The Friday Book*, p. 236.

# Select Bibliography

Like everyone who attempts to write seriously and at length about Stevenson's work, I have been greatly helped by Paul Maixner's *Robert Louis Stevenson: The Critical Heritage.*

Where it is not given, the place of publication is London.

Georges Van Den Abbeele, *Travel as Metaphor: From Montaigne to Rousseau* (Minneapolis, 1992).

Janet Adam Smith (ed.), *Henry James and Robert Louis Stevenson: A Record of Friendship and Criticism* (1948).

Robert Alter and Frank Kermode (eds), *The Literary Guide to the Bible* (Cambridge, Mass., 1987).

W. H. Auden, *The Dyer's Hand* (1963).

M. M. Bakhtin, *The Dialogic Imagination: Four Essays by M. M. Bakhtin*, ed. Michael Holquist, trans. Caryl Emerson and Michael Holquist (Austin, 1981).

——, *Rabelais and his World*, trans. Hélène Iswolsky (Bloomington, 1984).

John Barth, *Chimera* (Greenwich, Conn., 1972).

——, *The Friday Book: Essays and other Non-Fiction* (New York, 1984).

——, *Lost in the Funhouse* (1972).

Roland Barthes, *S/Z* (1992).

——, *Writing Degree Zero* (1967).

Charles Baudelaire, *Les Fleurs du Mal*, ed. Starkie (Oxford, 1974).

William Beckford, *Vathek* (Oxford, 1983).

Gillian Beer, *The Romance* (1970).

Walter Benjamin, *Charles Baudelaire: A Lyric Poet in the Era of High Capitalism*, trans. Harry Zohn (1985).

Bernard Bergonzi, *The Situation of the Novel* (1979).

Harold Bloom, *The Anxiety of Influence: A Theory of Poetry* (Oxford, 1975).

Peter Blos, *Son and Father: Before and Beyond the Oedipus Complex* (New York, 1985).

Jorge Luis Borges, *Labyrinths*, ed. Yates and Irby (Norfolk, Conn., 1962).

416     *R. L. S. and the Appearance of Modernism*

Wayne Booth, *The Rhetoric of Irony* (Chicago, 1974).

Malcolm Bowie, *Freud, Proust and Lacan: Theory and Fiction* (Cambridge, 1990).

Malcolm Bradbury, *The Modern World: Ten Great Writers* (1989).

——, *Possibilities: Essays on the State of the Novel* (Oxford, 1973).

Malcolm Bradbury and James McFarlane (eds), *Modernism 1890–1930* (1976).

A. A. Brill (ed.), *The Basic Writings of Sigmund Freud* (New York, 1938).

Peter Brooks, *The Melodramatic Imagination* (New York, 1985).

——, *Reading for the Plot: Design and Intention in Narrative* (New York, 1985).

Dennis Brown, *The Modernist Self in Twentieth Century English Literature* (1989).

Jenni Calder, *RLS: A Life Study* (1980).

Ian Campbell (ed.), *Nineteenth Century Scottish Fiction* (1979).

Peter L. Caracciolo (ed.), *'The Arabian Nights' in English Literature: Studies in the Reception of 'The Thousand and One Nights' into British Culture* (1988).

Richard Chase, *The American Novel and its Tradition* (Baltimore, 1983).

Monique Chefdor, Ricardo Quinones and Albert Wachtel (eds), *Modernism: Challenges and Perspectives* (Illinois, 1986).

G. K. Chesterton, *Robert Louis Stevenson* (New York, 1928).

Robert Con Davis (ed.), *The Fictional Father: Lacanian Readings of the Text* (Amherst, 1981).

Joseph Conrad, *Heart of Darkness* (1975).

——, *Lord Jim* (1966).

——, *The Nigger of the 'Narcissus'* (1955).

——, *The Secret Agent* (1983).

——, *The Shadow Line* (1985).

Frederick Crews, *The Sins of the Fathers: Hawthorne's Psychological Themes* (Berkeley, 1989).

David Daiches, *Stevenson and the Art of Fiction* (New York, 1951).

Daniel Defoe, *A General History of the Robberies and Murders of the Most Notorious Pyrates* (New York, 1972).

Edgar A. Dryden, *The Form of American Romance* (Baltimore, 1988).

Terry Eagleton, *Marxism and Literary Criticism* (1976).

Peter Faulkner (ed.), *A Modernist Reader: Modernism in England 1910–1930* (1986).

Jessica R. Feldman, *Gender on the Divide: The Dandy in Modernist Literature* (Cornell, 1993).

DeLancey Ferguson and Marshall Waingrow (eds), *RLS: Stevenson's Letters to Charles Baxter* (1956).

Leslie Fiedler, The *Collected Essays of Leslie Fiedler* (New York, 1971).

Joseph Frank, *The Widening Gyre: Crisis and Mastery in Modern Literature* (New Brunswick, NJ, 1963).

Carla Freccero, *Father Figures: Genealogy and Narrative Structures in Rabelais* (Ithaca, 1991).

J. C. Furnas, *Voyage to Windward: The Life of Robert Louis Stevenson* (1951).

Dorothy Van Ghent, *The English Novel: Form and Function* (New York, 1953).

Mirra Ginsburg (ed. and trans.), *A Soviet Heretic: Essays by Yevgeny Zamyatin* (Chicago, 1975).

Sandra M. Gilbert and Susan Gubar, *The Madwoman in the Attic* (New Haven, 1984).

Edmund Gosse, *Father and Son: A Study of Two Temperaments* (1964).

Elizabeth Grosz, *Sexual Subversions: Three French Feminists* (Sydney, 1989).

Moreton Gurewitch, *European Romantic Irony* (Ann Arbor, 1962).

David Harvey, *The Condition of Postmodernity: An Enquiry into the Origins of Cultural Change* (1989).

Ihab Hassan, *The Dismemberment of Orpheus: Toward a Postmodern Literature* (New York, 1978).

Frederick J. Hoffman, *Freudianism and the Literary Mind* (Baton Rouge, 1957).

Irving Howe, *Decline of the New* (New York, 1970).

——, *Selected Writings 1950–1990* (New York, 1990).

Ford Madox Hueffer, *Memories and Impressions* (1911).

Linda Hutcheon, *Narcissistic Narrative: The Metafictional Paradox* (1984).

B. Inhelder and J. Piaget, *The Growth of Logical Thinking from Childhood to Adolescence* (New York, 1958).

Christopher Isherwood, *Lions and Shadows* (1968).

A. Jefferson, and Robey, D. (eds), *Modern Literary Theory* (1983).

Gabriel Josipovici, *The Lessons of Modernism* (1987).

——, *The World and the Book* (1979).

Franz Kafka, *Wedding Preparations in the Country and other Prose Writings*, trans. E. Kaiser and E. Wilkins (1954).

Louis Kampf, *On Modernism: The Prospects for Literature and Freedom* (Cambridge, Mass., 1967).

Peter Keating, *The Haunted Study: A Social History of the Novel 1875–1914* (1989).

James Kerr, *Fiction against History: Scott as Storyteller* (Cambridge, 1984).

Robert Kiely, *Robert Louis Stevenson and the Fiction of Adventure* (Cambridge, Mass., 1964).

Søren Kierkegaard, *The Concept of Irony, with Constant Reference to Socrates* (1966).

Alanna Knight, *The Robert Louis Stevenson Treasury* (1985).

Philip Larkin, *Collected Poems*, ed. Anthony Thwaite (1988).

Michael Levenson, *A Genealogy of Modernism: A Study of English Literary Doctrine 1908–1922* (Cambridge, 1986).

Claude Lévi-Strauss, *Tristes Topiques* (New York, 1961).

David Lodge (ed.), *Modern Criticism and Theory* (1988).

——, *The Modes of Modern Writing: Metaphor, Metonymy, and the Typology of Modern Literature* (1979).

Frank McLynn, *Robert Louis Stevenson: A Biography* (1993).

Paul Maixner (ed.), *Robert Louis Stevenson: The Critical Heritage* (1981).

Paul de Man, *Blindness and Insight: Essays in the Rhetoric of Contemporary Criticism* (1983).

Thomas Mann, *Doctor Faustus: The Life of the German Composer Adrian Leverkühn*, trans. H.T. Lowe-Porter (New York, 1948).

——, *Lotte in Weimar*, trans. H. T. Lowe-Porter (1947).

——, *The Magic Mountain*, trans. H. T. Lowe-Porter (1988).

Robert Meek, *Ministering Angels* (1864).

George Meredith, *The Amazing Marriage* (1895).

——, *Evan Harrington* (1889).

W.J.T. Mitchell (ed.), *On Narrative* (Chicago, 1981).

D. C. Muecke, *The Compass of Irony* (1969).

——, *Irony* (1973).

Edwin Muir, *The Structure of the Novel* (1928).

Robert Musil, *The Man without Qualities*, trans. Wilkins and Kaiser (1960).

I. B. Nadel and F. S. Schwarzbach (eds), *Victorian Artists and the City* (New York, 1980).

Sandra Nadaff, *Arabesque: Narrative Structure and the Aesthetics of Repetition in '1000 Nights'* (Evanston, Illinois, 1991).

Andrew Noble (ed.), *Robert Louis Stevenson* (1983).

José Ortega y Gasset, *Meditations on Quixote* (New York, 1961).

Cyril Pearl, *The Girl with the Swansdown Seat: An Informal Report on Some Aspects of Mid-Victorian Morality* (1956).

Renato Poggioli, *The Theory of the Avant-Garde*, trans. Gerald Fitzgerald (Cambridge, Mass., 1968).

Richard Poirier, *The Performing Self* (Rutgers, 1992).

Ricardo J. Quinones, *Mapping Literary Modernism: Time and Development* (Princeton, 1985).

Wallace Robson, *The Definition of Literature and Other Essays* (Cambridge, 1984).

Margaret A. Rose, *Parody//Metafiction* (1979).

——, *Parody: Ancient, modern and post-modern* (Cambridge, 1983).

Jean-Jacques Rousseau, *Emile*, trans. Allan Bloom (1991).

Dianne Sadoff, *Monsters of Affection: Dickens, Eliot and Brontë on Fatherhood* (Baltimore, 1982).

Edward W. Said, *Beginnings: Intention and Method* (Baltimore, 1975).

Friedrich Schlegel, *Dialogue on Poetry and Literary Aphorisms*, trans. Behler and Struc (1968).

Walter Scott, *Old Mortality* (1954).

——, *Waverley* (1972).

Elaine Showalter, *Sexual Anarchy: Gender and Culture at the Fin de Siècle* (1992).

Susan Sontag, *A Susan Sontag Reader* (1982).

Stephen Spender, *The Struggle of the Modern* (1965).

Gertrude Stein, *Picasso: The Complete Writings*, ed. Edward Burns (Boston, 1970).

George Steiner, *Language and Silence: Essays 1958–1966* (1967).

Dolf Sternberger, *Panorama of the 19th Century* (Oxford, 1977).

Wallace Stevens, *The Necessary Angel: Essays on Reality and the Imagination* (1960).

Eugene Sue, *The Mysteries of Paris* (Sawtry, n.d.).

Stanley Sultan, *Eliot, Joyce and Company* (Oxford, 1987).

Roger Swearingen (ed.), *An Old Song and Edifying Letters of the Rutherford Family* (Paisley, 1982).

W. M. Thackeray, *Vanity Fair* (1971).

David Thorburn, *Conrad's Romanticism* (Yale, 1974).

Edward Timms and David Kelley (eds), *Unreal City: Urban Experience in Modern European Literature and Art* (New York, 1985).

William Veeder and Gordon Hirsch (eds), *Dr Jekyll and Mr Hyde after One Hundred Years* (Chicago, 1988).

Ian Watt, *Conrad in the Nineteenth Century* (1980).

—— (ed.), *Conrad: The Secret Agent* (1973).

Patricia Waugh, *Metafiction: The Theory and Practice of Self-Conscious Fiction* (1984).

Jeffrey Weeks, *Sex, Politics and Society* (1984).

H. G. Wells, *Experiment in Autobiography* (1934).

Allon White, *The Uses of Obscurity: The Fiction of Early Modernism* (1981).

# Index

Adam Smith, Janet  16, 144
Adams, Robert  83, 84–5
Archer, William  4, 16, 25, 26, 29, 86, 87, 93, 120, 125, 319
Auden, W. H.  79, 104, 105, 113, 142

Bakhtin, M. M.  13, 17, 140, 144, 181, 182, 194, 213, 214
Balzac, Honoré  15, 309
Barbey D'Aurevilly, J. A.  233
Barnes, Julian  48
Barrie, J. M.  384
Barth, John  322, 366, 369, 412, 414
Barthes, Roland  2, 12–13, 14, 16, 17, 18, 265, 270, 309, 310, 312, 313, 315, 316, 317, 329, 366, 408
Barzun, Jacques  282
Baudelaire, Charles  4, 100, 225, 231, 232, 257, 258, 262, 267
Baxter, Charles  42, 47
Beckett, Samuel  250, 265, 408
Beckford, William  142
Beebe, Maurice  1, 6, 11, 12, 14, 16
Beer, Gillian  150, 152, 178
Beethoven, Ludwig van  328, 330
Benjamin, Walter  231, 232, 267
Bennett, Arnold  213
Bergonzi, Bernard  151, 178
Bismarck, Prince von  155, 160, 161
Bleikasten, Andre  40, 42, 45, 47
Bloom, Harold  35, 36, 38, 39, 47, 62
Blos, Peter  19, 24, 25, 39, 40, 41, 46, 47, 80, 316
Boodle, Adelaide  81
Booth, Wayne  119, 143
Borges, Jorge Luis  3, 9, 90, 321–2
Boswell, John  253, 266
Bourdin, Martial  116
Bowditch, Nathaniel  331, 332, 333, 336
Bowie, Malcolm  16, 42, 44, 47
Bradbury, Malcolm  2, 4, 8, 13, 16, 34, 134, 137, 143, 144, 150, 151, 178, 225, 265, 320, 366

Brandes, Georg  4
Brooks, Peter  11, 12, 14, 17, 36, 276, 277, 278, 282, 315, 316
Brown, Dennis  249–50, 268
Brown, Norman  408
Browning, Robert  250
Bunner, H. C.  88, 89, 120, 141
Bunyan, John  353
Burns, Edward  16
Burns, Robert  157
Burton, Richard  83
Butler, Samuel  15

Calder, Jenni  204, 214, 216
Camus, Albert  122, 321
Cannon, Susan R.  213
Caracciolo, Peter  141
Cervantes-Saavedra, Miguel de  3
Chefdor, Monique  46
Chekhov, Anton  408
Chesterton, G. K.  86–7
Clarke Murray, J.  1
Collier, Peter  267
Collins, Wilkie  105, 265
Colvin, Sidney  9, 16, 28, 101, 222, 413
Conan Doyle, Arthur  230, 406
Conrad, Joseph  117–41 passim, 142–3, 179, 185, 222, 227, 229, 242, 250, 282, 287, 288, 317, 318, 321, 325, 326, 331, 335, 337, 341, 342, 345, 348–9, 353, 355, 356, 357, 364, 365, 366, 367, 368
Cunningham, Alison ('Cummy')  294, 360, 380, 414
Cunninghame Graham, R. B.  138
Curle, Richard  117

Daiches, David  81
Darwin, Charles  189
Davis, Robert Con  47, 80
Defoe, Daniel  69, 81, 198–9, 274
De Lauretis, Teresa  189
Derrida, Jacques  324, 366

Dickens, Charles 84, 105, 179, 222, 223, 224, 225, 229, 233, 265
Dingley, Robert 81, 367
Disney, Walt 174
Doré, Gustave 225, 266
Dostoevsky, Feodor 18, 182, 225
Dryden, Edgar 325, 366, 367
Dumas, Alexandre 88, 121

Eagleton, Terry 119, 143
Eliot, George 151, 165–6
Eliot, T. S. 85, 141, 229
Ellmann, Richard 2
Emerson, Caryl 17
Empson, William 3
Enfield, Henry 234
Esau (son of Isaac) 302, 303, 305, 316

Faulkner, Peter 16
Faulkner, William 41, 42, 45
Feldman, Jessica R. 100, 101, 142, 168, 267
Ferguson, Delancey 47
Fiedelson, Charles 2
Fiedler, Leslie 18, 19, 20, 39, 46
Findlay, Alexander 318, 336, 337, 338, 365, 367
Fitzgerald, Edward 312
Flaubert, Gustave 2, 11, 134
Fokkelman, J. P. 316
Ford, Ford Madox 19, 20, 46, 134, 309, 320
Formes, Karl Johan 323
Forster, E. M. 339, 358
Foucault, Michel 263
Fowler, Alastair 1, 50, 51, 72, 81, 320–1, 336, 366, 367
Frank, Joseph 148, 149, 150, 178
Freccero, Carla 21, 46
Freud, Sigmund 29, 38, 39, 45, 188, 200, 213, 215, 218, 249, 258, 266
Furnas, J. C. 83

Gaboriau, Emile 105, 106
Galland, Antoine 83
Garnett, Richard 5, 82
Garschine, Mme 18

Gaskell, Elizabeth 84
Gilbert, Sandra 23, 46
Gilbert, W. S. & Sullivan A. S. 87
Ginsburg, Mirra 47
Gosse, Edmund 24, 29, 81, 144, 168, 263
Graham, Kenneth 9, 16
Greenberg, Clement 12, 17, 26, 46
Grosz, Elizabeth 143, 368
Gubar, Susan 23, 45
Gurewitch, Morton 122, 143

Haddon, Trevor 25, 26, 33
Halèvy, Jacques-François 156
Handel, George Frederick 155, 156, 157, 172
Harvey, David 142
Hassan, Ihab 275, 315, 414
Hawthorne, Nathaniel 150, 324
Hazlitt, William 142
Heath, Stephen 220, 223, 251, 255, 266
Heine, Heinrich 122, 329
Henley, W. E. 159, 175
Hirsch, Gordon 265
Hoffman, Frederick J. 351, 367
Hofmannsthal, Hugo von 215, 221, 222
Hogg, James 249, 273
Holquist, Michael 17, 104, 142
Hosea 185
Housman, Laurence 219
Howe, Irving 27, 30, 32, 35, 46
Hueffer, Ford Madox *see* Ford, Ford Madox
Hugo, Victor 5, 7, 28
Hutcheon, Linda 90, 123, 142, 143

Ibsen, Henrik 4
Inhelder, B. 47
Ionesco, Eugene 408
Irwin, John T. 41, 47
Isaac 302, 316

Jacob (son of Isaac) 72, 302, 303, 305, 306, 316, 351, 367
James, Henry 6, 8, 16, 25, 33, 34, 89, 120, 140, 151, 271, 282

Jefferson, Ann 316, 329, 366
Jerrold, Blanchard 225, 233
Josipovici, Gabriel 85, 139, 140, 141, 144
Joyce, James 119, 250, 316

Kafka, Franz 19, 20, 21, 25, 40, 41, 42, 46, 81, 357
Kampf, Louis 2, 3, 10, 16, 34, 35, 47
Keating, Peter 6, 15, 16, 213
Keats, John 326, 340, 385
Kelley, David 142
Kermode, Frank 275
Kerr, James 414
Kiely, Robert 86–9, 94, 103, 105, 120, 141, 142, 196, 275
Kierkegaard, Søren 119, 143
Krafft-Ebing, Richard von 82
Kristeva, Julia 128

Lacan, Jacques 200, 310, 316
Lane, E. W. 84
Lang, Andrew 175, 324
Larkin, Philip 386, 414
Larson, Magali S. 266
Lathbury, D. C. & Mrs 88, 91, 121
Lawrence, D. H. 5, 30, 113
Le Gallienne, Richard 319
Lear, Edward 122
Levenson, Michael 1, 2, 16, 19, 20, 46
Lévi-Strauss, Claude 13, 17
Levin, Harry 1
Lodge, David 2, 17
Lunne, E. 142

Macherey, Pierre 119
Maixner, Paul 16, 46, 141–4, 177, 178, 268, 366, 414
Mallarmé, Stéphane 9, 82
Manheim, Leonard F. 80
Mann, Thomas 82, 119, 121, 122, 124, 330
Marks, Herbert 330, 342, 367
Marsh, Edward 47
Masson, David 142
Matthisohn, Friederich von 328, 330

McFarlane, James 2, 4, 7, 8, 13, 16, 265, 320, 366
McLynn, Frank 46, 81
Meek, Robert 323
Menikoff, Barry 90, 93, 102, 112, 141, 142
Meredith, George 85, 108, 142, 146, 156, 172, 173, 178, 324, 331, 335
Millais, John 9
Miller, Hillis 250
Miller, Karl 215, 268
Milton, John 76, 260, 314
Molière (Jean-Baptiste Poquelin) 8
Monroe, Harriet 159
Moore, George 8, 282, 293, 312, 313
Muecke, D. C. 1, 118, 120–5, 138, 143
Muir, Edwin 148, 178
Müller, Adam 120
Musil, Robert 123

Nabokov, Vladimir 3, 9
Nadel, Ira Bruce 225, 266
Noble, Andrew 16

Offenbach, Jacques 155
Ommundsen, Wenche 142
Ortega y Gasset, José 338, 367
Orwell, George 397
Osborne, Lloyd 52

Paley, William 106
Partridge, Eric 23
Payne, John 83, 141
Pearl, Cyril 266
Piaget, J. 47
Picasso, Pablo 10, 16, 140
Poe, Edgar Allan 104, 105, 219, 222, 225, 231, 265, 266, 310
Poggioli, Renato 46
Poirier, Richard 102, 142
Pollock, W. H. 89, 120
Pound, Ezra 82, 83, 141
Purcell, Edward 130, 133

Quiller-Couch, Arthur 376
Quinones, Ricardo 2, 10, 11, 12, 17, 46

Rabaté, Jean-Michel  80
Rabelais, François  3, 20, 21
Richardson, Samuel  279, 280
Richter, Jean Paul  143
Roberts, Batholomew  80
Robson, Wallace  51, 52, 67, 69, 72, 196, 214
Rodway, Allan  118
Rose, Margaret  119, 143
Rousseau, Jean-Jacques  213, 214

Sadoff, Dianne  80, 214
Said, Edward  13, 17, 22–3, 142
Saintsbury, George  86, 92
Schlegel, Friederich  1, 82, 120, 122, 124, 125, 127, 134, 135, 136, 140, 143
Scott, Walter  5, 8, 84, 133, 174, 178, 371, 372, 373, 383, 385, 418
Scudamore, Peter  80–1
Sedgwick, Eve Kosofsky  253
Shakespeare, William  76, 172
Sherry, Norman  117, 142
Showalter, Elaine  258, 260, 268
Sitwell, Mrs  18, 21, 52
Smollett, Tobias  55, 61, 62
Solger, Karl  120
Sontag, Susan  404, 408, 414
Spencer, Herbert  8
Spender, Stephen  2, 34, 47
Stein, Gertrude  10, 16, 147, 178
Steiner, George  408, 414
Sternberger, Dolf  267
Stendahl (Marie-Henri Beyle)  15, 36
Stevens, Wallace  35, 36, 47
Stevenson, R. A. M. (Bob)  22, 43, 234
Stevenson, Thomas  22, 40, 42, 47, 74
Stow, Randolph  384
Sue, Eugene  93, 105, 178, 225
Sultan, Stanley  141
Swearingen, Roger  7, 47

Thackeray, W. M.  84, 106, 152, 217
Thirlwall, Connop  134, 139, 143
Thomas, Ronald  218–22, 250, 263, 265, 269
Thomson, James  267
Thorburn, David  142
Timms, Edward  142, 230
Todorov, Tzvetan  322, 412
Torrens, Henry  84
Train, John  372
Trelawny, Edward John  81

Van de Grift, Fanny  18, 39, 52
Van Den Abbeele, Georges  33, 47, 189, 193, 199, 213
Van Ghent, Dorothy  14, 17
Veeder, William  217, 218, 220, 224, 232, 242, 243, 244, 247, 249, 253, 258, 261, 265–8, 366
Virgil  327, 330
Voltaire (François Marie Arouet)  8

Wachtel, Albert  46
Waingrow, Marshall  47
Watt, Ian  142, 366
Waugh, Patricia  221, 266
Weber, Carl Maria von  155, 156, 172, 323, 355
Weber, Henry  83, 84, 414
Weeks, Jeffrey  253, 268
Wells, H. G.  10, 16
White, Allon  335, 366, 367
White, Patrick  366
Wilde, Oscar  105, 109
Williams, Ioan  142
Williams, Raymond  104, 230
Woolf, Virginia  2, 320, 369
Wordsworth, William  249, 262
Worringer, Wilhelm  148, 149
Wyeth, N. C.  188, 213

Zamyatin, Yevgeny  32, 33, 47
Zangwill, Israel  319, 320